Actual Ethics

Actual Ethics offers a moral defense of the "classical liberal" political tradition and applies it to several of today's vexing moral and political issues. James Otteson argues that a Kantian conception of personhood and an Aristotelian conception of judgment are compatible and even complementary. He shows why they are morally attractive, and perhaps most controversially, when combined, they imply a limited, classical liberal political state. Otteson then addresses several contemporary problems—wealth and poverty, public education, animal welfare, and affirmative action—and shows how each can be plausibly addressed within the Kantian, Aristotelian, and classical liberal framework.

Written in clear, engaging, and jargon-free prose, *Actual Ethics* will give students and general audiences an overview of a powerful and rich moral and political tradition that they might not otherwise consider.

James R. Otteson is Associate Professor in and Chair of the Department of Philosophy at the University of Alabama. The author of *Adam Smith's Marketplace of Life,* he has held research fellowships at the Institute for Advanced Studies in the Humanities at the University of Edinburgh, at the Centre for the Study of Scottish Philosophy at the University of Aberdeen, and at the Social Philosophy and Policy Center, Bowling Green State University, Ohio. He has also received grants from the University of Alabama, the Atlas Foundation, and the Earhart Foundation.

For Stinkbug, Beetle, and Bear

Actual Ethics

JAMES R. OTTESON
University of Alabama

CAMBRIDGE
UNIVERSITY PRESS

CAMBRIDGE UNIVERSITY PRESS
Cambridge, New York, Melbourne, Madrid, Cape Town, Singapore, São Paulo

Cambridge University Press
40 West 20th Street, New York, NY 10011-4211, USA

www.cambridge.org
Information on this title: www.cambridge.org/9780521862714

© James R. Otteson 2006

First published 2006

Printed in the United States of America

A catalog record for this publication is available from the British Library.

Library of Congress Cataloging in Publication Data

Otteson, James R.
Actual ethics / James R. Otteson.
p. cm.
Includes bibliographical references and index.
ISBN 0-521-86271-x (hardback)—ISBN 0-521-68125-1 (pbk.)
1. Ethics. 2. Liberty. 3. Judgment (Ethics) I. Title.
BJ1012.O78 2006
171'.2—dc22   2005031227

ISBN-13 978-0-521-86271-4 hardback
ISBN-10 0-521-86271-x hardback

ISBN-13 978-0-521-68125-4 paperback
ISBN-10 0-521-68125-1 paperback

34.00

Contents

Acknowledgments

Little of what I say here is my own invention. What Newton said of himself is far truer of me: whatever I have been able to see has been by standing on others' shoulders. I have relied on numerous other people's work—so much so, in fact, that I could not hope to credit them all here. Among my central sources are Aristotle, David Hume, Adam Smith, Frédéric Bastiat, John Stuart Mill, and Albert Jay Nock: I hereby give them blanket credit for most of my good ideas.

A number of contemporary thinkers have also helped me to formulate my ideas, some knowingly, others unknowingly, and some no doubt unwittingly. They include Torin Alter, Randy Barnett, David Beito, Bradley Birzer, Donald Boudreaux, Nicholas Capaldi, Henry Clark, John Danford, Russell Daw, Richard Epstein, Samuel Fleischacker, Gordon Graham, Max Hocutt, Robert Lawson, Mark LeBar, Dennis LeJeune, Gordon Lloyd, Roderick Long, James R. Otteson Sr., P. Shannon Otteson, Maria Pia Paganelli, Tom Palmer, Steven Pinker, James Rachels, Stuart Rachels, Norvin Richards, Richard Richards, Peter Singer, Aeon Skoble, Thomas Sowell, Cass Sunstein, Richard Wallace, Walter Williams, and Bruce Yandle.

Max Hocutt, James Stacey Taylor, and Rosemary Tong all read earlier versions of the entire manuscript and made invaluable comments and suggestions.

I have also benefited from the advice of several exceptional former students, including Anne M. Donaldson, S. Cole Mitchell, Robin M. Preussel, Brett J. Talley, and Katherine I. Terry.

Of course, none of the people listed is in any way responsible for the errors contained in this book, or for the many ways in which I resisted their counsel. Only I am.

For their invaluable monetary and moral support while working on this book, I would also like to thank the Earhart Foundation, the Institute for Advanced Studies in the Humanities at the University of Edinburgh, and the Centre for the Study of Scottish Philosophy at the University of Aberdeen. I would also like to thank the University of Alabama for providing me a one-year leave, during which time I could work in places as wonderful, and wonderfully conducive to working, as Edinburgh and Aberdeen.

I would also like to thank my editor at Cambridge University Press, Beatrice Rehl, for numerous helpful suggestions.

Finally, I would like to thank my family for continuing to provide me inspiration and the motivation to *get back to work!* In this again, as in all things, they, and their love and support, are the sine qua non.

JRO
Tuscaloosa, Alabama

Preface

This book is about how you should live. Although it is written by a college professor, it is not primarily intended for other college professors. It is intended instead for the person who has decided to begin thinking a bit more carefully about the nature and justification of moral judgments and about the political principles a sound system of morality would imply.

The book is motivated in part by the fact that a lot of what gets written and taught about how you should live either ignores altogether or gives short shrift to an important moral and political tradition called the "classical liberal" tradition. I believe that this neglect is a mistake: the classical liberal tradition offers a compelling vision of what it means to be a respectable human being, of what a just political state is, and of what people should do to achieve their goals. Or at least I believe it is a compelling vision, and I hope in this book to convince you of that as well. In any case it is worth giving serious consideration. One reason it often isn't given such consideration is perhaps that there is no concise presentation of its fundamental principles that applies them to currently important moral and political topics. That is what this book aims to do.

One reason I believe the classical liberal tradition is compelling is that it is founded on simple, attractive principles that almost everyone endorses, implicitly if not explicitly, in everyday life. Because this tradition no longer receives the public attention it once did, however, there is something of a disconnection between the way people officially talk about morality and the way morality is actually practiced in people's real lives. But I think that our "private" morality has a lot more going for it than it is given credit for. One goal of this book, then, is to bring the simple principles of this private morality into the open so we can take a good look at them, evaluate them honestly, and trace out their consequences to see where they lead. Another goal is to uncover reasons and arguments supporting what is good about this morality, so that it can be defended if need be, and so that its adherents—as I hope you will become!—will have some confidence in what they believe or have come to believe.

GETTING STARTED

I argue in this book that individual freedom is required for success, and thus happiness, in life. We must develop good *judgment*—a central concept I take pains below to illuminate—and we can do so only when we enjoy the freedom to make decisions for ourselves and enjoy or suffer, as the case may be, the consequences of those decisions. As we shall see, that means that everyone has to leave us darned well alone. But that isn't the paradise it sounds like at first: it also means that others are not required to do anything for us and that they should not clean up our messes. Judgment cannot develop if we are not required to take responsibility for our decisions. If someone else takes the heat when we choose foolishly, there is no incentive for us to stop making similarly foolish decisions in the future. And given our natural laziness, we probably will not decide to take the hard way all on our own. But as we shall see, happiness will usually depend on having taken hard ways.

We already have, then, several pieces of the puzzle: freedom and its sometimes painful partner responsibility, judgment honed by experience, and then happiness. That was easy. Well, but as you suspected, it is not quite so easy. This all sounds a little too self-centered, doesn't it? It is all about how *I* can be happy—what about everyone else? What about poverty, the environment, animal rights, affirmative action, public education—in short, what about all the moral matters that concern others? Of course you wondered about these things: these constitute the core topics that have increasingly occupied our ethical attention for years, even decades. And we take them up in due course. But the attention they receive is often disproportionate to their actual importance. That is not to say that they are *un*important—rather that, as I argue, there are more important matters that require your attention before you get around to, or are properly prepared for, thinking about them.

I hope to convince you that we should indeed pay attention to our own lives and our own interests, and get them straight, before we start trying to "make the world a better place." That is not being selfish: it is being prudent. It is also a recognition of human nature, which we cannot get away from however much we dislike it, and also of the limits of our knowledge and benevolence. Luckily, however, part of that ineluctable human nature is to take a sincere interest in other people—especially our family and friends—which means that by paying attention to our own interests we will simultaneously pay attention to the interests of those others as well. So we do have a natural, though limited, benevolence. Like any other precious but scarce resource, we had better figure out how to use it wisely.

This is all fleshed out in the pages to come, but please be prepared to have some of your intuitions and background beliefs challenged. Please don't let yourself be put off by the arguments just because they might be different from what you have heard or thought before. Figuring out how to lead a good life is the most important thing we do: there is no time to pussyfoot around or sugarcoat the truth. So I take Emerson's advice and let my words hit like cannonballs, come what may. Your job is to engage what I say and evaluate my arguments on their merits, even if that means you take it upon yourself to refute me step by step.

MORAL COMMUNITY AND TALK ABOUT ETHICS

This book is also partly inspired by what I believe is the misleading way ethics, or applied or practical ethics, is often discussed in public forums such as daytime talk shows, news programs, and in newspapers, and as it is sometimes taught on college campuses. In such venues, discussions of these matters are often superficially framed as if there were only two, mutually irreconcilable sides between which one has to choose: the good side versus the bad side, the enlightened side versus the benighted side, the virtuous side versus the sinful side.

Discussions of these matters are usually more sophisticated in college classes, but they too can give some of the same misleading impressions. Sometimes these classroom discussions comprise a series of "issues," also presented as if there were only two opposing views about them (the "pro" and the "con"). Students are then required to read an article on each side of the issue, to talk—or *argue,* in the bad sense of the word—about them, and then to repeat on the test what they have read, perhaps adding a respectful word or two about the professor's own position. Now what, you may ask, is wrong with a course like that?

A course taught this way risks giving the false impressions that (1) there are only two sides to these questions and (2) there is really no reasonable way to resolve them, since there are arguments, responses, counterarguments, and so on ad infinitum on both sides. Such a course might also give the further false impressions that (3) life is made up of one major moral crisis after another and, most pernicious of all, (4) there is really no consensus about what a moral life is like or about how a person should live. Every one of these is false. The unintended but nonetheless frequent result of teaching a class like this is to foment division among the students that endangers the chance of forming any kind of moral community, to reinforce an unthinking moral relativism and defeatism, and to forever deaden many students to the possibility of substantive moral reasoning, judgment, and resolution.

This book argues that there is in fact widespread agreement on the basic elements of a morally respectable life, and furthermore that this agreement coalesces around the central principles of the classical liberal view. I try to make that case by drawing up a picture of such a life and showing how it applies to and addresses various of life's moral and political matters. I hope that by focusing less on abstract concepts, formal argumentation, and artificially stylized pro-and-con issues than on everyday moral sentiments and experiences the book gives rise neither to the false impressions nor to the confusion that other discussions can.

WHY WRITE — OR READ — THIS BOOK?

Peter Singer some time ago wrote an influential book called *Practical Ethics*. The book was small, but it packed a wallop: it has gone into a much-expanded second edition and is today among the most commonly used books in undergraduate college "ethics" and "applied ethics" courses, despite the proliferation of imitations defending similar positions. The book's success is perhaps somewhat surprising since it turns out to make recommendations that are often rather *im*practical, not to mention counterintuitive; but nevertheless Singer's book has come to occupy a central place in the canon of contemporary works used in such courses.

What does not exist, however, is a book that takes up many of the same issues and addresses them in a similarly nontechnical, readable way but that does *not* defend the same positions. This book is intended to be just such an alternative. That does not mean that this is an attempt to refute Singer point by point: that would be as tedious to read as it would have been to write. The subjects of concern in this book and in Singer's overlap, but they also diverge in a number of substantial ways; and although this book shares some common ground with Singer's and with others that take roughly "Singerian" lines, you will soon see that this book stakes out an overall position that is independent from, and at times quite at odds with, theirs.

What I offer here, then, is an alternative vision of what it takes to lead a good and happy life. I believe the vision offered herein is superior to that offered by the Singerians, particularly in regards to what is perhaps the most important issue that a book of this type should address, namely happiness. I only assert this now, but the rest of this book gives lots of reasons supporting my claim. And given the importance of happiness, the stakes are very high. The ancient Greek philosopher Aristotle (384–322 B.C.), one of the principal inspirations for the approach this book takes, says that happiness is the highest, ultimate goal in life, the thing for the sake of which everything else is chosen but that itself is chosen for the sake of nothing else.[1] High stakes indeed. That is why I wrote, and why I hope you read, this book.

PLAN OF THE WORK

The book has nine chapters, broken into three parts. The first part, comprising chapters 1 to 5, lays out what my overall position is. Chapter 1 sketches in general terms what I take to be human 'personhood,' or the thing about us that makes us morally valuable agents. I introduce here several of the concepts that I draw on in the rest of the book, in particular the nature, prerequisites, and importance of 'judgment.' This chapter in fact surveys many concepts, and it thus runs the risk of bombarding the reader. I try to develop an overall conception of 'personhood' and 'judgment,' fleshing it out with examples and illustrations, and occasionally contrasting it with alternative views. Because this chapter is an overview, however, its presentation is not exhaustive. I hope that it provides enough for you to get a clear picture of what the foundations and general implications of my view are, and for you to get a sense of how the view might handle problems or respond to objections. Each subsequent chapter of the book fills in more details of the outline sketched in this one.

In the second and third chapters I extend this notion of 'personhood' and its related concepts by drawing out the political implications I believe they have: the second chapter discusses systems of political organization that I believe are inconsistent with them, the third the system of political organization that I believe is entailed by them. To put my cards on the table: I argue that a proper conception of human 'personhood' implies

---

[1] In his *Nicomachean Ethics*, bk. I, chap. 7, pp. 7–10.

a state limited to certain specific functions. This is the "classical liberal" state I mentioned earlier. Despite the fact that its defenders are today in the minority, there is a lot of tradition, authority, and evidence on its side, not to mention, as I shall argue, moral attractiveness.

In the fourth and fifth chapters I address one of Peter Singer's central challenges, namely his set of arguments about what moral claims the existence of worldwide poverty makes on us. In chapter 4 I argue that Singer's position faces several difficult problems, and hence that our moral obligations concerning poverty do not quite square with his suggestions. In chapter 5 I present empirical evidence about which political and economic institutions are in fact most beneficial to the world's poor, and I argue that this evidence supports not the welfare state Singer recommended but rather the classical liberal state I defended in chapter 3. I take that as an additional, empirical reason to support the classical liberal state, over and above its coherence with the compelling "principled" conception of moral 'personhood' I argued for in chapters 1 and 2.

In Part II, I turn from the development of my position in general terms to its more practical application. Chapters 6 to 8 address by turns several of the central matters of concern in today's discussions of practical or applied ethics. There are any number of issues in applied ethics that might have been addressed, but unfortunately a selection had to be made. The fact that some issues are left unaddressed should not be taken to imply any sort of negative judgment about them—only that I couldn't very well write a two-thousand-page book. My hope, in any case, is that the concepts developed and defended in Part I combined with a selective application of them in Part II will allow you to get a pretty good idea of how a defender of my position would address other issues as well.

In chapter 6 I argue that public schooling should be abolished. Not that *education* should be abolished, only that *government funding* of it should be. I realize that this proposition may strike you as incredible—it did me too when I first encountered it. But the argument and evidence supporting this radical view eventually persuaded me. In this chapter I present the argument and evidence for your evaluation. Perhaps you will be surprised, as I was, at just how strong the case is.

Chapter 7 tackles the tangle of issues surrounding the nearly universal human practice of including some in their groups and excluding others from them. When is this morally objectionable and when not? When should the state step in, and when not? I argue that the notions of 'personhood' and 'judgment,' along with the classical liberal state they entail, give us a helpful roadmap to navigate these issues and develop plausible positions on them.

Chapter 8 broaches the topic of "rights," including whether there are any "natural" rights, and then proceeds to examine two areas where a common claim today is that we need to extend rights-based protections: to people who wish to engage in "alternative" lifestyles and to nonhuman animals. Although I remain something of an agnostic about the existence of natural rights (at least for the purpose of the discussion), I argue that the conceptual tools we have developed in the book nonetheless allow us to make some headway in these areas too.

Finally, Part III of the book is its conclusion, consisting of just one chapter. In chapter 9 I formally take up happiness. Throughout the book one of my arguments in support of classical liberalism is that there is no single conception of the good—or perhaps I should say, no single conception of the Good—that applies to everyone, and hence that no single conception of the good should be enforced by the state. Along the way I rely on a similar argument about happiness to justify my not saying anything substantive about it either – that is, until the end of the book. In this chapter I finally say what I believe can be said about what happiness consists of and how people can achieve it. My pluralism about 'goodness' limits what I can say about 'happiness,' but given human nature and the realities of human existence I believe that general contours of human happiness can be sketched.

LOTS AND LOTS OF CAVEATS

Before you read the book there are several things I should tell you up front so that you know what you are getting into.

First, this book does not pretend to lay out all the various positions on any given issue, objectively giving the chief arguments in support of and objections to each. There are several excellent books that do that already, including in particular Gordon Graham's *Eight Theories of Ethics* and James Rachels's *Elements of Ethics.*[2] This book is instead a largely one-sided presentation of the basic elements of the view I find most compelling. I put the arguments in the best light I can, and although I entertain objections at regular intervals, I do not exhaustively present or examine alternative

---

[2] See also Hugh LaFollette's anthology *Ethics in Practice* and Louis Pojman's anthology *The Moral Life*, both of which contain carefully reasoned discussions of most of the issues raised herein.

views. So please do not read my book thinking it gives you an overview of all, or even several, reasonable positions on the issues it takes up. It should not therefore be read in lieu of other books, such as Singer's *Practical Ethics,* that argue their own points of view; it should rather be read in addition to them.

Second, I proceed on the assumption that many of the people reading this book will not be familiar with its positions, with the premises on which those positions rest, or with the implications they have. For that reason I have written it largely as a *primer* or *introduction* to the position and, as I mentioned, a complement or perhaps counterweight to more prevalent views such as Singer's. Hence the book is not the final word: it is only the first word, or perhaps the first few words. I invite the reader to continue the investigation of the matters discussed herein. To assist in that endeavor, I provide at the end of each chapter a bibliography listing all the works I refer to or rely on in the text and footnotes, as well as other works taking various positions that you can consult to examine the issues further. If you are reading this book as part of a college course, your professor will no doubt also stand ready to assist you with further reading.

One other note in this connection. Because it is meant to be a primer, this book may at times strike you as containing simply what common sense or "the wisdom of the ages" would recommend. (I certainly hope what I say will comport with common sense, though that is not the point of this potential objection.) But just because something has a long pedigree, or when stated seems obviously true, does not mean that it is unimportant or not worth repeating. Arithmetic has a long pedigree, and its elements, when stated, seem obviously true; but everyone still needs to be taught it before moving on—you can't master calculus, or even algebra, without it. Or take grammar: you cannot write good prose, or appreciate good literature, without having first mastered the basic rules of grammar; they are no less important for being elementary, and they are the necessary first step. The same is true about many issues in politics and morality. Yet, as is increasingly the case with grammar,[3] too often people are *not* made aware of the fundamentals involved. That is, they do not know exactly what the proper principles are and hence are unsure about, or make mistakes in, thinking about how to apply them. People proceed right on to try to write moral and political poetry without basic moral and political grammar. The result can be mistakes that could have been avoided. So in this book, and especially in Part II, I draw out the conclusions of what

---

[3] See David Mulroy's excellent *The War against Grammar,* esp. chap. 4.

I believe and hope are our commonsense but still important—and often forgotten or neglected – moral principles, supplemented with what some recent empirical evidence has shown or suggested, in the hopes that readers can use those principles and that evidence as foundations for further reflection and investigation.

Third, I draw liberally on the ideas and research of other people. If I can claim originality, it is perhaps in the book's particular organization and presentation; but this book would not have been possible without the work of a great deal of other people. I list in the Acknowledgments many of those people; I also give credit in the text where appropriate. But the general disclaimer is necessary at the beginning.

Finally, a cautionary word about the book's style and method. I have striven to make the book interesting and engaging to read. That means that, as I mentioned earlier, I have tended to avoid formal argumentation, abstract constructions, and artificial formulations, and to focus instead on presenting an overall picture of a good and just life, on simple principles and commonsense judgments, and on everyday examples. It also means that I have interspersed some humor throughout the book. In so doing I have followed the lead of Shaftesbury, the late-seventeenth-century philosopher, politician, and raconteur, when he wrote: "I am sure the only way to save men's sense or preserve wit at all in the world is to give liberty to wit. Now wit can never have its liberty where the freedom of raillery is taken away, for against serious extravagances and splenetic humours there is no other remedy than this."[4] Writing with humor (or *attempting* to write with humor) runs certain risks, however: humor can be misunderstood, it can be mistakenly taken literally, and it can even be found offensive by some who might think that politics and morality are no laughing matters. If so, why, one might ask, use it at all? Here is Shaftesbury's answer:

[W]it will mend upon our hands and humour will refine itself, if we take care not to tamper with it and bring it under constraint by severe usage and rigorous prescriptions. All politeness is owing to liberty. We polish one another and rub off our corners and rough sides by a sort of amicable collision. To restrain this is inevitably to bring a rust upon men's understandings. It is a destroying of civility, good breeding and even charity itself, under pretence of maintaining it.[5]

---

[4] Anthony Ashley Cooper, Third Earl of Shaftesbury (1671–1713), *A Letter Concerning Enthusiasm to My Lord *****, contained in his 1711 *Characteristics of Men, Manners, Opinions, Times*, p. 12.

[5] *Sensus Communis, an Essay on the Freedom of Wit and Humour in a Letter to a Friend*, in *Characteristics*, p. 31.

For some readers, moreover, avoidance of formal argumentation is the same as, or tantamount to, weakness in argumentation. Professional academics, and professional philosophers in particular, are trained to look for and find fault in arguments—and we are very, very good at it. Shaftesbury anticipated this risk as well: "It is certain that in matters of learning and philosophy the practice of pulling down is far pleasanter and affords more entertainment than that of building and setting up. Many have succeeded to a miracle in the first who have miserably fallen in the latter of these attempts. We may find a thousand engineers who can sap, undermine and blow up with admirable dexterity for one single one who can build a fort or lay the platform of a citadel."[6] Although I would not claim that my book *quite* counts as a "miracle" of "building and setting up" (that was humor), nevertheless I did decide that writing an introductory-level book that is enjoyable, and indeed provocative, to read was worth the risk of leaving some professional academics ultimately unsatisfied. You may in the end judge that I erred *too* much on the side of readability, simplicity, and raillery. If so, go write your own book. (That was humor again.)

Bibliography

Aristotle. *Nicomachean Ethics,* 2nd ed. Terence Irwin, trans. Indianapolis, Ind.: Hackett, 2000 (ca. 350 B.C.).

Graham, Gordon. *Eight Theories of Ethics.* London and New York: Routledge, 2004.

LaFollette, Hugh, ed. *Ethics in Practice: An Anthology.* Cambridge, Mass.: Blackwell, 1997.

Mulroy, David. *The War against Grammar.* Portsmouth, N.H.: Boynton/Cook, 2003.

Pojman, Louis P., ed. *The Moral Life: An Introductory Reader in Ethics and Literature.* New York: Oxford University Press, 2000.

Rachels, James. *The Elements of Moral Philosophy,* 4th ed. New York: McGraw-Hill, 2002.

Shaftesbury, Third Earl of (Anthony Ashley Cooper). *Characteristics of Men, Manners, Opinions, Times.* Lawrence E. Klein, ed. Cambridge: Cambridge University Press, 1999 (1711).

Singer, Peter. *Practical Ethics,* 2nd ed. Cambridge: Cambridge University Press, 1993.

---

[6] *Miscellany III,* in *Characteristics,* p. 395.

PART I

WORKING OUT THE POSITION

1

Personhood and Judgment

To be human is to think and to imagine, to express one's thoughts and imaginings, and to make decisions and take actions based on one's thoughts and imaginings. Although there are exceptions to this, exceptions we discuss below, still the conception of human nature as characterized by a rich mental life and the ability to contemplate and act on that mental life captures the heart of it.

However persuasively some have argued that human beings are only marginally different from other animals,[1] G. K. Chesterton was right that the cave paintings in southern France refute them decisively.[2] Those images were painted deep inside many different dark caves tens of thousands of years ago, then were forgotten for thousands of years, before they were found again only recently. The images are primitive, as one would expect, but they are nonetheless unmistakable in their portrayals of bears, bison, mammoths, panthers, rhinoceroses, ibexes, hyenas, horses, insects, owls, aurochs, and other animals, not to mention men, women, and children—in short, many of the most important parts of those humans' everyday experience. In addition to paintings, there are engravings, carvings, stencils, and finger tracings. We do not know for sure who made them or why, or exactly why they were put just where they were, but the images are able to reach across the millennia and to

---

[1] For one recent example among many, see Richard Dawkins's *A Devil's Chaplain,* esp. chaps. 5 and 6.

[2] In the first two chapters of his 1925 *The Everlasting Man,* "The Man in the Cave" and "Professors and Prehistoric Men."

communicate clear and obvious meaning to us. Indeed, their expressive power is almost haunting.

As Chesterton rightly points out, however old these paintings are and whoever made them, what is unmistakable is that they were painted by human beings just like us. Those people's circumstances may have been dramatically different from ours, but their reactions to those circumstances were just what ours would have been. They wanted to express and record their experiences for the same reasons we do today. And their remarkable ingenuity in not only finding these seemingly inaccessible locations but also in employing such a degree of artistic and technical sophistication has required a rethinking of what human life was like twenty thousand years ago. Thus the essential humanity of these paintings is immediately recognizable. Indeed, this propensity to create may be one of the central defining features of humanity. As the Scottish philosopher Adam Ferguson (1723–1816) put it,

We speak of art as distinguished from nature; but art itself is natural to man. He is in some measure the artificer of his own frame, as well as his fortune, and is destined, from the first age of his being, to invent and contrive. He applies the same talents to a variety of purposes, and acts nearly the same part in very different scenes. He would be always improving on his subject, and he carries this intention where-ever he moves, through the streets of the populous city, or the wilds of the forest.[3]

This suggests not only that there *is* something that is essentially human, but also that it is unique among the living things on earth. No other animal on earth makes cave paintings.

It is frequently maintained that the chimpanzee has the mental development and ability of a three- or four-year-old human being; in some respects—like problem-solving ability—this is probably roughly accurate, although it is difficult to get a precise measure of such things. But chimpanzees do not make paintings that approximate those ancient cave paintings, only, perhaps, less well. A three-year-old child does. In fact, no chimpanzee ever spontaneously attempts to make any kind of representation of itself or its life or its relationships with other chimpanzees. I say "spontaneously" because some chimps have been trained by persistent and patient human dedication to take paint brushes and make images with them on paper or canvass. Elephants, similarly, have been taught to grasp a brush in their trunks and make strokes on canvass with

---

[3] In his *Essay on the History of Civil Society*, p. 12. For recent evidence of the universality of the human artistic inclination, see Dutton's "Aesthetic Universals."

them. There may be a handful of other animals capable of responding to similar training—though not many, since, among other things, a prehensile appendage is required—but the point to highlight is that this is *training:* it is much closer to the instinctive, and nonreflective, process involved in stimulus-response conditioning than it is to the "free play of deliberative faculties," as the German philosopher Immanuel Kant (1724–1804) put it,[4] that humans engage in. Painting is more difficult and thus more indicative of intelligence than, say, "training" a plant to grow in a certain way or "training" wood to bend or warp in a certain direction. Hence these animals obviously have intelligence—so much so, in fact, that they may be able to recognize pictures of themselves or their own images in mirrors. But they do not on their own—that is, without sustained, concerted human intervention—make any representations of their experiences. No other animal on earth makes cave paintings.

KANTIAN PERSONHOOD

I bring this up not to initiate a discussion of precisely what the difference between human and nonhuman animals is. We shall investigate that in a bit more detail later in the book. I have instead a different, though related, point to make here. It is this: The cave paintings are reflective of, partly constitute, and point toward the fact that human beings have *personhood.* Drawing on Kant again, we can divide objects in the world roughly into two categories: *things* and *persons.* A 'thing' is something that we may use to serve our purposes, without bothering to worry about its own interests—generally because a 'thing' *has* no interests. So, for example, a screwdriver is a 'thing': we are not required to ask its permission when we want to use it. A human being, on the other hand, is a 'person,' which means, approximately, that it is something that has its own deliberate purposes and exercises judgment with respect to them. It follows, Kant believes, that a 'person' may not be used to serve other people's purposes without his permission. This is a foundational premise of the argument I wish to make, and of the "classical liberal" moral and political position I defend in this book: the nature of personhood is such that 'persons' may not be used against their will to serve other people's ends.

Kant is one of the founders of this classical liberal tradition, and hence we should take a moment to look at his justification of this crucial claim. Kant's position is that autonomy or freedom is necessary for an individual

---

[4] In his 1790 *Critique of Judgment.*

to be a 'person.' "Rational beings," Kant says, "are called persons inasmuch as their nature already marks them out as ends in themselves, i.e., as something which is not to be used merely as a means and hence there is imposed thereby a limit on all arbitrary use of such beings, which are thus the objects of respect."[5] An awful lot is packed into that sentence; let's unpack it a bit. A 'person,' unlike a 'thing,' has the capacity both to construct rules of behavior for himself and to choose to follow them; hence, Kant argues, a person must be treated as an *end*, not merely as a *means*. Of course persons may be treated as means—when one pays someone else to mow one's lawn, for example—but persons may never be treated *merely* as means. Respecting the lawnmower's personhood would entail, for example, making him an offer and allowing him either to accept or not as he judges fit; allowing him to choose is a recognition that he has his own 'ends' or goals or purposes—he is a person, in other words, not a thing. On the other hand, forcing the lawnmower to mow one's lawn against his will would be treating him merely as a means—a means to *my* ends—and thus treating him as a thing, not a person. From this consideration Kant derives this version of his famous "categorical imperative," which he argues is the supreme rule of morality: "Act in such a way that you treat humanity, whether in your own person or in the person of another, always at the same time as an end and never simply as a means" (G, p. 36).

Kant extends the argument by linking the notion of a 'person' with the notions of *worth* and *respect*. The only thing whose existence has "absolute worth," Kant says, is "man, and in general every rational being" (G, p. 35). Everything else has a value or worth relative only to a person who values it. Kant's argument is that because only the rational being can be subject to a moral law, only such a being warrants our respect as an 'end in itself.' The rational being alone is "autonomous"—that is, capable of making free choices—and hence alone has "dignity":

> Reason, therefore, relates every maxim of the will as legislating universal laws to every other will and also to every action toward oneself; it does so not on account of any other practical motive or future advantage but rather from the idea of the dignity of a rational being who obeys no law except what he at the same time enacts himself. (G, p. 40)

Kant goes so far as to say that "everything has either a price or a dignity" (ibid.), which means that everything that is not a person has a price; only persons, insofar as they are persons, have a dignity, meaning in part

---

[5] From Kant's 1785 *Grounding for the Metaphysics of Morals*, p. 36. Hereafter referred to as G.

that they are not, or should not be, for sale at any price. "Now morality is the condition under which alone a rational being can be an end in himself, for only thereby can he be a legislating member in the kingdom of ends. Hence morality and humanity, insofar as it is capable of morality, alone have dignity" (G, pp. 40–41). Individual human beings have a dignity because of their natures as beings of a certain kind (namely, rational and autonomous), and this fact about them entails that these individuals must be respected, both by themselves and by others.

Kant is notoriously difficult to understand—as you no doubt noticed!—and his complicated argument, not to mention his dense prose, has given rise to continuing reinterpretation. You'll be glad to hear that we will not attempt to work through all of Kant's argument here. Instead, I wish to focus on one main conclusion: the Kantian conception of rational nature implies that my using you against your will to achieve an end of mine would be immoral because it would violate your dignity as a person. It would not only use you simply as a means to my end, but by making you adopt my "maxim" or rule of behavior, it destroys your autonomy. Importantly, the end or goal I wish to achieve by using you, whether good or bad, is irrelevant: given the nature of a person's essential humanity, *any* use of it simply as a means is a disrespecting of it.[6] So even if the reason that I enslaved you was to force you to use your keen intellect to search for a cure for cancer, I have still violated your dignity as a rational being—and therefore, according to the Kantian argument, I have acted immorally. That is the bedrock moral principle on which most of the rest of this book is based.

PERSONHOOD AND PURPOSES

One thing indicative of personhood, therefore, is having *ends:* purposes, goals, aspirations, things you want to accomplish. They need not be grand and lofty, like realizing world peace; they can be quite pedestrian and local, like getting in a workout today. The point is, you, unlike screwdrivers, have them. But dogs and horses have purposes in some sense, as do perhaps mice and even earthworms; one might even argue that oak trees and lichens do as well. In fact, the idea that *everything* in nature has a purpose is a venerable one indeed, dating back at least to the ancient Greek philosopher Aristotle (384–22 B.C.). What distinguishes a person's interests from those of dogs, mice, and oak trees, however, is that they

---

[6] See Robert S. Taylor, "A Kantian Defense of Self-Ownership."

are, or can be, deliberate and intentional. Oak trees' purposes, if they have them—and modern biology has tended to steer away from ascribing purposes to things in nature—would have been given to them by something else, such as God or nature (or perhaps Nature). Persons, on the other hand, are capable of giving themselves purposes. Persons are usually aware of their purposes and they often intentionally develop new ones; they might decide against some they have had for a long time or redirect those they already have. So after having had a good philosophy class, she decided to become a philosophy professor; after a mid-life religious conversion, he quit his lucrative job and gave away all his material possessions; and after having a baby she used the leadership skills she had developed as a banking executive to organize a Mom's Group to support other new mothers. In each of these cases the person's actions are motivated by the purposes that the person individually created and developed. They got ideas about what they wanted to do, they imaginatively fleshed out in their minds both what they wanted and what would be required to accomplish what they wanted, and they set about directing their everyday activities accordingly. Those are the hallmark characteristic activities of 'persons,' exactly what is missing in 'things.'

Now we must be careful not to overstate our ascription of deliberateness to the purposes of persons. That is why I said that persons are "usually" or "can be" aware of their ends and "often" change them on purpose. What this gets at is that sometimes even proper persons are unaware of what they are doing or where their lives are going, at least momentarily; and they might well not be aware of why their purposes changed or what the ultimate origin of their purposes is. We all know people who have religious beliefs but are not really sure why they have them, who become lawyers because that is what was expected of them, who buy only certain brands of shoes or clothing because that is what the cool people wear, or, what is especially evident in my line of work, who go to college because, well, that's just pretty much what everyone expected them to do after high school. In any or all of these cases one might argue that the agents' purposes were not their own and were instead given to them by someone or something else. Fair enough. But that still would not disqualify the agents in question from personhood, however, because even in the cases in which one is doing what others have told one to do, or is drifting sleepily through life, or is just not paying attention, it is still the case that one *could* be aware. One can always stop and think, focus one's attention—or just snap out of it. Those nonhuman animals or plants that one might like to say have purposes cannot be made conscious of their purposes as purposes. That is clear in the case of oak trees, but even in the case of, say, dogs, the dog loves its master and will do whatever it can to sneak into the car and go for a ride, but the dog does not and cannot be made to understand that it has or is acting out of respect for interests. If you are not sure about this, talk it over with your dog, and see if you can get him to understand that he is an agent acting out of respect to ends. Let me know how you fare.

TWO COMPLICATIONS

You may be wondering whether the distinction between 'persons' and 'things,' and the relegation of nonhuman animals to the category of 'things,' implies that we may use nonhuman animals for our purposes. I address this question squarely in chapter 8, but let me tell you now the position I will defend: yes, it does mean we may use them, but it does not mean that we may act cruelly or inhumanely toward them. The level of care and concern we should display toward all animals should track their intelligence and their abilities to sense and perceive. Thus we should be more solicitous about a chimpanzee than about a cow or a snail, and more solicitous still about a human being. The questions of whether in fact chimpanzees and perhaps a few other kinds of animals might count as 'persons,' exactly how much care we should display toward them, whether we should consider them to have "rights," and so on are crucial to delimiting the exact boundaries of the conception of personhood in play here. They will, again, be addressed in chapter 8. For our present purposes, however, what is needed is to see that *human beings* are 'persons' and not 'things,' and hence the moral injunction against using them against their will applies to them (if also to other beings as well).

But not so fast. The other thing you will wonder about is whether my definition of personhood means that some *humans* do not count as 'persons.' What about children and mental incompetents? I return to this concern below, after I have described what I mean by 'judgment' and how it can and should be used in difficult cases such as these. And before proceeding I should point out that the fact that there might be some exceptions to the general description of human 'personhood' does not mean that the description does not still apply to all the other cases. But the short answer to the question posed is that there are no hard and fast rules about human exceptions from personhood and that instead *judgment* is required. Children and mental incompetents are indeed the principal exceptions, but in most of those cases what to do—that is, who should make decisions for them—is fairly obvious. We might say, then, that the paradigmatic exemplar of a 'person' is a normally functioning human adult. The closer a being, any being, approximates this exemplar, the stronger is its claim to respect as a 'person.' In most cases there will be little doubt as to whether the individual in question is in fact a person or not, even if it will turn out to be difficult, even impossible, to give a perfect and exceptionless definition of the exact boundary.[7] Thus the conception of personhood described here should be sufficient to cover the majority of cases: it will allow us to tell in most cases whether a being in question is a 'person,' and, if not, which persons should be in charge of making decisions for them.

But there will nevertheless be cases where people of good faith will disagree—cases of particularly mature teenagers, say, or of an increasingly forgetful and confused grandmother. In hard marginal cases like these, there are, I suggest, no universally applicable rules yielding unique decisions that can be relied on. I wish there *were* such rules—it would make things a lot easier; but unfortunately there are not. I invite you to try to formulate one if you're not sure; I bet you won't be able to come up with a rule that is not subject to falsifying exceptions. If I am right, then in such cases *good judgment* will instead have to be exercised. The next question, then, is what exactly is this 'judgment,' and what makes it *good* as opposed to *bad?*

JUDGMENT, FREEDOM, AND RESPONSIBILITY

So human beings, or at least most of them, are 'persons,' and therefore they have purposes that are or can be deliberate. The other distinctively human feature is that they have a power that allows them to recognize their ends, including the relative ranking of their ends; to assess their current situations, including the opportunities and resources available to them; to estimate the relative chances of success at serving their ends that various available actions would provide; and finally to decide what to do based on a judgment taking all these variables into account. I wrap all of this into one term: *judgment.* To have judgment is to be able to do all this, and if something is a person, then it has judgment. Judgment is not, however, an all-or-nothing thing: it is a skill and, like other skills,

---

[7] Donald E. Brown, for example, cites the features I suggest among the "universal" features of humanity. See Brown's *Human Universals* and "Human Universals and Their Implications."

to be good at it you need to practice and exercise it. Also like other skills, judgment is something that some people will develop better than others. That fact is reflected in the everyday experience that you would go to some people for advice but emphatically not to others; you trust some people's judgments about even your most important life decisions, whereas you also know people whose judgment you would not trust as far as you could throw them. The relevant point, though, is that every person has judgment and that it can be bettered by concerted practice. That too distinguishes persons from things.

If judgment is a skill that can get better by practice—or worse by disuse or misuse—what is required to make it better? Judgment requires two things: freedom and responsibility. It first requires the freedom to exercise it, the freedom to make decisions about oneself and one's life. If someone else is making my decisions for me, then I am not going to develop any judgment—in the same way that if someone else pays all my bills for me, I will not develop any sense of value or economy. A former professor of mine put it this way: people start cleaning up after themselves about the time everyone else stops cleaning up after them. That captures an important truth, but it is only half of the truth. The other half is that you need to be held accountable for your decisions too. If you are allowed to decide for yourself how to use your credit card, but then, when you have run the balance up to its limit, someone else pays the bill, you will not be developing your judgment. If you never clean up your messes or dress appropriately or open the door for another when you should, but no one ever calls you on it, then, well, so what? What difference will it make to me that I am imprudent, inconsiderate, rude, or selfish, if those I care about do not require me to change? If no one embarrasses me by pointing out my bad behavior, if no one shuns or avoids me, if no one chastizes me, if no one cuts my gravy train off, then I have little or no incentive to change; and being naturally lazy, as most of us are to some extent or other, chances are I won't change if I don't have to. Good judgment develops, in other words, not only by enjoying the freedom to exercise it, but also by being required to take responsibility for its exercise.

Another way of making the same point: if you were going to create your own new religion, one requiring people to sacrifice and change their otherwise everyday behavior, it would help to have a hell. Promises of good things to come if one behaves the way your religion prescribes will take you some distance, more with some people and less with others; but your efforts will be considerably aided if you also have punishment for bad behavior. The example of religion also highlights the role of instruction in developing good judgment. We can give people the list of specific rules by which the religion requires them to live, or the general maxim we wish them to apply; but people will also have to interpret the rules or the maxim, figure out how to apply it to their own cases, when exceptions should be allowed and when not, and so on. For all these tasks, their own judgment will be necessary, and getting them to develop it wisely and then to use it is likely to be more successful if you offer both the carrot and the stick.

Why would that be? Couldn't we rely on people's benevolence, innate goodness, or on their sense of virtue, perhaps properly instructed by those who already possess good judgment? The answer, I suggest, is "no, we can't." Let me justify my answer by reference to what I call *natural necessity,* or the idea that allowing things to take their "natural" course imposes incentives on people to which they will, sooner or later, respond, and that it is sometimes *only* when these natural incentives are felt that people respond at all, let alone properly. The nineteenth-century philosopher and evolutionary biologist Herbert Spencer—the contemporary of Darwin who actually coined the phrase "survival of the fittest"—wrote that it is a mistake to protect people from the natural consequences of their decisions: "The ultimate effect of shielding men from the effects of folly," wrote Spencer, "is to fill the world with fools."[8] That is put in typical Victorian prose, which sounds a bit harsh to our ears, but it contains a kernel of truth nonetheless. That kernel is that human beings respond to incentives. If a particular course of action leads to a felt reduction in their well-being, then they will tend to avoid it in the future; if, on the other hand, a particular course of action leads to no such reduction, then they have no incentive to avoid it in the future. The unstated premise in the argument is that when a reduction in well-being is *personally* experienced, as opposed to being experienced by others, the individual concerned is much more likely to amend his future behavior. Calling this a response to *natural necessity* emphasizes, then, that we must sometimes let nature take its course, allowing the consequences

---

[8] See http://www.bartleby.com/66/50/54950.html. Partly on the strength of this and similar claims, Spencer has been unjustly maligned by history as a "Social Darwinist"—despite his repeated, and at the time radical, arguments for equal treatment of women and slaves and his denunciations of the treatment of women and slaves and of the British class system. For a good discussion of Spencer and how history has smeared his name, see Roderick T. Long's "Herbert Spencer: The Defamation Continues," http://www.lewrockwell.com/orig3/long3.html.

of people's actions to be experienced by them—even if they are bad or uncomfortable or lead to a reduction in well-being, and even if we could intervene and protect the people in question from enduring the consequences. That is precisely how we learn from mistakes and develop a sense about what sorts of things we should shun or avoid and what we should seek out—in other words, how we develop good judgment. And it is what will create the motivation necessary to act on what our judgment indicates.

Let me illustrate with a concrete example. My wife has a friend who tells her that one of her children "just will not eat anything but mayonnaise sandwiches" and that the friend fears for her daughter's health. Your heart might go out to this parent, tragically burdened, as she apparently is, with a gustatorial freak of nature. But of course it's not *literally* true that the girl won't eat anything but mayonnaise sandwiches. So what is the best way to address this girl's potential health problem? Let her go a day without eating, and then see how long her natural freakishness holds out. That is what I mean by letting natural necessity work. Similarly, I suggest, with adults: we sometimes hear how some people are incapable of finding work, of preparing themselves for an interview, of finding adequate housing on their own, of negotiating the purchase of a car, even of finding the best cell phone plan or buying a digital camera.[9] But of course people are capable of doing these things, if given the chance and allowed to develop their judgment. They might not be good at such things at first, especially if someone else has been doing it for them all this time, but they will catch on—and sooner than you think, once the natural necessity of finding out ways to increase their well-being and avoid ways of diminishing it is brought to bear on them.

To respect someone's personhood, then, requires *both* giving him freedom *and* holding him accountable for what he does with that freedom. That is the only way he will be able to develop judgment; and the possession of judgment, and allowing others to develop it, is integral to personhood.

Respecting personhood will therefore entail respecting the choices a person makes. That means we will have to let a person take drugs, visit prostitutes, listen to bad music, read romance novels, and say stupid or offensive things, just as much as it means we will have to let him invent

---

[9] The last two examples come from psychology professor Barry Schwartz, writing in the January 22, 2004, *New York Times*. Schwartz's full argument is found in his *The Paradox of Choice: Why More Is Less*.

and sell new pharmaceuticals, operate a business, write symphonies, and publish his blog of witty and incisive political commentary. It does *not* mean, however, that we should yield to the common injunctions not to be "judgmental" because it hurts people's feelings. Yes, it can hurt people's feelings—but sometimes that is exactly what's required! What the denizens of daytime talk shows say to the contrary notwithstanding, forming and communicating judgments of one another is a crucial and integral part of the process of developing judgment and thus of the fabric of shared moral community. In addition to damming the feedback people need from others to develop their judgment, keeping our judgments to ourselves can have the adverse effects of isolating us from others and of weakening or even gradually dissolving the social bonds that connect and hold together the members of a community.[10] If someone is misbehaving or acting improperly or doing something we disapprove of, we absolutely should let our awareness of that affect our behavior. As the case may be, we should speak up and let the person know, we should stop being his friend, we should ignore or avoid or move away from him, we should make him pay his own bills. If you're just being catty or captious, well, that is not exactly polite and you should probably stop—perhaps that is the element of truth in admonitions not to be "judgmental." But we should resist the mistake of taking the reasonable advice not to be needlessly fault-finding as reason to refrain from judging altogether. If you don't exercise your judgment you are not fully realizing your own personhood; the corollary to this is that the more you try not to judge others, the less do you respect *their* personhood, while possibly allowing your own to atrophy. There is, then, no contradiction between holding, on the one hand, that a person should be allowed to make decisions about his own life, that it is not our place to intercede forcibly, and that he should face the natural consequences of his decisions and actions, while also holding, on the other hand, that if the person is making bad decisions, we can, and perhaps should, tell him so. Both follow from, and are instances of, respecting both his and our own personhood.

It should be emphasized that nature, as one might put it somewhat anthropomorphically, is a harsh mistress: she has a way of getting what is her due in the end. Bad decisions have bad consequences, and nature

---

[10] Robin Dunbar argues that sharing of such judgments—what is often somewhat pejoratively referred to as "gossip"—is crucial to maintaining social order in human communities, in just the way that mutual grooming is crucial to maintaining order in great ape communities. See his *Grooming, Gossip, and the Evolution of Language*, chap. 4.

will make sure that the costs of bad decisions are borne somewhere by someone. As the publicist and social critic Albert Jay Nock wrote in 1931,

But unfortunately Nature recks little of the nobleness of prompting any human enterprise. Perhaps it is rather a hard thing to say, but the truth is that Nature seems much more solicitous about her reputation for order than she is about keeping up her character for morals. Apparently no pressure of noble and unselfish moral earnestness will cozen the sharp old lady into countenancing a breach of order. Hence any enterprise, however nobly and disinterestedly conceived, will fail if it be not also organized intelligently.[11]

Having, for example, a government program to pay people after they lose their jobs sounds like a good idea, motivated by the "noble and unselfish moral earnestness" Nock speaks of. But sometimes people lose their jobs because they decided not to bother developing the skills necessary to keep their jobs or to get new ones. It takes work, after all, to develop skills or learn new ones. If such a government program exists, and if it pays people money regardless of the reasons for their having lost their jobs (as is often the case for such programs), the program does not, alas, erase or annihilate the consequences of not developing those skills: it only shifts the costs onto other people—in this case, the taxpayers paying for the program. The point is that sooner or later *someone* will pay for bad decisions. So the question, then, is not whether we can escape paying for them, because we can't, but rather how best to minimize the costs. And the best long-term strategy for minimizing bad decisions, I suggest, is to connect as directly as possible the consequences of decisions to the person or persons making them. To whatever extent this link between freedom and responsibility is severed, there will be a corresponding diminution of the incentives to avoid bad decisions: we are far less motivated to economize, consider options carefully and thoroughly, and discipline ourselves if we know that someone else will pick up the tab.

I said earlier that one of the abiding features of human nature is laziness. Though some of us suffer from this more than others, we all tend to be relentless economizers of our own energy: we do not want to put out any more effort than is necessary to achieve our goals, and we tend to look for ways to get the biggest results with the smallest effort. This means, for example, that we tend not to undertake the difficult and laborious tasks of weighing options, considering the long-term effects of our actions, and disciplining ourselves to act in accordance with what we judge to

---

[11] From "American Education," first published in the May 1931 *Atlantic Monthly;* reprinted in *The State of the Union,* p. 174.

be right—unless some natural necessity requires us to do so. Weighing, considering, and disciplining all take effort and energy, and so people will be inclined to expend that effort and energy only when it seems to them that it will pay off in the form of giving them something they want whose value (to them) outweighs the cost of the effort. That is why we should often let natural necessity take its course.

Here, then, are the steps of the argument so far: people need to develop judgment to realize their personhood; to develop judgment, people must have both the freedom to use it by making decisions for themselves and the responsibility of suffering or enjoying the consequences of their decisions; and they will be motivated to exercise their judgment only if the consequences involved connect up with their personal scheme of desires, goals, and ambitions. The last step in this chain of inferences is natural necessity; or rather it is the first step on the road to good judgment.

It is of course difficult, perhaps even in some cases impossible, to ensure that the consequences of a person's decisions redound only on himself, since human beings form networks of associations over which those consequences, good and bad, can propagate. Hence one might object that my suggestion that we let natural necessity work is impracticable, perhaps even unjust, precisely because people's actions almost always have some effect on others. Shouldn't we rather *protect* people from the (bad) effects of other people's actions? Yes! That is precisely my argument. The way to protect people from others' bad decisions is precisely by making sure, as far as we can, that the consequences of A's actions affect only A, that the consequences of B's actions affect only B, and that, unless they mutually agreed otherwise, ne'er the twain shall meet. Thus we should strive to maintain the connection between decision (or freedom) and consequences (or responsibility) as much as possible. Not only is that the way to respect people's personhood—both of the actors and of those affected by their actions—but it also allows to operate the natural incentives that give people the motivations necessary to develop their judgment properly, and hence, we can hope, to make fewer bad decisions in the future.

NATURAL HUMAN MOTIVATION

I do not wish to suggest that human beings are exclusively self-interested in any narrow or pernicious sense. Indeed, I take it as all but self-evident that they routinely consider the interests of others in making their decisions. The contrary position, often called egoism, is one of the most frequently refuted views in moral philosophy. Contemporary philosophers who refute egoism often take the theory to amount to the claim that one is morally required to disregard others' interests, to stab them in the back when it suits one and one can get away with it, and generally to take every opportunity to advance oneself without any regard for others. I am not sure who actually holds such a view,[12] but, regardless, it must be distinguished from the argument I am making here. Although the "self-interested" human being is indeed concerned with his own interests first and foremost, nevertheless these interests routinely and regularly involve the interests of others. So they are "his own" in the innocuous sense that it is the individual who has them, and additionally the claim is that the individual is naturally partial to his own interests; but I am certainly not supposing that all human beings are by nature wickedly selfish.

On the contrary, I subscribe to the belief that human beings are naturally sociable. They seek out the company of other people and they look for ways to develop long-lasting and deep bonds with others. They moreover frequently sacrifice their narrowly conceived "selfish" interests for the sake of others with whom they have formed such bonds, including spouses, siblings, children, and friends. Thomas Hobbes (1588–1679) famously, or perhaps infamously, argued that wherever human beings "live without a common power to keep them all in awe, they are in that condition which is called war, and such a war as is of every man against every man."[13] He further argued that in the natural state of humanity,

there is no place for industry, because the fruit thereof is uncertain, and consequently, no culture of the earth, no navigation, nor use of the commodities that may be imported by sea, no commodious building, no instruments of moving and removing such things as require much force, no knowledge of the face of the earth, no account of time, no arts, no letters, no society, and which is worst of all, continual fear and danger of violent death, and the life of man, solitary, poor, nasty, brutish, and short.[14]

---

[12] This view is not held by Aristotle or Adam Smith, who are sometimes implicated; not even Ayn Rand, who goes so far as to give her moral view the deliberately provocative name "the virtue of selfishness," can be characterized this way. It is also a mistake to ascribe this view to contemporary sociobiologists such as E. O. Wilson or to free-market economists such as Milton Friedman or F. A. Hayek. Perhaps Max Stirner or some neoclassical economists are examples. For these authors' works, see the bibliography; for a general discussion of the issues involved, see James Rachels's *Elements of Moral Philosophy*, chaps. 5 and 6; for a recent example of an attempt to refute "egoism," see Stuart Rachels, "Nagelian Arguments against Egoism"; for a discussion of some aspects of neoclassical economics, see Wikipedia's entry "Homo Economicus," http://en.wikipedia.org/wiki/Homo_economicus.

[13] *Leviathan*, part I, chap. xii, p. 76.

[14] Ibid.

That last line is one of the most famous in all of Western philosophy, trailing perhaps only René Descartes's "cogito ergo sum" ("I think; therefore I am") and Socrates's "the unexamined life is not worth living." One can understand why Hobbes would think that mankind's natural state was so nasty and brutish: he wrote *Leviathan,* after all, in 1651, just after the English civil war and the execution of its sitting monarch, Charles I, and the deep religious and political divisions among the people of England— not to mention the unhygienic squalor in which most people lived at the time[15]—cannot have given a very good impression of mankind's "natural" state. Nevertheless, although the apparent ease with which mankind can be provoked to aggression and atrocity cannot be gainsaid, I think everyday experience points against Hobbes. Surely far more common than war and fighting, even as common as those are, is the neighborliness of local communities, the charity and respect shown toward strangers, the caring, love, and concern among spouses, family members, and friends, and the tenderness, love, and sacrifice shown by parents toward their children. And all of this takes place without a "power to keep them all in awe" forcing them to be courteous, loving, and respectful of one another on pain of punishment or death.

To focus on one particularly prominent example: no one, I believe, who has had children, or been around those who have them, can doubt the genuine sacrifices that parents routinely and regularly make for their children. It is sometimes claimed that parents act lovingly toward and sacrifice for their children because by doing so they are really, albeit indirectly, serving their own self-interests—by, say, increasing the chance that their children will care for them in their old age or by just making their lives more enjoyable by not having unhappy children around.[16] Such explanations are based on the implausible narrowly self-interested conception of human motivation that I mentioned earlier. The evidence for human altruism is contained in human sociality, which is everywhere around us. Consider, for example, that almost everyone would rather be with others than be alone; we all have times when we like to be by ourselves, but there are very, very few people who prefer long-term solitude to having close and loving relations with others. Moreover, I take the fact that when you meet eyes with a stranger, say, walking down the sidewalk,

---

[15] For a graphic and arresting glimpse of conditions in the England of Hobbes's day, see Lawrence Stone's *The Family, Sex and Marriage in England 1500–1800.*

[16] See Gary S. Becker's *Treatise on the Family,* chaps. 5 and 6, and Richard A. Posner's *Sex and Reason,* chaps. 7–9.

your first inclination is to smile—not to growl or threaten—as anecdotal but still telling further evidence of our disposition toward both sociality and benevolence.

Now the explanation for the existence of this human altruism is contested and has seen considerable discussion in recent years. Evolutionary biologists, for example, often try to account for it by recourse to something they call "kin selection," whereby the presence of a genuine concern for the well-being of one's kin might have increased the chances of the survival of the genotype shared among the kin, and thus would have been selected for. The idea is that what gets selected for is copies of genes, regardless of the individual housing the copies. Since an individual's siblings and parents, for example, carry genes that are very similar to its own, the hypothesis is that what might be selected for is not only an interest in *oneself* reproducing—because, after all, that is putting all one's eggs in one basket—but rather an interest in *both* oneself *and* one's near relatives surviving. The theory of kin selection would predict moreover that the further one gets away from oneself—that is, as the "coefficient of relatedness" declines—the less concern an individual would have for another.

Whether this is the correct explanation of human altruism or not,[17] it shows the general consensus that this *is* a feature of humanity that must be explained. Moreover, the theory of kin selection indicates a further aspect of this human altruism that is relevant here: it is limited. We do not feel a universal benevolence toward others, and hence we cannot be counted on or expected to act in a generally beneficent way. Some biologists have attempted to apply a mathematical precision to the descending levels of concern we naturally have as the coefficient of relatedness declines—claiming that an individual should, for example, be willing to sacrifice itself to save two siblings, four nephews, or eight cousins, since siblings share 50 percent of one's own genes, nephews 25 percent, cousins 12.5 percent, and so on[18]—but it strikes me as implausible that genes

---

[17] It is not universally accepted. For recent discussions, see Buss, *The Evolution of Desire,* esp. chap. 12; Dawkins, *The Selfish Gene;* Kitcher, *Vaulting Ambition,* chap. 3; Ridley, *The Origins of Virtue,* esp. chap. 1; Sober and Wilson, *Unto Others;* E. O. Wilson, *Consilience,* esp. chap. 8; J. Q. Wilson, *The Moral Sense,* esp. chap. 2; and Wright, *The Moral Animal,* esp. chap. 7. I draw on all these works in my discussion.

[18] As did, for example, William Hamilton, in his 1964 papers "The Genetical Evolution of Social Behaviour I" and "The Genetical Evolution of Social Behaviour II," both collected in *The Narrow Roads of Gene Land.* For sustained criticism of this enterprise, see Kitcher's *Vaulting Ambition.*

could determine behavior with anything like this much precision. (Even one of the strongest natural desires human beings have—to have sex— does not determine how often, or even whether, a person will have sex, with whom, and so on.) It is much more reasonable to say that our genes determine parameters, or "reaction norms," within which our behavior can fall; the exact course of anyone's behavior will be somewhere in that range—that much we can know—but *exactly* where it will fall cannot be predicted by knowing one's genes. Relating this to the case of altruism, we can say that our genes suggest a *familiarity principle:* our interest in and con- cern for others naturally declines as our familiarity with them declines. So we are principally concerned with ourselves, then with our closest fam- ily and friends (for whom our concern might approach, equal, perhaps occasionally even exceed that for ourselves), then with other friends, then with acquaintances, then, finally, strangers.[19] Outside these circles of con- cern altogether might be people we view as enemies, say, from hostile or warring tribes; people we view as not really being human, as, for exam- ple, slaveholders commonly view their slaves; or animals and other living things that we do not consider as deserving of concern approaching what other humans deserve.

This brief discussion of human motivation suggests another claim, which will also come into play later in our study: a proposed system of moral or political order that is premised on universal benevolence or on an absence, even in the long run, of self-interest is a nonstarter. We might be able to extend benevolence (by extending familiarity), and we can probably find ways to channel natural self-interest so that it maximizes its constructive tendencies and minimizes its destructive tendencies, but it is exceedingly unlikely that we will ever get rid of self-interest or inculcate

---

[19] This principle is accepted by most evolutionary biologists and evolutionary psychologists today, but it was already articulated carefully by Adam Smith in his 1759 *Theory of Moral Sentiments* (hereafter referred to as TMS). For discussion, see James R. Otteson, *Adam Smith's Marketplace of Life,* chap. 5. The idea has Stoic origins. For example, the Stoic Hierocles (fl. ca. A.D. 100) wrote, "Each one of us is as it were entirely encompassed by many circles. . . . The first and closest circle is the one which a person has drawn as though around the centre, his own mind. . . . Next . . . contains parents, siblings, wife, and children. The third one has in it uncles and aunts, grandparents, nephews, nieces, and cousins. . . . The next circle includes other relatives, and this is followed by the circle of local residents, then the circle of fellow-tribesmen, next that of fellow-citizens, and in the same way the circle of people from neighbouring towns, and the circle of fellow- countrymen. The outermost and largest circle, which encompasses all the rest, is that of the whole human race" (in Long and Sedley, *Hellenistic Philosophers,* vol. I, p. 349). I thank Leonidas Montes for this reference.

a universal benevolence. Human beings just aren't constructed that way: their care and concern starts with themselves and declines as its object recedes from them, and even if we can find ways to extend this care and concern, there appears to be no chance of making it extend equally even to their family and friends, let alone to all mankind. Thus however intellectually appealing a moral "cosmopolitanism" might be, whereby each of us views every other one of us as deserving of equal concern and consideration, it is, as we might put it, naturally impossible for us to put that into practice because it is inconsistent with fundamental principles of our nature. Again, that is not to say that we cannot concern ourselves with other people's interests: obviously, we do that every day. The claim is rather that it is extremely unlikely for most people under ordinary circumstances that they could act on the principle that everyone's interests have exactly as much weight as everyone else's. And hence it would be imprudent to design political institutions that presuppose anything other than a predominance of self-interest motivating most people most of the time.

Just how unlikely would it be that we could change the balance of people's motivations from self-interest to benevolence, or extend their natural concern to all mankind? It would be like trying to teach tigers not to attack and kill their natural prey. With concerted, persistent—and coerced, one might add—effort, you might make some headway in getting them to jump through hoops or stand on their hind legs, but if you let a baby wild boar loose in your trained Siberian tiger's habitat, well, I think we both know what would happen. Similarly, there are human beings who have achieved an extraordinary regard for others—Mother Teresa, for example, or St. Francis of Assisi—but those people were so extraordinary that we call them saints! If we tried to institute a social policy whereby, say, parents were to regard every child as equally deserving of their time and concern as their own children were—something approximating what Plato (427–347 B.C.) imagined in Book V of his *Republic*—however zealously we tried to persuade parents to follow the policy, when they came upon children that they recognized as their own, well, again I think we both know what would happen.

My conclusion, then, is that we should accept the facts of expanded but still limited natural self-interest, of natural but also limited benevolence, and of the governance of both by the familiarity principle. If we couple this claim with those I made earlier about the need for natural necessity in developing judgment and the requirement that we respect personhood, we begin to get an idea about what kinds of political institutions would be suitable—or, if not quite that yet, then at least what political institutions would be *un*suitable—for human beings constituted as they actually are.

I would like to introduce a distinction that is crucial to my discussion of judgment, freedom, and responsibility and that plays a large role in the drawing out of political implications in this book. That distinction is between *positive virtue,* on the one hand, and *negative justice,* on the other. The positive virtues are those actions and behaviors that one ought to engage in to be a *fully* good person, those activities that go above and beyond the minimal call of duty. I call them "positive" because they typically require a person to *do* something: you must take positive action to fulfill them. Negative justice, however, concerns principally those minimal actions and behaviors that one must *refrain from* in order for a society to survive and for social relations to exist at all. To be moderate, or courteous, or loyal, for example, requires that you engage in only those activities you should, and only to the degree that you should, that you take the interests and well-being of others into proper consideration when you act, and that you stand by your friends when they need you, even if it would profit you to betray them. Exemplifying these virtues makes a person admirable, and a society filled with such persons is one each of us would probably like to live in. But society could survive and social relations could exist even if people were not moderate, courteous, or loyal. It might not be the most attractive society, but as long as people aren't assaulting, enslaving, or stealing from one another, the society could soldier on. On the contrary, if people in your society *are* assaulting, enslaving, or stealing from one another—or defrauding or reneging on contracts with one another, which are forms of stealing—then your society is not long for this world. Adam Smith captured the distinction well when he wrote that benevolence "is the ornament which embellishes, not the foundation which supports the building [of society], and which it was, therefore, sufficient to recommend, but by no means necessary to impose. Justice, on the contrary, is the main pillar that upholds the whole edifice" (TMS, p. 86). The key point is that to act justly, as opposed to being positively virtuous, usually what one has to do is simply refrain from taking certain actions (such as assaulting or stealing). That is why this conception of justice is called "negative." Smith again: "We may often fulfil all the rules of justice by sitting still and doing nothing" (TMS, p. 82).

Now this "negative" conception of justice is a controversial one,[20] and it admits of exceptions. One principal cluster of exceptions is the keeping of contracts or promises: even on this minimal conception of justice, it is unjust to renege on contracts because that is tantamount to theft; but fulfilling contracts usually means that once you have voluntarily entered into a contract you must take positive action to fulfill it. Yet even in cases of contracts it might still be possible for one to fulfill the rules of justice by doing nothing—if one simply refrained from making promises or entering into contracts in the first place. The more difficult objection one might raise, however, is that acting "justly" toward another might sometimes require actually *doing something for* the person rather than simply *not doing something to* him. I acknowledge this alternative conception of justice, but I resist it nonetheless. I wish to say instead that the things one might be inclined to include in the broader, "positive" conception of justice—such as charity, compassion, courtesy, or generosity—are indeed traits we would like others, and ourselves, to have, but that are not *necessary* for the maintenance of a peaceful society. They would thus come under the definition I gave of "positive virtue," not of "negative justice." At this point the distinction may seem merely verbal, but in fact it has significant implications: because we usually endorse coercion to enforce justice, exactly what counts as 'justice' will be of considerable moment.

I suggested that negative justice is crucial to maintaining a good social order because no society whatever can survive if it is not recognized and enforced, coercively if necessary. On the other side, however, all sorts of untoward consequences can be attendant on attempting to enforce coercively the rules of positive virtue. Attempting to force charity, compassion, generosity, and so on by legislation would require comprehensive oversight and observation of people's behaviors, including their private behaviors, and a vast bureaucracy to collect, monitor, and assess the information on their personal situations, associations, and relationships. People in such a society would soon be spending more time spying on each other than producing goods, services, or wealth. Moreover, and just as worrying, the systematic substitution of the *state's* judgments of what

---

[20] For classic discussions of the distinction between "negative" and "positive" conceptions of justice, see Isaiah Berlin's 1969 "Two Concepts of Liberty" and Gerald McCallum's 1967 "Negative and Positive Freedom." For more recent discussions that defend positions different from mine, see Samuel Fleischacker's *A Third Concept of Liberty* and Stephen Holmes and Cass R. Sunstein's *The Cost of Rights*. For an illuminating recent discussion, see Max Hocutt's "Sunstein on Rights" and Sunstein's reply, "Confusing Rights: A Reply to Hocutt."

counts as the minimum allowable charity, compassion, or generosity for that of each individual would lead, if our argument so far has been right, to a gradual decline in individuals' own abilities to judge. Smith says that a government charged with the vague goal of enforcing positive virtue would soon institute something like a society-wide "inquisition" (TMS, p. 105), endeavoring to peer into the inner thoughts of people, asking neighbors to spy and give evidence on their neighbors, and so on. Perhaps that could indeed lead to the condition Hobbes described, and perhaps there is further supporting evidence in other historical examples, including in the twentieth century, of where societies based on systematic oversight of their members' behavior and private relations can lead.[21]

I recommend instead, therefore, the Smithian conclusion that society should restrict its use of coercive power to enforcing adherence to the rules of negative justice. Leave the encouraging of positive virtue to other means. If it should turn out that the "other means" of encouraging virtue—we discuss what those are in due course—turn out not to be as successful or effective as we would like, still a society organized around an exact administration of justice will at least be a safe and peaceful one in which we can carry on with the business of our lives.

THE RULES OF JUSTICE

What exactly *are* the rules of 'justice,'[22] then? This has of course been a subject of central philosophical concern since Socrates (470–399 B.C.), and there have traditionally been roughly two ways of addressing the question. First, there has been the method of Socrates and his student Plato, whereby one tries to arrive at a definition of justice by means of a kind of a priori, or purely logical, deduction or intellectual apprehension. According to this method, we ask ourselves what the *concept* of justice inherently includes. Perhaps we entertain a series of proposed definitions, finding fault with each of them successively, until we arrive by process of elimination at a faultless definition. On the Platonic view, this definition would be one that explains why every instance of justice (or injustice) is in fact just (or unjust); it would therefore be of universal applicability, it would be fixed and unchanging, and it would serve as an exemplar,

---

[21] See, for example, Friedrich A. Hayek's *The Road to Serfdom.*
[22] From here on, when I speak of "justice," I mean "negative justice."

paradigm, or template by which to determine whether future actions or decisions were just.

The second traditional method of figuring out what justice is, is connected more generally with Plato's student Aristotle. For Aristotle, determining what counts as justice is a rather more empirical and pragmatic affair. His view is roughly that we investigate conceptions of justice historically held, we examine those currently in practice in our own and in other communities, and then—here is the crucial part—we look to see what works. The criterion "what works" is a bit vague, but it means roughly which conceptions of justice allow human beings to flourish, to have peaceable and beneficial relations with others, and to make their lives better, whereas conceptions of justice under which people can't do those things, or not as easily or well, would be conceptions that *do not* "work." On this account of justice, it is not an a priori, timeless, changeless entity that we apprehend intellectually, but is instead an operational or provisional concept that we discover empirically and pragmatically. So what counts as 'justice' in one place may or may not be the same thing as 'justice' in another place: whether 'justice' will be universal or not is an open question, to be resolved, if at all, by empirical investigation.

Now there is considerable scholarly debate as to how exactly to characterize Socratic or Platonic and Aristotelian notions of justice, as well as their respective scientific or philosophical methods, but we need not concern ourselves with those debates here.[23] What is relevant to our purposes is the rough distinction between a priori, or purely logical, investigation and a posteriori, or based on empirical data, investigation. I favor the latter over the former. Indeed, I am skeptical that there exists any universal form of justice out there somewhere awaiting discovery. What I am more confident about is that human beings seem to have a nature, that the world seems to have a nature, and that if we want to figure out how human beings should behave given their ends, we will need to see what their and the world's natures are. That means empirical investigation, and a lot of it.

What indeed has empirical investigation disclosed? Is there anything we can say in general about an empirically grounded human 'justice'? It turns out there is. Historical investigation converges on a concept of justice that is indeed nearly universal, centering on, as I suggested earlier,

---

[23] The literature on Platonic and Aristotelian justice is vast. Accounts I recommend are Richard Kraut's "The Defense of Justice in Plato's *Republic*" and Fred D. Miller Jr.'s *Nature, Justice, and Rights in Aristotle's Politics*.

three things: protections of oneself, protections of one's liberty, and protections of one's property. If this seems familiar, it is probably because it is the conception on which the Declaration of Independence is based, and it is the driving motivation for what has become known as "classical liberalism."[24] The idea is that a government is created to protect people's lives, liberty, and property and that it is justified in using coercive powers both to support itself in those activities and to punish infractions of those principles, but that it is not justified in doing anything else. In the next two chapters I investigate this conception of government in more detail, and I argue—and, I hope, will convince you—that it is indeed the conception of government we should support. Here, however, I limit my claim to the argument that this basic, "negative" conception of justice is the *minimum* that must be recognized and enforced by any society for it to survive. As I have argued, if people in your society are routinely assaulting one another, stealing from one another, and enslaving one another, then your society either is or will shortly become a state of war, not really a society at all. That is the sense in which we can say that justice is "universal": human nature is sufficiently fixed and human experience is sufficiently similar that all human societies, whatever else is true about them and however else they will vary in their details, will have to respect these rules of justice. If you would like therefore to call this justice "natural," and think of it as "natural law," please do. Just keep in mind that it is an empirically discovered generalization, like Newton's "laws" of motion, not a law in the sense of a rule that was handed down by a lawgiver, divine or otherwise.

The conclusion I suggest is that society is justified in requiring its members to abide by the rules of justice, for otherwise there would be no society; but beyond that it should take no action, for otherwise it would disrespect or imperil people's personhood. Although we might justifiably feel and communicate disapprobation at a person's injustices or his vices, we are justified in forcibly correcting or punishing only his injustices. As should be clear, however, that certainly does not mean that we are powerless in the face of vice: we can remonstrate with the vicious person, try to persuade him, exhort him, plead with him, argue with him; we can shun, avoid, or ignore him; we can even organize others to do any

---

[24] The qualifier "classical" is used in part to distinguish this version of liberalism from the "progressive" liberalism that gained currency in Britain and America in the late nineteenth century and is largely what is still meant today by the term "liberalism."

or all of these things with us. But if he persists in behaving in ways we consider vicious, at the end of the day we must recognize his freedom to do so. All we have left to do is make sure that the consequences of his actions are, as much as possible, restricted in their effects to him alone.

JUSTICE AND THE POND CASE

Let me illustrate my use of the distinction between positive virtue and negative justice, along with the political implications I'm suggesting it has, with a concrete example. The philosopher Peter Singer argues that we have a moral duty to give to poor people overseas; moreover, he considers great personal sacrifice in this regard—amounting even to everything a person has to the point of "marginal utility," or until the next unit given away would make the giver worse off than the recipient—not as "supererogatory," or above and beyond the call of duty, but rather as obligatory; and he suggests that the state ought to take money from private hands and redistribute it to this end.[25] His argument seems to presuppose a *one-place* conception of morality: either one is moral or one is immoral. If one does not help distant suffering people, one is immoral; if one does, one is (at least on this count) not immoral. Yet we tend to recognize in our everyday dealings with people something like the *two-place* conception I have been describing. We say that I disagree with what you say, but that you have a right to say it; we say that you are wasting your life doing what you do, but that it is your business to do so; we say that you are making a mistake to pay so much money for a car, but that it is your money. Yet we do *not* say that you should not kill an innocent person, but that it is your business; we do not say I think you should not rape people, but that it is your business; we do not say I think you should not steal from others, but that it is your business. I suggest that this way of looking at people and their actions reflects the distinction between *positive virtue* and *negative justice:* however disagreeable we may find it, we allow people to be vicious, or to fail to be "positively virtuous," as long as they are not unjust; but the moment they cross the line of injustice we feel justified in stepping in. We may express disapproval of viciousness, and we may attempt—through exhortation, persuasion, rebuke, and so on—to change the vicious person's behavior. But we do not initiate force because the vicious person is doing no "real and positive hurt," as Adam

---

[25] See Singer's *Practical Ethics,* chap. 8.

Smith puts it (TMS, p. 79 and passim), to anyone—except perhaps to himself, which, as a 'person,' he is entitled to do. On the other hand, murder, rape, and theft all do "real and positive hurt" to unwilling others and thus are all breaches of justice; hence our initial reaction that one ought to intervene in such cases is justified.

A brief yet necessary digression is in order. Although we might have a rough sense of what constitutes "real and positive hurt" based on what has been said so far, the term is nevertheless somewhat vague. Can it do the important moral work we are asking it to do? Here is Smith's gloss on it, which is worth quoting at length:

> Beneficence is always free, it cannot be extorted by force, the mere want of it exposes to no punishment; because the mere want of beneficence tends to do no real positive evil. It may disappoint of the good which might reasonably have been expected, and upon that account it may justly excite dislike and disapprobation: it cannot, however, provoke any resentment which mankind will go along with. The man who does not recompense his benefactor when he has it in his power, and when his benefactor needs his assistance, is, no doubt, guilty of the blackest ingratitude. The heart of every impartial spectator rejects all fellow-feeling with the selfishness of his motives, and he is the proper object of the highest disapprobation. But still he does no positive hurt to any body. He only does not do that good which in propriety he ought to have done. He is the object of hatred, a passion which is naturally excited by impropriety of sentiment and behaviour; not of resentment, a passion which is never properly called forth but by actions which tend to do real and positive hurt to some particular persons. His want of gratitude, therefore, cannot be punished. To oblige him by force to perform what in gratitude he ought to perform, and what every impartial spectator would approve of him for performing, would, if possible, be still more improper than his neglecting to perform it. (TMS, pp. 78–9)

Smith distinguishes here between two scenarios: (1) not doing a good deed for someone, as, for example, not doing a favor for someone who has done you a favor in the past, and (2) deliberately doing something bad to someone, which entails taking an action designed to damage a person. Both are blameworthy. But the former, the failure of "positive virtue," is *only* blameworthy; the latter, which Smith interchangeably calls "positive evil" and "positive hurt," is, according to Smith, *both* blameworthy *and* punishable. Does this explanation, then, clear up exactly what will count as real and positive hurt, and thus deserve punishment, and what won't? For the most part, yes. There will still be hard cases; we shall consider some in a moment. But this distinction will serve us well in the majority of cases. Let us see how by looking at Peter Singer's famous hypothetical scenario, the Pond Case.

Singer asks us to imagine a person walking past a shallow pond in which a young child is drowning.[26] As Singer frames it, the person does not wade in to help the child—perhaps because he is in a hurry, perhaps because he does not want to get his clothes dirty, or perhaps because he believes others will take care of the child. Singer would have us judge the passerby to be immoral if he does not help the child. And surely he is blameworthy. But the two-place picture I am recommending enables, I believe, a more accurate judgment: we can say that the person is *vicious* and thus blameworthy, but he is not *unjust* and thus not punishable. That is, we disapprove of his behavior, but, because he himself did no "real and positive hurt" to the child—he refrained from doing the child a good turn, but he was himself not the cause of the child's distress or suffering—he committed no injustice. We should therefore refrain from initiating force against him (by throwing him in jail, for example).

It is important to emphasize that if a person *caused* another's suffering, that is a different matter altogether: that is to breach the rules of justice. Now, some would argue that a more expansive notion of "causation" might actually include the do-nothing passerby in the causal chain leading up to the child's drowning.[27] I think that definition of causation is *too* expansive, however, because the child would (by hypothesis) have drowned whether the do-nothing passerby were there or not. So if there had been no passerby at all, the child would have drowned; if the passerby was there and did nothing, the child still would have drowned. I suggest that a theory of causation that counts as "causes" actions or events whose presence or absence makes no material difference is not a good theory. Instead, what seems required is a theory of causation by which the only actions or events that count as "causing" something to happen are those for which it is the case that, at a minimum,[28] had they not been there or had they not acted the way they did, the event in question would not have happened either. That certainly fits better with our everyday notion of causation, and I believe it will capture our considered judgments in the majority of cases. So the do-nothing passerby did not *cause* the child's

---

[26] He first posed this scenario in his "Famine, Affluence, and Morality."

[27] For an excellent discussion of competing causal theories at work in legal matters, including detailed defenses of the view I am about to reject, see Hart and Honoré's *Causation in the Law.* I thank James Taylor for helpful discussion here.

[28] Depending on the case, there may be other factors necessary as well, such as deliberate intention. Thus the criterion I offer is necessary but may not be sufficient to establish "causation." See again Hart and Honoré; for a shorter introduction to the issues, see Honoré's article "Causation in the Law" in the *Stanford Encyclopedia of Philosophy.*

predicament, hence did *no positive hurt* to the child, hence committed *no injustice,* and hence is *not justifiably punishable.*

On the account I suggest, no amount of viciousness by itself turns it into injustice. Singer's Pond Case gets much of its intuitive appeal because it is so extreme—such a small amount of effort to alleviate such a large amount of suffering. We are tempted to think that perhaps police action is warranted after all if the passerby does nothing. But my suggestion is that one should not be held punitively responsible for something one did not do. That leads to the conclusion that an inactive passerby might be horribly vicious, but not jailably unjust.

We examine Singer's argument in more detail in chapter 4, but the implication for the time being is that there should be no laws requiring a person to help a drowning child, and no laws to punish a person if he fails to help. More generally, we should legally or coercively punish only breaches of justice; failures to fulfill positive virtue fall outside the state's proper purview. That does not mean that we have no recourse against the unhelpful passerby, however. Because of his viciousness, such a person would, as Smith said, be "the proper object of the highest disapprobation." This disapprobation might take the form of any of the tools at our moral disposal: shunning, shaming, public condemnation, and so on. These measures can be extremely psychologically punishing. And though this kind of viciousness would not license forcible corrective action, the recriminations it would license would nonetheless provide a significant disincentive to engage in a large range of the behavior we would like to discourage.

EXPERIMENTS AND INDIVIDUALITY

In an unjustifiably neglected 1875 essay entitled "Vices Are Not Crimes," Lysander Spooner argued that because "vices" are "acts by which a man harms himself or his property," the vicious person should not be punished by anyone else for them; but whereas "crimes" "are those acts by which one man harms the person or property of another," those should indeed be punished.[29] Spooner's conception of "crimes" maps pretty closely onto the conception of injustice I have been pursuing: it involves doing positive hurt to others, on Spooner's account to their "person or property." Spooner's conception of "vice" is actually a bit narrower than what I have

[29] In the *Lysander Spooner Reader,* pp. 23–47.

been suggesting, since it does not include the failure to do the "good offices" to others that full "positive virtue" would require. Nevertheless, his distinction cuts at the same joint, as it were, as does my distinction and underscores its importance by reiterating its connection to forcible state action. The argument Spooner gives for this distinction, and thus for its obvious political implications, echoes an argument John Stuart Mill had made in his classic 1859 essay *On Liberty,* namely, that human life is largely an experiment conducted by each individual to discover what course or path or direction his life should take to make him happy. Both Spooner and Mill believed that happiness was the ultimate goal, but both held to the Aristotelian belief that what was required for happiness could not be ascertained through a priori analysis but had rather to be discovered by a posteriori investigation. That meant that each individual would have to figure out for himself by trial-and-error experimentation what would make him happy.[30]

Now it is true that empirical observation could specify rough parameters that would hold for all, or almost all, people. For example, given the constitution of the human body we can know that ingesting certain substances, such as mercury, can be unhealthy or even fatal, whereas regular ingestion of other substances, such as fruits and vegetables, is nutritious and even necessary for good health. Or, given the constitution of human psychology, we can know, for example, that prolonged isolation from other human beings will tend to be detrimental to one's well-being, whereas loving and close associations with others are usually necessary for one to flourish. There are many other generalizations that observation can recommend, and we usually do well to follow them. But we must not overestimate the usefulness of these kinds of recommendations, since they leave a world of questions unanswered. Take diet: should breakfast, lunch, or dinner be your biggest meal? Will you do best with a big, hearty breakfast, a light, continental one, or none at all? Should you be a vegetarian? Or take sociability: yes we need bonds to other people, but *which* other people? Should you get married? Now? To *this* person? And of course, yes, we are biologically driven to find means to survive and to pass on our genes, but what means to these ends should one avail oneself of? Should you be a lawyer, an accountant, a plumber, a philosophy professor? Should you travel and live the life of a bohemian, or should you settle down and start a family? How many kids should you have? If we

---

[30] See Chandran Kukathas's *The Liberal Archipelago.*

can know generally that exercise is good for everyone, does that mean that you should run marathons, practice martial arts, go for daily walks, lift weights thrice weekly?

You will have to answer these questions, as well as indefinitely more such, at some point in your life, and the point of listing them like this is to bring several things to the fore. First, no one else can answer these questions for you. You will have to answer them for yourself, and you will have to do so by experimentation, not sitting in your office and trying to deduce things from the "concept of humanity" (or whatever). Second, if you are to have a shot at leading a happy life, the rest of us will have to let you conduct these experiments. We can restrict you from impinging on other people's similar experiments—that is, we can require you to observe the rules of justice—but we must resist the temptation so many of us feel to run other people's lives or make their decisions for them because we are sure we know better than they do. We must instead let them find their own way.

Third, and just as important, there is no single path that will be good for everyone. The mistake of Platonic investigations into "the good" is precisely to believe that there is just *one* good that, once discovered, can be applied to everyone, perhaps coercively if people resist. But I submit that it is emphatically not the case that there is one good for everyone—something that can already be seen from the fact that there is no single answer to any of the above questions that will hold for everyone. It does not even hold at the level of human biology. Consider something as pedestrian as bread, allegedly the most basic staple of the human diet: almost everyone eats it, but it is not good for everyone. Some are gluten-intolerant, for example, and hence should not eat bread at all; others would do better with certain kinds of bread but not others; some will need to eat more bread than meat, others the reverse. There simply is no single prescription that can capture the good in this case for everyone. This may seem like a trivial example, and perhaps it is,[31] but it applies generally, including to much more important areas. Which religion one should subscribe to, which organizations one should join, with whom one should have close and intimate relationships, which activities one should engage in: these are not trivial matters, and yet they too admit of no single good answer that holds for everyone.

---

[31] On the other hand, Jared Diamond claims that agriculture is "the worst mistake in the history of the human race." See his essay by that name, http://www.agron.iastate. edu/courses/agron342/diamondmistake.html.

Let me emphasize the point by indicating one potential political implication it has. The claim that no single good, or no single good course of
life, applies to everyone would undercut, to take one example, a central
premise of much of what the Food and Drug Administration and the
United States Department of Agriculture claim to do. The FDA operates
on the assumption that it can know exactly how much of any given drug
is going to be helpful to you, and it has concretized its prescriptions in
extremely precise rules, all of which are enforced with the power of the
federal government. But in practice it is impossible for it to know how
much of any drug is right for you, when you should take a drug and
when not, how long you should take a drug, and so on. There is no single rule for all people in such cases; what is good for any individual can
only be guessed, let alone known, on the basis of detailed knowledge
of the individual in question. You have a bad cough: should you take a
codeine-based cough suppressant? How much? Perhaps you are allergic
and should take something else; or perhaps this is exactly what you need,
but you have a naturally high tolerance to it and so require higher than
average doses. The FDA's rules might reflect averages or norms, but of
course averages and norms will fail or be inapplicable in a substantial
number of individual cases.[32]

Similarly with the USDA. Its "food pyramid" currently prescribes six to
eleven daily servings of bread, cereal, rice, or pasta; two to three servings
daily of meat, poultry, fish, dried beans, or nuts; two to three servings
of milk, yogurt, or cheese; and only "sparing" use of fats and sweets. Is
this the right diet for everyone? Of course not. Some people will need
far more protein (certain kinds of athletes, for instance), while others
could become seriously ill from that much milk product; and consider
the apparent success of the Atkins diet, which recommends far higher
intakes of meat and fat and far lower intakes of breads, pastas, and other
carbohydrates. Again, the point is that there can be no knowing which
of these various paths is the best for any individual except on the basis of
detailed knowledge of the constitution of each person individually. Since
generally no one else has that much knowledge of any person except the
person himself—and, let us not forget, no one else has the motivation
to get it right that the person in question does—that means that each

---

[32] Sometimes this can even be a matter of life and death. See, for example, Roger Feldman
and Mark Pauley's *American Health Care,* Elaine Feuer's *Innocent Casualties,* and Robert
Higgs's *Hazardous to Our Health?* See also the continuously updated FDA watchdog Web
site http://www.FDAReview.org, administered by economists Daniel Klein and Alexander
Tabarrok.

of us will have to figure it out for ourselves, perhaps with the aid of our personal physician, nutritionist, or trainer. Even with the help of such experts, however, we will make frequent mistakes. How well can people do laying down rules for you when they have never met you and know nothing about you whatsoever?[33]

Much of your life will hence be constituted by successive experiments to see what works for you. These experiments will yield results that can direct your future action. If you are a person of good judgment, you will tend to use the results to direct your future action; if you are a person of poor judgment, you will tend not to pay attention to the results and either keep trying things out anew or trying things that have already proved unsuccessful. My argument is that in order to determine what will make you happy in life you will have to develop judgment; in order to develop judgment you will have to have the freedom, within the bounds of justice, to experiment, and the consequences of your decisions will have to be borne by you. I repeat that this last part, about bearing the consequences oneself, is necessary for developing judgment. Indeed, the overall acumen with which you wield your judgment will in large part be a function of the degree to which you have in your life been required to assume responsibility for the consequences of your decisions. Respecting your experiments in life and holding you responsible for them is, then, both the only way to enable you to achieve happiness and a matter of respecting your personhood. Hence insofar as we infringe on someone's liberty to experiment within the bounds of justice, we both diminish his chances of discovering his path to happiness and we treat him rather as a 'thing' than a 'person.'

HELPING OTHERS

One might wonder whether the argument so far entails that one should not help others. If someone in our family is in a bad way, or someone we know is down on his luck, am I saying that it would be wrong to help out

---

[33] For a detailed discussion of the way politics perversely influences the adoption of official nutritional standards, see Marion Nestle's *Food Politics*. For an informative and entertaining discussion making broadly similar points, see Brad Edmonds's *There's a Government in Your Soup*. I note that the federal government is once again rewriting its official nutritional guidelines as I write. See Gail Russell Chaddock's "A Capital Food Fight over Diet Guidelines," http://www.csmonitor.com/2004/0917/p03s01-uspo.htm; for a discussion critical of the government's efforts in this regard, see Robert E. Wright's "Are Dietary Guidelines a Public Good?" http://www.fee.org/publications/the-freeman/article.asp?aid=4471.

such people? Of course not. What my argument implies is that before you can know whether help is required in any given case, you have to know a lot of details about the case. In particular, you have to know *why* the person is in a bad way, *why* the person is down on his luck. Suppose my uncle is being evicted from his apartment. Just telling me that does not tell me what, if anything, I should do about it. Depending on the situation and the reasons for the eviction, perhaps I should let him move in with me; perhaps I should co-sign a loan with him on a house; perhaps I should lend him fifty bucks; perhaps I should put him in touch with a good attorney; or perhaps I should do absolutely nothing because he needs to learn that he cannot continue to waste his money on booze and drugs. Not everyone who asks for help really needs or deserves it, after all, and sometimes the best thing we can do for someone is to say "no." The point is that familiarity with the person in question and his situation and history is required to exercise good judgment in the case. Sometimes good judgment will indicate help, sometimes not; and even when it does indicate help, further judgment will be required when determining what kind of help is best. Asking for a single rule or a single policy in regards to all people who are in a bad way would thus be showing blindness to the real, and material, differences in people's situations. So a policy such as "Give whatever you can to anyone who comes to you for help, no questions asked" is a misguided one, however well intentioned. It is akin to a parent adopting a policy such as "Feed my children whatever they ask for, no questions asked." Need one spell out the disaster to which this would lead? (Think: all ice cream, all the time.) But a similar point obtains with adults who are asking for help. The rule here, as elsewhere, is: *use your judgment.* Adopting the one-size-fits-all policy is easier, and perhaps can assuage guilt or gratify the need to feel as if we are helping others. But that is not the best policy to adopt if one is interested in doing what can actually help those who need it.

Now, the recommendation to "use your judgment" might strike you as a platitude, but it will turn out not to be so because of the political implications it will have. I shall flesh out these implications later, but here is an indication: because, as I argue below, good judgment relies on "local knowledge"—that is, on knowledge of the particular situation in question—and because government agencies typically do not and cannot have the requisite local knowledge, it will follow that helping others is a job that is better left to individuals and local (private) groups than to governments. So I argue that if you agree with my characterization of the nature of good judgment, the prerequisites of its development, and the necessity of using it on a case-by-case basis, then you will have to conclude that a great deal of what governments in America currently do, or try to do, they shouldn't.

To return now to the main thread of the argument, it also follows, on the other side as it were, that we must allow others to give help even when we think their help is unnecessary or unproductive. If you think it is time for your parents to finally cut your sister off, because she has been a mooch for just too long, but your parents just keep on giving her breaks, giving her the benefit of the doubt, and—not least—giving her money, what recourse do you have? There are lots of things you might do to persuade them to stop—threaten not to visit at Christmas next year?—but in the end your parents are entitled to continue helping if they wish. To use the terminology we have developed, it may be vicious of them to do so but it is not unjust. Of course, if they took *your* money away from you to give it to your sister, that would be a different matter. But it is a fact of human life that people disagree about who deserves help from others, what kind of help should be given, how long it should be given, and so on. Respecting people's personhood entails respecting their judgment about such matters, whether we agree with it or not. It does *not* entail, however, that we allow them to force us to follow their judgment— on the contrary. Respecting our personhood requires that they honor our judgments about whether and how to help.[34] Thus, observing the limits of our freedom and the scope of others' freedom in this way has the added benefit of allowing for a proliferation of different charitable organizations and aid efforts that will reflect the diversity of human belief and judgment, not to mention the benefit of simultaneously engaging the natural mechanism of sorting and culling for efficiency that is created by securing the link between freedom and responsibility.

HARM AND DRAWING LINES

It follows from what I have argued that what counts as good for you cannot be known in advance but can be discovered only by trial-and-error experimentation. Should you therefore try everything? Lord no! The whole point of developing judgment is to obviate the need to try everything by ruling some things out of contention. The ancient Delphic maxim of "Know thyself" is important precisely because it tells you the first step in

---

[34] This also constitutes an argument against government welfare programs. More on that below.

leading a successful, meaning happy, life. If you do not know yourself, you will not know what you should do. It is that simple. But knowing yourself means knowing not only your abilities, desires, and interests; it also means knowing your peculiar weaknesses. If you discover, for example, that you have a penchant for chocolate, or a worryingly strong liking of gambling, or a weakness for alcohol, you should take that into account when deciding what to do with yourself. So you should probably avoid working at a Hershey's packaging plant, you should probably vacation somewhere other than Las Vegas, and you might want to consider avoiding bars and other places where you might come into contact with the objects of your weakness. The simple yet profound wisdom enshrined in the Delphic Oracle issues from its awareness that we all have our own unique set of peccadilloes, and hence we must come to know them thoroughly if we are to have a chance of mastering them.

This raises the question, however, of exactly what counts not just as harm to oneself, but as harm to others. I have argued that as long as a person does no "positive hurt" to another we have no justification in forcibly preventing him from doing what he wants or in forcibly punishing him for what he does. In *On Liberty*, Mill argued that "one very simple principle" was to guide interaction between individuals and their societies: "the sole end for which mankind are warranted, individually or collectively, in interfering with the liberty of action of any of their number, is self-protection. That the only purpose for which power can be rightfully exercised over any member of a civilized community, against his will, is to prevent harm to others."[35] This has accordingly become known as Mill's "harm principle," and although it captures my argument so far, it has come under attack on the grounds that the distinction between harming oneself and harming others is not so clear as one might initially think. Take the examples I have given above. If you eat so much chocolate that you become morbidly obese, one is inclined to say that you are endangering only yourself. But what about your family members who might have to care for you, or perhaps support you when you become unable to support yourself? What about taxpayers who might have to pick up the tab of your medical bills if medical treatment is subsidized by the state? Or consider gambling or drinking: if you have dependents, the problem is clear enough; but even if you do not, is it so obvious that your more distant family members or your friends are not affected by watching you gamble or drink your life away? And similarly with other vices. Where exactly,

---

[35] *On Liberty,* chap. 1, p. 13.

then, do we draw the line between actions that affect only oneself, and thus are not proper objects of external coercive control, and actions that also affect others, and thus do properly come within the scope of external coercive control?

No single reply can be given to this question that would settle it once and for all; indeed, there are instances in which it is difficult, even impossible, to settle on definite answers. But it does not follow from that that the distinction is not a sound one and worth using. There is no clear dividing line between *child* and *adult*, but that does not mean it is not useful and wise to distinguish—and treat differently—children and adults. Similarly, there is no clear dividing line between *sapling* and *tree*, between *day* and *night*, or between *black* and *white:* in each case there are instances on the margins that reasonable people may either disagree about or simply be unable to classify. But that doesn't mean that there are not clear, unambiguous, and generally recognized instances of children and adults, saplings and trees, days and nights, black and white, and so on. And the difficulty of identifying or categorizing some examples does not by any means entail that it is not important, indeed perhaps crucial, to identify, categorize, and treat accordingly the other 95 percent of examples. Thus although some would claim that if a principle does not work in the hard cases, it should be abandoned altogether,[36] I suggest on the contrary that *no* principle works in all cases, and hence we should adopt the principle or principles that turn out to cover the majority of cases.

We can if we like simply stipulate when, for, say, legal purposes, a person counts as an 'adult' or 'major' as opposed to a 'child' or 'minor'; and although the precise date selected will involve some arbitrariness, it will presumably be motivated by the criteria relevant to the purpose at hand. So, for example, we might consider you an 'adult' at the age of sixteen for the purpose of driving a car, because that is approximately when you become able to handle a car; at age eighteen for serving in the military and voting, for similar reasons; at age twenty-one for consuming alcohol; and so on. Similarly, we may settle on certain ages when we agree legally to consider a person as being able to give informed consent—for marriage, say, or for entering into a binding contract—and again one expects, or

---

[36] Like Mill: "Strange it is, that men should admit the validity of the arguments for free discussion, but object to their being 'pushed to an extreme,' not seeing that unless the reasons are good for an extreme case, they are not good for any case" (*On Liberty*, chap. 2, p. 24). I thank James Taylor for this reference.

hopes, that the age selected will be informed largely by actual experience of when people tend to be capable of handling such responsibility.

A similar claim can be made on behalf of the "positive harm" criterion, and I would like to suggest that it implies what I will call the General Liberty principle. *Positive harm* will have occurred when you or some other unwilling person has suffered an injustice, which means having been injured in life, liberty, or property; any other kind of harm—disappointment, for example, irritation, or frustration—would be dubbed *negative harm*. In the former case someone has injured or taken˙ something that belongs rightfully to another; in the latter case someone has (say) merely refrained from giving or offering to another person something that was rightfully the former's. Is there "harm" in both cases? The critic of the distinction will charge that there is indeed harm in both, and will hence discredit the distinction on grounds of ambiguity. But we can concede that there is harm in both cases while nevertheless maintaining that although two kinds of harm are possible, only one of them requires or allows forcible action.[37]

One way to emphasize the difference between the cases, as well as to avoid the appearance of a merely circular definition, is by relying on a principle that I call *third-party interference:* if the action in question prevents two third parties from exchanging, contracting, or associating with one another, or from buying from and selling to one another, then we have probably crossed the line from negative harm to positive harm; if not, then you have probably done no positive harm and hence no punitive action is warranted against you. So suppose, for example, that you start a business that competes with mine, and you take away some of my customers. Well, you certainly have "harmed" me. But this would be harm only in the negative sense because you did not prevent me from interacting with anyone who was also willing to interact with me. None of the customers who went to you, in other words, was forced to do so. You therefore committed no *third-party interference,* and thus you did not run afoul of the injunction against positive harm. Focusing in this way on whether A's actions prevent B and C from freely associating with one another, as opposed to whether A's actions simply "harm" B, both disambiguates the two kinds of "harm" that might be involved and brings to the fore the personhood of everyone involved. If C wants to deal with B

---

[37] There has been a great deal of discussion of the "harm principle." For a discussion I find instructive, see Richard Epstein's *Principles for a Free Society,* chap. 3 and the references contained therein.

rather than A, his personhood requires that we respect that decision, even if A would have been better off had C decided to go the other way.

The General Liberty principle would hold, then, that so long as one does no positive harm to another, one is free to decide and do what one likes. Moreover, given the crucial necessity of freedom for developing one's judgment, one's personhood, and indeed one's happiness, the general default setting would be to assume that people are acting within their rights under the General Liberty principle except when there is clear evidence to the contrary that they are committing positive harm, and thus injustice, to others. This line will not be perfectly definite in all cases, as critics charge, but it is clear enough, I believe, to adjudicate the overwhelming majority of human interaction. That is all that can be hoped for from a moral or political principle, and I attempt to show in the coming chapters that the General Liberty principle is indeed capable of shouldering the burden I suggest it can. For the small percentage of cases that are marginal, more difficult to assess, and left indeterminate by the General Liberty principle, we can only rely on the good judgment of the individuals in question or of those charged to adjudicate the cases.

NONPERSON HUMANS?

The argument now raises once again the question broached earlier of what we are to do about those who cannot make decisions about their own lives. Are they not 'persons'? The paradigmatic exceptions to the General Liberty principle are of course children and mental incompetents. What is it exactly that makes them different from 'persons,' and where exactly do we draw the line between a mental "competent" and a mental "incompetent"? There will again always be marginal instances that can be decided only on a case-by-case basis, using our informed judgment. I suggest that the rule of thumb should be that we not restrict a person's liberty because he makes bad decisions, but only if he is incapable of making reflective or considered decisions at all. Because using and exercising our judgment is constitutive of the process of developing it, we should err on the side of caution and thus liberty. We should therefore not take away a person's liberty until there seems to be clear evidence, persuasive to any reasonable impartial observer, that the person in question is not capable of exercising judgment. Children are not initially capable of exercising judgment, and hence they are justifiably governed by their parents; as they grow older and develop their judgment, the parents' rules should relax, until finally the parents should give the children complete freedom.[38] My argument implies a similar conclusion in the case of mental incompetents: the degree to which another may substitute his judgment for theirs depends on and is inversely proportional to the degree to which their judgment is able to function.

Now, this general rule may not be able to give specific guidance for any particular case, but it does, I believe, provide a sound foundation on which to base particular judgments.[39] And one reason I am not pursuing the exact boundaries between proper persons and nonpersons is because I want to motivate your agreement that normally functioning adults are 'persons' and hence fall under the scope of my argument about freedom and responsibility. If your principal worry is about hard cases on the margins, then you've already accepted the central and most important part of my argument.

SUMMARY

To conclude, finally, this long chapter, let me summarize its argument. Human beings are 'persons,' and respect for their personhood entails the principle of General Liberty, which requires that we grant them the widest possible scope of personal liberty that is at the same time compatible with the similar liberty of every other person. 'Justice' names this respect; 'injustice' names violations of it. Violations of justice should be punished, whoever the people are who perpetrate them; but failures to achieve positive virtue are not crimes and must therefore be left to the realm of persuasion, not coercion, and addressed by personal and individual initiative. Persons must moreover be held responsible for the consequences of their decisions, because allowing them to shift the responsibility for their actions onto unwilling others would be both a breach of 'justice' and an obstacle to their own development of judgment, which itself is integral to personhood. Finally, individuals will have to negotiate their own ways through life on the search for happiness; because developing good judgment is necessary for making wise choices about one's happiness, just as we want others to respect our judgment, we must do the same for others—as long as they do no positive harm to unwilling others.

[38] For a discussion I find instructive about freedom, children, and parents, see Jennifer Roback Morse's *Love and Economics*.
[39] It will also provide some guidance when it comes to the question of nonhuman animals, whether they count as 'persons,' and to what extent we are justified in governing them. To that issue I turn in chapter 8.

Bibliography

Aristotle. *Nicomachean Ethics,* 2nd ed. Terence Irwin, trans. Indianapolis, Ind.: Hackett, 2000 (ca. 350 B.C.).

Aristotle. *Politics.* C. D. C. Reeve, trans. Indianapolis, Ind.: Hackett, 1998 (ca. 350 B.C.).

Becker, Gary S. *A Treatise on the Family,* enlarged ed. Cambridge: Harvard University Press, 1993.

Berlin, Isaiah. "Two Concepts of Liberty." In *Four Essays on Liberty.* Oxford: Oxford University Press, 1969.

Brown, Donald E. *Human Universals.* New York: McGraw-Hill, 1991.

Brown, Donald E. "Human Universals and Their Implications." In *Being Humans: Anthropological Universality and Particularity in Transdisciplinary Perspectives.* Neil Roughley, ed. New York: Walter de Gruyter, 2000.

Buss, David M. *The Evolution of Desire: Strategies of Human Mating,* rev. and exp. ed. New York: Basic Books, 2003.

Chaddock, Gail Russell. "A Capital Food Fight over Diet Guidelines." *Christian Science Monitor,* September 17, 2004. Http://www.csmonitor.com/2004/0917/p03s01-uspo.htm, accessed December 12, 2005.

Chesterton, G. K. *The Everlasting Man.* Ft. Collins, Colo.: Ignatius, 1993 (1925).

Dawkins, Richard. *The Selfish Gene,* 2nd ed. Oxford: Oxford University Press, 1990.

Dawkins, Richard. *A Devil's Chaplain: Reflections on Hope, Lies, Science, and Love.* New York: Houghton Mifflin, 2003.

Diamond, Jared. "The Worst Mistake in the History of the Human Race." *Discover Magazine* (May 1987): 64–66. Http://www.agron.iastate.edu/courses/agron342/diamondmistake.html, accessed December 12, 2005.

Dunbar, Robin. *Grooming, Gossip and the Evolution of Language.* London: Faber and Faber, 1996.

Dutton, Denis. "Aesthetic Universals." In *The Routledge Companion to Aesthetics.* Berys Gaut and Dominic M. Lopes, eds. New York: Routledge, 2001.

Edmonds, Brad W. *There's a Government in Your Soup: Why There's Too Much Government in Your Kitchen, and What You Can Do about It.* Lincoln, Neb.: iUniverse, 2004.

Epstein, Richard A. *Principles for a Free Society: Reconciling Individual Liberty with the Common Good.* Reading, Mass.: Perseus, 1998.

Feldman, Roger D., and Mark V. Pauley, eds. *American Health Care: Government, Market Processes, and the Public Interest.* New Brunswick, N.J.: Transaction, 2000.

Ferguson, Adam. *An Essay on the History of Civil Society.* Fania Oz-Salzberger, ed. Cambridge: Cambridge University Press, 1995 (1767).

Feuer, Elaine. *Innocent Casualties: The FDA's War against Humanity,* rev. ed. New York: Dorrance, 1998.

Fleischacker, Samuel. *A Third Concept of Liberty: Judgment and Freedom in Kant and Adam Smith.* Princeton, N.J.: Princeton University Press, 1999.

Friedman, Milton. *Free to Choose.* New York: Harcourt Brace Jovanovich, 1980.

Friedman, Milton. *Capitalism and Freedom.* Chicago: University of Chicago Press, 1982.

Hamilton, William D. *Narrow Roads of Gene Land: The Collected Papers of W. D. Hamilton,* vol. 1: *The Evolution of Social Behavior.* Sarah Brunney, ed. Oxford: Freeman, 1996.

Hart, H. L. A., and Tony Honoré. *Causation in the Law,* 2nd ed. Oxford: Oxford University Press, 1985.

Hayek, F. A. *The Constitution of Liberty.* Chicago: University of Chicago Press, 1978.

Higgs, Robert. *Hazardous to Our Health? FDA Regulation of Health Care Products.* Oakland, Calif.: Independent Institute, 1995.

Hobbes, Thomas. *Leviathan.* Edwin Curley, ed. Indianapolis, Ind.: Hackett, 1994 (1651/1668).

Hocutt, Max. "Sunstein on Rights." *The Independent Review* 10, no. 1 (Summer 2005): 117–32.

Holmes, Stephen, and Cass R. Sunstein. *The Cost of Rights: Why Liberty Depends on Taxes.* New York: Norton, 1999.

"Homo Economicus." *Wikipedia, the Free Encyclopedia.* Http://en.wikipedia.org/wiki/Homo_economicus, accessed December 12, 2005.

Honoré, Antony. "Causation in the Law." *Stanford Encyclopedia of Philosophy* (Winter 2001). Edward N. Zalta, ed. Http://plato.stanford.edu/archives/win2001/entries/causation-law, accessed December 12, 2005.

Kant, Immanuel. *Critique of Judgment.* Werner S. Pluhar, trans. Indianapolis, Ind.: Hackett, 1995 (1790).

Kant, Immanuel. *Grounding for the Metaphysics of Morals.* James W. Ellington, trans. Indianapolis, Ind.: Hackett, 2000 (1785).

Kitcher, Philip. *Vaulting Ambition: Sociobiology and the Quest for Human Nature.* Cambridge, Mass.: MIT Press, 1985.

Kraut, Richard. "The Defense of Justice in Plato's *Republic.*" In *The Cambridge Companion to Plato,* ed. Richard Kraut. Cambridge: Cambridge University Press, 1992.

Kukathas, Chandran. *The Liberal Archipelago: A Theory of Diversity and Freedom.* Oxford: Oxford University Press, 2003.

Long, A. A., and D. N. Sedley. *The Hellenistic Philosophers,* 2 vols. Cambridge: Cambridge University Press, 1987.

Long, Roderick T. "Herbert Spencer: The Defamation Continues." August 28, 2003. Http://www.lewrockwell.com/orig3/long3.html, accessed December 12, 2005.

McCallum, Gerald. "Negative and Positive Freedom." *Philosophical Review* 76 (1976).

Mill, John Stuart. *On Liberty.* Stefan Collini, ed. Cambridge: Cambridge University Press, 1989 (1859).

Miller, Fred D., Jr. *Nature, Justice, and Rights in Aristotle's* Politics. Oxford: Oxford University Press, 1997.

Morse, Jennifer Roback. *Love and Economics: Why the Laissez-Faire Family Doesn't Work.* Dallas, Tex.: Spence, 2001.

Nestle, Marion. *Food Politics: How the Food Industry Influences Nutrition and Health.* Berkeley: University of California Press, 2002.

Nock, Albert Jay. *The State of the Union: Essays in Social Criticism.* Charles H. Hamilton, ed. Indianapolis, Ind.: Liberty Press, 1991.

Otteson, James R. *Adam Smith's Marketplace of Life.* Cambridge: Cambridge University Press, 2002.

Plato. *Republic,* 2nd ed. G. M. A. Grube, trans., rev. by C. D. C. Reeve. Indianapolis, Ind.: Hackett, 1992 (ca. 380 B.C.).

Posner, Richard A. *Sex and Reason.* Cambridge: Harvard University Press, 1992.

Rachels, James. *The Elements of Moral Philosophy,* 4th ed. New York: McGraw-Hill, 2002.

Rachels, Stuart. "Nagelian Arguments against Egoism." *Australasian Journal of Philosophy* 80, no. 2 (June 2002): 191–208.

Rand, Ayn. *The Virtue of Selfishness: A New Concept of Egoism.* New York: Signet, 1989 (1964).

Ridley, Matt. *The Origins of Virtue.* New York: Penguin, 1996.

Schwartz, Barry. "A Nation of Second Guesses." *New York Times,* January 22, 2004, p. A27.

Schwartz, Barry. *The Paradox of Choice: Why More Is Less.* New York: Ecco, 2004.

Singer, Peter. "Famine, Affluence, and Morality." *Philosophy & Public Affairs* 1, no. 3 (Spring 1972): 229–43.

Singer, Peter. *Practical Ethics,* 2nd ed. Cambridge: Cambridge University Press, 1993.

Smith, Adam. *An Inquiry into the Nature and Causes of the Wealth of Nations.* Indianapolis, Ind.: Liberty Classics, 1981 (1776).

Smith, Adam. *The Theory of Moral Sentiments.* Indianapolis, Ind.: Liberty Classics, 1982 (1759).

Sober, Elliott, and David Sloan Wilson. *Unto Others: The Evolution and Psychology of Unselfish Behavior.* Cambridge: Harvard University Press, 1998.

Spooner, Lysander. "Vices Are Not Crimes." In *The Lysander Spooner Reader.* George H. Smith, ed. San Francisco: Fox and Wilkes, 1992 (1875).

Stirner, Max. *The Ego and Its Own.* David Leopold, ed. Cambridge: Cambridge University Press, 1995 (1844).

Stone, Lawrence. *The Family, Sex and Marriage in England 1500–1800.* London: Penguin, 1979.

Sunstein, Cass. "Confusing Rights: A Reply to Hocutt." *The Independent Review* 10, no. 1 (Summer 2005): 133–38.

Taylor, Robert S. "A Kantian Defense of Self-Ownership." *Journal of Political Philosophy* 12, no. 1 (March 2004): 65–78.

Wilson, Edward O. *On Human Nature.* Cambridge, Mass.: Harvard University Press, 1978.

Wilson, Edward O. *Consilience: The Unity of Knowledge.* New York: Knopf, 1998.

Wilson, James Q. *The Moral Sense.* New York: Free Press, 1993.

Wright, Robert. *The Moral Animal: Why We Are the Way We Are.* New York: Pantheon, 1994.

Wright, Robert E. "Are Dietary Guidelines a Public Good?" *The Freeman: Ideas on Liberty.* November 2002. Http://www.fee.org/publications/the-freeman/article.asp?aid=4471, accessed on December 12, 2005.

2

A Matter of Principle, Part One

The Betrayal of Personhood

I argued in the previous chapter that human beings are 'persons,' which I defined as something able to develop ends deliberately and exercise judgment with respect to them. I also argued that one could not be a 'person' without judgment, and hence that in order to respect people's personhood we had to respect their judgment. That meant that we must grant each other not only a wide scope of freedom to exercise, develop, and fine-tune our judgment, but also the responsibility of accepting the consequences, good or bad, of the decisions we make and the actions we take. This view of human personhood, along with the privileges and responsibilities it entails, has political implications, some of which I suggested in chapter 1. In this and the next chapter I propose to spell out those implications a bit more carefully. My ultimate goal is to persuade you that only a government limited in certain specific ways is consistent with human personhood. In this chapter I argue that certain familiar forms of government are *not* consistent with personhood as I have described it; in the next chapter I lay out what form I believe *is* consistent. I hope in the end to give you strong reason, based both on moral principle and, later, on empirical evidence to endorse this kind of limited government.

SOCIALISM?

Every society has some form of organization or other, and there are probably indefinitely many potential schemes of organization. One useful scale on which to place most forms is according to the extent to which they allow individuals to make decisions for themselves. This scale will run the gamut from totalitarianism on one end to anarchism on the other.

A limited, constitutional republic, such as what was created in America in 1789, would fall between totalitarianism and anarchism, rather nearer to the latter; social democracy and socialism, by contrast, would fall rather nearer to totalitarianism. We cannot survey every form on this scale, but some expansion of our notion of 'personhood' will enable us to see which kinds of government organization would be ruled out by respect for this personhood, if not all those that would be ruled in.

Let us begin with socialism, at least since the second half of the nineteenth century an influential conception of government. Perhaps we should first ask what exactly socialism is. According to the account offered by Karl Marx (1818–83), socialism is the stage of natural human social progress that succeeds capitalism and precedes communism. It is the stage during which the monopoly on private property enjoyed by the few under capitalism is broken, private property is abolished, and society is governed, coercively where necessary, by a centralized authority that makes all decisions about production, housing, education, and so on for all the citizens. Marx's account holds that socialism will then eventually develop into "communism," where the harmony and cooperation that was enforced under socialism now takes place spontaneously, and the competition and "alienation" regnant under capitalism gives way to something like a universal brotherhood. The coercive state apparatus that arose under socialism, now no longer necessary, merely "withers away."[1] Here is how the Communist Party of Great Britain (CPGB) puts it in its party platform today:

Through society reabsorbing the functions of the state the need for it withers away. Democracy (a form of the state) negates itself and gives way to general freedom. The higher stage of communism is a free association of producers. Everybody will contribute according to their ability and take according to need. Real human history begins and society leaves behind the "realm of necessity." In the realm of freedom people will become rounded, fully social individuals who can for the first time truly develop their natural humanity.[2]

There are other accounts of what exactly socialism is, and I shall not quibble about names. For our purposes the central distinguishing features of socialistic states are that the state claims most, if not all, activities of its members as falling within its proper purview, its decisions about

[1] This famous and oft-repeated phrase actually comes from Friedrich Engels's 1877 essay *Anti-Dühring*.

[2] Http://www.cpgb.org.uk/documents/cpgb/prog_transition.html (accessed December 12, 2005).

these matters are made centrally, and those decisions are enforced coercively. I thus use the term "socialism" quite broadly: it would include everything from the former Soviet Union to China under Mao and still today, from Nazi Germany to Uganda under Idi Amin. There are many regimes in the world today that would count,[3] and many more that are either close or heading in that direction.[4] Under this kind of state the individual officially has little substantive freedom to decide for himself what his schooling will be, what job he will take, how much he should produce and when and in what way, and possibly even whom he will marry, how many children he will have, what religion, if any, he will subscribe to, and so on. Historically, attempts at such total control have usually failed to become fully realized because people, being recalcitrant 'persons,' find ways to express themselves despite the attempted oversight. So they develop black markets or "shadow economies," take unofficial or illegal liberties, conduct cash-only or other untraceable exchanges, meet or conduct illegal religious ceremonies in secret, and so on. It is enough, however, that under a socialist state people's activities are centrally directed, and deviations from those directions are punished when discovered.

The justifications for this attempted total control over the individual usually fall under two heads. First is the idea that there is some single good for everyone or for all of society, which only the "most advanced" intellectuals, as Marx and Friedrich Engels (1820–95) put it in their 1848 *Manifesto of the Communist Party*,[5] are qualified to apprehend and interpret. This claim serves the dual purpose of justifying why these particular people should be in charge as well as justifying their pervasive use of force or threats of force—if what they are enforcing is actually the good, after all, what possible grounds can we have to object? Now, if you are inclined to reject out of hand such claims to authority, consider that this is not unlike what most versions of Christianity hold. Most Christians, that is, are quite happy to have God tell them what to do, no matter what it involves—including destroying property, imprisoning others, or even killing innocents (remember the story of Abraham and his son Isaac, Genesis 22: 1–14). Why? Well, presumably because they believe that God actually does know what the good is; if He does and I disagree with what

---

3 See R. J. Rummel's *Death by Government*, chap. 1, and *Saving Lives, Enriching Life*, chap. 1.
4 See Goldfarb, *Freedom in the World 2004*, and Gwartney and Lawson, *Economic Freedom of the World 2004*.
5 In Tucker, *The Marx-Engels Reader*, p. 484.

He says, then it is not God but I who am wrong. A similar logic lies behind the socialist argument. There are experts or intellectuals who know what the good is, so you should follow what they say: by hypothesis, then, if you have other ideas, well, since they are right, you must be wrong. Now putting it that way is an exaggeration since it portrays these government elites as if they made claims to infallibility.[6] A perhaps more charitable way to put their argument might be that, while no one is infallible, still some people are better positioned to understand the movement of history, the dynamics that give rise to historical and social change, the perversions and ideologies created by various political regimes, and thus the best courses of action to take to realize proper human social ends. Here again is the Communist Party of Great Britain, this time on "leadership":

The leadership of the Communist Party is its vanguard in terms of theory, politics and organisation. It constitutes its general staff. No movement can survive without a permanent body of leaders through which it can ensure continuity. Without authoritative and influential leaders who have been steeled over a long period of time and are able to work collectively together, no class can wage a serious struggle for power. If the proletariat wishes to defeat the bourgeoisie, it must train from among its ranks its own proletarian class politicians who should not be inferior to the bourgeois politicians. Our Party attaches great importance to the cultivation of leaders, their theoretical knowledge, revolutionary energy and political instinct and experience.[7]

The other main justification for the socialistic state rises out of criticisms of the "capitalist" order. The bill of particulars against capitalism is long, but it typically includes charges that it concentrates society's wealth in the hands of a few while impoverishing the rest; that it "alienates" (Marx's term) workers from their work, from their fellow workers, even perhaps from their own true humanity; and that it subverts the natural order by pitting people against one another in a ruthlessly competitive struggle for life, rather than allowing people to live with one another in a cooperative harmony. Capitalism, Marx claimed, turns money from being a mere tool into a "fetish" in which people desire, almost erotically, simply more and more money as an end unto itself; it creates an "ideology" or complex of concepts and slogans that simultaneously provides its

---

[6] Though some would defend even this strong charge. See, for example, economist Thomas Sowell's *The Vision of the Anointed*.

[7] Http://www.cpgb.org.uk/documents/cpgb/prog_party.html#leadership (accessed December 12, 2005). I should note that I use the CPGB site only because it states its aims and justifications with frankness and lucidity. Similar sentiments can be found in many other places.

own justification and secures unquestioning faith; and it divides society into classes whose interests are artificially opposed and who therefore struggle endlessly, and pointlessly, against one another.[8]

Most of these charges are, or are based on, empirical claims, and so they will be decided by empirical investigation, not a priori speculation. In the last few decades an enormous amount of empirical investigation has in fact been undertaken on these and related claims, and it turns out that the evidence points strongly against most of these charges. In chapter 5 I present the evidence rebutting them. Here, however, I take up the separate but I believe equally important question of whether a socialist or centralized state is compatible with respecting people's personhood. Even if it is true that, as I argue in chapter 5, systems of government that protect private property and allow capitalist or quasi-capitalist markets to operate actually benefit all economic classes of people, including the poor, it might nevertheless be objected that moral principle trumps material well-being. That is, one might argue that respecting the dignity and worth of 'persons' is the prime moral directive, and that although empirical economic considerations might also be important, they take second place to human dignity. Thus the *first* question to be addressed is: is the socialist or centralized state compatible with respecting the personhood of its members?

The answer is no. The essence of personhood, recall, is the capacity to develop deliberate ends and to exercise judgment with respect to them. The twin integral prerequisites of this personhood were the freedom to exercise judgment and the responsibility of oneself facing the consequences of one's judgment. No exception was made for cases of bad judgment. On the contrary, people must be able both to make and to face the consequences of their mistakes if they are to develop their

---

[8] See Marx's "Estranged Labour" and "Private Property and Communism," from his *Economic and Philosophic Manuscripts of 1844* (pp. 70–93 in Tucker, *Marx-Engels Reader*) and the *Grundrisse* (pp. 224–93 in Tucker). For good recent discussion of Marxian claims, see Arnold's *Marx's Radical Critique of Capitalist Society,* Brudney's *Marx's Attempt to Leave Philosophy,* Cohen's *Karl Marx's Theory of History,* and Elster's *Making Sense of Marx.* For sophisticated defenses of similar positions, see Christman's *The Myth of Property* and Cohen's *Self-Ownership, Freedom, and Equality.* Finally, for a clear presentation of standard worries about markets and market economies, see Rebecca M. Blank's "Viewing the Market Economy through the Lens of Faith." I draw on all these works in my discussion. In the bibliography at the end of this chapter I also list a number of other works that address and critically evaluate these claims, including those by Barnett, Bastiat, Bethell, de Jasay, Epstein, Friedman, Lester, Machan, Narveson, Nock, Rasmussen and Den Uyl, Rothbard, and Robert Paul Wolff.

judgment, and thus their personhood and humanity, at all. Impinging on individuals' freedom to decide, and either absolving them from facing the undesirable consequences of their bad decisions or not allowing them to enjoy the desirable consequences of their good decisions, are all instances of disrespecting their judgment, thus their personhood, thus their humanity. It is to treat them as *things* and not *persons*. But this is what socialistic states do. They proceed on the assumption that you are not in fact the person best positioned to take action on your own behalf—indeed on the assumption that you might be deluded about what is in your own best interest, blinded perhaps by your class interests or the self-serving ideologies your regime or class has inculcated in you. That is why you are not trusted to make decisions about your own life. So the state must assume responsibility for educating you, the state must provide for your retirement, the state must tell you which kinds of employment contracts you may enter into and which not, it must tell you on which conditions you may buy a home, buy a car, receive medical care, or get a loan, which foods, drugs, associates, partners, tools, machines, books, movies, music, art, language, and political and religious positions are acceptable for you and which are not—all because you cannot, or cannot properly, do these things by yourself.

Are you incapable of making such decisions on your own? Leading one's own life and taking responsibility for one's decisions are not easy things to do, and we might sometimes find the security of having others make decisions for us a comforting and attractive proposition. However natural that attraction might be, it does not mean that we are not *capable* of taking responsibility for ourselves—a quite different, and much stronger, claim. I argued in chapter 1 that there are two clear cases of people who are in fact incompetent to do so: children and mentally infirm adults. Although we presume that children will in time develop the relevant abilities, they don't have them when they're children—which is why they are rightly guided by others who *do* have such abilities, as are infirm adults who also lack, and may never regain, the abilities. I also argued, however, that these two groups of people were exceptions to the paradigmatic group of what I called 'persons,' and the central identifying characteristic of persons is precisely that they *do* possess the abilities to order their own purposes and goals, to assess and weigh options for achieving them, to choose courses of action, and to interpret and respond to the consequences attendant on their choices. These abilities constitute 'judgment,' which I argued was an integral part of personhood. What this means is that unless you are a child or a mental incompetent, you are a person: you possess judgment, you are capable of guiding your own life, and if we wish to respect your personhood we must let you do so. That means that socialistic states are out.

I personally find it offensive that others presume I am incompetent to make these decisions on my own.[9] But what is perhaps an even greater affront is the underestimation of the average person—the worker or "proletarian" that such states claim to support. Nobody is perfect, of course; people make lots of mistakes, and I suppose it is true that the lower one's IQ is the more mistakes one will make; it might even be true that the "intellectuals" and "experts" who would be the rulers in a socialistic state tend to have high IQs. But it does not follow from any of that that anyone other than you is the best person to run your life. Still less does it follow that they have any justified authority to run your life. Let them have the highest IQ in the world, let them have read hundreds, even thousands of books, and let them have the best possible intentions: Do they know what *your* talents are and what opportunities are available to you? Do they know your proclivities, your likes and dislikes, your peccadilloes and idiosyncrasies, your hopes and dreams and fears, your ambitions and failings, your loves and hates? They don't know mine either. That fatally undercuts the premise on which their claim to authority over others is based.

We can call this the *local knowledge argument*. Economist Robert Lucas won the 1995 Nobel Prize in economics for having shown how local knowledge effects macroeconomic patterns on the basis of microeconomic decisions. But this argument was formulated already by Adam Smith in his 1776 *Wealth of Nations*. Smith wrote, "What is the species of domestick industry which his capital can employ, and of which the produce is likely to be the greatest value, every individual, it is evident, can, in his local situation, judge much better than any statesman or lawgiver can do for him."[10] The argument is that because you know your own circumstances—including your own talents and desires, as well as the resources and opportunities available to you—better than anyone else does, you are better positioned than anyone else to make decisions about which actions you should take to achieve your goals. Suppose a

---

9 I don't think it matters, but in case you were wondering (as one sympathetic to Marxism might), my personal view cannot be explained by a privileged upbringing. I am the first person in my family to graduate college, I come from a "broken" home without a father, and I was raised by a single working mother in conditions of relative poverty.

10 *Inquiry into the Nature and Causes of the Wealth of Nations*, p. 456 (hereafter referred to as WN).

company is offering $30,000 per year for people to do a specific job. Is it worth it? The local knowledge argument holds that there is no single answer to that question that holds for everyone. Instead, each person must ask whether the job is worth it *to himself.* Thus only you can answer that question for yourself because to do so requires a judgment based on knowledge of your purposes, opportunities, and so on that only you possess. Moreover, you can answer it only for yourself; I would have to answer it for myself and only myself, and similarly for everyone else. And the argument applies to everything else you (and I) do.

The argument also implies what we might think of as concentric circles of knowledge. Outside yourself, your closest family members or friends will have the best chance of making good decisions for you, then more distant family members or friends, and so on, until we get to absolute strangers, who will not have much of a chance at all. Thus if you were to become for some reason incapacitated, this is the rough order of authority we should follow for making decisions for you. This again is the *familiarity principle* from chapter 1: one's knowledge of, interest in, and, one might also add, one's natural benevolence for another varies directly with one's familiarity with that other. The important point to focus on here is that the "experts" in charge of a centralized state—the legislators, state regulators, government bureaucrats, and so on—are all in the furthest position from you, in a circle far from you in the center. They have no personal knowledge of you or your unique particular circumstances, and that renders them unfit to make decisions for you. Since they are in precisely the same position of ignorance with respect to the overwhelming majority of people in their society, the local knowledge argument undercuts their authority to rule not just with respect to this or that particular issue, but generally. As Smith puts it: "But the law ought always to trust people with the care of their own interests, as in their local situations they must generally be able to judge better of it than the legislator can do" (WN, p. 531).

I do not suggest that each of us has an infallible God's-eye view of ourselves, that we know everything about ourselves, that we never suffer from self-deception, or that we do not make mistakes. People in fact routinely make mistakes about their own situations, misjudging themselves or their motivations, overestimating their own successes or virtues, or minimizing their failings.[11] Moreover, in cases of long, intimate association

---

[11] For an intriguing recent discussion of the possible evolutionary bases of self-deception, see Wright, *The Moral Animal,* chap. 13.

it sometimes happens that someone else can know something about you before you do. A longtime close friend or spouse might realize you are tired and need a nap before you do, for example, as a parent can tell that her child's crankiness is due to having missed his afternoon snack before the child even realizes he is hungry. But those are limited and exceptional cases. Specifically, they are limited in at least two ways: first, the number of people who might have that kind of intimate knowledge about any given person is very small, and almost certainly does not include anyone in the state claiming authority over him; and second, even among those who do possess such knowledge of another, they will not have access to the complete package of motivations, desires, purposes, and so on that each individual does about himself. Even granting, then, that people sometimes deceive themselves and make mistakes, the general claim holds that each of us knows more about himself than anyone else does.

Perhaps even more important, each of us has a far greater stake in the outcome of our actions than anyone else does. If you make a mistake that leads to bad consequences, it is likely to be *you* who suffers the consequences. As I argued in chapter 1, this is as it should be because it provides a natural incentive to get things right: you do not want to suffer, so when you take actions that lead you to suffer, however slightly, you have an automatic, or "natural," incentive to mark what happened, remember it, and make adjustments for the future as necessary. But no one else has similar incentives in your case, and the farther away the decision maker is from you, the more likely he is to be unconcerned with the consequences of his decisions as they materialize in your life. This can be shown by the fact that people are inclined to take far greater risks when they are insulated from the consequences than when they suffer the consequences themselves.

Two concrete examples illustrate the point. There is a great deal of evidence—indeed, more than two millennia of it—that a fundamental building block of education is the mastery of grammar. Grammar is to reading and writing as arithmetic is to statistical reasoning, balancing a checkbook, or figuring out gas mileage: you can't do the one, or at least not well, without the other. For some time now, however, educators in the United States have tended to disdain the teaching of grammar. One reason for doing so is the common belief that teaching "Standard English" accepts or endorses the legitimacy of an unjust imperialism or unjustly neglects to recognize the legitimacy of dialects of English. Yet the movement away from teaching grammar has coincided with a decline in students' abilities to read and write, and there is evidence of a causal, not merely correlative, relation between the two.[12] Despite the evidence, which has been available for some time now, teachers and administrators persist in eschewing teaching grammar. Why? The answer given by one teacher of English as a second language gives a clue. As reported by classics professor David Mulroy, when asked about it, this teacher said "that she carefully refrained from criticizing nonstandard English in the classroom and felt that it was important to do so. Then she added as a humorous aside, a throw-away line, that 'of course' she policed her own daughters' grammar with fanatical vigilance." Mulroy concludes: "It was, I thought, a moment of truth. People who use 'good grammar' do not hesitate to force it on the children they love"[13]—the implication being that they are not nearly so concerned with the children they *do not* love. Here we see at work the incentives involved in severing decision making from consequence suffering: it is one thing when *your* children suffer the consequences of my decisions, another thing entirely when it is *my own* children.

A second example illustrating the point comes from a recent ecological disaster that took place in Lake Michigan near Milwaukee, Wisconsin. According to the *Milwaukee Journal Sentinel,* in May and June, 2004, the Milwaukee Metropolitan Sewerage District (MMSD) "dumped an unprecedented 4.6 billion gallons of raw sewage" into Lake Michigan.[14] The dumping was not a mistake or error, however, but was rather the MMSD's policy: when their sewage system receives a lot of rainwater—as it did because of "intense back-to-back storms and almost unrelenting rain"—then it is programmed simply to dump the untreated sewage into Lake Michigan. In this case the dumping resulted in the extended closure of miles of beaches, though the full damage to the Lake Michigan ecosystem is not yet determined. The Michigan Department of Natural Resources (MDNR) has considered punishing the district, but the relevant statutes give an exception to municipalities during "the most dire weather emergencies," which of course the MMSD is claiming this was.

[12] See Mulroy, *The War against Grammar,* chaps. 1–3, and Coulson, *Market Education,* chaps. 2 and 6.

[13] Mulroy, *The War against Grammar,* pp. 87–8.

[14] "Sewage Dumped in May: 4.6 Billion Gallons: Amounts Top Any Yearly Total since Tunnel Opened," *Milwaukee Journal Sentinel,* May 29, 2004 http://www. jsonline.com/news/metro/may04/232813.asp (accessed December 12, 2005). See also the June 4, 2004, article in the *Janesville* (Wisconsin) *Gazette,* "DNR Issues Notices of Violations for Lake Michigan Sewage Dumping," http://www.gazetteextra.com/sewagedumping060304.asp (accessed March 15, 2005), and Christopher Westley's "Milwaukee's Mess," http://www.mises.org/fullstory.asp?control=1538 (accessed December 12, 2005).

Whatever the MDNR decides, what is clear is that no one will be jailed for this disaster, and since government officials are by long-standing tradition and legal precedent immune to prosecution for what they do in their official capacities,[15] the people responsible for the disaster will not be held legally responsible.

Now compare that situation with one that took place in 1989, when the Exxon oil tanker *Valdez* ran aground near Alaska's Prince William Sound, dumping some 11 million gallons of oil into the ocean. Exxon was sued in court, found guilty of negligence, and has paid since 1989 over $3 billion in clean-up costs and restitution to affected fishermen, industry, and so on. The Exxon disaster was the subject of an enormous firestorm in world-wide press coverage, and still today people readily call up profoundly negative associations with the name "Valdez." But there is a good chance you never heard about the Milwaukee disaster, since it was covered almost exclusively in local and regional papers, never making it into the national press. And that is despite the fact that the Milwaukee disaster released some *four hundred times* as much pollution as did the *Valdez,* and into a lake a fraction of the size of the north Pacific Ocean. The Exxon disaster has led not only to extensive punishments of the company and the ship's captain, but also led to industry-wide changes in business operations. It was an accident, the result indeed of negligence of a very high order. But the Milwaukee disaster was fully foreseen, and was part of the predicted and intentional planning. Why the difference? Why, one might ask, would the MMSD willingly and knowingly take such a spectacular risk of destroying or damaging a vital natural habitat—not to mention the chief supply of fresh water for millions of people? A large part of the answer, I suggest, is that the politicians making the decision *knew* that they could not be held responsible. And they haven't been. The divorce between their freedom to decide and the responsibility for the consequences of their decisions provided them little or no incentive, no 'natural necessity,' to look for alternative, better ways to handle things, to buy insurance against mistakes, or to accept responsibility for their risky behavior. And so they didn't.

Incentives matter, in other words. Just imagine all the creative ideas you could come up with for, say, running a company if you did not have to

---

[15] For summaries of the relevant legal precedents, see http://www.november.org/razorwire/rzold/17/17024.html or http://www.peoples-law.org/individual-rts/civil-rights/Federal_law.htm#Immunity%20from%20Suit (both accessed December 12, 2005).

pay for any losses out of your own pocket. You could let your imagination run wild: maybe let the janitors be the board members, or require everyone to be paid the same, or decide that it has to be run as an absolute democracy with every employee having an equal vote, or require that the company's employees reflect the exact ethnic or religious proportions of the surrounding population, or require that each employee must produce as much as he can but be paid only as much as (you judge) he needs, or decree that the minimum pay anyone should receive is $20 an hour. The point is that not only are third parties not positioned to know as much about you and your situation as you are, and are thus not as well positioned as you to make decisions about your life; but they also do not face the incentives that discipline them, whether they will or no, to pay attention to the actual results of the actions they decide to take. That makes for a dangerous combination.

It may also go some way toward explaining the otherwise unfathomable indifference authoritarian leaders often display toward the suffering and misery of their people. How can a Lenin or a Stalin or a Pol Pot possibly be so cruel, so inhumane, so pitiless and merciless? Part of the explanation, I suspect, lies in the fact that they did not *themselves* endure any of the suffering caused by their decisions and actions, and neither did their own loved ones or friends. When, on the other hand, there is a real chance that a political leader might not be reelected, might be fired, or even hanged or guillotined, well *then* they smarten up fast. Until that point, however, we can only pin our hopes on their benevolence—and we need not belabor just how weak that can be in the face of their own self-interest.

The conclusion is that a socialist state is incompatible with a society of human beings—that is, a society of *persons*—because it robs them of the opportunities to exercise judgment and to deliberate about ends that are constitutive of personhood. It treats them the way slavery treats its charges, as mere *things*. Slaveholders indeed have sometimes defended their practice by claiming that it was in the best interest of the slaves themselves, since, it is alleged, those inferior creatures just are not capable of directing their own lives in a "civilized" or "truly human" fashion. I suggest we should reject the socialistic argument for exactly the same reasons we reject that of slavery's apologists. The further facts that the leaders of a centralized state (1) do not have the local knowledge required to make good decisions about individuals' lives and (2) do not have the proper incentives to discipline them to continually seek out what is best for people to do not only explain why government agencies are so typically unintelligent (more on that below), but also provide additional reason why we should leave the direction of people's lives as much as possible to the people themselves.

THE AMERICAN WELFARE STATE: A "MIDDLE WAY"?

Since at least the era of Franklin Delano Roosevelt and the New Deal, the United States has embarked on a path attempting to steer a so-called middle way between the extremes of socialism, on the one hand, and of "horse-and-buggy-era" classical liberalism (as FDR called it[16]), on the other. The idea has been that since socialism has its "excesses"—abusive tyranny, mainly—and since classical, Lockean, minimal-state, or "night-watchman" liberalism has its own excesses—great disparities in wealth chief among them—perhaps the wise thing to do is to steer a middle path. Perhaps, then, we can allow the classical liberal scheme of markets, competition, and private property, out of deference to the apparent reality that this is the best engine for the creation of material prosperity; while at the same time hemming those markets in, limiting competition, and weakening private property rights when doing so leads to socially desirable ends or when other undesirable consequences would otherwise ensue. This is the welfare state: it allows private property, but it taxes it and may revoke or confiscate it on demand; it allows markets, but it has rules about what kinds of goods may be sold, under what conditions they may be sold, what kind of employment contracts are allowable, and so on; and it redistributes wealth from the wealthy to the poor in an effort to narrow, if not close altogether, the gap between them.

Many people today believe that such a system, at least as it exists in theoretical descriptions, is the perfect embodiment of compromise between the highest, if unattainable, moral and political goals (socialism) and the actual, if selfish and ugly, reality of human nature (capitalism). I suspect, however, that many more people accept the welfare state not because of any theoretical or moral commitments but rather because that is just what they are used to. As the great Scottish philosopher David Hume (1711–76) argued, political power rests not on physical force but on belief, and belief itself is largely determined by habit.[17] Why do people obey the king's soldiers? Because everyone knows—that is, everyone

---

[16] At a press conference on May 31, 1935. See http://www.bartleby.com/73/1763.html (accessed December 12, 2005).

[17] In his essay, "Of the Origin of Government," contained in the collection *Essays Moral, Political, and Literary,* pp. 37–41.

believes—that they are in charge. Why do they believe that? Because it has always been so. Why, in turn, do the king's soldiers obey the king? Because they believe that he is in charge; and besides, *everyone* obeys the king. Similarly, in America today, many people follow what the president says, what their senators and representatives say, what the people who staff all those bureaus and agencies and offices say, because they believe that those people are in charge. Why do they believe that? Well, everyone does—right? Besides, it has always been that way—right? In an 1884 essay entitled "The Great Political Superstition,"[18] the English philosopher and biologist Herbert Spencer (1820–1903) claimed that despite their republican pretenses the English had never truly rid themselves of the old and publicly denigrated idea of the "divine right of kings," according to which the king claimed authority to rule either because he was appointed by God or because he *was* a god. That may have been the earlier "great political superstition," but according to Spencer the great political superstition of his own day was "the divine right of parliaments": whereas earlier there were no limits on the *king's* authority to rule, now there is no limit on *parliament's* authority to rule. Were he alive today, Spencer would probably claim that Americans got rid of the "divine right of kings" in 1776 only to replace it with the "divine right of Congress" in the 1930s.[19] Though perhaps possessed of a grain of truth, Spencer's claim strikes us today, especially in America, as an exaggeration. But looking at the long list of current government agencies (contained in the Appendix to this chapter) and listening to the seemingly boundless promises of contemporary politicians nevertheless gives one pause.

---

[18] Contained in Spencer's *The Man versus the State*, pp. 123–66.

[19] American sociologist William Graham Sumner (1840–1910) explicitly makes just this claim in his 1901 essay "The Bequests of the Nineteenth Century to the Twentieth." Sumner writes there: "During the nineteenth century the state, as it was inherited from the eighteenth century, has undergone great improvement. The nineteenth century inherited from the eighteenth vague notions of political beatification. To abolish kings and get a 'republic' would, it was expected, bring universal and endless peace and happiness. Then the idea was to get the 'rights of man' declared and sworn to. Then the result was to come from universal suffrage in the republic. Then democracy was to be the realizer of hope and faith. It was thought that a democracy never would be warlike or extravagant in expenditure. Then faith was put in a constitutional government, whether republican or monarchical. Next hope turned to representative institutions as the key to the right solution. The century ends with despondency as to each and all of these notions. Now [that is, in 1901] social democracy and state socialism seem to be the divinities which are to beatify us. The faith that beatification is possible and that some piece of political machinery can get it for us seems to be as strong as ever" (*On Liberty, Society, and Politics*, p. 377). For a penetrating contemporary discussion of this phenomenon, see Daniel Klein's "The People's Romance."

Welfare and Forced Labor

But let us ask whether a welfare state is compatible with respecting humanity's personhood. The answer, I believe, is, again, no. Stripped to its essentials, a welfare state is a merely *partially realized* socialistic state. It may not claim its members' *entire* lives to be under its proper purview, but it does claim enough of their lives to impede, and thus be inconsistent with, their personhood. Allowing you to have some, limited say over your life is better, to be sure, than allowing you none at all, but it is still inferior to allowing you full say. It is like using forced labor on your farm, but allowing your wards to do what they want in the evenings and on the weekends—and then defending the practice on the grounds that it strikes the perfect balance between the extremes of total (tyrannical) control and total (anarchistic) freedom. Actually, this comparison is more apt than you might think. Economist Robert Lawson has estimated for me that in 2004 Americans had to work nearly six months out of the year to pay their total government burden, which includes federal, state, and local taxes, costs of compliance with government rules, and costs of government regulation.[20] In other words, almost *50 percent* of America's gross national product is consumed by the state in its various guises. Indeed, according to the Tax Foundation, Americans pay more in taxes than they do for food, clothing, and shelter combined.[21] How different is that from a slavery in which you have to work for the slaveholder for only half the year? Or in which you work for him from 8 A.M. to noon, and then, after lunch, you can begin work for yourself? Even if it were true—which it is not—that all that money you had to work for to pay your debt to the state went to good ends?

A few considerations about likening paying one's debt to the state to slavery are in order.[22] First, people who must labor to pay taxes are not subject to the physical and emotional abuse that is often characteristic of actual slave trades. So we should take care not to minimize or trivialize the horrors of slave trading. Moreover, a taxed person in a welfare state can, unlike the slave, move away if he objects to the taxation. (This is the familiar "America: love it or leave it!" position.) That is a fair point, but

---

[20] Lawson should know: he is the principal economist on the annually compiled *Economic Freedom of the World*.

[21] Http://www.taxfoundation.org/taxfreedomday.html (accessd December 12, 2005).

[22] The following discussion of taxation and slavery draws on the discussions of several others, including Feser, Haworth, Kymlicka, Michael, Nozick, Jonathan Wolff, and Robert Paul Wolff.

I think it is often exaggerated. Consider this scenario. A large company decides to buy your town lock, stock, and barrel; perhaps it's discovered that under your town are large oil reserves and the company wants to capitalize on them. It approaches your town council, negotiates a price, and, despite the protestations of you and a few other dissenting citizens, closes the deal. The company promptly begins charging you a premium for driving on "its" roads, shopping in "its" stores, and living in one of "its" houses; it reorganizes "its" schools according to its lights and forces you to pay for the schools whether your children go there or not; it develops numerous rules about what kinds of businesses it will allow and what not; it charges premiums on some businesses and gives subsidies (paid for by you) to others; and so on. Naturally, you protest again: you did not agree to the company buying your town, your land, your house, and the rest; you do not (let us say) agree with much of what the company does with its money, and hence you do not want to contribute to its profits; and you never consented to pay the company's premiums—indeed, you openly and publicly refused your consent. Now suppose that, on hearing your complaints, a fellow town citizen responds: "Look, this is just what the company *does.* Everybody knows that. It's done it in other towns for a very long time. Anyway, I like sending my kids to their schools 'for free.' And besides, if you don't like it, you can always just move." Consider what your reaction would be. I suspect you would not feel particularly consoled. Yes, you can, technically, move: if you have enough money, you can uproot your family, sell your house (after paying another premium to the company), and move somewhere else—to another town that is also owned by this same company or by another one in nearly exactly the same way. That is the scenario that a person in America who objects to taxation faces today. There is not the physical brutalization often involved in chattel slave trade, but the extent to which people's choices are constrained in a contemporary welfare state such as America is often unappreciated.

A brief historical digression and elaboration on this point. The seventeenth-century philosopher John Locke (1632–1704) had argued in his 1690 *Second Treatise of Government* that a legitimate government must rest on the consent of the governed. But consent can come in two guises, Locke argued: *express,* which is clear enough, and *tacit,* which presents, as Locke says, a "difficulty."[23] If a person expressly consents to a government's authority—by, say, taking a public oath of

---

[23] John Locke, *Second Treatise of Government,* §119, p. 347. Other references to Locke's *Second Treatise* are to paragraph and page in this edition.

allegiance—then, Locke argues, there is no question as to the government's legitimate authority over him. On the other hand, Locke argued that in the absence of such public declarations, one can also "tacitly" consent to a government's authority:

> every Man, that hath any Possession, or Enjoyment, or any part of the Dominions of any Government, doth thereby give his *tacit Consent*, and is as far forth obliged to Obedience to the Laws of that Government, during such Enjoyment, as any one under it; whether this his possession be of Land, to him and his Heirs for ever, or a Lodging only for a Week; or whether it be barely travelling freely on the Highway; and in Effect, it reaches as far as the very being of any one within the Territories of that Government. (§119, p. 348)

This might capture the sentiment of the claim that if I enjoy the privileges and immunities of living under a government's jurisdiction, then I have ipso facto given my consent, even if "tacitly," to what that government does. And thus I have no legitimate grounds to resist my government's actions, for example, when it taxes me. But that notion of consent is far too broad—indeed, it is so broad as to lose all connection to anything one might legitimately call "consent" at all. David Hume addressed the Lockean argument in his essay "Of the Original Contract" and, to my mind, refuted it. It is worth quoting at length:

> Should it be said, that, by living under the dominion of a prince, which one might leave, every individual has given a tacit consent to his authority, and promised him obedience; it may be answered, that such an implied consent can only have place, where a man imagines, that the matter depends on his choice. But where he thinks (as all mankind do who are born under established governments) that by his birth he owes allegiance to a certain prince or certain form of government; it would be absurd to infer a consent or choice, which he expressly, in this case, renounces and disclaims.
>
> Can we seriously say, that a poor peasant or artisan has a free choice to leave his country, when he knows no foreign language or manners, and lives from day to day, by the small wages which he acquires? We may as well assert, that a man, by remaining in a vessel, freely consents to the dominion of the master; though he was carried on board while asleep, and must leap into the ocean, and perish, the moment he leaves her. (p. 475)

Hume here reiterates the two central points in my argument above. First, it seems implausible—Hume says "absurd"—to claim that a person has "consented" to a government to which he has never expressly given allegiance and whose authority over him he now expressly denies. Second, the "love it or leave it" response is a Hobson's choice, which is no choice at all. In other words, if one of the options offered is not a realistic possibility, then it is a mere pretense to claim that one's taking the other option is an act of free, voluntary consent.

To return, then, to the issue of taxation and slavery, perhaps one is inclined to say that a better comparison would be between taxation and *theft*, both being instances—so one might argue—of A taking away from B what was rightfully B's and not A's to take. But the theft analogy does not fully capture the situation, since paying taxes is something that one must do continuously, with every transaction of goods, services, or commodities, and forever; it is not a one-time loss, as theft usually is. Moreover, the notion of theft might presuppose a controversial notion of (natural?) property rights: A can only "steal" something from B if B rightfully "owned" it in the first place. But an objector might argue that the state, not individuals, owns everything, and hence that in taxation the state is merely taking what was its own in the first place. Since paying one's government debt is enforced by coercion or the threat of coercion, however, and since one's ability to vote, if one has that ability, is negligible in altering the governmental burden—each person's vote is statistically insignificant in almost every election, and in any case the majority of people setting and enforcing actual tax policy are unelected government employees over whom no citizen has any direct control—perhaps the proper way to think of people's legal responsibility to pay the governmental burden is as *forced labor*. However you decide to work, and however much work you do, federal, state, and local governments in America will take about half of whatever you make. They do this whether you agree they should or not and whether you consent or not, and they have a considerable array of coercive punitive measures they can bring to bear on you if you try not to comply. Thus you are forced to give a portion of the fruits of your labor to others against your will to serve their ends, not yours. That is virtually the *definition* of "forced labor."

Most people are inclined to accept that forced labor is wrong, even if they resist the suggestion that state taxation is relevantly similar to it. In the next chapter I argue that despite the similarity to forced labor, the state is still justified in taxing its citizens—but only for a narrow, specifically limited purpose. That one purpose is a corollary to the argument I wish to make here, which is that when you are forced to pay a portion of what you earn to someone else, you are to that extent not free to use your own judgment: you are not allowed to decide for yourself to what uses or purposes your money or labor will be put, and you are not allowed to decide for yourself whether the uses or purposes to which that demanded portion of your money is put are worthwhile or justified.

Taking these decisions away from you therefore restricts the scope of your judgment. And doing that, as I have argued, is an affront to your personhood. My suggestion, then, is that to whatever extent the state makes decisions about your life for you, to that same extent does it disrespect your personhood and thus your humanity. If it does that only a little bit, then you are better off than many other people in the world whose states are more oppressive; but it still does it that little bit. Just as you would reject, and rightly so, forcing someone to work against his will even for only "a little bit" of his day, for the same reasons you should reject a state that substitutes its judgment for an individual person's, even a little bit.

As I mentioned, however, it is easy to underestimate the extent to which welfare states such as America's resemble in effect the socialistic state more than a "middle road" between totalitarianism and anarchism. To give an idea, consider first the description Alexis de Tocqueville (1805–59) gave of the peculiar brand of "despotism" growing in America in the 1830s:

Thus, after taking each individual by turns in its powerful hands and kneading him as it likes, the sovereign extends its arms over society as a whole; it covers its surface with a network of small, complicated, painstaking, uniform rules through which the most original minds and the most vigorous souls cannot clear a way to surpass the crowd; it does not break wills, but it softens them, bends them, and directs them; it rarely forces one to act, but it constantly opposes itself to one's acting; it does not destroy, it prevents things from being born; it does not tyrannize, it hinders, compromises, enervates, extinguishes, dazes, and finally reduces each nation to being nothing more than a herd of timid and industrious animals of which the government is the shepherd.[24]

Moving forward in history only a few decades, consider next the list of ten things that Marx and Engels claimed in the *Communist Manifesto* are required to establish socialism:

1. Abolition of property in land and application of all rents of land to public purposes.
2. A heavy progressive or graduated income tax.
3. Abolition of all rights of inheritance.
4. Confiscation of the property of all emigrants and rebels.
5. Centralization of credit in the banks of the state, by means of a national bank with state capital and an exclusive monopoly.

---

[24] *Democracy in America*, vol. 2, pt. 4, chap. 6, p. 663. Be sure to read the rest of Tocqueville's chapter, too.

6. Centralization of the means of communication and transport in the hands of the state.

7. Extension of factories and instruments of production owned by the state; the bringing into cultivation of waste lands, and the improvement of the soil generally in accordance with a common plan.

8. Equal obligation of all to work. Establishment of industrial armies, especially for agriculture.

9. Combination of agriculture with manufacturing industries; gradual abolition of all the distinction between town and country by a more equable distribution of the populace over the country.

10. Free education for all children in public schools. Abolition of children's factory labor in its present form. Combination of education with industrial production, & c., & c.[25]

The United States currently fully embraces 2 and 10, and it has gone some considerable way toward realizing 1, 3, 4, 6, 7, and 9. Consider, finally, all the departments, agencies, offices, and bureaus, listed in the Appendix to this chapter, that the American federal government currently comprises. You may be surprised to see just how many departments of the federal government there are that are dedicated to monitoring, recording, regulating, and controlling so many areas of human life.[26] This gives, I think, a strong—and indeed sobering—indication of just where we fall on the spectrum between totalitarianism and anarchism.[27]

My claim is not that all of these state programs and agencies are bad in themselves, that they have only bad effects, or that they do no good. My argument here is rather that *whatever* their consequences, they disrespect people's personhood. Their effects, whether good or bad, are irrelevant to that claim—in the same way that it would be irrelevant if a thief defended his practices on the grounds that he helps the economy by spending his stolen money or circulating his pilfered goods. Now, a thief does not in fact help the economy. It is an old fallacy, still unfortunately widely believed, that mere circulation of goods or spending of money helps the economy, regardless of how it is spent or cir-

---

[25] In Tucker, *Marx-Engels Reader*, p. 490.

[26] See Brian Finegan's *The Federal Subsidy Beast* for details.

[27] Consider also the 2005 U.S. Supreme Court decision in *Kelo v. New London* (http://straylight.law.cornell.edu/supct/html/04-108.ZS.html, accessed December 12, 2005), which grants local governments the legal right to seize people's private property by eminent domain and transfer ownership of it to other private interests whenever the local government believes it would be a good idea to do so. See Jeff Jacoby's "Eminent Injustice in New London."

culated. The fallacy was brilliantly exposed by the nineteenth-century French economist Frédéric Bastiat (1801–50) in his 1850 essay "What Is Seen and What Is Not Seen."[28] Bastiat there entertains, and then demolishes, the proposition that someone who breaks other people's windows helps the economy by making work for the glazier. As Bastiat explains, the new work for the glazier is "what is seen"; "what is not seen," however, and thus is usually forgotten, is the lost opportunity represented by what the window's owner *would have otherwise spent his money on*—which, since he would rather have done that than pay for a new window, would have led to better opportunity and thus satisfaction for him. This has become known as the "broken window fallacy," and a version of it lies behind the thief's supposed rationalization of his own destructive practices. But suppose, contrary to fact, that the thief *did* help the economy: his practice would still be theft and therefore unjust. Similarly, I claim, with government programs. I think most of them are in fact demonstratively counterproductive, but even if they were not, they would still disrespect the personhood of those whose personal judgment they distrust and abridge.

"NEGATIVE" AND "POSITIVE" LIBERTY

Bastiat wrote elsewhere that the state "is the great fictitious entity by which everyone seeks to live at the expense of everyone else."[29] In this he was echoing the French *philosophe* Voltaire (1694–1778), who had said in the eighteenth century that the state is merely a device for taking money out of one set of pockets and putting it into another.[30] *Oh, come on!* you might think. Those remarks might make for provocative rhetorical flourishes, but they cannot be taken literally—or if they *are* taken literally, then they are either exaggerated or outright false. Right? Well, just how exaggerated are they?

Let us try to get a handle on this by looking at some influential recent discussions. In a seminal 1969 essay entitled "Two Concepts of Liberty," political theorist Isaiah Berlin distinguished what he called *negative* from *positive* liberty. The "negative" concept of liberty is usually associated with what John Locke defended in his *Second Treatise of Government,* which

---

[28] Contained in his *Selected Essays on Political Economy*, pp. 1–50.
[29] In his essay, "The State," contained in *Selected Essays on Political Economy*, p. 144. Compare the surprisingly similar sentiments expressed by V. I. Lenin in his 1918 *The State and Revolution*, chap. 1.
[30] Quoted in Albert Jay Nock's "Anarchist's Progress," pp. 40–1.

holds that the government should be strictly limited in the scope of its power to defending person and private property, enforcing voluntary contracts, and punishing violations of person, private property, or contracts. On this conception, liberty is the "negative" freedom to do as one pleases with one's person or private property, as long as one does not violate the similar freedom of everyone else. This conception of freedom is essentially the General Liberty principle I defended in chapter 1. The "positive" concept, on the other hand, holds that a person is truly free only when he has the *resources required* to enable him to be what he wants and can be. This conception requires the state or others to take "positive" action to provide people who otherwise would not have the relevant means with whatever they need. This may require state-provided health care, education, unemployment insurance, business loans, monopolies, or other goods, services, or guarantees.

This second, "positive" freedom sounds to me rather more like *capacity* or *power*, as in the distinction between saying that you are *free* to outrun a horse, but you are not *capable* of it: it strikes me as a confusion to say that because you are not *able* to outrun a horse, you are not "free" to do so. (Of course you are: go ahead and try.) And if you really wanted to be able to go faster than a horse, and I could provide you with the means—suppose I have a motorcycle right here that you could use—still it would seem a confusion to say that I am limiting your freedom by not lending you my motorcycle. I may be acting selfishly or ungenerously, but I am not coercing you; so I have not limited your freedom. A concrete recent example also makes the point. In 2001, President George W. Bush issued an Executive Order limiting federal funding for stem-cell research on the grounds that the federal government should not fund something that many people have deep moral reservations about. (On that criterion, an awful lot of what the government does would be unacceptable, but put that to one side for now.) For this decision Bush was widely criticized as having restricted stem-cell research itself, or for having 'tied one hand behind the backs' of researchers.[31] Without judging Bush's decision itself, it seems that this criticism displays the same confusion between power or capacity, on the one hand, and freedom, on the other. Bush did not ban the research or ban private donations to support it; hence he did not

---

[31] Here is a typical example: http://www.cnn.com/2004/ALLPOLITICS/06/07/stem.cell. ap/index.html (accessed March 15, 2005). See also Ronald Bailey's "Do We Really Need the Feds? Funding Stem-Cell Research without Uncle Sam," http://www.reason. com/rb/rb082405.shtml (accessed December 12, 2005).

limit the freedom of the researchers or the potential donors or other supporters. He only removed one source of financial support for it—and even then only partially, since there is still some federal support for it. Regardless, whatever else we might think of Bush's actions or the reasons for them, I suggest that although researchers might now be less *able* to do what they want, they are still *free* to do so if they choose and can find the means. "Positive freedom," then, seems more accurately called "capacity" than "freedom"; "negative freedom" has I think the stronger claim to being rightly called "freedom."

Nevertheless, the defenders of "positive" freedom have claimed that they are in fact advocating the only real freedom, namely, the freedom to do things. What good does it do a pauper, they ask rhetorically, to be "free" to start a business? *True* freedom, they contend, requires that the state provide people with the background, training, and other resources necessary to make it in fact possible for anyone to start a business. Indeed, some defenders of "positive" freedom have argued that the provision of certain basic needs or "necessary goods" is actually required by a proper respect for personhood.[32] So where I have suggested that it violates personhood to limit people's choices about how to work, what to do with their money, and so on, several thinkers have turned the focus away from those who *pay* the money and provide the goods to those who *receive* them and argued that respect for their (that is, the recipients') personhood entails providing them with "basic needs" such as food, clothing, shelter, education, and health care if we are able to do so.[33] I disagree and argue

---

[32] See, for example, Joseph Raz's *The Morality of Freedom* and the collection of essays contained in Gillian Brock's edited collection *Necessary Goods* (see especially Copp's, Goodin's, O'Neill's, and Sterba's contributions).

[33] Exactly what counts as a "basic need" is a subject of discussion. Here is David Copp's fairly typical definition, which he adapts from David Braybrook: "Any credible analysis of the concept of a basic need would imply that all or most of the following are either basic needs or forms of provision for a basic need: the need for nutritious food and water; the need to excrete; the need otherwise to preserve the body intact; the need for periodic rest and relaxation, which I presume to include periodic sleep and some form of recreation; the need for companionship; the need for education; the need for social acceptance and recognition; the need for self-respect and self-esteem; the need to be free from harassment" (in *Necessary Goods*, p. 124). Copp says that his list "is perhaps not complete, and it may contain some redundancy," and he adds that although the state cannot directly provide citizens with several of these things (such as self-respect and companionship), its duty nevertheless is to *enable* citizens to meet their basic needs, if not *provide* them the needs outright (ibid.). Cf. the Universal Declaration of Human Rights adopted by the United Nations General Assembly in 1948, which, in addition to the standard life, liberty, and property, includes among everyone's "universal rights" such things as "a right to social security" (Article 22), "the right to . . . periodic holidays

to the contrary that having the state provide even "basic" or "necessary" goods—rather than, or in addition to, having the state secure 'justice' as described in chapter 1—is an infringement, and thus disrespecting, of the personhood *both* of the person who is called on to provide the goods *and* the recipient of the goods. To make that case, I turn now to examine in a bit more detail one recent attempt to argue that a proper respect for persons' freedom entails the provision of a substantial range of goods.

A "Third" Concept of Liberty?

Samuel Fleischacker has recently offered what he calls a "third concept of liberty," which he argues successfully navigates between the Scylla of Berlin's "positive" liberty and the Charybdis of his "negative" liberty, enjoying the benefits of both but the liabilities of neither. In his thus aptly named *Third Concept of Liberty,* Fleischacker argues that his "third" concept is a prudent middle way: it requires the government to provide citizens with basic necessities to free them for leading lives with ample opportunity for activities that are "phronetic"—that is, judgment-developing, named after *phronesis,* Aristotle's word for *judgment;* but it also requires the government to limit itself by not making *all* decisions for its citizens, in this way allowing scope for citizens to exercise their *phronesis.*

Fleischacker argues that "phronetic activity" is an essential element of leading a flourishing, truly human life—that without it no person can be happy or, as Fleischacker puts it, have a life filled with "proper pleasures." I think he is right about that, and his argument bears a striking similarity to the one I developed in this and the previous chapter about 'personhood' and what it entails. But the political conclusions Fleischacker reaches do not follow from the premises, and indeed, as I shall try to show, they are inconsistent with those premises. It is important to spend this time on Fleischacker's argument because his is a particularly sophisticated and

with pay" (Article 24), and "the right to a standard of living adequate for the health and well-being of himself and his family" (Article 25); and it declares, "Everyone has the right to education. Education shall be free, at least in the elementary and fundamental stages" (Article 26). Several other "fundamental human rights" are included; see the entire list at http://www.un.org/rights/50/decla.htm (accessed December 12, 2005). For criticism, see, for example, Antony Flew's short essay "The Artificial Inflation of Natural Rights," http://www.fee.org/publications/the-freeman/article.asp?aid=3297 (accesssed December 12, 2005), and Max Hocutt's *Grounded Ethics,* chap. 15. For another recent list of "basic needs" that the author believes the state should provide for everyone, see Cass Sunstein's *The Second Bill of Rights.* For criticism, see Max Hocutt's "Sunstein on Rights."

powerful defense of a commonly held position—namely, that a welfare state is justified or even required by a proper conception of human personhood. Thus if I can show that Fleischacker's argument is problematic, then I hope to have also cast doubt on other arguments claiming to support similar conclusions.[34]

Fleischacker argues that if judgment is crucial to personhood and that certain circumstances—such as leisure time, health care, and education—are necessary to cultivate judgment, then it follows that the state ought to look after those circumstances. But that does not follow. Grant, for example, that I should exercise more, or that we should all exercise more, or even that exercising more is crucial to everyone's overall well-being: it does not follow from any of that that the government must take over direction of everyone's exercising. Or grant Plato's belief that what children read (or listen to) has considerable influence on the kind of adults they become; grant even that what children read (or listen to) is of greater influence on them than any other single factor: still it does not follow that the state must therefore take over direction of what children read (or listen to).[35] Another argument is required to link the two. One would need to show that what is crucial for human judgment must *therefore* be provided by the state. But I suggest that there is no such argument, at least not one that does not simultaneously entail disrespecting people's personhood.

Fleischacker's argument makes a transition that is common in arguments defending the welfare state, but the transition masks a problem. "A minimal condition for participation in a sphere of phronetic activity, especially if one's work life lacks any interesting tasks," Fleischacker writes, "is that one have the *time* to discover, and develop the skills for, such a sphere. It follows that from the importance of judgment and its proper pleasures we can resuscitate the old liberal idea that government needs to ensure adequate *leisure* for its citizenry."[36] As I showed above,

---

34 My discussion here is based in part on my "Private Judgment, Individual Freedom, and the Role of the State" in the *Journal of Social Philosophy* and my review of Fleischacker's book in the *Review of Metaphysics*.

35 For an attack on "rock music" in the spirit of Plato, and thus contrary to my argument, see Allan Bloom's chapter "Music" in his *The Closing of the American Mind*.

36 *A Third Concept of Liberty*, p. 116 (emphasis in orginal). All other references to Fleischacker are to this book, on the page given in parentheses. Incidentally, Fleischacker claims that contemporary Americans have increasingly less leisure time, basing his claim on Juliet Schor's *The Overworked American*. But Schor's conclusions must be compared with the contrary (and to my mind convincing) evidence found in Robinson and Godbey's *Time for Life* and in Cox and Alm's *Myths of the Rich and Poor*.

however, that conclusion does *not* follow. Here is another example of the *non sequitur:* "More active [as opposed to "passive"] preferences use and therefore develop our capacity for choice itself—for intelligent, which is to say phronetic, choice. So the political powers that be must guarantee us substantial opportunities to satisfy these preferences because otherwise we will lose our freedom" (p. 118). And again:

> As a society, we are obligated to put every resource we can muster into prevent-ing and overcoming the circumstances that make children unable to grow up with good characters, and to provide insurance to adults against events that "dis-lodge" them from so much as having control over their own characters, from retaining the virtues that enable them to handle and appreciate luck at all.... [I]t is not appropriate to let luck provide whatever it takes to insure that peo-ple not get entrenched in starvation, in slavery, in illness or despair sufficient to "corrupt... desire, expectation, and thought," in miseries sufficiently "crushing and prolonged" to break their self-command. The material security to prevent such disintegration of virtue is the "guaranteed minimum" of political economists. This minimum we as a society must supply, must distribute to each, not expect each to earn for himself. (pp. 234–35)

Finally, Fleischacker concludes: "To hold each responsible for his or her own acts, to expect people to work for their own ends, we must provide them with the means that allow for responsibility: the means of health, leisure, and education by which they can judge intelligently of their lives and their conditions" (p. 235). As Fleischacker makes clear, when he says "we" must provide such things, he means that the *state* must do it. But why the state? Why not families? Why not churches? Why not other voluntary organizations?[37] Any of these might be called for, depending on the circumstances. Indeed, depending on the circumstances of a par-ticular case, perhaps what is called for is precisely *no* help from anyone: perhaps the individual needs to face this hardship on his own. This last consideration provokes perhaps the most important question: Shouldn't we expect individuals themselves to figure out ways to provide for their needs—especially given the importance of their having opportunities to develop their phronesis? Barring exceptional cases, such as children and infirm adults, the default expectation should be that a 'person' is both capable of and responsible for directing his own life, for facing and sur-mounting challenges, and for pursuing cooperative arrangements with

---

[37] We should not underestimate or discount what voluntary clubs and organizations can do. See David Beito's *From Mutual Aid to the Welfare State* and *The Voluntary City* and Fred Foldvary's *Public Goods and Private Communities* for extensive descriptions of actual cases. See also Flew's *Social Life and Moral Judgment,* chap. 3.

others to help secure his ends. Thus state action is neither the necessary nor the only possible implication of the importance of human phronesis.

When Fleischacker turns, then, to make his political recommendations, he faces the further, more substantial problem that the wish to extend private phronesis is incompatible with the endorsement of an expansive welfare state.

To allow for "the judgment that we need for truly free choices," Fleischacker argues that the state must do all of the following (pp. 238–9): (1) provide "good information about the options among which one is choosing," (2) provide "a thorough education in the skills of interpretation and the assessment of evidence," including education in "the skills of aesthetic interpretation" and in applying "those skills to the decisions [people] need to make about running their own lives," (3) provide "access to rich, clear, and clearly organized facts about products and jobs," and (4) provide "centralized computer services open to everyone" where such information will be available at no cost to the user. So far Fleischacker's list is not very different from some of what federal, state, and local governments routinely do, or attempt to do, in America today. But Fleischacker is not finished yet. To alleviate problems he believes economic markets lead to, the state must also ensure (5) that all citizens are raised "from childhood on with adequate nutrition, shelter, and health care," (6) that citizens know "they would receive considerable aid in unemployment," (7) that they know they "could take any job in the country because funds [are] available to transport them there," (8) that they are "well trained in evaluating evidence and [have] easy access to a large amount of information about their opportunities," and (9) that they have "sufficient leisure to reflect on their lives and alter them if necessary," on the order of "six weeks a year, or a several-month sabbatical every few years." (Duty (8) might be encompassed by some combination of (1)–(3); if so, we can eliminate it from the list. On the other hand, duties (1) and (3) require not only that the state provide information, but also that it procure or generate it; and duties (6) and (7) require not just that the state notify citizens of services, but also that it actually provide the services. That suggests that we should perhaps increase Fleischacker's list.)[38]

The government that could undertake to do all that is a large one indeed, and it thus seems Fleischacker's "third," "true" concept of

---

[38] I should note that Fleischacker's description of what the state should provide its citizens is not particularly unusual among contemporary political theorists. For another recent version, see Cass Sunstein's *The Second Bill of Rights*.

freedom would be considerably closer to the socialist model than to any classical liberal model. For consider what would be required to actually effect the tasks Fleischacker believes the state must undertake. It would require extensive state-supported educational programs, nationalized health care, nationalized information and transportation systems, and systematic national oversight of businesses' vacation policies, benefits packages, retirement offerings, employment contracts, and working conditions. Moreover, the requirements to provide adequate overall conditions for all children would require extensive central planning of economic resources and educational policies. And all this state apparatus would have to be supported by taxation, entailing large-scale redistribution of wealth, and be executed and directed by an extensive information-gathering agency, entailing the procurement of a great deal of detailed information about all citizens.

The problem is that all this state action would compromise the protection of human judgment—which was the initial, and indeed paramount, concern. Consider what Fleischacker says about the importance of the freedom to judge, which entails freedom from governmental and other third-party interference. One thing he argues that recent democratic theorists have gotten right is the importance of autonomy and independence. "Still," says Fleischacker, "in the end what matters is independence itself, not the mode of reaching it, and it is far from clear that participation in government is the only way to develop that quality" (p. 248).[39] Part of the reason for Fleischacker's skepticism here is the kind of people who are in government:

Arrogant, self-deluded, and otherwise morally incompetent people abound who participate well in communal government. Political activists, kibbutz leaders, school and church board members—anyone who has spent a significant amount of time with such people knows plenty who are shallow, ambitious, and vain, whose service to their cause or community is a means of self-promotion or, at best, a distraction from personal failings. (pp. 248–9)

Fleischacker concludes—tellingly—that it "is indeed quite possible that, in modern societies, we develop and exercise our communally oriented virtues *better* by 'private' than by 'public' activities" (p. 249; emphasis in original). Fleischacker goes on to claim, even more strongly: "We legislate most successfully for ourselves, we govern our own lives most fully,

[39] For a criticism of democracy based on an argument similar to Fleischacker's here, see Gordon Graham's *The Case against the Democratic State*.

by controlling how we individually run our most important individual decisions, not by participating in group attempts to coordinate human actions" (p. 251). He elaborates, "It should be clear that the condition 'not being coerced by anyone else' [which Fleischacker endorses] rules out any use of judgment to coerce others. So it is the government's business, of course, to stop killing, theft, rape, assault, and the like: the whole libertarian program for government action is brought in by that condition." But note well his next sentence: "The point of my list of conditions is to go *beyond* the libertarian program" (p. 325 n. 26; emphasis in original). That, I suggest, is the problem in a nutshell.

To make clearer the problem I see, let me focus for a moment on this single sentence of Fleischacker's: "As soon as judgment is recognizably in place—the person has her basic biological needs met, has the experience and mental training to reflect on ends as well as means, and is not being coerced by anyone else—what one does with one's judgment is none of any government's business" (p. 264). Here we see both of Fleischacker's concerns: enabling judgment, on the one hand, and allowing scope for its practice, on the other. But we also see the seeds of the position's undoing. For there is no way, I suggest, that the state can do all the things Fleischacker has argued are necessary for making sure that "judgment is recognizably in place" in every citizen while simultaneously allowing for all citizens to use that judgment however they see fit. The state cannot, after all, produce the education, health care, food, transportation, information, and so on ex nihilo: rather, it can provide them only indirectly, by drawing on the labor, services, and money of others. And of course the labor, services, and money of others must be produced by the people themselves. Thus in calling for "the government" to provide these things for those who do not already have them, one is actually calling on the state to make one group of people provide them for another. If the state taxes or demands the labor of some to provide for others, the former are to that extent no longer free to use their judgment as they see fit. The alternative—allowing people to provide such services to others as they privately judge proper—is precisely *not* what Fleischacker argues for; he is rather arguing for whichever group of people is running the relevant branch of the state to *override* others' judgments and make them pay or labor as the group sees fit. Perhaps Bastiat and Voltaire were on to something after all.

One might respond here that perhaps Fleischacker's argument is that although the government may not poke its nose into what I do with my judgment privately, it may justifiably concern itself with what I do with my goods and services. In other words, it may regulate my (public) economic activity, even as it respects my (private) judgment about other matters. This response founders on two problems. First, it relies on an untenable distinction between public actions and private judgment. My goods and services are produced by my labor, and my labor is inherently connected with my private judgment. They cannot be separated, since the former are simply products or extensions of the latter. So granting the state oversight of my goods, services, and labor is in effect granting it oversight of a large part of the functioning of my judgment, and since judgment just is deciding for oneself, that is in effect to damage my judgment itself. Second, this reply overlooks the full scope of the range of activities that Fleischacker, as well as other theorists defending similar positions, actually say falls within the proper purview of the state, as well as what would be required to provide for those activities. They could not be created except by extensive impingement on the private judgment of individuals.

Using language drawn from Immanuel Kant, Fleischacker says that it is the free play of the deliberative faculties culminating in passing judgment that chiefly defines who we are and makes our lives worth living. Remove or limit the opportunities to do this and human life correspondingly suffers. I agree: to the extent that one person or one group substitutes its notion of the good life for that of others, then to that same extent the others' opportunities for phronetic activities are curtailed, thereby diminishing free choice and imperiling human flourishing. I conclude, therefore, that it is inconsistent to ask the state *both* to provide such an extensive list of services to its citizens *and* to give them a wide scope of private space in which to exercise their phronetic powers.

One final way of making this point is by pointing out that people's actions under "negative" liberty are *compossible*, meaning that every person can fully exercise his negative freedom simultaneously with everyone else, and no one will be interfering with anyone else's similar exercise. This is the sentiment captured in Adam Smith's remark that one can "fulfil all the rules of justice by sitting still and doing nothing."[40] On the other hand, "positive" liberty is *not* compossible: it is not possible for everyone to exercise "positive" liberty, because such exercise by some will necessarily be at the expense of others. This is a fundamental contradiction involved in the welfare state, what makes it inherently inimical to a true respect for personhood.

[40] *Theory of Moral Sentiments*, p. 82.

The Judgment of Recipients of Aid

The contradiction is also made apparent by considering not only the ways in which a welfare state limits the phronetic activity of those it requires to *provide* services—by not allowing them the opportunity to judge whether to provide the service, and if so how much, in what way, and so on—but by considering how it limits the phronetic activities of the *recipients* of these services—by depriving them of the opportunity to make important life decisions on their own. Depending on how extensive the final list of the state's tasks is, there may in fact turn out to be embarrassingly little scope for people's private phronesis. Individuals would not judge the structure or content of their or their children's education, for example, which doctors to see or which medical treatments to pay for, or which information is important or proper or necessary to know; they may not have final say in which foods to eat, which exercises or sports or hobbies to engage in or refrain from, or even, perhaps, whether or how many children to have.

If you find it implausible to suggest that such matters might come within the ambit of a Fleischackerian state's authority, consider to what lengths government programs have gone in the American welfare state once they have been implemented. A critic of the 1990 Americans with Disabilities Act, to take one recent example, would have been laughed out of court had he suggested that it might lead to overweight people suing movie theaters and airlines for not providing seats big enough to accommodate the "disability" of being obese; yet there have been such cases.[41] Another example, taken at random: when the United States Forest Service was founded in 1905 to "improve and protect the forests" of America, it is safe to say that no one then dreamed that by 1991 the service would have constructed 360,000 miles of roads (eight times the length of the entire American Interstate Highway System, making it the largest single road-construction agency in the world), that its 2001 budget would total $5.3 billion, and that it would employ some 38,000 people.[42] Some other facts. According to the Congressional Budget Office, the total budget of the U.S. federal government has increased significantly in recent decades: in 1962, total outlays were $106.6 billion (18.8% of gross domestic product); in 1970, $195.6 billion (19.3%); in 1980, $590.9 billion (21.6%); in 1990, $1,253 billion (21.8%); in 2000, $1,789 billion (18.4%);

---

[41] See, for one example, "Woman Says Dairy Fired Her over Weight," *New York Times,* February 18, 1999.
[42] See Bethell's *The Noblest Triumph,* chap. 18, and O'Toole's *Reforming the Fire Service.*

and in 2003, \$2,158 billion (19.9%).[43] Total spending on federal regulatory activity alone (that is, not including other areas of spending)
increased from \$1.9 billion in 1960 to \$30.1 billion in 2003 in constant
1996 dollars, a real increase of 1,584 percent. Federal employees staffing
the regulatory agencies went from 70,080 in 1970 to 195,284 in 2003, an
increase of 279 percent.[44] And total pages in the *Federal Register,* where all
federal regulations are listed, increased from 12,792 in 1960 to 75,795
in 2003, an increase of 593 percent.[45] A final indicator: the number of
people holding "executive titles" in the federal government (that is, people who report "directly to the Senate-confirmed positions of secretary,
deputy secretary, undersecretary, assistant secretary and administrator")
was seventeen in 1960, then grew to thirty-three in 1992, fifty-one in
1998, and sixty-four in 2004: almost a quadrupling.[46] According to the
U.S. Census Bureau, however, from 1960 to 2000 the American population increased from 180,671,158 to 272,690,813—a mere 50 percent
increase.[47] So the increase in population cannot nearly account for the
huge growth in American federal government staffing, spending, and
regulation. A look at other aspects of the federal government reveals
remarkably similar trajectories.

My suggestion, then, is that the inevitable drift of such government
programs is almost always to extend, not limit, their scope. Once agencies
are created with the express but quite general purpose of making sure
that all people have whatever is required for proper phronesis, I do not
think there is any way we can say in advance which areas of life they would
consider outside their legitimate purview.

[43] See http://www.cbo.gov/showdoc.cfm?index=1821&sequence=0#table1 (accessed December 12, 2005). Economist Robert Higgs argues that federal expenditures are
substantially higher than the Budget Office's estimates, both in real terms and as
a percentage of American wealth; see Higgs's "Lies, Damn Lies, and Conventional
Measures of the Growth of Government," http://www.independent.org/tii/media/
pdf/tir_09_1_9_higgs.pdf (accessed December 12, 2005).
[44] See Dudley and Warren, "Regulatory Spending Soars," http://wc.wustl.edu/Reg_Budget_final.pdf (accessed December 12, 2005). See also Higgs, "Lies, Damn Lies, and Conventional Measures of the Growth of Government," and Crews, *Ten Thousand Commandments.*
[45] The number of pages increases almost daily. For running updates, see http://www.
access.gpo.gov/su_docs/fedreg/frcont03.html (accessed December 12, 2005).
[46] See "Agencies Getting Heavier on Top," *Washington Post,* July 23, 2004, http://www.
washingtonpost.com/wp-dyn/articles/A7590-2004Jul22.html (accessed December 12,
2005).
[47] See http://eire.census.gov/popest/archives/pre1980/popclockest.txt (accessed December 12, 2005).

Might such an agency decide that a person's nutrition, for example, is a critical factor affecting whether he is able to exercise his phronesis properly—a bad diet can incapacitate a person, after all—and thus that it must specify which foods and medicines and supplements each person must eat or take? This is not too far from where the U.S. Food and Drug Administration now stands: the FDA's 2005 budget is $1.8 billion, and it now claims oversight over all foods and drinks consumed by human beings; all medicines, medications, biologics, and nutritional supplements taken epidermally, orally, anally, intravenously, or otherwise; all devices, packages, or utensils for the administration of foodstuffs, medicines, medications, biologics, or supplements; as well as animal feed and drugs, cosmetics, radiation-emitting products (such as cell phones, lasers, and microwave ovens), and "combination products."[48]

Or might such an agency decide that parents within a certain range of income can only *properly* care for their children—and hence properly provide the necessary environment for cultivating phronesis in them—if they are limited to having, say, only two children? Consider, to take one example among many that might be chosen, what the Department of Children and Family Services (DCFS) of Illinois describes as among the services it provides in just one branch of its activities: "therapeutic intervention and support, homemaker services, psychological evaluations, attending to the child's personal needs of clothing and special equipment if needed, programs transitioning teens to self-sufficiency, alcohol and substance abuse diagnosis, pregnant and parenting teen services."[49] The Illinois DCFS describes one of its programs, called "Wraparound," as providing "counseling, advocacy, mentoring, psychological or psychiatric services, therapeutic recreation, and other services" for children and their families. Here is a further description of Wraparound:

Oftentimes children and their families have needs that cross agency boundaries. Interagency cooperation is an integral part of the wraparound planning process. It is essential that all services are developed cooperatively and are coordinated in a child and family team. The team shares responsibility, expertise, and mutual support while *designing creative services that meet an individual's strengths and needs across home, school, and community.* A wraparound plan is continually reviewed and modified based on the child and family's developing strengths and evolving needs.

[48] For the FDA's budget, see http://www.fda.gov/oc/oms/ofm/budget/documentation.htm; for its claimed oversight, see http://www.fda.gov/default.htm (both accessed December 12, 2005).

[49] Http://www.state.il.us/dcfs/otherServices/index.shtml (accessed December 12, 2005).

Wraparound interventions are flexible because the approach is multifaceted, *taking all aspects of the child's history and current life situation into account.* (emphasis added)

The Illinois DCFS elaborates that it achieves Wraparound's aims with "planning and services [that] are comprehensive, addressing needs in three or more life domain areas. These life domains are: family, living situation, educational/vocational, social/recreational, psychological/ emotional, medical, legal, and safety/crisis."

I do not mean to single out the Illinois DCFS, as it is typical among similar agencies in other states. And I also do not mean to insinuate that its agents are evil or underhanded or have sinister intentions. Not at all: I am sure they have only the best intentions. My point rather is simply to illustrate the scope of this one branch of this one state agency's authority and the range of services and resources it is prepared to engage, and to suggest that if it were given the charge of protecting all children's phrone-sis or judgment, as well as the authority and means to back up its decrees coercively, then I think things like one day mandating how many children people may have, or any number of other similarly intrusive mandates, are very real possibilities. Given numerous historical precedents, partic-ularly in the twentieth century, it seems naïve, even dangerously so, to think that the state would instead voluntarily limit its authority to what the theorist antecedently believes would be appropriate.

BETRAYING PERSONHOOD

An indefinite encroachment of state decision making into areas otherwise left to individuals' own phronesis is not a problem, however, if one thinks that people are not 'persons' and that their choices therefore *may* be cir-cumscribed to ensure that they do not choose badly or incorrectly. But that is not the view I have argued for here. I believe instead that people are 'persons' and should be treated as such. And as I argued in the previous chapter, it is a crucial part of taking individual judgment seriously that one allow people to make bad choices and to suffer the consequences. That is, after all, the only way one can learn. How can one develop, adjust, and fine-tune one's judgment if one does not have the opportunity to fail? Thus if making mistakes is necessary for improving and developing one's judgment, and if this judgment is integral to personhood, what follows is that the proper government is one protecting "negative," but not "positive," liberty. Calling on the state to take positive steps toward fostering individual judgment—as opposed to merely protecting the liberty of individuals to develop and exercise it on their own—introduces a means that is significantly, even fatally, destructive of the desired end. The welfare state, therefore, fails to meet our moral standards, in just the way socialistic states did.

If the socialist and the welfare state both betray personhood, however, then whaich form or forms of government do not do so? Which political options does respect for personhood leave us with? Those questions bring us to chapter 3.

APPENDIX TO CHAPTER 2

U.S. Federal Government Agencies, 2003

The U.S. federal government in 2003 spent a total of $2.14 trillion, and, not including military personnel, it had 1,745,013 employees.[50] For comparison, the company with the highest revenues in the world was Wal-Mart Stores; its total worldwide gross revenues in 2002 were $245 billion. Wal-Mart's revenues beat its nearest worldwide competitor, General Motors, by about one-third—and yet Wal-Mart had only about *one-tenth* of the federal government's expenditures. Wal-Mart employs 355,500 people, approximately one-fifth as many as the federal government's nonmilitary employment. And the 2003 total market value of Wal-Mart's assets was estimated at $372 billion. To put that into perspective, in 2003 the U.S. federal government could have bought all of the world's largest corporation—land, buildings, equipment, inventories, everything—almost six times over.

Two notes about what follows. First, with one exception I do not provide total budget outlays for each agency. The exception is military spending, which many erroneously believe is the bulk of what the government does. In 2003 the federal government spent approximately $459 billion on the military—a not inconsiderable sum, to be sure, but in the end only about one-fifth of its total budget. Second, I do not include state or local government agencies, all of which, of course, have their own budgets.

---

[50] On April 28, 2005, the U.S. Congress passed a budget for 2005 of $2.56 trillion—already an increase of fully 20 percent over the 2003 budget, despite the "cuts" that some critics highlight and lament. See "Congress Passes Budget with Cuts in Medicaid and in Taxes," *New York Times*, April 29, 2005.

80 Working Out the Position

Agencies of the U.S. Federal Government in 2003

Accounting and Auditing Policy Committee
Acquisition Department
Acquisition and Assistance Management Services
Administration and Resource Management
Administration for Children and Families
Administration on Aging
Administrative Committee of the Federal Register
Administrative Law Judges
Administrative Office of the U.S. Courts
Administrator
Advanced Technology Program
Advisory Council on Historic Preservation
Aeronomy Laboratory
African Development Foundation
African and Middle Eastern Reading Room
AgExport Services Division
Agency for Healthcare Research and Quality
Agency for Toxic Substances and Disease Registry
Agricultural Labor Affairs Coordinator
Agricultural Marketing Service
Agricultural Research Service
Air Combat Command
Air Education and Training Command

Air Force Agency for Modeling and Simulation
Air Force Audit Agency
Air Force Center for Environmental Excellence
Air Force Civil Engineer Support Agency
Air Force Communications Agency
Air Force Cost Analysis Agency
Air Force Historical Research Agency
Air Force Historical Support Office
Air Force Information Warfare Center
Air Force Inspection Agency
Air Force Institute of Technology
Air Force Legal Services Agency
Air Force Logistics Management Agency
Air Force Material Command
Air Force Medical Operations Agency
Air Force Medical Support Agency
Air Force News Agency
Air Force Office of Scientific Research
Air Force Office of Special Investigations
Air Force Office of Survivor Assistance
Air Force Personnel Center
Air Force Real Property Agency
Air Force Research Laboratory

Air Force Reserve Command
Air Force Reserve Officer Training Corps
Air Force Reserve Personnel Center
Air Force Safety Center
Air Force Services Agency
Air Force Space Command
Air Force Special Operations Command
Air Force Studies and Analyses Agency
Air Force Technical Application Center
Air Intelligence Agency
Air Mobility Command
Air National Guard
Air Resources Laboratory
Air University
Air Weather Service
Aircraft Technology
Albuquerque Operations Office
American Battle Monuments Commission
American Folklore Center
American Forces Information Center
American Indian Liaison Office
American Indian and Alaska Native Affairs Desk
American Memory
Ames Laboratory
Ames Research Center
Anacostia Museum and Center for African American History and Culture

Animal and Plant Health
Inspection Service
Antitrust Division
Appalachian Regional
Commission
Architect of the Capitol
Architectural and
Transportation
Barriers Compliance
Board
Archives of American
Art
Arctic Research
Commission
Argonne National
Laboratory
Armed Forces
Radiobiology
Research Institute
Armed Forces
Retirement Home
Army Financial
Management
Army Materiel
Command
Army Medical
Department
Army Research
Laboratory
Army Review Boards
Agency
Arthritis and
Musculoskeletal
Interagency
Coordinating
Committee
Arthur M. Sackler
Gallery
Arts and Industries
Building
ArtsEdge
Asian Division Reading
Room
Associate Administrator
for Commercial Space
Transportation
Atlantic Oceanographic
and Meteorological
Laboratory

Barry M. Goldwater and
Excellence in
Education Foundation
Benefits Review Board
Bettis Atomic Power
Laboratory
Board of Contract
Appeals
Board of Governors of
the Federal Reserve
System
Board of Veterans'
Appeals
Border and
Transportation
Security
Branch of
Acknowledgement
and Research
Broadcasting Board of
Governors
Brookhaven National
Laboratory
Building and Fire
Research Laboratory
Bureau of
Administration
Bureau of African
Affairs
Bureau of Alcohol,
Tobacco, and
Firearms
Bureau of Arms Control
Bureau of Citizenship
and Immigration
Services
Bureau of Consular
Affairs
Bureau of Democracy,
Human Rights, and
Labor
Bureau of Diplomatic
Strategy
Bureau of East Asian
and Pacific Affairs
Bureau of Economic
Analysis
Bureau of Educational
and Cultural Affairs

Bureau of Engraving
and Printing
Bureau of European and
Eurasian Affairs
Bureau of Indian
Affairs
Bureau of Industry and
Security
Bureau of Intelligence
and Research
Bureau of International
Labor Affairs
Bureau for International
Narcotics and Law
Enforcement Affairs
Bureau of Justice
Assistance
Bureau of Justice
Statistics
Bureau of Labor
Statistics
Bureau of Land
Management
Bureau of Legislative
Affairs
Bureau of Medicine and
Surgery
Bureau of Naval
Personnel
Bureau of Near Eastern
Affairs
Bureau of
Nonproliferation
Bureau of Oceans and
International
Environmental and
Scientific Affairs
Bureau of Political
Military Affairs
Bureau of Population,
Refugees, and
Migration
Bureau of Prisons
Bureau of Public Affairs
Bureau of Reclamation
Bureau of Resource
Management
Bureau of South Asian
Affairs

Bureau of
Transportation
Statistics
Bureau of Western
Hemisphere Affairs
Bureau of the Census
Bureau of the Public
Debt
Business Reference
Services
Cataloging Directorate
Cataloging Distribution
Service
Cataloging Policy and
Support Office
Cataloging in
Publication Division
Center for Biologics
Evaluation and
Research
Center for the Book
Center for Cost and
Financing Studies
Center for Devices and
Radiological Health
Center for Drug
Evaluation and
Research
Center for Earth and
Planetary Studies
Center for Faith-Based
Initiatives
Center for Food Safety
and Applied Nutrition
Center for Information
Technology
Center for Organization
and Delivery Studies
Center for Outcomes
and Effectiveness
Research
Center for Practice and
Technology
Assessment
Center for Primary Care
Research
Center for Quality
Improvement and
Patient Safety

Center for Scientific
Review
Center for Veterinary
Medicine
Centers for Disease
Control and
Prevention
Centers for Medicare
and Medicaid Services
Central Intelligence
Agency
Chemical Safety and
Hazard Investigation
Board
Chemical Science and
Technology
Laboratory
Chief Financial Officers
Council
Chief Information
Officer
Chief Information
Officers Council
Chief of Naval
Operations
Chief Procurement
Officer
Children's Literature
Center
Citizens' Stamp Advisory
Committee
Civil Division
Civil Rights Division
Climate Diagnostics
Center
Climate Monitoring and
Diagnostics
Laboratory
Clinical Center
Coastal Habitat
Conservation
Programs
Cognitive, Neural, and
Biomolecular Science
and Technology
Division
Cold Regions Research
and Engineering
Laboratory

Command, Control,
Communications,
Computers
Commandant of the
Marine Corps
Commission of Fine Arts
Commission on Security
and Cooperation in
Europe (Helsinki
Commission)
Committee on Foreign
Investment in the
United States
Committee for the
Implementation of
Textile Agreements
Committee for Purchase
from People Who Are
Blind or Severely
Disabled
Commodity Futures
Trading Commission
Community
Development
Financial Institutions
Fund
Community Relations
Service
Compliance Review
Staff
Congressional Budget
Office
Congressional Research
Service
Construction
Engineering Research
Laboratories
Consumer Product
Safety Commission
Contract Reform and
Privatization Office
Cooper-Hewitt National
Design Museum
Coordinating Council
on Juvenile Justice
and Delinquency
Prevention
Corporate Programs
Division

Corporation for
National and
Community Service
Cotton, Oilseeds,
Tobacco, and Seeds
Division
Council of Economic
Advisors
Council on
Environmental
Quality
Courts of Appeal
Criminal Division
Critical Infrastructure
Assurance Office
Customer Service:
Departmental
Account
Representative
Division
Dairy, Livestock, and
Poultry Division
D.C. Circuit
Defense Acquisition
University
Defense Administrative
Support Center
Defense Advanced
Research Projects
Agency
Defense Commissary
Agency
Defense Contract Audit
Agency
Defense Contract
Management Agency
Defense Contract
Management District
International
Defense Contract
Management District
West
Defense Contribution
Center
Defense Courier Service
Defense Energy Support
Center
Defense Finance and
Accounting Service

Defense Human
Resources Activity
Defense Industrial
Supply Center
Defense Information
Systems Agency
Defense Intelligence
Agency
Defense Legal Services
Agency
Defense Logistics
Agency
Defense Logistics
Information Service
Defense Logistics
Support Command
Defense National
Stockpile Center
Defense Nuclear
Facilities Safety
Board
Defense Prisoner of
War/Missing
Personnel Office
Defense Reutilization
and Marketing Service
Defense Security
Cooperation Agency
Defense Security Service
Defense Supply Center
Columbus
Defense Supply Center
Philadelphia
Defense Supply Center
Richmond
Defense Technical
Information Center
Defense Threat
Reduction Agency
Delaware River Basin
Commission
Democratic Caucus
Democratic Leadership
Democratic Whip
Department of
Agriculture
Department of the Air
Force
Department of the Army

Department of
Commerce
Department of Defense
Department of Defense
Education Activity
Department of
Education
Department of Energy
Department of Health
and Human Services
Department of
Homeland Security
Department of Housing
and Urban
Development
Department of the
Interior
Department of Justice
Department of Labor
Department of the Navy
Department of the Navy
Environmental
Program
Department of State
Department of
Transportation
Department of the
Treasury
Department of Veterans
Affairs
Departmental Account
Representative
Division
Departmental Appeals
Board
Departmental
Representative
Division
Deputy Chief Financial
Officer
Director, Marine Corps
Staff
Directorate for
Command, Control,
Communications, and
Computer Systems
Directorate of
Educational Policy
and Development

Directorate of Integration
Directorate for Intelligence
Directorate of Management
Directorate for Manpower and Personnel
Directorate for Operations
District Offices
Division of Contracting and General Services
Division of Endangered Species
Division of Energy and Mineral Resources
Division of Environmental Contaminants
Division of Federal Aid
Division of Federal Employees' Compensation
Division of Finance
Division of Forestry
Division of Habitat Conservation
Division of Health Assessment and Consultation
Division of Health Education and Promotion
Division of Health Studies
Division of Information Technology Management
Division of Law Enforcement
Division of Longshore and Harbor Workers' Compensation
Division of Policy and Directives Management
Division of Public Affairs

Division of Realty
Division of Toxicology
DLA Office of Operations Research and Resource Analysis
Document Automation and Production Service
Domestic Policy Council
Drug Enforcement Administration
Dryden Flight Research Center
Economic Development Administration
Economic Research Service
Economics and Statistics Administration
Educational Partnerships Program
Eighth Circuit
Eighth U.S. Army
Electronics Division
Electronics and Electrical Engineering Laboratory
Eleventh Circuit
Eleventh Wing
Employee Benefits Security Administration
Employees' Compensation Appeals Board
Employment Standards Administration
Employment and Training Administration
Endangered Species Committee
Energy Efficiency and Renewable Energy
Energy Information Administration
Energy Sciences Network

Energy Security and Assurance Program
Enforcement Center
Engineering Materials and Physical Science
Environmental Measurement Laboratory
Environmental Protection Agency
Environmental Research Laboratories
Environmental Studies Program Information System
Environmental Technology Laboratory
Epidemiology Program Office
Equal Employment Opportunity Commission
Equal Employment Opportunity Office
Ernest Orlando Lawrence Berkeley National Laboratory
Ethics Office
European Command
European Reading Room
Evidence-Based Practice Centers
Executive Office for Asset Forfeiture
Executive Office for Immigration Review
Executive Office of the President
Executive Office for United States Attorneys
Executive Office for United States Trustees
Executive Office for Weed and Seed
Export Administration Review Board

Export-Import Bank of the United States
Facilities and Leadership
Family Policy Compliance Office
Farm Credit Administration
Farm and Foreign Agriculture Services
Farm Service Agency
FBI Laboratory
Federal Accounting Standards Advisory Board
Federal Aviation Administration
Federal Bureau of Investigation
Federal Communications Commission
Federal Computer Incident Response Center
Federal Crimes Victim Division
Federal Deposit Insurance Corporation
Federal Depository Library Program Administration
Federal Duck Stamp Office
Federal Election Commission
Federal Emergency Management Agency
Federal Energy Management Program
Federal Energy Regulatory Commission
Federal Executive Board
Federal Executive Institute and Management Development Centers

Federal Financial Institutions Examination Council
Federal Financing Bank
Federal Highway Administration
Federal Housing Finance Board
Federal Interagency Committee on Education
Federal Interagency Committee for the Management of Noxious and Exotic Weeds
Federal Job Announcement Search
Federal Judicial Center
Federal Junior Duck Stamp Conservation and Design Program
Federal Labor Relations Authority
Federal Laboratory Consortium for Technology Transfer
Federal Lands Highway Office
Federal Law Enforcement Training Center
Federal Library and Information Center Committee
Federal Maritime Commission
Federal Mediation and Conciliation Service
Federal Mine Safety and Health Review Commission
Federal Railroad Administration
Federal Relay Service
Federal Research Division

Federal Reserve Bank of Atlanta
Federal Reserve Bank of Boston
Federal Reserve Bank of Chicago
Federal Reserve Bank of Cleveland
Federal Reserve Bank of Dallas
Federal Reserve Bank of Kansas City
Federal Reserve Bank of Minneapolis
Federal Reserve Bank of New York
Federal Reserve Bank of Philadelphia
Federal Reserve Bank of Richmond
Federal Reserve Bank of San Francisco
Federal Reserve Bank of St. Louis
Federal Retirement Programs
Federal Retirement Thrift Investment Board
Federal Supply Service
Federal Technology Service
Federal Trade Commission
Federal Transit Administration
FedWorld Information Network
Fermi National Accelerator Laboratory
Fernald Environmental Management Project
Fifth Circuit
Financial Crimes Enforcement Network
Financial Management Service

Information Analysis and Infrastructure Protection
Information Electronics and Surveillance Department
Information Management and Information Technology
Information Operations
Information Resource Center
Information Resources Management College
Information Security Oversight Office
Information Technology Laboratory
Information Technology Solutions
Information/Publications
Infrastructure
Infrastructure Protection and Computer Intrusion Squad
Inspector General
Installations and Logistics Department
Institute for Federal Printing and Electronic Publishing
Institute of Museum and Library Services
Institute for Telecommunications Sciences
Insurance Service
Inter-American Foundation
Internal Revenue Service
International Cultural Property Protection
International Field Office

International Trade Administration
J. William Fulbright Foreign Scholarship Board
James Madison Memorial Fellowship Foundation
Japan Documentation Center
Japan-United States Friendship Commission
Jet Propulsion Laboratory
Johnson Space Center
Joint Board for the Enrollment of Actuaries
Joint Chiefs of Staff
Joint Forces Command
Joint Forces Staff College
Joint Military Intelligence College
Justice Information Center
Justice Management Division
Kansas City Plant (Allied Signal, Inc.)
Kennedy Space Center
Knolls Atomic Power Laboratory
Langley Research Center
Law Library of Congress
Lawrence Livermore National Laboratory
Legal Services Corporation
Library of Congress
Library of Congress Online Public Access Catalog
Loan Guaranty Service
Local History and Genealogy

Local Offices
Logistics Directorate
Los Alamos National Laboratory
Management Assistance Team
Management Service Office
Manpower and Reserve Affairs
Manufacturing Engineering Laboratory
Manufacturing Extension Partnership
Manufacturing Technology Division
Manuscript Division
Mapping and Analysis for Public Safety
Marine Corps Combat Development Command
Marine Corps Recruiting Command
Marine Corps Systems Command
Marine Corps Uniform Board
Marine Expeditionary Units
Marine Mammal Commission
MarineLink Websites
Maritime Administration
Market Access Compliance
Marketing and Regulatory Programs
Marshall Space Flight Center
Materials Management Service
Materials Science and Engineering Laboratory

Materials Science and Technology Division
Mathematical, Computer, and Information Sciences Division
Measurement and Standards Laboratories
Mechanics and Energy Conversion Science and Technology Division
Medical Science and Technology Division
Medicare Payment Advisory Commission
Merit Systems Protection Board
Miamisburg Environmental Management Project
Microform Reading Room
Migratory Bird Conservation Commission
Mike Moroney Aeronautical Center
Mine Safety and Health Administration
Minerals and Geology Management
Minerals Management Service
Minority Business Development Agency
Missile Defense Agency
Mississippi River Commission
Moffett Federal Airfield
Morris K. Udall Scholaiship and Excellence in National Environmental Policy Foundation

Motion Picture and Television Reading Room
Motor Carrier and Highway Safety
NASA Centers
NASA Headquarters
National Aeronautics and Space Administration
National Agricultural Library
National Agricultural Statistics Service
National Air and Space Museum
National Arboretum
National Archives and Records Administration
National Bipartisan Commission on the Future of Medicare
National Cancer Institute
National Capital Planning Commission
National Cemetery Administration
National Center on Birth Defects and Developmental Disabilities
National Center for Chronic Disease Prevention and Health Promotion
National Center for Complementary and Alternative Medicine
National Center for Environmental Health
National Center for Health Promotion and Disease Prevention

National Center for Health Statistics
National Center for HIV, STD, and TB Prevention
National Center for Infectious Diseases
National Center for Injury Prevention and Control
National Center for Minority Health and Health Disparities
National Center for Research Resources
National Center for Toxicological Research
National Chaplain Center
National Climatic Data Center
National Commission on Libraries and Information Science
National Communications System
National Conservation Training Center
National Council on Disability
National Credit Union Administration
National Criminal Justice Reference Service
National Defense University
National Drug Intelligence Center
National Economic Council
National Education Research Policy and Priorities Board

National Endowment for the Arts

National Endowment for the Humanities

National Energy Technology Laboratory

National Environmental Satellite, Data, and Information Service

National Eye Institute

National Finance Center

National Gallery of Art

National Geophysical Data Center

National Guard

National Guideline Clearinghouse

National Heart, Lung, and Blood Institute

National Highway Traffic Safety Administration

National Human Genome Research Institute

National Human Resource Management Center

National Ice Center

National Imagery and Mapping Agency

National Immunization Program

National Indian Gaming Commission

National Information Resource Management Center

National Information Technology Center

National Infrastructure Protection Center

National Institute on Aging

National Institute of Alcohol Abuse and Alcoholism

National Institute of Allergy and Infectious Diseases

National Institute of Arthritis and Musculoskeletal and Skin Diseases

National Institute of Biomedical Imaging and Bioengineering

National Institute of Child Health and Human Development

National Institute of Corrections

National Institute on Deafness and Other Communication Disorders

National Institute of Dental and Craniofacial Research

National Institute of Diabetes and Digestive and Kidney Disease

National Institute on Disability and Rehabilitation Research

National Institute on Drug Abuse

National Institute on Early Childhood Development and Education

National Institute on the Education of At-Risk Students

National Institute on Educational Governance

National Institute of Environmental Health Sciences

National Institute of General Medical Sciences

National Institute of Justice

National Institute of Mental Health

National Institute of Neurological Disorders and Stroke

National Institute of Nursing Research

National Institute for Occupational Safety and Health

National Institute on Postsecondary Education

National Institute of Standards and Technology

National Institute on Student Achievement, Curriculum, and Assessment

National Institutes of Health

National Interagency Fire Center

National Invasive Species Council

National Labor Relations Board

National Law Enforcement and Corrections Technology Center

National Library of Education

National Library of Medicine

National Library Service for the Blind and Physically Handicapped

National Marine Fisheries Service

National Mediation Board

National Mine Health
and Safety Academy
National Museum of
African Art
National Museum of
American History
National Museum of the
American Indian
National Museum of
Natural History
National Nuclear
Security
Administration
National Ocean Service
National Oceanic and
Atmospheric
Administration
National Oceanographic
Data Center
National Park
Foundation
National Park Service
National Petroleum
Technology Office
National Portrait Gallery
National Postal Museum
National Quality
Program
National Railroad
Passenger
Corporation (Amtrak)
National Renewable
Energy Laboratory
National Research and
Development
Centers
National Response
Center
National Rural
Development
Partnership
National Science
Foundation
National Security
Agency/Central
Security Service
National Security
Council

National Severe Storms
Laboratory
National Technical
Information Service
National
Telecommunications
and Information
Administration
National Training
Center
National Transportation
Library
National Transportation
Safety Board
National War College
National Weather
Service
National Wetlands
Inventory
National Wild Horse
and Burro Program
National Wildlife Refuge
System
National Zoo
Natural Resources
Conservation Service
Naval Expeditionary
Warfare
Naval Petroleum/Shale
Reserves
Naval Research
Laboratory
Naval Space Science and
Technology Program
Office
Navigation Center
Navy Science and
Technology Ship
Office
Nevada Operations
Office
Nevada Test Site
New Brunswick
Laboratory
Newspaper and Current
Periodical Room
Nonproliferation and
Disarmament Fund

North American
Waterfowl and
Wetlands Office
North Atlantic Division
Northern Command
Northwest Power
Planning Council
Nuclear Regulatory
Commission
Nursing Service
Oak Ridge Institute for
Science and
Education
Oak Ridge National
Laboratories
Oak Ridge Operations
Oak Ridge Operations'
Environmental
Management Program
Oakland Operations
Office
Occupational Health
and Environmental
Services
Occupational Safety
and Health
Administration
Ocean Atmosphere and
Space Department
Office of Acquisition
and Materiel
Management
Office of Acquisition
and Property
Management
Office of Administration
Office of Administrative
Law Judges
Office of Advanced
Scientific Computing
Research
Office of Aircraft
Services
Office of Allowances
Office of American
Indian Trust
Office of Asset
Management

Office of the Assistant
Secretary for
Administration and
Management
Office of the Assistant
Secretary for Policy
Office of the Associate
Administrator for
Airports
Office of the Associate
Administrator for
Science
Office of the Associate
Attorney General
Office of the Attorney
General
Office of Authentication
Office of Bilingual
Education and
Minority Languages
Affairs
Office of Biological and
Environmental
Research
Office of Boating Safety
Office of Bridge
Technology
Office of the Budget
Office of Budget and
Management
Services
Office of Budget and
Program Analysis
Office of Business
Innovations
Office of Business
Liaison
Office of the Chief
Economist
Office of the Chief
Financial Officer
Office of the Chief
Information Officer
Office of Children's
Health
Office of the Circuit
Executive

Office of Citizen Services
and Communications
Office of Civil Rights
Office of Civilian
Radioactive Waste
Management
Office of the Clerk
Office of the
Commissioner
Office of
Communications
Office of Community
Oriented Policing
Services
Office of Community
Planning and
Development
Office of Compliance
Office of the
Comptroller
Office of the
Comptroller of the
Currency
Office of Congressional
Affairs
Office of Congressional
and
Intergovernmental
Affairs
Office of Congressional
and Legislative Affairs
Office of Congressional
and Public Affairs
Office of the
Coordinator for
Counterterrorism
Office of Crisis Planning
and Management
Office of Defense
Programs
Office of Defense Trade
Controls
Office of Departmental
Operations and
Coordination
Office of the Deputy
Attorney General

Office of the Director
Office of Disability
Employment Policy
Office of Dispute
Resolutions
Office of Domestic
Finance
Office of Economic
Adjustment
Office of Economic
Impact and
Diversity
Office of Educational
Research and
Improvement
Office of Elementary
and Secondary
Education
Office of Enforcement
Office of Environment,
Safety, and Health
Office of Environmental
Management
Office of Environmental
Policy and
Compliance
Office of Equal
Opportunity
Office of Equal
Opportunity
Programs
Office of Ethics
Office of the Executive
Secretariat
Office of Extramural
Research, Education,
and Priority
Populations
Office of Fair Housing
and Equal
Opportunity
Office of Faith-Based
and Community
Initiatives
Office of Federal
Contract Compliance
Programs

Office of Federal Housing Enterprise Oversight

Office of Federal Programs

Office of Field Policy and Management

Office of Finance: Electronic Funds Transfer Enrollment and W-9 Forms

Office of Financial Management

Office of the First Lady

Office of FirstGov

Office of Fissile Materials Disposition

Office of Fossil Energy

Office of General Counsel

Office of Genomics and Disease Prevention

Office of Global Programs

Office of Government Ethics

Office of Governmentwide Policy

Office of Health Care Information

Office of Hearings and Appeals

Office of the Historian

Office of Housing/Federal Housing Authority

Office of Human Resources

Office of Independent Oversight and Performance Assurance

Office of Indian Education Programs

Office of Information

Office of Information Management

Office of Information and Privacy

Office of Information Resources Management

Office of the Inspector General

Office of Insular Affairs

Office of Intelligence Policy and Review

Office of Intergovernmental and Interagency Affairs

Office of International Affairs

Office of International Information Programs

Office of Justice Programs

Office of Labor Relations

Office of Labor-Management Standards

Office of Law Enforcement

Office of Lead Hazard Control

Office of the Legal Advisor

Office of Legal Counsel

Office of Legal Policy

Office of Legislation and Congressional Affairs

Office of Legislative Affairs

Office of the Majority Leader

Office of Management

Office of Management and Administration

Office of Management and Budget

Office of Managing Risk and Public Safety

Office of Migrant Education

Office of Migratory Bird Management

Office of Multifamily Housing Assistance Restructuring

Office of National AIDS Policy

Office of National Drug Control Policy

Office of National Service and Educational Partnerships

Office of Naval Research

Office of the Naval Inspector General

Office of Nonproliferation and National Security

Office of Non-Public Education

Office of Nuclear Energy, Science, and Technology

Office of Occupational Safety and Health

Office of Oceanic and Atmospheric Research

Office of Overseas Schools

Office of the Pardon Attorney

Office of Pavement Technology

Office of Performance Budgeting

Office of the Permanent Representative to the United Nations

Office of Personnel

Office of Personnel Management

Office of Planning and Performance Management

Office of Policy Development and Research

Office of Policy and External Affairs

Office of Policy and International Affairs

Office of Policy, Management, and Budget

Office of Portfolio Management

Office of Postsecondary Education

Office of Procurement

Office of the Procurement Executive

Office of Professional Responsibility

Office of Program Operations and Management

Office of Program and Policy Services

Office of Protocol

Office of Public Affairs

Office of Public Health Preparedness

Office of Public and Indian Housing

Office of Reform Assistance and Dissemination

Office of Regional Operations

Office of Regulatory Affairs

Office of Research and Development

Office of Research and Technology Applications

Office of Risk Assessment and Cost-Benefit Analysis

Office of Satellite Data Processing and Distribution

Office of Science

Office of Science and Technology

Office of Science and Technology Policy

Office of Scientific and Technical Information

Office of the Secretary

Office of the Secretary of Defense

Office of the Secretary of Energy Advisory Board

Office of Security and Emergency Operations

Office of the Senior Coordinator for International Women's Issues

Office of Small Business Programs

Office of Small and Disadvantaged Business Utilization

Office of the Solicitor

Office of the Solicitor General

Office of the Speaker of the House

Office of Special Actions

Office of Special Counsel

Office of Special Education Programs

Office of Special Education and Rehabilitative Service

Office of the Special Trustee for American Indians

Office of Surface Mining Reclamation and Enforcement

Office of System Safety

Office of Technology Assessment

Office of Technology Services

Office of Thematic Programs

Office of Thrift Supervision

Office of Tribal Services

Office of Trust Responsibilities

Office of Under Secretary for Arms Control and International Security Affairs

Office of the Under Secretary of Defense (Comptroller)

Office of the Under Secretary of Defense for Acquisition and Technology

Office of the Under Secretary of Defense for Personnel and Readiness

Office of the Under Secretary for Economic, Business, and Agricultural Affairs

Office of the Under Secretary for Global Affairs

Office of the Under Secretary for Management

Office of the Under Secretary for Public Diplomacy and Public Affairs

Office of Urban Affairs

Office of the Vice President of the United States

Office for Victims of
  Crime
Office of Vocational
  and Adult Education
Office of Women's
  Business Ownership
Office of Worker and
  Community
  Transition
Office of Workers'
  Compensation
  Programs
Offshore Minerals
  Management Program
Ohio Field Office
Operational Plans
  Interoperability
  Directorate
Operations
Overseas Private
  Investment
  Corporation
Overseas Security
  Advisory Council
Pacific Air Forces
Pacific Command
Pacific Marine
  Environmental
  Laboratory
Pacific Northwest
  National Laboratory
Pacific Ocean
  Division
Panama Canal
  Commission
Pantex Plant: Nuclear
  Weapons Assembly
  and Disassembly
  Facility
Pasture Systems and
  Watershed
  Management
  Research Lab
Patent and Trademark
  Office
Peace Corps
Pension Benefit
  Guaranty Corporation

Pentagon Force
  Protection Agency
Performing Arts
  Reading Room
Photoduplication
  Service
Physical Medicine and
  Rehabilitation
  Service
Physical Sciences
  Science and
  Technology Division
Physics Laboratory
Planning and
  Environment
Plans, Policies, and
  Operations
Policy Planning Staff
Postal Rate Commission
Preservation Directorate
Preservation
  Reformatting Division
President's Council on
  Integrity and
  Efficiency
President's Council on
  Sustainable
  Development
President's Foreign
  Intelligence Advisory
  Board
Presidio Trust
Princeton Plasma
  Physics Laboratory
Printing Procurement
  Department
Prints and Photographs
  Reading Room
Processes and Prediction
  Division
Product Innovation
  Division
Production Department
Production Estimates
  and Crop Assessment
  Division
Program Support Center
Programs and Resources

Property Management
Public Building Service
Public Health Program
  Office
Quality Control and
  Technical Department
Radio and TV Marti
  (Español)
Radio Free Asia
Radio Free
  Europe/Radio
  Liberty
Railroad Retirement
  Board
Ralph J. Bunche Library
Rare Book and Special
  Collections Reading
  Rooms
Real Estate Assessment
  Center
Recorded Sound
  Reference Center
Regulatory Information
  Service Center
Rehabilitation Services
  Administration
Research, Education,
  and Economics
Research Facilities
Research and Special
  Programs
  Administration
Richland Operation
  Office
Risk Management
Rocky Flats Field Office
Rural
  Business-Cooperative
  Service
Rural Community
  Development
Rural Development
Rural Housing Service
Rural Utilities Service
Safety Division
Saint Lawrence Seaway
  Development
  Corporation

Bibliography

"Agencies Getting Heavier on Top: 47 Executive Titles Created Since 1960." *Washington Post*, July 23, 2004, p. A27. Http://www.washingtonpost.com/wpdyn/articles/A7590-2004Jul22.html, accessed December 12, 2005.

Arnold, N. Scott. *Marx's Radical Critique of Capitalist Society: A Reconstruction and Critical Evaluation*. Oxford: Oxford University Press, 1990.

Bailey, Ronald. "Do We Really Need the Feds? Funding Stem-Cell Research without Uncle Sam." *Reason Online*, August 24, 2005. Http://www.reason.com/rb/rb082405.shtml, accessed December 12, 2005.

Barnett, Randy E. *The Structure of Liberty: Justice and the Rule of Law*. New York: Oxford University Press, 2000.

Bastiat, Frédéric. *The Law*. In *Selected Essays on Political Economy*. Irvington-on-Hudson, N.Y.: Foundation for Economic Education, 1995 (1850).

Bastiat, Frédéric. "The State." In *Selected Essays on Political Economy*. Irvington-on-Hudson, N.Y.: Foundation for Economic Education, 1995 (1848).

Bastiat, Frédéric. "What Is Seen and What Is Not Seen." In *Selected Essays on Political Economy*. Irvington-on-Hudson, N.Y.: Foundation for Economic Education, 1995 (1850).

Beito, David T. *From Mutual Aid to the Welfare State: Fraternal Societies and Social Services, 1890–1967*. Chapel Hill: University of North Carolina Press, 2000.

Beito, David T., ed. *The Voluntary City: Choice, Community, and Civil Society*. Ann Arbor: University of Michigan Press, 2002.

Berlin, Isaiah. "Two Concepts of Liberty." In *Liberty: Incorporating Four Essays on Liberty*. Oxford: Oxford University Press, 2002 (1969).

Bethell, Tom. *The Noblest Triumph: Property and Prosperity through the Ages*. New York: St. Martin's Press, 1998.

Blank, Rebecca M. "Viewing the Market Economy through the Lens of Faith." In *Is the Market Moral? A Dialogue on Religion, Economics, and Justice*. Washington, D.C.: Brookings Institution, 2004.

Bloom, Allan. *The Closing of the American Mind*. New York: Touchstone, 1987.

Brock, Gillian, ed. *Basic Needs: Our Responsibilities to Meet Others' Needs*. New York: Rowman & Littlefield, 1998.

Brudney, Daniel. *Marx's Attempt to Leave Philosophy*. Cambridge, Mass.: Harvard University Press, 1998.

Christman, John. *The Myth of Property: Toward an Egalitarian Theory of Ownership*. New York: Oxford University Press, 1994.

Cohen, G. A. *Self-Ownership, Freedom, and Equality*. Cambridge: Cambridge University Press, 1995.

Cohen, G. A. *Karl Marx's Theory of History*, expanded ed. Princeton, N.J.: Princeton University Press, 2000.

"Congress Passes Budget with Cuts in Medicaid and in Taxes." *New York Times*, April 29, 2005.

Copp, David. "Equality, Justice, and the Basic Needs." In *Basic Needs: Our Responsibilities to Meet Others' Needs*. Gillian Brock, ed. New York: Rowman & Littlefield, 1998.

Coulson, Andrew J. *Market Education: The Unknown History.* New Brunswick, N.J.: Transaction, 1999.

Cox, W. Michael, and Richard G. Alm. *Myths of the Rich and Poor: Why We're Better Off Than We Think.* New York: Basic Books, 1999.

Crews, Clyde Wayne, Jr. *Ten Thousand Commandments: An Annual Snapshot of the Federal Regulatory State, 2002 Edition.* Washington, D.C.: Cato Institute, 2002.

"DNR Issues Notices of Violations for Lake Michigan Sewage Dumping." *Janesville* (Wisconsin) *Gazette,* June 4, 2004. Http://www.gazetteextra.com/ sewagedumping060304.asp, accessed March 13, 2005.

Dudley, Susan, and Melinda Warren. "Regulatory Spending Soars: An Analysis of the U.S. Budget for Fiscal Years 2003 and 2004." Fairfax, Va.: Mercatus Center, and St. Louis, Mo.: Weidenbaum Center, 2004. Http://wc.wustl.edu/ Reg_Budget_final.pdf, accessed December 12, 2005.

Elster, Jon. *Making Sense of Marx.* Cambridge: Cambridge University Press, 1985.

Engels, Friedrich. *Anti-Dühring.* In *Karl Marx and Friedrich Engels: Collected Works,* vol. 25. Moscow: Progress Publishers, 1987 (1877).

Epstein, Richard. *Simple Rules for a Complex World.* Cambridge, Mass.: Harvard University Press, 1997.

Feser, Edward. "Taxation, Forced Labor, and Theft." *The Independent Review,* 5, no. 2 (Fall 2000): 219–35.

Finegan, Brian J. *The Federal Subsidy Beast: The Rise of a Supreme Power in a Once Great Democracy.* New York: Alary, 2000.

Fleischacker, Samuel. *A Third Concept of Liberty: Judgment and Freedom in Kant and Adam Smith.* Princeton, N.J.: Princeton University Press, 1999.

Flew, Antony. "The Artificial Inflation of Natural Rights." *The Freeman: Ideas on Liberty,* December 1989. Http://www.fee.org/publications/the-freeman/article. asp?aid=3297, accessed December 12, 2005.

Flew, Antony. *Social Life and Moral Judgment.* New Brunswick, N.J.: Transaction, 2003.

Foldvary, Fred. *Public Goods and Private Communities: The Market Provision of Social Services.* New York: Edward Elgar, 1994.

Friedman, David. *The Machinery of Freedom: A Guide to Radical Capitalism,* 2nd ed. LaSalle, Ill.: Open Court, 1989.

Goldfarb, Michael. *Freedom in the World 2004: Global Freedom Gains Amid Terror, Uncertainty.* Washington, D.C.: Freedom House, 2004. Http://www. freedomhouse.org/research/survey2004.htm, accessed December 12, 2005.

Goodin, Robert E. "Vulnerabilities and Responsibilities: An Ethical Defense of the Welfare State." In *Basic Needs: Our Responsibilities to Meet Others' Needs.* Gillian Brock, ed. New York: Rowman & Littlefield, 1998.

Graham, Gordon. *The Case against the Democratic State.* Exeter: Imprint Academic, 2002.

Gwartney, James, and Robert Lawson. *Economic Freedom of the World 2004.* Vancouver, B.C.: Fraser Institute, 2004. Http://www.freetheworld.com/2004/ efw2004complete.pdf, accessed December 12, 2005.

Haworth, Alan. *Anti-libertarianism: Markets, Philosophy, and Myth.* New York: Routledge, 1994.

Higgs, Robert. "Lies, Damn Lies, and the Growth of Government." *The Independent Review* 9, no. 1 (Summer 2004): 147–53. Http://www.independent.org/tii/media/pdf/tir_09_1_9_higgs.pdf, accessed December 12, 2005.

Hocutt, Max. *Grounded Ethics: The Empirical Bases of Normative Judgments.* New Brunswick, N.J.: Transaction, 2000.

Hocutt, Max. "Sunstein on Rights." *The Independent Review* 10, no. 1 (Summer 2005): 117–31.

Hume, David. "Of the Origin of Government." In *Essays Moral, Political, and Literary.* Eugene F. Miller, ed. Indianapolis, Ind.: Liberty Fund, 1987.

Jacoby, Jeff. "Eminent Injustice in New London." *Boston Globe,* June 26, 2005. Http://www.boston.com/news/globe/edition_opinion/oped/articles/2005/06/26/eminent_injustic_in_new_london, accessed December 12, 2005.

Jasay, Anthony de. *Justice and Its Surroundings.* Indianapolis, Ind.: Liberty Fund, 2002.

Klein, Daniel. "The People's Romance: Why People Love Government (as Much as They Do)." *The Independent Review* 10, no. 1 (Summer 2005): 5–37. Http://www.independent.org/pdf/tir/tir_10_1_1_klein.pdf, accessed December 15, 2005.

Kymlicka, Will. *Contemporary Political Philosophy: An Introduction,* 2nd ed. Oxford: Oxford University Press, 2001.

Lenin, Vladimir Ilyich. *The State and Revolution.* In *Marx, Engels, Marxism,* 6th English ed. Moscow: Foreign Languages Publishing House, 1964 (1918).

Lester, J. C. *Escape from Leviathan: Liberty, Welfare, and Anarchy Reconciled.* New York: St. Martin's, 2000.

Locke, John. *Second Treatise of Government.* Peter Laslett, ed. Cambridge: Cambridge University Press, 1988 (1690).

Machan, Tibor. *Individuals and Their Rights.* LaSalle, Ill.: Open Court, 1989.

Marx, Karl. "Estranged Labour" and "Private Property and Communism," from his *Economic and Philosophic Manuscripts of 1844.* In *The Marx-Engels Reader,* 2nd ed. Robert C. Tucker, ed. New York: Norton, 1978 (1844).

Marx, Karl. *Grundrisse.* In *The Marx-Engels Reader,* 2nd ed. Robert C. Tucker, ed. New York: Norton, 1978 (1857–8).

Marx, Karl, and Friedrich Engels. *Manifesto of the Communist Party.* In *The Marx-Engels Reader,* 2nd ed. Robert C. Tucker, ed. New York: Norton, 1978 (1848).

Michael, Mark A. "Redistributive Taxation, Self-Ownership, and the Fruit of Labour." *Journal of Applied Philosophy* 15, no. 2 (1998): 350–71.

Mulroy, David. *The War against Grammar.* Portsmouth, N.H.: Boynton/Cook, 2003.

Narveson, Jan. *The Libertarian Idea.* Philadelphia, Pa.: Temple University Press, 1992.

Nock, Albert Jay. "Anarchist's Progress." In *The State of the Union.* Charles H. Hamilton, ed. Indianapolis, Ind.: Liberty Press, 1991 (1927).

Nock, Albert Jay. "On Doing the Right Thing." In *The State of the Union.* Charles H. Hamilton, ed. Indianapolis, Ind.: Liberty Press, 1991 (1924).

Nock, Albert Jay. *Our Enemy, the State,* exp. ed. Tampa Bay, Fla.: Hallberg, 2001 (1935).

Nozick, Robert. *Anarchy, State, and Utopia.* New York: Basic Books, 1974.

O'Neill, Onora. "Rights, Obligations, and Needs." In *Basic Needs: Our Responsibilities to Meet Others' Needs*. Gillian Brock, ed. New York: Rowman & Littlefield, 1998.

O'Toole, Randal. *Reforming the Fire Service: An Analysis of Federal Budgets and Incentives*. Brandon, Ore.: Thoreau Institute, 2002. Http://www.ti.org/Fireng.doc, accessed December 12, 2005.

Otteson, James R. Review of Samuel Fleischacker's *Third Concept of Liberty: Judgment and Freedom in Kant and Adam Smith*. *Review of Metaphysics* 52, no. 2 (December 2000): 426–28.

Otteson, James R. "Private Judgment, Individual Liberty, and the Role of the State." *Journal of Social Philosophy* 33, no. 3 (Fall 2002): 491–511.

Rasmussen, Douglas B., and Douglas J. Den Uyl. *Liberty and Nature: An Aristotelian Defense of Liberal Order*. La Salle, Ill.: Open Court, 1991.

Rasmussen, Douglas B., and Douglas J. Den Uyl. *Norms of Liberty: A Perfectionist Basis for Non-perfectionist Politics*. University Park: Penn State University Press, 2005.

Raz, Joseph. *The Morality of Freedom*. Oxford: Clarendon, 1986.

Robinson, John P., and Geoffrey Godbey. *Time for Life: The Surprising Ways Americans Use Their Time*. University Park: Penn State University Press, 1997.

Rothbard, Murray N. *The Ethics of Liberty*. New York: New York University Press, 1982.

Rummel, R. J. *Death by Government*. New Brunswick, N.J.: Transaction, 1994.

Rummel, R. J. *Saving Lives, Enriching People*. 2001. Http://www.hawaii.edu/powerkills/WFA.BOOKSAVING.PDF, accessed December 12, 2005.

Schor, Juliet B. *The Overworked American: The Unexpected Decline of Leisure*. New York: Basic Books, 1991.

"Sewage Dumped in May: 4.6 Billion Gallons: Amounts Top Any Yearly Total since Tunnel Opened." *Milwaukee Journal Sentinel*, May 29, 2004. Http://www.jsonline.com/news/metro/may04/232813.asp, accessed December 12, 2005.

Smith, Adam. *An Inquiry into the Nature and Causes of the Wealth of Nations*. Indianapolis, Ind.: Liberty Classics, 1981 (1776).

Smith, Adam. *The Theory of Moral Sentiments*. Indianapolis, Ind.: Liberty Classics, 1982 (1759).

Sowell, Thomas. *The Vision of the Anointed: Self-Congratulation as a Basis for Public Policy*. New York: Basic Books, 1996.

Spencer, Herbert. *The Man versus the State: With Six Essays on Government, Society, and Freedom*. Indianapolis, Ind.: Liberty Classics, 1981.

Sterba, James P. "From Liberty to Universal Welfare." In *Basic Needs: Our Responsibilities to Meet Others' Needs*. Gillian Brock, ed. New York: Rowman & Littlefield, 1998.

Sunstein, Cass. *The Second Bill of Rights: FDR's Unfinished Revolution and Why We Need It More Than Ever*. New York: Basic Books, 2004.

Sunstein, Cass. "Confusing Rights: A Reply to Hocutt." *The Independent Review* 10, no. 1 (Summer 2005): 133–38.

Tocqueville, Alexis de. *Democracy in America*. Harvey C. Mansfield and Delba Winthrop, eds. and trans. Chicago: University of Chicago Press, 2000 (1835, 1840).

United Nations General Assembly. Universal Declaration of Human Rights. 1948. Http://www.un.org/rights/50/decla.htm, accessed December 12, 2005.

Westley, Christopher. "Milwaukee's Mess." June 14, 2004. Http://www.mises.org/story/1538, accessed December 12, 2005.

Wolff, Jonathan. *Robert Nozick: Property, Justice, and the Minimal State.* Stanford: Stanford University Press, 1991.

Wolff, Robert Paul. *In Defense of Anarchism.* Berkeley: University of California Press, 1998 (1970).

"Woman Says Dairy Fired Her over Weight." *New York Times*, February 18, 1999.

Wright, Robert. *The Moral Animal: Why We Are the Way We Are.* New York: Pantheon, 1994.

3

A Matter of Principle, Part Two

Personhood Writ Large

Where on earth does the argument so far leave us? If, as I argued in the previous chapter, socialistic states are morally unacceptable, and if likewise the welfare state, even when it officially recognizes the importance of judgment, still violates people's personhood, what is left? Can we have *no* state? Does the conception of personhood I have defended entail *anarchism*—and, if so, does that not constitute a reductio ad absurdum refutation of it?

There are indeed many who would argue for anarchism, or something approximating it, on the basis of the premises I have defended. Economists Bruce Benson, Walter Block, and Hans-Hermann Hoppe, political theorists Anthony de Jasay, Fred Foldvary, and David Friedman, law professors Randy Barnett and Robert Ellickson, and philosophers J. C. Lester, Tibor Machan, Jan Narveson, and Robert Paul Wolff[1] are among those who have recently defended positions that approximate the anarchist or "anarcho-capitalist" view that the only legitimate form of social organization is one that includes no coercive state. And numerous historical figures from many disparate disciplines have argued for similar positions. There are in fact more defenders of this view than one might think, especially given how little they are publicly discussed today; the list of recent advocates above is but a fraction of the authors it would not take you long to discover if you looked into it. I mention these thinkers not because that settles the matter but rather to suggest that a view held

---

[1] See the bibliography for information about these thinkers' works.

by a large number of intelligent and thoughtful people and defended by argument and evidence—not mere intuition—is not a likely candidate for a reductio refutation. Just because it is new to you does not mean it is absurd or without plausible foundation.

But I defend instead the form of government that draws on the tradition running back through the Magna Carta, signed in 1215 by King John of England, setting limits, even if principally in name, on his power over nobles and freemen; through the Declaration of Arbroath, signed in 1320 by the nobles of Scotland, declaring its independence from English rule and Robert the Bruce its rightful king, by which America's 1776 Declaration of Independence was partly inspired; through the English Petition of Right in 1628, which reaffirmed the principal state limitations imposed by the Magna Carta, in particular the supremacy of duly enacted laws to all men, including even the king; through the English Levellers of the 1640s, who risked their lives to demand freedom of conscience and individual liberty for all English freemen;[2] through the 1689 English Bill of Rights, reaffirming the principles that no one is above the law and that everyone is entitled to free speech and his own religion; through John Locke in his 1690 *Two Treatises of Government,* in which he argued for the "natural right" to equal freedom of all people, including slaves, as well as the "natural right" to private property; through the eighteenth-century Scotsmen David Hume and Adam Smith, who realized that the most important thing for a government to do if it wants its citizens to flourish was protect private property and little else;[3] and through Thomas Jefferson, John Adams, James Madison, Patrick Henry, Thomas Paine, and other American founders who drew on this "classical liberal" tradition in realizing that a legitimate government would need to be rigorously limited in scope and power to be consistent with respecting people's lives, liberty, and property—not to mention their sacred honor.

I suggest that the government that is consistent with respecting people's personhood, *all* people's personhood, is one that refuses to privilege one person or group above another, is skeptical about one person or group's ability to know the good for anyone else, and disallows one person or group from coercing others into adopting beliefs, behaviors, or ends against their will. This government works to secure people in their *lives,* so that they can be free from murder and assault; in their *liberty,* so that

---

[2] See Otteson's *The Levellers,* esp. the Introduction to vol. 1.

[3] For excellent historical discussions of the British aspects of this tradition, see Dumont's *Essays on Individualism,* Macfarlane's *The Origins of English Individualism,* and Pipes's *Property and Freedom,* chap. 3.

they can work, exchange, believe, and associate as they judge fit in cooperation with others who also judge fit; and in their *property*, so that they
can be free from theft and fraud and can work to make life for themselves
and for those they care about better with a reduced risk that the fruits
of their endeavors will be taken from them. This government therefore
has as its sole aim to secure what was described in chapter 1 as 'justice.'
Anything above or beyond that is up to individuals themselves, alone or
in voluntary associations with others. To the question, then, of what is
left if socialism and welfare-statism are rejected because they violate personhood, the answer I offer is the simple, yet I believe inspiring, vision
of free and independent individuals who take no and brook no violation
of personhood, who thus meet each other as equals in personhood, and
who seek to provide for themselves and for those they care about a good
and happy life.

This classical liberal tradition is a long and venerable one, drawing as it
does on centuries of experience and the combined judgment of countless
thinkers. For an excellent overview, see Jim Powell's *Triumph of Liberty*,
which contains short biographies of more than sixty leading figures of the
last two thousand years of this tradition. The political vision these brave
souls advocated—and many of them paid dearly, sometimes with their
lives, for their beliefs—entails an individual freedom and responsibility
that can be bracing, but every human society that has striven for it has
also found it invigorating and enlivening.

On the other hand, the classical liberal society might not seem as
exciting as a Sparta under Leonidas, a Macedonia under Alexander, a
France under Napoleon, or a Germany under Bismarck: a "nation of
shopkeepers," as it has been called,[4] where people, as Voltaire put it,
mainly tend their own gardens,[5] might not fire the heart the way fighting
and winning wars and territory, vanquishing heathens, or bringing God's
wrath to the pagans might. It might, in other words, not allow sufficient
scope for the human drive to be grandly heroic, as some people have
objected. This is a fair point, inasmuch as humans—some of them, at
least—really do seem to revel in conquering, vanquishing, appropriating,
and so on. According to the argument defended in the first two chapters,
however, unless acting in self-defense, all of that would constitute flagrant

---

4 Adam Smith first used this phrase to describe the liberal commercial society he recommended in the *Wealth of Nations* (p. 613). Since then, some, such as apparently Napoleon,
  have used it as a mocking epithet to denigrate societies that celebrate common people
  instead of venerating "great men" (like Napoleon, of course).
5 In the final line of his 1759 *Candide*. See also Nock's essay "On Doing the Right Thing."

violations of others' personhood. But aside from that, does the classical liberal state not in fact offer opportunities to satisfy this drive? What about entrepreneurship? Be the first person on earth to be worth one hundred billion dollars; figure out how to make faster-than-light travel a reality, which some physicists now think might be possible after all;[6] discover a new source of energy and bring it to market; and so on. There are literally numberless possibilities for entrepreneurial innovation in the classical liberal society, and there will be for the indefinite future. As economist Julian Simon has argued, the *ultimate* natural resource is not land or coal or water or even the sun—remember that humans have had all these things since the beginning, even when they did not use them or know how to use them. Indeed, there are places today that are full of natural resources but are still poor (such as Russia for the past several decades), and others that have virtually no resources but are quite wealthy (such as Hong Kong). So none of these natural resources is the "ultimate" resource. Instead, Simon argued, the ultimate resource is *human ingenuity.* It is the resourcefulness of "people—skilled, spirited, and hopeful people who will exert their wills and imaginations for their own benefit, and inevitably they will benefit not only themselves but the rest of us as well."[7] And as long as there are people around, *that* resource will not ever run out; nor will it run out of need for it or opportunities to exercise itself. Such entrepreneurial possibilities might, then, it would seem, offer continuing opportunities for heroism, valor, and noble action.[8]

If that kind of innovative and competitive activity is not your cup of tea, however, how about boxing or football? Or chess?

BRASS TACKS

Two important implications follow from the fact that the first duty of the state is, as I argued in chapter 2, to secure justice. The first is that

[6] See, for example, http://news.bbc.co.uk/1/hi/sci/tech/781199.stm (accessed on December 13, 2005).

[7] *The Ultimate Resource 2*, p. 589.

[8] An interesting side note is that *Cato's Letters* no. 65, written by Thomas Gordon in 1721, argues that true martial valor can only be produced in a society under a government limited in the ways I have described. The letter begins, "Sir, I have shewn in my last [letter], that trade and naval power are produced by liberty only; and shall shew in this [letter], that military virtue can proceed from nothing else ... " (in *Cato's Letters*, vol. 1, p. 450). A fascinating recent account of the incredible ingenuity human beings can muster to address problems they face is Erik Larson's *The Devil in the White City*, which recounts the efforts of Daniel H. Burnham and others in attempting to stage the 1893 World's Fair in Chicago.

if the state pursues anything beyond that, regardless of how good its intentions or the ends to be served are, it contradicts and thus undercuts its own reason for being. The core of the 'justice' that the state must secure is to protect each individual's personhood. As shown in chapters 1 and 2, that means that each person must have his person, his liberty, and his legitimately acquired private property protected. To protect this personhood, the state will have to have principally three things: (1) an agency to make public rules about what counts as property, what counts as transfer, what constitutes ownership, what the punishments are for violation, and so on; (2) a system to adjudicate impartially the inevitable disputes that arise among citizens, most of which will concern property and contracts; and (3) defensive agencies to protect people's life, liberty, and property and to enforce duly enacted punishments for the violation of them. That prescription should sound pretty familiar: it is the essence of what America's founders created to begin the United States of America, and it constitutes the core of the classical liberal tradition on which they drew to do so. Now the system of government entailed by respecting personhood is not identical with that described in the U.S. Constitution: other forms might satisfy it as well, and indeed the form described in the Constitution might deviate from it in some details. The important thing is that on this account the state's sole reason and justification for existing is to protect people's personhood by establishing, maintaining, and administering the three duties that together constitute justice.

Suppose, however, by way of illustrating the limits this conception places on state activities, that politicians decide that because some people do not have the wherewithal to allow them to retire comfortably, a state-run pension system must be set up to support people in their retirement years. Put to one side for the moment the objection that such a system would almost certainly end up, as virtually all such programs have, as a Ponzi scheme that merely robs Peter to pay Paul, hence will inevitably run out of Peters, and hence will inevitably collapse.[9] Note instead that

---

9 Here is the U.S. Securities and Exchange Commission's explanation of "Ponzi scheme": "Ponzi schemes are a type of illegal pyramid scheme named for Charles Ponzi, who duped thousands of New England residents into investing in a postage stamp speculation scheme back in the 1920s. Ponzi thought he could take advantage of differences between U.S. and foreign currencies used to buy and sell international mail coupons. Ponzi told investors that he could provide a 40% return in just 90 days compared with 5% for bank savings accounts. Ponzi was deluged with funds from investors, taking in $1 million during one three-hour period—and this was 1921! Though a few early investors were paid off to make the scheme look legitimate, an investigation found that Ponzi had only purchased about $30 worth of the international mail coupons. Decades later,

precisely in robbing Peter it has violated his personhood: Peter was not asked whether he wanted to contribute to Paul's retirement fund or how much he wanted to contribute. If the government implements such a policy, then, it systematically violates the personhood of those it forces willy-nilly to pay for it. It also violates the personhood of those on behalf of whom, also willy-nilly, it requires payment, for the recipients now are no longer respected in their capacities to make decisions, take actions, and face consequences for themselves. By thus undertaking such an endeavor the state would act in violation of its own purpose and indeed would act at cross-purposes to itself. It would in this way face the fatal problems raised in chapter 2's discussion of the welfare state.

This problem arises *generally*, that is, regardless of what the state might decide to do other than secure justice. The problem is illustrated in William Graham Sumner's brilliant 1883 essay, "The Forgotten Man."[10] Sumner points out that "when we come to the proposed measures of relief for the evils which have caught public attention," a curious phenomenon often ensues, namely:

> As soon as A observes something which seems to him to be wrong, from which X is suffering, A talks it over with B, and A and B then propose to get a law passed to remedy the evil and help X. Their law always proposes to determine what C shall do for X or, in the better case, what A, B and C shall do for X. As for A and B, who get a law to make themselves to do for X what they are willing to do for him, we have nothing to say except that they might better have done it without any law, but what I want to do is look up C. I want to show you what manner of man he is. I call him the Forgotten Man. Perhaps the appellation is not strictly correct. He is the man who never is thought of. He is the victim of the reformer, social speculator and philanthropist, and I hope to show you before I get through that he deserves your notice both for his character and for the many burdens which are laid upon him. (p. 202)

Sumner goes on to argue that C, the "forgotten man," is the poor stiff who does everything right: he works hard, saves his money, lives within

the Ponzi scheme continues to work on the 'rob-Peter-to-pay-Paul' principle, as money from new investors is used to pay off earlier investors until the whole scheme collapses" (http://www.sec.gov/answers/ponzi.htm). Be sure also to read the SEC's description of "pyramid schemes," http://www.sec.gov/answers/pyramid.htm (both sites accessed December 13, 2005). Although the SEC and the Federal Trade Commission vigorously pursue the "fraudsters" who conduct such "fraudulent multi-level marketing programs" in the business marketplace, they turn a blind eye to such programs that the government itself runs—such as Social Security, which, by the SEC's definition, counts as a virtual paradigm case of both a "pyramid scheme" and a "Ponzi scheme."

[10] Contained in the collection *On Liberty, Society, and Politics*, pp. 201–22.

his means, meets his family obligations, and does not ask others to support him. Yet despite his virtue—indeed, *because* of it—he is systematically punished by the activists who revile him for (1) having more than some others, as he inevitably will, and (2) for being concerned primarily with himself and his own. He is accordingly made to pay for others who have not worked to cultivate the virtues he has. Sumner believes this to be profoundly unjust to this "forgotten man." One might add to Sumner's charge of injustice that the activists' policy is counterproductive because it introduces incentives for even the once-industrious forgotten man to stop working so hard: after all, if others get rewarded for not working, and he gets punished for working, then only a fool, he might understandably think to himself, would continue to work. And if enough of these forgotten men stop working, then neither will there be the wherewithal to relieve the "evil" "from which X is suffering" nor will the forgotten men themselves enjoy the fruits of their former labor that they once did. So *everyone* would be worse off.

But we can see that Sumner's charge of profound injustice is exactly right. A and B are quite entitled by the scope properly accorded their personhood under the General Liberty principle to undertake to help X, but when they ask the state to coerce C (and D, E, F, and so on) into doing so as well, as opposed to their trying merely to persuade C (and D, E, F, and so on) to do so voluntarily, they ignore and dismiss C's (and D's, E's, F's, and so on) personhood and therefore act unjustly. And in complying with A and B's wishes, the state abandons its prime duty and indeed works against it.

The second important implication of the fact that the state's only duty is to secure justice is that taxation for purposes other than this single one are also acts of injustice. The anarchists and anarcho-capitalists mentioned above will argue, with more justification than one might initially think, that *all* taxation is illegitimate, in precisely the way that all slavery is illegitimate. And they usually argue that taxation is at bottom a form of slavery along the lines I sketched in chapter 2. I would like to argue, however, that the minimal classical liberal state I have described is nevertheless defensible on two grounds: not only does historical investigation suggest that this state is in fact the most conducive to human flourishing, and in particular to the flourishing of individual human judgment, but also, and perhaps more important, this is the only condition that *all* persons require to pursue their ends, *whatever* their ends are. Whatever their individual respective goods are, and whatever means they will find to secure them, they will be able to do so only once justice has been secured, or has been secured to the extent possible given that it must be implemented by fallible human beings. I therefore follow Hume, Smith, and the classical liberal tradition generally in concluding that this is the duty, but the only one, of the state. That would mean that the state is justified in taxing its citizens for the maintenance of the agencies required for securing justice, which I suggest are those three described earlier, and that taxation for anything else constitutes an unjustifiable violation of personhood.

A Contradiction?

An important objection must be addressed here. Previously, I argued that taxation on persons was tantamount to forced labor, and hence unjustified; here, however, I suggest that the state may, after all, tax to support the institutions required to secure 'justice,' and it may collect those taxes coercively if necessary. Aren't these two positions inconsistent? How can I have it both ways?

I take this to be an important problem. Before suggesting my proposed solution, I would first point out that this objection underscores the crucial moral importance of what I have called this book's bedrock moral principle, namely, the imperative to respect personhood: if a government (or any other agency or group) does *not* respect personhood, then it has to go—period. If you agree with me on that, as I hope you do, then the lion's share of my challenge in convincing you to support a minimal, limited government is already won. But let me now address the objection squarely. I believe the classical liberal state can indeed be justified on the following grounds: its purpose is to secure the conditions required for the exercise of personhood, and it may do nothing else, since, as I have argued, anything else would threaten or undermine those same conditions. As I suggest above, the minimal protections of life, liberty, and property can be supported and endorsed by all persons, regardless of whatever their ends and purposes are, because these protections are necessary to pursue *any* ends or purposes. Anything else a state would do, however, will *conflict* with the ends or purposes of at least *some* persons. Hence the classical liberal state is justified, but nothing beyond it is.

To summarize my argument, then: if I am right that (Premise 1) morality requires us to recognize each other's 'personhood,' if I am right that (P2) this means observing 'justice' in all our interactions with others, and, finally, if I am right that (P3) "observing justice" comprises respecting and protecting each other's life, liberty, and property, then (Conclusion 1) the minimal classical liberal state is justified, (C2) nothing beyond this state is justified, and (C3) it may tax its citizens to support it in this protection but for nothing else. I apologize for that somewhat schematic formulation, but I want to be clear about where I end up and how I got there.

Two further objections—one from each direction, as it were—will be raised and should also be addressed. The first one is from the anarcho-capitalists: if respecting personhood is your bedrock moral principle, what about the person who does not want any government at all? That is, what do you do about the person who in fact wants to have a go at securing justice himself or by employing private protection agencies, and does not want to pay the state for doing so? I think the answer to this objection is, and must be: let him go. Respect for personhood entails that we must respect people's decision to take even this extreme step. If he does not want to pay taxes to the state to provide justice for him, he may opt out; but of course he thereby also gives up the right to ask the state to save him if things go south. Now this policy of allowing people to opt out could potentially lead to the proliferation of free-riders—people opting out of paying for state protections but enjoying them nonetheless—but I think we will simply have to allow that possibility and do our best not to let them free-ride. Coercing them to subscribe to a state against their wishes is more to be avoided because it *certainly* violates personhood; striving to make sure potential free-riders are not able to free-ride has at least the chance of not violating anyone's personhood, and we should err on the side of caution where personhood is concerned.

SOCIAL POWER VERSUS POLITICAL POWER

The other main objection that will have occurred to you comes from the welfare-statists and the socialists. It is that the classical liberal state might be, as Samuel Fleischacker puts it, "breathtakingly callous towards the poor."[11] *Do* the poor suffer especially under such a state? Are they left to languish while others—the rich, perhaps, or the "propertied classes," to use a Marxian term—are allowed to prosper? Are the poor left without opportunities to improve or succeed because those already in the know or already with some wherewithal have first access to the opportunities and are able to exploit them before the poor have a chance? In short, by

---

[11] *A Third Concept of Liberty*, p. 3.

embracing the classical liberal state are we abandoning the least among us and thus turning our backs on a significant part of our moral obligations?

In chapter 5 I shall present evidence showing that, contrary to what one might expect, *everyone*, including in particular the poor, prospers under states approximating the classical liberal one, and indeed that they prosper more under such states than under any other known kind. What kind of government is most conducive to people's flourishing is an empirical question, after all, and it turns out that considerable empirical evidence exists showing the close correlation between the classical liberal state and increasing material prosperity, again especially among the poorest of society. Since I have not yet presented that evidence, however, I do not rely on it here. And in any case, since no state is perfect, even under the best conditions there will still be people who face hardship and difficulty and need the assistance of others. However much we might be able to minimize human suffering, we shall never eradicate it altogether, and hence there will always be occasion to exercise our virtues of generosity and benevolence.

To restate the question, then, what can we do about the poor and downtrodden in the classical liberal state? To answer this question let me introduce a distinction exploited by Sir Henry Sumner Maine, Albert Jay Nock, Franz Oppenheimer, Herbert Spencer, William Graham Sumner, and others[12] between *social means* and the correlated concept of *social power*, on the one hand, and *political means* and the correlated concept of *political power*, on the other. The idea is this. Roughly speaking, there are just two ways to accomplish things in cooperation with others, using either social means or political means. Social means are those that employ the voluntary agreements of free and independent people and depend on the resources developed and created by individuals working honestly for them and earning them legitimately. Now by using the words "honestly" and "legitimately," I do not mean to beg any questions: all I mean is that the resources were created, earned, or exchanged for without impinging on or disrespecting anyone's personhood at any stage. They are the result of voluntary associations of people seeking to serve their local ends. Included in the voluntary associations employing social power are all the clubs, relief agencies, churches, charities, and other eleemosynary organizations that people form to help others and to which they make voluntary contributions out of their own resources.

---

[12] See the bibliography for information about these thinkers' works. For a contemporary account using this distinction, see Thomas Sowell's *Applied Economics,* chap. 1.

There has indeed been in the United States an astonishing array of such organizations, despite the federal government's growing attempt, at least since the 1930s or so, to assume their roles. David Beito's *From Mutual Aid to the Welfare State: Fraternal Societies and Social Services, 1890–1967* provides an excellent discussion of those that existed especially among black communities in the South, and his edited *The Voluntary City* canvasses the surprising number and effective scope of such associations even today. But the peculiar inclination of Americans to form such voluntary associations has a longer pedigree. It was noted, for example, by Tocqueville in *Democracy in America:*

Americans of all ages, all conditions, all minds constantly unite. Not only do they have commercial and industrial associations in which all take part, but they also have a thousand other kinds: religious, moral, grave, futile, very general and very particular, immense and very small; Americans use associations to give fêtes, to found seminaries, to build inns, to raise churches, to distribute books, to send missionaries to the antipodes; in this manner they create hospitals, prisons, schools. Finally, if it is a question of bringing to light a truth or developing a sentiment with the support of a great example, they associate. Everywhere that, at the head of a new undertaking, you see the government in France and a great lord in England, count on it that you will perceive an association in the United States. (vol. 2, pt. 2, chap. 5, p. 489)

By contrast to these instances of employing social means to effect desired ends, *political means* are those that employ a coercive apparatus to take money, goods, or services from one group of people, whether they concur or not, and deliver them to another group of people—or even deliver them right back to the people from whom they were taken (after the coercing agency has taken its cut). Instances of using political means include all the government agencies providing welfare, relief, loan subsidies, food, shelter, and so on. In America, the federal government is so expensive and its services so extensive (see the Appendix to chapter 2) that it can finance its activities only by taking the bulk of its revenues from the largest portion of its citizens, the middle class.[13] That means that the majority of Americans are today subject to the devices of political means.

Social means draw on "social power" in the sense that it requires people to take individual, personal initiative to help others. If a tornado flattened

---

[13] Although it is often claimed that such programs are financed by the rich for the benefit of the poor, in fact there are not enough "rich" to support all the programs; hence the middle class, and even the poor, are made to finance them themselves. A classic presentation of this perhaps surprising reality is Bertrand de Jouvenel's *The Ethics of Redistribution*, Lecture II.

your neighbor's house, you yourself must go and help clean up, buy potable water, put him up in your own house, and so on. This power is called *social* because it relies on the power that individuals voluntarily working together—that is, socially—can generate. By contrast, political means draw on "political power" in the sense that it uses force or the threat of force to get people to comply. If the Federal Emergency Management Agency arrives to help your neighbor with his tornado-flattened house, it does not ask your permission to draw on your money to help and it does not ask you your opinion about how to use that money; likewise, if it helps out flood victims a thousand miles away, it similarly does not hesitate to take your money and use it as it sees fit. This power is called *political* because typically it is only through politics that one group of people can unilaterally command and use the resources of another group of people without being jailed or shot for it.[14]

Given the nature of personhood as I have described it, however, and given what respecting it entails, I suggest that employing political means and political power for things such as poor relief or disaster relief is an unjust violation of it. How badly the victims need the help or how good people's ends are in using the resources thus extracted does not change the fact that to take it involuntarily from others is to violate the latter's personhood and to treat them, as well as the fruits of their judgment and actions, as mere tools to your or someone else's ends. That treats them again as if they were *things*—which they are not. If the man who robbed you at the ATM used the money to pay for his child's life-saving operation, it was still theft, it still violated your personhood, and it was thus still wrong. If a person in such a desperate situation had merely *asked* you for money, you might well have given it to him; that would have been to respect both his and your personhood. But taking it from you against your will, even for a good end, is a violation of personhood. The same conclusion holds, I suggest, with the use of political means to make use of people's lives, liberty, or property.

Now, opposing the use of political means for this kind of relief does not mean, however, opposing *all* kinds of relief for those who need it. On the contrary—and this cannot be emphasized enough—it means only that such cases as require the help of others are all matters of social means and

---

[14] There are groups other than the state that use political means as well—the Mafia and other crime syndicates, muggers, rapists, and so on—but their activities are usually illegal. On the other hand, the operations of FEMA can sometimes resemble illegal extortion and payoffs; see, for a recent example, the *Washington Post*'s "Report Calls Payments by FEMA Questionable."

social power. So the objection is *only* to the use of political means, *not* to provision of help generally. My argument is that when help is required, social means, and social means only, should be employed. People who need help, families that need shelter, infants who need formula, children who need operations, students who need scholarships, adults who need a second chance, laid-off workers who need new job training—in these cases and any others like them, if help is required, then take action! Do not wait for someone else to do it. Do not shift your personal moral responsibilities onto distant agencies or unknown third parties and believe that you have thereby fulfilled *your* duty. If in any particular situation moral responsibility attaches to the doing of something, then that responsibility can be assumed only by individuals—which means by you and me. So let us roll up our sleeves and get to work.

That is the real import of the social power/political power distinction. There is a fairly widespread view that advocates of a limited government such as what I have defended are, in Fleischacker's words, "breathtakingly callous" toward those who need help. A former professor of mine once mentioned that he could not respect people advocating a limited government because they are "indifferent to the suffering" of others.[15] I may not ever be able to gain that professor's respect, but I want to make sure that my position is plain: I am not indifferent to people's suffering, I am not callous toward the poor, and, more to the point here, I do not think the classical liberal state disrespects or disregards them. On the contrary. As I mentioned earlier, in chapter 5 I show that a classical liberal state is actually *better* for the poor than welfare states (or socialistic states). Here, however, my argument is that in order to fulfill one's moral obligations to helping others, one must employ social means, not political means. That *does not* mean turning your back on them. Indeed, it means facing them full square—and *yourself* doing something about it. Go help clean up, go buy formula and diapers and deliver them, write a check out of your own account to help toward the tuition, start a learn-to-read program in your garage, and so on. Here is yet another wide-open space for exercising your entrepreneurial and imaginative genius: find out where help is needed, and do what you can. My argument is that not only will you in this way be respecting the personhood of everyone concerned—your own, that of the recipients, and that of unknown others from whom you will not be

---

[15] For a recent repetition of this charge, see Rebecca M. Blank's "Viewing the Market Economy Through the Lens of Faith." For another, rather mean-spirited example, see Brian Barry's review of Robert Nozick's *Anarchy, State, and Utopia.*

taking resources to serve your ends—but you will also be fulfilling your own moral responsibilities in the only way possible, by actually fulfilling them yourself.

Putting this responsibility on the shoulders of individuals, on your shoulders and mine, has moreover the additional beneficial consequence of making sure we are aware of the costs of taking actions. For some these costs may incline them to adopt a callous indifference to others' suffering, but evidence supports the hunch that most people will take the opposite tack of deciding to go ahead and help others: charitable donations tend to go up, for example, when taxes are lowered. Requiring you and me to make individual personal sacrifices does, however, encourage us to start making the proper demands on those who solicit our help and to make judgments about who should be supported, to what extent, and exactly how. Some of those who ask for help, after all, simply do not deserve it. The world is full of conmen, charlatans, and just plain lazy bums who are more than happy to tug on our sentimental heart strings for all they are worth, and milk us for all we are worth, to support their corrupt or shiftless lifestyles. The real tragedy about such people is that they can siphon funds that could and should have gone to someone who truly needed it. Government welfare agencies are spectacularly bad at distinguishing those who need and deserve help from those who do not, but that should not surprise us: it is not *their* money, after all.[16] But precisely because it is your money and my money, you and I will have the strong incentive indeed to separate the deserving from the undeserving, to discover and help only the former while sniffing out and sending the latter packing.

The classical liberal, then, is not by any means indifferent to the poor. He claims only that the moral responsibility to help those who deserve it attaches to individuals, not to the state, and thus that it falls within the scope of social power, not political power. Respect for personhood entails this schema of individual responsibility, even if it would be far easier simply to tell those who deserve your help, "I already gave to the state; take it up with them." The alternative method of relying on political

---

[16] There is an enormous literature demonstrating the systematic, not just occasional, waste of resources endemic to government programs. For a classic account, see Buchanan and Tullock's *The Calculus of Consent;* for more recent discussions, see Bandow's *The Politics of Plunder,* Sowell's *Basic Economics,* Tanner's *The Poverty of Welfare,* and Tullock, Seldon, and Brady's *Government Failure.* See also reporter John Stossel's ABC News Special, *Freeloaders,* http://www.intheclassroom.com/cgi-bin/storefront.cgi?page=prod&prod=1005 (accessed December 13, 2005).

power has the effects not only of pitting people against one another in their struggle to get their piece of the governmental pie and encouraging potential helpers to see others merely as undeserving hangers-on, but also of robbing people of the opportunity to take actions fulfilling their own individual moral duty.

Political power is justified only in the enforcement of justice. Everything else—all the requirements of charity, benevolence, altruism, generosity, liberality, munificence, and magnanimity—are left to the discretion, and duty, of individuals, to you and to me. If you want to save the world, then, do not lobby Congress: give of your own time and money, start your own charity (or your own business, for that matter), convince others to join you in your efforts. Only in that way can you respect the personhood of your would-be beneficiaries, of your would-be co-donors, and, it should not go unnoticed, of yourself—for a person who violates the personhood of others cannot but demean himself in the doing.

ONE FINAL PUTSCH: NO SUCH THING!

Let us look at one more objection to the classical liberal state I have defended, this one from law professors Stephen Holmes and Cass R. Sunstein. In their recent book *The Cost of Rights,* Holmes and Sunstein claim not that the classical liberal state does not in fact respect personhood or that it does not in fact have the generally beneficial effects I have suggested, but rather that there is really no difference between "negative" liberty and "positive" liberty after all. What is their argument for this counterintuitive claim? They begin with the unobjectionable premise that rights cost money; that is, enforcing people's "negative" liberty has costs, because one has to pay for the police or military to defend them, for the courts and impartial judges to adjudicate disputes about them, and so on. Therefore, conclude Holmes and Sunstein, there is no such thing as purely "negative liberty," all liberty is created and maintained by the state, all "rights" are merely provisionally held at the pleasure of the state, and individuals can have no legitimate grounds on which to protest that the state is violating their "rights."

Whoa there just a minute! How do those conclusions follow? The answer is: they don't. The argument of Holmes and Sunstein's book is constituted by one reasonable claim—enforcing rights costs money—and then a seemingly endless series of non sequiturs. Yes, enforcing rights, or the freedoms you are entitled to under the General Liberty principle entailed by your personhood, is, or can be, costly. But it does not follow from that that you have only such rights as you can pay for (is there no such thing as an unenforced right?), that the state alone creates rights (what about, for example, the Declaration of Independence, which claims that government is instituted among men to enforce pre-existing, or "natural," rights?), that only the state is justified in protecting rights (may one not employ self-defense, then, before the police arrive?), that only the state is able to protect rights (again, what about self-defense, or the American Revolutionary War, for that matter?), or that since the state currently undertakes to defend rights it is justified in taxing for whatever it deems fit (so there can be no such thing as justified civil disobedience— ever?). Some of Holmes and Sunstein's conclusions might turn out to be plausible, but, despite what they assert, none of them simply follows from the fact that protecting rights costs money.[17]

One central thesis of Holmes and Sunstein's warrants individual treat- ment. They assert that all rights are "positive," and that there is no real distinction between alleged "negative" rights and "positive" rights. Their evidence for this is that there are marginal cases where it is difficult to say what kind of right they are; for example: "the right of legislative ini- tiative, the right not to be denied a job because of sexual preference, the right to return to a job after taking unpaid maternity leave, the right to interstate travel, freedom of testation, and the right to inform authori- ties of a violation of the law."[18] Moreover, they claim, in America today it is one and the same government that protects both kinds of rights. To the first point: although Holmes and Sunstein's "ramshackle inventory" (their words, not mine: see p. 39) is indeed bewilderingly drawn up—one might suspect that they are intentionally trying to muddy the waters—I think that the "positive"/"negative" distinction nevertheless makes con- siderable headway in sorting it out. The notion of having sovereignty over your own life, liberty, and property and having the "negative" freedom to do with those things whatever you like consistent with everyone else's hav- ing the same freedom provides a simple and plausible criterion by which to categorize most of the "rights" Holmes and Sunstein list. Even putting that aside, however, the bare existence of difficult marginal cases does not imply that there are not nonetheless clear examples of each respective kind. As I argued in chapter 1, it is sometimes difficult to say whether a given particular specimen counts as a "boy" or as a "man," but that does

[17] See also Hocutt's "Sunstein on Rights."
[18] *The Cost of Rights*, p. 38. Holmes and Sunstein give numerous other examples as well; see all of the first chapter, "All Rights Are Positive."

not mean there are no such things as boys, that there are not clear, unambiguous examples of boys, or that all boys are really men; there will be cases in which people of good faith will have trouble deciding whether a given particular specimen counts as a "sapling" or a "tree," but again that does not mean that there is no such thing as a sapling, that there are not clear, unambiguous examples of saplings, or that all saplings are really trees, and so on. Similarly, it is perfectly reasonable to distinguish a state protecting people from aggression from one providing people benefits, even if there are some cases of "protection" that are hard to distinguish from "benefit" and vice-versa.

To the second point: a single entity can of course attempt to protect either "negative" or "positive" rights, or neither, but that is irrelevant to the question of whether or not there are "negative" rights. The fact that the state in America currently undertakes to enforce all sorts of "positive" rights has no bearing on *whether* it should do so or whether it is justified in doing so. Moreover, Holmes and Sunstein do not consider the argument raised earlier that all actions within the scope of "negative" liberty are compossible, whereas those within the scope of "positive" liberty are not: that seems a clear distinction between them, and a good at least initial reason to believe both that "negative" liberty is not simply a figment of several hundred years' worth of people's imagination and that it is not incoherent to criticize a state for overstepping its legitimate bounds by not respecting only "negative" liberty. The notions of "negative" and "positive" liberty are, to borrow the terminology of French philosopher René Descartes (1596–1650), both *clear* and *distinct:* their respective content seems clear, and the differences between them render them distinct from one another. Merely asserting that one exists and the other does not therefore cuts no ice.

I might add that *The Cost of Rights* repeatedly disparages classical liberalism, dismissing it as a "fiction" and charging that it is unrealistic, but Holmes and Sunstein never take up the arguments or evidence offered on behalf of the position, and they ignore the entire historical tradition that classical liberalism draws on and embodies. They call its supporters names, they suggest that no "serious" thinker entertains the idea anymore (an amazing claim, especially given that Richard Epstein, one of the foremost defenders of this tradition today—and certainly a serious thinker if there ever was one—is a member of the same law school faculty as Sunstein), and they proceed to make their own case using the argument-by-avalanche method wherein they seem to believe that if they just assert that their view is true enough times then eventually you will assent out of sheer exhaustion. The argument of Holmes and Sunstein's book is thus quite unpersuasive, even if it has been influential (Sunstein is considered one of the leading legal academics in America today, often appearing on television, for example). I hope that what you have read so far in this book will give you reason to consider the classical tradition more seriously than Holmes and Sunstein are willing to do, even if you end up rejecting it as well.

MAKING FRIENDS AND INFLUENCING PEOPLE

My argument, then, is that only the limited, "classical liberal" state is consistent with respecting people's personhood—*all* people's personhood, not just that of the "intellectuals" or the "experts"—and that this conception of the state enjoys the support of a long intellectual and historical tradition. In response to worries about what kind of condition that leaves 'the least of us' in, I have argued that social power should be pursued on their behalf, not political power, because only social power is consistent with their personhood. Finally, I suggested that this kind of state may hold the key to general prosperity; in the next chapter I offer an explanation for why social power, or private enterprise, is in fact a more promising means to satisfy our desires than state provision of them will be.

What, however, does this conception allow us by way of changing people's behavior? If people are greedy, selfish, or otherwise vicious, if they engage in self-debasing activities, or if they do not take proper regard for the consequences of their actions, what avenues do respect for personhood and the classical liberal state allow us to pursue? I briefly addressed this matter in chapter 1, but it is worth mentioning here John Stuart Mill's felicitous list of several of the available options. In *On Liberty*, Mill says that if you find that a person is being any of these things,

These are good reasons for remonstrating with him, or reasoning with him, or persuading him, or entreating him, but not for compelling him, or visiting him with any evil in case he do otherwise. To justify that, the conduct from which it is desired to deter him, must be calculated to produce evil to some one else. The only part of the conduct of any one, for which he is amenable to society, is that which concerns others. In the part which merely concerns himself, his independence is, of right, absolute. Over himself, over his own body and mind, the individual is sovereign. (p. 13)

If the person in question violates justice, in other words, then we are justified in "visiting him with evil," but only then. If we wish to change his conduct in matters dealing with virtue and vice, only the use of rhetorical weapons is consistent with respecting him as a person.

One great virtue of the classical liberal state that warrants underlining is a consequence of the principle of General Liberty, and provides another way to address society's moral failings. The principle of General Liberty allows people to pursue many different paths; it also allows people to make associations with others who are of like mind. Thus not only are poor-relief societies, philanthropic associations, salvation societies, and moral uplift unions of all manner and stripes allowed, but so are cooperatives, communes, theocracies, and even socialist communities—such as Robert Dale Owen's 1824–7 New Harmony, Indiana.[19] Want to establish a community in conformity with your religious or political or moral views? Go right ahead. Fancy abolishing private property and enforcing strict equality? Feel free. Are you a bohemian wanting to found an art colony? By all means. A homosexual or free love or nudist community? Amish? Puritan? Anti-technology Luddite? Yes, yes, yes, and more power to you. As long as no one is forced to join or support any of these ventures, they are all perfectly consistent with the classical liberal state. Indeed, it is a fair bet that they would flourish in such a state like nowhere else as people successively investigate various ways of living; historically it has always been the freest societies that were the most vibrant (not to mention wealthiest, which helps considerably). And since people who dislike or disagree with you are not forced to go along with you, they have no right to stop you—just as you have no right to stop them in their pursuits. They might try to change your mind, as you might theirs, but at the end of the day we can all go home and disagree in peace. The wide scope of possibility and human diversity the classical liberal state allows is indeed one of its greatest virtues. (And it should not go unnoticed that one would *not* be allowed to form a New Freedom classical liberal community within a socialist state.) You can therefore also address society's failings by creating your own subsociety: found a community according to your lights, and use your social power to encourage others to join it. That is an easier, and perhaps also more effective, way of realizing your goals than trying to remake *all* of society according to your plan. And you might find that it answers your need to conquer, vanquish, and act heroically, only in this case with innovative, imaginative, and rhetorical—not martial—arts.

[19] For discussion of Owen's New Harmony project, see Bethell's *The Noblest Triumph*, chap. 9.

POLITICAL EXCEPTIONS TO JUSTICE?

What I hope to have given here are fundamental principles that can enable us to negotiate and make judgments about most of the problems and issues usually thought to fall under the scope of "ethics" or "morality." In chapters 6 to 9, I address several of these other areas and I lay out how I think these principles apply. Before closing the discussion of "principled" reasons to support the classical liberal state, however, I would like to make another important point. In the Preface I remarked that there is often a significant disconnection between private morality and public, or publicly endorsed, morality. Here we can perhaps bring out an important instance of this disconnection.

You may have been taken aback at my suggestion that, on the one hand, people should be allowed to engage in activity we all know is wrong or foolish, and, on the other hand, that people should be left to face the consequences of their decisions, even if they are bad or degrading or cause suffering. But even if that offends your sensibilities, I would bet the farm that that is precisely what *you* do and believe, though perhaps implicitly, in your own life. If the person next to you on the bus is riveted with an assemblage of metallic accoutrements that make you think—privately, to yourself—something like "What's *wrong* with that guy?" you do not decide he should be apprehended and forcibly taken in for moral re-education, do you? Well, why not? Or if your co-worker is wasting all her income on bad movies and gambling rather than on John Ford movies and great books, you do not forcibly take over management of her finances. Again, why not? Because it is none of my business, you say. Precisely. Other people should enjoy the same freedom of judgment that you do, even if they use that freedom unwisely. If you know that your neighbor sits at home by himself every night getting drunk, you may feel sorry for him, you may even try talking him into getting some help; but you do not break down his door and bodily haul him into a treatment clinic. If your friend drives a big SUV that you are certain she does not need for herself and her one child, while you can afford only a small, cramped sedan for yourself and your three children, do you go to her and demand that she stop wasting her money on herself and instead give it to you? If you know someone who is working for a company that you think does not pay him enough for what he does, do you get your friends together, march over to the company's management, and inform them that if they do not pay him more you will begin a campaign of theft and assault on the company's property? Or inform your friend that you will not let him work there anymore and will if necessary physically prevent him from doing so? If a relative of yours decides to have risky plastic surgery, now for the twelfth time, and you think it is absurdly vain and wasteful of her to do so, do you inform her that if she tries to go through with it you will have to lock her up in your basement for a period of time, and that you will do the same to any plastic surgeon who agrees to perform the operation? Of course you do not do these things; you would not even consider them. Again, why?

My argument has been predicated not on the belief that people make decisions *well,* but rather that they are able to make them *at all.* And you may have noticed that the areas where you already believe people should be left free and unmolested to make their own decisions—although not necessarily free of your informing them of your disapproval!—are precisely the areas covered by our 'justice' as defined above. You let them decide what to do with their lives, with their liberty, and with their property. On the other hand, if they begin impinging on other people's lives, liberty, or property, then you will think you are indeed justified in taking action. The same point is made by looking at it from this other side: you do not personally assault or imprison, steal from, or make false promises with those you care about. Or if you do it is only when you have convinced yourself that this is a sufficiently extraordinary case that you are justified in making an exception. But it is precisely the fact that you believe it is an *exception requiring special justification* that proves my point. If you violate the three cardinal rules of justice, you will probably feel guilty about it and try to hide, deny, or rationalize it. The only time you would do it consistently and regularly would be when you do it in concert with others, and even then you will probably invent a myth or story to justify what you are doing.

This suggests in what sense we might here be dealing with a disconnection from publicly endorsed morality. The vast majority of us routinely observe the rules of justice as I have described them in our everyday dealings with people, but the farther out the affected people are from us, the less scrupulous we can tend to be in observing them. And the large and anomalous arena of human life we tend to regard as a complete exception is: politics. Consider: you probably endorse, tacitly if not explicitly, violations of all three rules of justice in political action. Do you endorse policies or politicians who take money away from one group of people, whether they agree or not, and give it to another group of people? Do you endorse policies or politicians who restrict the range of acceptable behavior persons can engage in even when they neither do nor pose a threat of positive harm to others? Do you endorse policies or politicians who prohibit persons from making voluntary contractual arrangements with others even when they neither do nor pose a threat of positive harm to others?[20]

If you think about it for a moment, my guess is that you will probably realize that you do in fact support such policies or politicians, at least in some cases. Most likely you will support some restrictive policies and oppose others, and you may have a story to tell about why in political matters you selectively enforce only the rules that you far more consistently observe, and demand others observe, in your own private life. You may, for example, think of yourself as subscribing to a kind of Robin Hood morality, whereby it is all right to steal from "the rich" to give to "the poor." Or perhaps you will, like FBI sniper Lon Horiuchi, claim that assassinating unarmed, innocent people may be necessary "for the good of the country" and justified if one is "just following orders."

PEOPLE ARE PEOPLE

During an armed standoff between federal agents and the Weaver family in Ruby Ridge, Idaho, in 1992, Federal Bureau of Investigation Special Agent Lon Horiuchi, who was hiding in the woods outside the Weavers' cabin under the orders (of questionable legality) to shoot any armed man he saw, spotted through a window Vicki Weaver, the wife of the owner of the property. She was not under suspicion for any crime, was unarmed, and, when Horiuchi saw her through the scope on his rifle, was standing in the doorway of the cabin holding her ten-month-old baby. Horiuchi shot her through the head, killing her instantly, whereupon she collapsed in a heap on top of the baby. The baby survived, but after more than a decade now of unsuccessful attempts to prosecute Horiuchi for murder or even manslaughter, he is not only still a free man, but the federal government has provided him tens of thousands of dollars' worth of

---

[20] An instance of this that has just come across my desk: A man in New Hampshire recently engaged in a deliberate act of civil disobedience, and was duly jailed. His crime was to give another adult a mutually voluntary manicure—but without the "license" that the New Hampshire Board of Cosmetology (yes, there is such an agency) legally requires before anyone may give another a manicure. See P. Gardner Goldsmith's "Nailing Free Enterprise," http://www.fee.org/vnews.php?nid=7110 (accessed March 15, 2005). The number of cases wherein the state prevents otherwise willing adults to engage in peaceful exchanges is surprisingly large. For overviews, see James Bovard's *Lost Rights* and Peter McWilliams's *Ain't Nobody's Business If You Do.*

taxpayer-funded government attorneys, has paid all his other legal bills, and has maintained its official defense of his actions that whether what he did was wrong or not is irrelevant, since all that matters is whether he was acting under the authority granted him by the relevant federal agencies. But we should not need recourse to the Nuremberg trials and the My Lai courts-martial to tell us that "I was just following orders" is not a justifiable excuse to kill unarmed, unaccused, and unthreatening noncombatants. Though some doughty souls are still trying to bring Horiuchi to justice, the federal government has pledged its continuing support of him and its continuing intention to shield him from any prosecution. At the time of this writing, Special Agent Horiuchi continues to be on the payroll and an employee in good standing of the FBI.[21]

I raise this troubling case for two reasons. The first is that it supports my claim that we would not endorse violation of the three central rules of justice unless we had a rationale at hand that we believed justified taking exception to the rules. I say this on the assumption and expectation that you will share my view that if Horiuchi had not been in the employ of a federal agency—that is, if he had not been part of the state—there is no question his actions would have been punished as crimes. Otherwise, the gravity of deliberately assassinating an unarmed, innocent civilian requires condemnation and punishment, regardless of what else was going on in the situation. I predict that if you have any inclination at all to defend Horiuchi's actions or any sympathy for what he did, it will be motivated by your belief that government agents either do or perhaps should enjoy an exception to the standard rules of justice by which you hold yourself and everyone else accountable. Would any *civilian* be able to walk away unprosecuted and unpunished from having done what Horiuchi did?

The second reason I bring it up is because it is indicative of what I believe is the danger of making such exceptions. There is a handful of rationales that have been used throughout history to justify horrific and otherwise unimaginable injustices, "for the good of the country" and "I was just following orders" principal among them. These have served as cover for acts far surpassing in scope and scale Special Agent Horiuchi's actions. Take a moment to survey in your mind several of human history's most notorious and brutal raids, wars, or other large-scale criminal actions, and ask yourself how many of them were justified at the time, both

---

[21] For a range of perspectives on the Horiuchi case, see Aronson, "Back to Ruby Ridge," Blackman and Kopel, "The Ruby Ridge Prosecutions," and Bovard, *Lost Rights*.

by those who perpetrated them and by the groups they represented, by just such rationales. Confine, even, your consideration to only those more spectacular atrocities that took place during the twentieth century.[22] You may well be surprised at what you discover. When you hear, then, politicians or government agents making recourse to these familiar choruses, it seems prudent to be on alert and mark well what they are meant to justify.

I would like to submit for your consideration the proposition that we should not make any moral exceptions for state action, and that we should hold politicians and other government agents to the same standards of conduct, to the same standard of 'justice,' to which we hold ourselves, everyone we know, and indeed everyone else who is not an agent of the state. Being part of the government gives one no special exemption from the rules of morality, and it gives one no special wisdom to know how to adjudicate the difficult cases from afar. And in any case the mandate to respect people's personhood is still in place. Individuals may make bad or foolish or even absurd decisions, but until they begin to impinge on your rightful arena of freedom, or on that of others, you have no more justification in forcibly restricting them than they do you. Government agents are people just like everyone else: they are just as prone to selfishness, passions, stupidity, short-sightedness, superstitions, and bigotry as everyone else is; if history is any indication, we should probably add to this list a susceptibility to megalomania, and, given their positions of power (not to mention all the bombs and the really big guns), a capability of mass destruction to boot. These are all reasons we should, if anything, be *more* exacting in our oversight of the actions of state agents and in our insistence that they follow the rules of justice to the letter.

Poor Persons

Poor people are 'persons' too, however, and so the nagging question recurs: what are wealthier people's obligations to them? If respect for personhood forbids state-sanctioned violations of the rules of justice, even when the ends that the violations would serve are good, then we would seem to have a large and important concern as yet unaddressed. How do poor people fare under a state strictly limited to respecting personhood? What are our duties toward poor people? What are poor people's

---

[22] For a rehearsal of the grisly facts of the twentieth century, see R. J. Rummel's *Death by Government*.

prospects under the classical liberal state? Let us finally take up this cluster of questions in the next chapter.

Bibliography

Aronson, Barton. "Back to Ruby Ridge: Why Idaho Shouldn't Be Prosecuting FBI Agent Lon Horiuchi." *FindLaw's Legal Commentary*, December 29, 2000. Http://writ.news.findlaw.com/aronson/20001229.html, accessed December 13, 2005.

Bandow, Doug. *The Politics of Plunder: Misgovernment in Washington*. New Brunswick, N.J.: Transaction, 1990.

Barnett, Randy E. *The Structure of Liberty: Justice and the Rule of Law*. New York: Oxford University Press, 2000.

Barry, Brian. Review of *Anarchy, State, and Utopia*. *Political Theory* 3, no. 3 (August 1975): 331–6.

Beito, David T. *From Mutual Aid to the Welfare State: Fraternal Societies and Social Services, 1890–1967*. Chapel Hill: University of North Carolina Press, 2000.

Beito, David T., ed. *The Voluntary City: Choice, Community, and Civil Society*. Ann Arbor: University of Michigan Press, 2002.

Benson, Bruce. *The Enterprise of Law: Justice without the State*. San Francisco, Calif.: Pacific Research Institute, 1990.

Benson, Bruce. *To Serve and Protect: Privatization and Community in Criminal Justice*. New York: New York University Press, 1998.

Bethell, Tom. *The Noblest Triumph: Property and Prosperity through the Ages*. New York: St. Martin's Press, 1998.

Blackman, Paul, and David Kopel. "The Ruby Ridge Prosecutions." Independence Institute, 2000. Http://i2i.org/SuptDocs/Waco/rrprosec.htm, accessed March 15, 2005.

Blank, Rebecca M. "Viewing the Market Economy through the Lens of Faith." In *Is the Market Moral? A Dialogue on Religion, Economics, and Justice*. Washington, D.C.: Brookings Institution, 2004.

Block, Walter. *Defending the Undefendable*, 2nd ed. San Francisco, Calif.: Fox and Wilkes, 1991.

Bovard, James. *Lost Rights: The Destruction of American Liberty*. New York: Palgrave Macmillan, 1995.

Bovard, James. "Ruby Ridge: The Coverup Continues." Fairfax, Va.: Future of Freedom Foundation, 2001. Http://www.fff.org/freedom1101g.asp, accessed December 16, 2005.

Buchanan, James T., and Gordon Tullock. *The Calculus of Consent*. Ann Arbor: University of Michigan Press, 1962.

Dumont, Louis. *Essays on Individualism: Modern Ideology in Anthropological Perspective*. Chicago: University of Chicago Press, 1986.

Ellickson, Robert. *Order without Law: How Neighbors Settle Disputes*. Cambridge, Mass.: Harvard University Press, 1994.

Fleischacker, Samuel. *A Third Concept of Liberty: Judgment and Freedom in Kant and Adam Smith*. Princeton, N.J.: Princeton University Press, 1999.

Foldvary, Fred. *Public Goods and Private Communities: The Market Provision of Social Services*. New York: Edward Elgar, 1994.

Friedman, David. *The Machinery of Freedom: A Guide to Radical Capitalism,* 2nd ed. LaSalle, Ill.: Open Court, 1989.

Hocutt, Max. "Sunstein on Rights." *The Independent Review* 10, no. 1 (Summer 2005): 117–32.

Holmes, Stephen, and Cass R. Sunstein. *The Cost of Rights: Why Liberty Depends on Taxes*. New York: Norton, 1999.

Hoppe, Hans-Herman. *Democracy: The God That Failed: The Economics and Politics of Monarchy, Democracy, and Natural Order.* New Brunswick, N.J.: Transaction, 2001.

Jasay, Anthony de. *Justice and Its Surroundings*. Indianapolis, Ind: Liberty Fund, 2002.

Jouvenel, Bertrand de. *Ethics of Redistribution*. Indianapolis, Ind.: Liberty Fund, 1990 (1952).

Larson, Erik. *The Devil in the White City: Murder, Magic, and Madness at the Fair That Changed America*. New York: Vintage, 2004.

Lester, J. C. *Escape from Leviathan: Liberty, Welfare, and Anarchy Reconciled*. New York: St. Martin's, 2000.

Macfarlane, Alan. *The Origins of English Individualism*. Oxford: Basil Blackwell, 1978.

Machan, Tibor. *Individuals and Their Rights*. LaSalle, Ill: Open Court, 1989.

Maine, Sir Henry Sumner. *Ancient Law*. New Brunswick, N.J.: Transaction, 2001 (1861).

McWilliams, Peter. *Ain't Nobody's Business If You Do: The Absurdity of Consensual Crimes in Our Free Society*. Los Angeles, Calif.: Prelude, 1996.

Mill, John Stuart. *On Liberty*. In *J. S. Mill: On Liberty and Other Writings*. Stefan Collini, ed. Cambridge: Cambridge University Press, 1992 (1859).

Narveson, Jan. *The Libertarian Idea*. Philadelphia, Pa.: Temple University Press, 1992.

Nock, Albert Jay. "On Doing the Right Thing." In *The State of the Union*. Charles H. Hamilton, ed. Indianapolis, Ind.: Liberty Press, 1991 (1924).

Nock, Albert Jay. *Our Enemy, the State,* expanded ed. Tampa Bay, Fla.: Hallberg, 2001 (1935).

Nozick, Robert. *Anarchy, State, and Utopia*. New York: Basic Books, 1974.

Oppenheimer, Franz. *The State*. New York: Black Rose, 1975.

Otteson, James R., ed. *The Levellers: Overton, Walwyn and Lilburne,* 5 vols. Bristol: Thoemmes, 2003.

Pipes, Richard. *Property and Freedom*. New York: Vintage, 2000.

Powell, Jim. *Triumph of Liberty: A 2,000 Year History Told through the Lives of Freedom's Greatest Champions*. New York: Free Press, 2001.

"Report Calls Payments by FEMA Questionable: Investigators Cite $31 Million Disbursed in Florida." *Washington Post*, May 19, 2005, p. A25.

Rummel, R. J. *Death by Government*. New Brunswick, N.J.: Transaction, 1994.

Simon, Julian L. *The Ultimate Resource 2*. Princeton, N.J.: Princeton University Press, 1998.

Smith, Adam. *An Inquiry into the Nature and Causes of the Wealth of Nations*. Indianapolis, Ind.: Liberty Classics, 1981 (1776).

Sowell, Thomas. *Applied Economics: Thinking beyond Stage One.* New York: Basic Books, 2004.

Sowell, Thomas. *Basic Economics: A Citizen's Guide to the Economy.* New York: Basic Books, 2003.

Spencer, Herbert. *The Man versus the State: With Six Essays on Government, Society, and Freedom.* Indianapolis, Ind.: Liberty Fund, 1981 (1884).

Stossel, John. *Freeloaders.* ABC News Special. Http://www.intheclassroom.com/cgi-bin/storefront.cgi?page=prod&prod=1005, accessed December 13, 2005.

Sumner, William Graham. "The Forgotten Man." In *On Liberty, Society, and Politics: The Essential Essays of William Graham Sumner.* Robert C. Bannister, ed. Indianapolis, Ind.: Liberty Fund, 1992 (1883).

Sumner, William Graham. "Socialism." In *On Liberty, Society, and Politics: The Essential Essays of William Graham Sumner.* Robert C. Bannister, ed. Indianapolis, Ind.: Liberty Fund, 1992 (ca. 1880).

Tanner, Michael. *The Poverty of Welfare: Helping Others in Civil Society.* Washington, D.C.: Cato, 2003.

Tocqueville, Alexis de. *Democracy in America.* Harvey C. Mansfield and Delba Winthrop, eds. and trans. Chicago: University of Chicago Press, 2000.

Trenchard, John, and Thomas Gordon. *Cato's Letters: Or Essays on Liberty, Civil and Religious, and Other Important Subjects,* 2 vols. Ronald Hamowy, ed. Indianapolis, Ind.: Liberty Fund, 1995 (1720–3).

Tullock, Gordon, Arthur Seldon, and Gordon L. Brady. *Government Failure: A Primer in Public Choice.* Washington, D.C.: Cato, 2002.

Voltaire. *Candide.* New York: Penguin, 1990 (1759).

Wolff, Robert Paul. *In Defense of Anarchism.* Berkeley: University of California Press, 1998 (1970).

4

The Demands of Poverty

I argued in chapters 2 and 3 that only the limited, "classical liberal" state is consistent with respecting people's personhood. In that way I claimed to have made a "principled" case: because respecting personhood is the bedrock moral principle, disrespecting it is wrong regardless of other considerations. At the end of chapter 3, however, I suggested that the argument left one central question as yet unaddressed: What about the poor? I argued that respect for personhood meant allowing only social, not political, power to be employed to help others. But perhaps restricting the state so that it secures and enforces 'justice' will benefit only those who already have (substantial?) private property. Again, where does it leave the poor? What exactly is our obligation to give to those who have less than we? If the poor suffer unduly under the classical liberal state, perhaps "general welfare" ought to supersede or trump the "principled" case made earlier.

I propose to tackle this cluster of questions in two ways. First I examine philosopher Peter Singer's influential argument about our moral duty of famine relief. Singer argues that wealthy people in the West are morally obligated to give a large portion of their money to poor people elsewhere in the world, and the reach of the obligation Singer presses is surprisingly extensive. The influence of the Singerian argument warrants scrutinizing it closely, which we will accordingly do to see what we can make of it. The second way to address these questions, which follows naturally from the first, is to investigate the empirical matter of which institutions, political structures, and programs do actually and in fact benefit the poor most—that is, which allow the poor to themselves become wealthy. In the next chapter I survey the considerable research done in the last several decades into precisely this question by economists, political scientists, and historians, and see what it can tell us. In this chapter, let us look at Singer.[1]

THE SINGERIAN ARGUMENT

Peter Singer's famine relief argument has come to be enormously influential since its first publication in 1972.[2] His argument is widely anthologized, frequently assigned in undergraduate ethics classes, and has been the subject of a number of (largely sympathetic) philosophical treatments.[3] The argument's influence is easy to understand: it is a simple and powerful statement of an ethical position that many find intuitively attractive, if hard to adopt. Indeed, some opposition to the Singerian position focuses not on any flaws it might have but only on the impracticality of the position it encourages. But the position has its flaws. After summarizing Singer's argument, I lay out three problems with it: (1) the principle on which the argument is based requires knowledge that people cannot reasonably be supposed to have; (2) the position relies on an untenable notion of "value"; and (3) the position conflates two notions of morality that ought to be kept separate, namely, justice and virtue. Although I principally address Singer's formulation of this position, I note that the problems I raise are generalizable and apply to similar positions adopted by a number of others.

Singer's argument is motivated by this single, fundamental principle: "if it is in our power to prevent something very bad from happening, without thereby sacrificing anything morally significant, we ought, morally,

---

[1] What follows is based in part on my "Limits on Our Obligation to Give"; see also my "Private Judgment, Individual Liberty, and the Role of the State."

[2] Peter Singer, "Famine, Affluence, and Morality" (hereafter referred to as FAM). Singer has somewhat enlarged his argument in his *Practical Ethics,* pp. 218–46.

[3] FAM is included, to take one example, in Feinberg and Shafer-Landau's popular textbook *Reason and Responsibility: Readings in Some Basic Problems of Philosophy.* Peter Unger's *Living High and Letting Die* is a book-length elaboration and defense of Singer's position. Unger's book was the subject of an also largely sympathetic symposium in *Philosophy and Phenomenological Research* in 1999; see in particular Fred Feldman's "Comments on *Living High and Letting Die.*" James Rachels's *The Elements of Moral Philosophy,* chap. 6, defends a Singerian position, as does Garrett Cullity's "International Aid and the Scope of Kindness" and *The Moral Demands of Affluence* (though Cullity is also critical of parts of the Singerian argument); see also Susan James's "The Duty to Relieve Suffering" and John M. Whelan Jr.'s "Famine and Charity." For discussions of several of these issues from a variety of viewpoints, see Aiken and LaFollette's edited collection, *World Hunger and Moral Obligation.*

to do it" (FAM, p. 24). Accepting this principle means Singer's battle is already partly won. There is in fact great suffering going on in the world—"suffering and death from lack of food, shelter, and medical care" (ibid.)—and anyone reading Singer is most likely in a position to help if he chose. So the argument applies to you and me: if either of us can alleviate the suffering and dying of others with only a relatively insignificant sacrifice, then, according to Singer's principle, we ought morally to do so. Singer drives the point home with what I called in chapter 1 the Pond Case: "if I am walking past a shallow pond and see a child drowning in it, I ought to wade in and pull the child out. This will mean getting my clothes muddy, but this is insignificant, while the death of the child would presumably be a very bad thing" (ibid.). The Pond Case[4] purports to show that all of us already accept Singer's principle, since, as Singer maintains, this principle is what motivates our intuitive agreement that a passerby ought to save the child. All that remains, then, is to point out the many other cases that fall under the scope of the principle.

Before raising my objections, I should note that Singer himself addresses a few obvious ones. The first is that the Pond Case and the case of starving poor people in East Bengal (Singer's example, which I will call Overseas Aid Cases) are in fact dissimilar because in the latter the people in question are very far away from us. Singer concedes that his principle takes "no account of proximity or distance," but he argues that this is irrelevant because a person's physical distance from us is itself irrelevant to whether we ought to help him if we can (FAM, p. 25).[5] I argue in chapter 9 that psychological propinquity, which is not unrelated to physical distance, is indeed a relevant factor for determining obligations. But let's table that for now and instead consider the second objection Singer entertains, that the cases are dissimilar because in the Pond Case the passerby is, by hypothesis, the only person who can help the child, whereas any number of people might be in a position to help a starving Bengali. Singer concedes this fact as well, but he argues that it too is irrelevant: if we changed the Pond Case so that there were, say, twenty passersby, Singer argues that *each* of them would still be morally obligated to save the child, regardless of what the others did. And the same holds true for people starving in Bengal.[6]

---

[4] Unger has a number of cases intended to make points similar to that of the Pond Case; see *Living High and Letting Die*, chap. 2.

[5] Cullity argues more thoroughly for the irrelevancy of distance than does Singer; see "International Aid and the Scope of Kindness," pp. 108–9.

[6] FAM, pp. 25–6.

Another objection is *vagueness*. Singer says that we should help as long
as our helping does not sacrifice "anything morally significant." But what,
one might ask, counts as "morally significant"? One person might think
that saving his clothes from getting muddy is morally significant, while
another might think that nothing short of giving away almost everything
would count. Singer addresses this concern by distinguishing a "strong"
from a "moderate" version of his principle (FAM, p. 32). The strong version maintains that one ought to prevent suffering "unless in doing so we
would be sacrificing something of a comparable moral significance"; the
moderate version maintains that we ought to prevent suffering "unless, to
do so, we had to sacrifice something morally significant" (ibid.). Although
the strong version is the one Singer thinks is correct, he proposes instead
the moderate version—which he thinks is "surely undeniable" (ibid.)—to
allow for some variation in personal judgments of moral significance.
Thus the Singerian position can be restated this way: one ought to prevent the suffering of others unless in one's judgment doing so would sacrifice something morally significant. This version simultaneously avoids
the slippery-slope-style objection and nevertheless maintains the radical
change in most of our lives that Singer believes is required.

A final common objection is raised by John Arthur, who argues that
two important concepts of common morality—*rights* and *deserts*—are left
out of Singer's account.[7] We have a *right* to our bodies, for example, which
entails rights to the fruit of our bodies' labor; that means no one else has
a right to that fruit. Moreover, common morality acknowledges that we
deserve the fruit of our labors. Although we are often called on to share
that fruit with our family or close friends, common morality usually does
not oblige us to share with strangers what we have legitimately acquired
or made. Arthur argues that not only do the poor have no right to others'
money, but the nonpoor also need not feel guilty for not giving to the
poor what the nonpoor legitimately acquired and hence deserve. But the
Singerian need not argue that the poor have a *right* to someone else's
honestly acquired wealth, and he may concede that a person deserves
what he honestly acquired. All the Singerian needs to argue is that a
person with wealth is morally blameworthy if he does not voluntarily give
some of it to people who desperately need it. It is perfectly consistent
to hold that, on the one hand, A has no right to B's money, while, on
the other hand, that B is nevertheless blameworthy if he gives none of
it to A.

---

7 In "World Hunger and Moral Obligation: The Case against Singer."

CENTRAL PROBLEM NUMBER ONE: KNOWLEDGE

Let me now turn to the problems I believe defeat the Singerian argument. The first is that one thing that distinguishes the Pond Case from Overseas Aid Cases is the *knowledge* that the agent in question can reasonably be supposed to have in each case. In the Pond Case, the agent can—in just the few moments he has to evaluate the situation—ascertain with reasonable certainty whether the child has any hope to live or any better means available to survive, other than by his hand. He can know this whether others are passing by or not, simply by scanning quickly to see whether anyone else is preparing to wade in. The agent can also know with a high level of certainty just *what* help is required—whether, say, wading in to grab the child, using the nearby shepherd's hook, or throwing him a life preserver. Finally, the agent can also be sure that his help would indeed *be* help: he can be certain that no unintended and unforeseen bad consequences would ensue from his saving the child (barring of course the exotic possibilities that the saved child might, for example, grow up to be the next Stalin). It is partly because of the certainty with respect to these considerations that we would judge inaction as morally blameworthy. In Overseas Aid Cases, however, one cannot have anything like the same level of certainty in regard to any of the three considerations: one cannot know whether those who are suffering have other means of help available, one cannot know precisely what help is required, and one cannot be certain whether the help one is contemplating would indeed be beneficial.

Now these may initially seem like quibbles, but reflection shows they aren't. Take the first consideration. One of the things that makes the Pond Case so powerful is the knowledge that without the agent's action the child will die. But this knowledge is itself powerful because one assumes that the child has no other, and hence no better, means available to survive: if I do not wade in to rescue the child now, the child will die. But such knowledge is absent in Overseas Aid Cases. You typically will not know whether there are other, perhaps better, ways to aid starving people far away than by giving money to the charity presently asking for it. There are, after all, any number of ways in which help might be given: there are numerous relief agencies, many supplying different kinds of help (food, shelter, medical supplies, books); there are government agencies providing various kinds of help; and there are often local groups working to help. Moreover, some aid agencies might be more efficient than others, or even less corrupt than others. Recent scandals of United Way charities are a case in point. William Aramony, former president of United Way, was convicted in 1995 for stealing some $600,000 from the charity's funds to subsidize a lavish personal lifestyle.[8] And several heads of local United Way chapters have come under fire for taking a salary and benefits package that seems exorbitant for a nonprofit charity, often worth in excess of $200,000 per year.[9] If there are in fact other, better means of helping, then giving to this charity might thus in fact be counterproductive: giving money to an inefficient charity would mean less money available for an efficient charity, which could mean that less total suffering is alleviated.

It is not that one could not commence an investigation of the matter and become better acquainted with some of the facts, but I do maintain that one cannot reasonably be supposed to know all the relevant facts, as one can be supposed in Pond Cases. Such an investigation would be, first of all, a time-consuming process that many are simply not in a position to undertake. More important, however, some of the relevant facts would remain stubbornly unavailable to any given potential donor. Some details of local conditions, circumstances, and needs will be ascertainable only on a first-hand, local basis. And because they change frequently, any information gathered and sent to an American donor—even with the quickness of the internet—may well be outdated by the time the potential donor is able to take action. Hence the vast majority of people who are tapped for donations to overseas aid agencies cannot be reasonably supposed to have the facts that are necessary to make a properly informed judgment about what is best to do. And that means they cannot know whether this particular request from this particular agency represents the only or even the best way to help suffering people. Indeed, if an American is in possession of facts that allow him to know how he can help locally, then the uncertainties accompanying Overseas Aid Cases may mean that he should *not* give the money to overseas aid agencies, even if there is a chance that the overseas suffering is greater than what he can help to alleviate locally.

Now why exactly is the degree of certainty such an important factor? I may not *know* whether I am the best swimmer around, after all, but I should still wade in to help the drowning child. True enough, but that

---

[8] See "Ex-President of United Way Guilty of Fraud," *Chicago Tribune*, April 4, 1995; and "United Way Admits to 'Excesses,' Says Laws May Have Been Broken," *Chicago Tribune*, April 4, 1992.

[9] See, for one example, "Salary of United Way's Detroit Chief Questioned," *Chicago Tribune*, March 18, 1992. Another case has been the misappropriation of donated monies for the recent tsunami relief efforts in Indonesia. See "Graft Fears Stalk Indonesia Tsunami Aid Efforts."

point fails to bring Pond Cases and Overseas Aid Cases together. Regardless of other circumstances, in the Pond Case there is little doubt that I will accomplish what needs to be done, namely, saving the child; but I cannot even be *reasonably* sure that my giving money to this charity will in fact prevent suffering. My money *might* help, but it might also go to paying staff or administrative costs, or it might support an otherwise inefficient charity. I cannot know for sure. One might respond here that to avoid the force of my objection, one need only add the requirement that, in addition to helping overseas poor, my moral obligations include first investigating which relief agencies are efficient at getting money to the people who need it. This is a reasonable suggestion, but note two things. First, there are no similar additional requirements in the Pond Case: we don't require the passerby to investigate whether his wading in would be more efficient than another's doing so. Hence the cases are still differentiated by this criterion. Moreover, the requirement that a person investigate the relative effectiveness of relief agencies—aside from being a time-consuming activity that, as I suggested above, not everyone is reasonably in a position to undertake—does not in the end eliminate the uncertainty; it only relocates it. The United Way charities, for example, made impressive claims about their efficiency while its leaders were spending on themselves. Perhaps their similar claims today are in fact credible, but I would not know for sure. And how could I find out? Not, obviously, by simply asking the charities themselves. By contrast, however, it is immediately obvious what help the drowning child requires, and it will be readily ascertainable whether there are other, better means of helping the child. Although it might be true, then, that the differences in certainty in the end are merely matters of degree, the different degrees between these cases can justify different actions in each.

Turn now to the second consideration: is it always clear exactly *what* should be done about the suffering in third-world countries? Unfortunately, no.[10] To begin, different kinds of suffering require different kinds of aid: where one natural disaster might leave the local residents most in need of potable water, another might leave them in need of penicillin or other medical supplies. In one place foodstuffs are required, elsewhere seeds for future crops are best. In one place building materials for storm shelters are needed, elsewhere building materials for irrigation

---

[10] To be contrasted with the Singerian position on what is to be done is, for example, that of economist Julian L. Simon; see Simon's "Introduction" to his edited *The State of Humanity*, esp. pp. 24–7.

or damming systems. And this is not just a matter of some having more knowledge than others. Among charitable agencies claiming first-hand knowledge, some will argue that what is best for the residents of one location is birth control devices and fertility education, others that books and school supplies are most important, others again that scholarships for foreign study are in their best long-term interests. Still others will argue that what is most required is political action—lobbying one's own government for trade sanctions or aid, perhaps, or protesting the needy people's government for greater respect for human rights. Indeed, some will argue that in some cases what is required is no action whatsoever.[11] This partial list offers an already bewildering array of choices, and it is exceedingly difficult to know which is best. In Singer's example of Bengal, one could make plausible arguments for *any one* of these options as the best for helping current and future Bengalis. For a potential American donor, then, it is anything but clear whether giving money to the organization now asking for it is the best thing for him to do—especially considering that some groups argue not only that their own is the best strategy for helping, but that others' strategies are in fact counterproductive, or even immoral.

Similar uncertainties do not beset the agent in the Pond Case. There can be little doubt that what is required is bodily taking the child out of the water. A few thoughts might still occur to the passerby—whether he should take off his coat, whether he should take the child to the north or south edge of the pond—but these can be assessed and decided in the few moments it takes to reach the child. The uncertainties attendant on Overseas Aid Cases are far more numerous, involve indefinitely more possible courses of action and resulting effects, and hence cannot be assessed in the same on-the-spot fashion.

Finally, the third consideration is the degree to which the passerby in question can know that his help would in fact be beneficial. A person who wishes to alleviate the suffering of others must think about which factors affect the suffering of the people in question, and he must hence investigate which causes, including which actions he himself might undertake, would mitigate the suffering. It follows that such a person must recognize the distinction between the long-term and short-term effects of available courses of action, and recognize the importance of considering both. Any course of action that leads on balance to an increase in suffering in the long run would seem prima facie to be avoided, even if it led to a short-term decrease.

---

[11] See John Kekes's "On the Supposed Obligation to Relieve Famine."

A potential American donor must therefore consider, for example, the real possibility that sending money might sustain a moribund political system, leading to perhaps a short-term decrease but long-term increase in the number of people that die. Monetary aid now might temporarily buoy an incompetent government, with the result that the government extends and entrenches—rather than retracts or abolishes—its inefficient policies. A few months or years later, then, the country is in worse shape than it was and more people are suffering than would have been if the government or citizens had heeded the early warning signs and made or demanded the necessary changes. Tom Bethell, for example, argues in his *The Noblest Triumph* that the U.S. policy of giving money to third-world countries has actually "retarded economic development" there for just these reasons.[12] A similar scenario is possible with a corrupt rather than an incompetent government: in this case foreign aid might assuage the citizens' suspicions about their leaders, putting off a change of leadership until after more damage has been done.[13] Red Cross and other well-intentioned Western aid to Leninist Russia in 1921 is a case in point. As Stéphane Courtois catalogues in gruesome, grisly detail in his edited *The Black Book of Communism: Crimes, Terror, Repression,* over the two subsequent years, more than five million Russians died of hunger from a famine deliberately created by the Russian government.[14] But, again, there are no such worries in the Pond Case: wading into the pond will save the child's life, which is good; no further considerations are necessary.

Singer's Pond Case is also powerful in part because of the unstated assumption that the child is innocent. What could a child have done to deserve such a fate? Similarly, what could far-away, starving children possibly have done to deserve their suffering? Yet money given to charities does not always go to starving children; sometimes it does not even go to their parents. Sometimes it instead goes to childless adults, or ends up in the hands of government officials, military officers, or business conglomerates. But those people may not deserve the money. They might, after all, be the *reason why* children are suffering: their corruption, plundering, or other irresponsibility might be exactly what has caused the conditions that lead to poverty. In such a situation, giving money might

---

[12] See chap. 13.

[13] See also David Osterfield's "The Failures and Fallacies of Foreign Aid," http://www.fee.org/vnews.php?nid=2191, and "Leftist Uses U.S. Aid for 'Dictatorship.'"

[14] See esp. pp. 122–31.

in fact exacerbate the problem of starvation and suffering rather than alleviate it.

And again this is no mere rationalization. We know, for example, that there is enough food produced in the world today to feed every single inhabitant adequately, all six-billion-plus of them.[15] Moreover, there is strong empirical evidence suggesting that a chief cause of poverty world-wide is inefficient or counterproductive governmental policies, evidence I present in detail in chapter 5. The annually published *Economic Freedom of the World*[16] shows the strong correlation between economic prosper-ity and certain kinds of governmental policies (can you guess which?), and between economic privation and other policies: almost all countries approximating one kind of policies are wealthy or becoming so, almost all not approximating that kind of policies are poor or becoming so—and their relative wealth or poverty closely tracks the degree to which they do or do not have proper government policies. It is thus reasonable for a person to be more skeptical about giving money to relief agencies work-ing in foreign countries than he would be to wading in and pulling a child to safety, especially when considering places such as Bengal, where governmental policies are a principal cause of the poverty. In its 2004 report, *Economic Freedom of the World* ranks Bangladesh (where East Bengal is located) 83rd out of 123 countries examined in having governmen-tal policies favorable to economic prosperity; since 1975, Bangladesh's ranking has been as high as 69th and as low as 93rd. Given such poli-cies, Bangladesh is one of the world's poorer countries: according to the World Bank, its per capita gross domestic product in 2001 was $1,610 (for comparison, that of the United States, which ranks third on the EFW index, was $34,320). Neighboring India, which contains West Bengal, was ranked 68th on the index, and it had a per capita gross domes-tic product of $2,840. So how could morality possibly require that we simply send money over, without first straightening out these political matters—or at the very least investigating them? The point again is not that such an investigation is not possible: it is instead to underline the dif-ferences between the Pond Case, where no such investigation is required, and the Overseas Aid Case, where such an investigation is required. The

---

[15] Singer recognizes this; see *Practical Ethics,* p. 236. For current evidence, see the *FAO Quar-terly Bulletin of Statistics* or the *FAO Monthly Bulletins,* both put out by the United Nations Food and Agricultural Organization. See also Lomborg's *The Skeptical Environmentalist,* chap. 3.

[16] Http://www.freetheworld.com.

implication is that the basis for moral judgments about the former do not necessarily apply to the latter.

Before leaving this third consideration, I should note that Peter Unger's response to what he calls the "thought of the disastrous further future" does not answer my argument.[17] The objection Unger considers in his *Living High and Letting Die* is that giving starving children food now will only allow them to grow up and have more starving children in the future. Unger has two responses. First, he says that actual population statistics show that "the thought of the disastrous further future is little better than an hysterical fantasy"; second, he says that even if that thought were true, it would be irrelevant to the case at hand. Unger supplies no argument for the first response; he cites an article by Nobel-laureate economist Amartya Sen on the topic and then reasserts that it is nevertheless irrelevant. But why is it irrelevant? I have argued that a consideration of long-term consequences is closely connected with a concern for alleviating suffering. If it turned out that one course of action could be seen by reasonable prediction to lead to an increase in overall suffering, then this would seem to be a good reason to avoid that course of action. Thus we have to look at the population data after all, and here Unger stands on shaky ground.

In the article cited by Unger, Sen summarizes his own and others' research data that suggest that, contrary to Malthusian predictions, increasing economic prosperity leads to decreasing, not increasing, birth rates.[18] Sen argues that the data suggest that despite increasing worldwide population—although the rate of increase is decreasing: in fact, according to the World Bank, estimates are now that worldwide population will ultimately stabilize of its own accord, perhaps even sometime in this century[19]—there is no reason to think that we are in for a global disaster. Indeed, the production of food has stayed ahead of the production of human beings, despite the fact that human beings have been reproducing

---

[17] Unger, *Living High and Letting Die*, pp. 36–9. Cullity ("International Aid and the Scope of Kindness," p. 125) and Whelan ("Famine and Charity," p. 156) also consider and reject this objection on grounds similar to those of Unger.

[18] Amartya Sen, "Population: Delusion and Reality." Citations of Sen's article are on the page given in parentheses. For Malthus's argument, see his 1803 *Essay on the Principle of Population*.

[19] *World Development Report 1994*, pp. 210–11. For a dissenting discussion, see, for example, http://www.prb.org/Template.cfm?Section=PRB&template=/Content/Content-Groups/Datasheets/2005_World_Population_Data_Sheet.htm, accessed December 13, 2005.

at breathtaking speeds, and despite the further fact that the majority of
the reproduction is taking place in some of the poorest areas of the world,
such as China and India. But Sen's data do not support Unger's case. In
the first place, they suggest that, if anything, we should be *less* concerned
about the impending fate of people presently in conditions of poverty,
since, as economist Julian Simon was fond of putting it, things are looking better and better. In addition, Sen argues that what continues to keep
poor nations poor is neither lack of food, for there is more than enough,
nor overcrowding, for there are more crowded places that are nevertheless richer. Instead, the problem has to do with "political disruption,
including wars and military rule" (p. 65). Sen argues that contraceptives,
better education, and better health care would all decrease birth rates,
but that even a decreasing birth rate would not alleviate suffering until the
"food problem . . . [is] seen as one part of a wider political and economic
problem" of third-world countries (p. 66). Thus Sen's argument substantiates my claim that the concerns of an American—even one otherwise
committed to helping alleviate suffering—of exacerbating the situation
by unintentionally propping up an inefficient or corrupt government are
legitimate and can justify hesitation to give.

The argument, then, is that there are uncertainties in Overseas Aid
Cases that cannot be overlooked and quite possibly cannot be avoided,
and that these uncertainties can justify inaction that in Pond Cases would
be unjustifiable. Depending on the particulars of the Overseas Aid Case at
hand, giving money to the charity asking for it might be morally required,
not giving money might be morally required, or an (indefinite) suspen-
sion of the decision of whether to give until more facts become available
might be morally required. Or, indeed, perhaps nothing whatsoever is
morally required. In light of the combined effect of these sources of
uncertainty—even if any one of them were overcome—one cannot maintain in advance, as Singerians do, that giving to overseas aid agencies
is always morally required. Even a weak and qualified claim, such as
although one cannot know for sure, one can be *reasonably* certain that
giving money to one of the *more reputable* charities will *probably* lead to the
reduction in suffering of *someone* in the *relatively near* future, is falsified
by the three kinds of uncertainty. But none of this uncertainty applies to
Pond cases. That means that the cases are different. It also means that
Singer's principle that one ought to prevent something very bad from
happening if one can do so without sacrificing something (comparably)
morally significant fails as well. Maybe the people suffering something
very bad deserve to suffer it; maybe our preventing the very bad thing

would lead in fact to worse consequences down the road; maybe the people suffering it do not want help; and so on.[20] Surely we should not simply ignore such possibilities. Because we cannot know these things in Overseas Aid Cases, Singer's principle is false, and the Pond Case therefore does not suffice to show that we are morally obligated to give.

I emphasize that I have *not* shown that one should not give to charities. My argument is rather that the immorality of inaction in Pond Cases does not entail the immorality of inaction in Overseas Aid Cases, because the cases differ in significant ways. Effective charitable giving remains based on local knowledge, and if Singer's Pond Case shows anything, it is that moral action itself requires individual judgment based on local knowledge.

CENTRAL PROBLEM NUMBER TWO: VALUE

One source of the Singerian position's strength is the fact that we intuitively think that a wealthy person's enjoyment from, say, buying a new compact disc simply cannot be so valuable that it outweighs the suffering of a person starving. Singer construes the comparison in economic terms: \$15 is worth much more to the starving person than it is to the music lover. Singer gives the following list of items that he thinks are less important to a wealthy American than their monetary value would be to a poor foreigner: "stylish clothes, expensive dinners, a sophisticated stereo system, overseas holidays, a (second?) car, a larger house, private schools for our children, and so on."[21] Such interpersonal comparisons of value intuitively seem unproblematic, especially when such extreme cases are compared. But can one articulate this notion of comparative value in a coherent way?

In a word: no. One of the central discoveries that led to modern economics was what is called the subjective theory of value—the notion that a thing's "value" be sought not in the thing itself or in any objective criterion or standard, but, rather, simply in what any individual is willing to sacrifice in order to get it. This notion of value allows us to understand otherwise paradoxical phenomena. For example, two people with exactly the same amount of money may make entirely different judgments about whether the product they are contemplating is worth the price. I may be willing to spend \$5,000 for an Amy LeJeune Harper painting, but not \$5,000 for

---

[20] See Kekes's "On the Supposed Obligation to Relieve Famine," esp. pp. 506–7.
[21] *Practical Ethics*, p. 232.

an autographed Nolan Ryan rookie baseball card; on the other hand, you would not pay $5,000 for a Harper, but you would gladly pay $5,000 for the Nolan Ryan card. One employer might be willing to pay a worker only $7 per hour to do something for which another employer is willing to pay the same worker $10 per hour. What accounts for these differences? The longtime mistake was to think that there is some objective value in the painting, card, or work that the prices are trying to approximate. On the contrary, discrepancies in judgments about what things are worth merely reflect the fact that a thing's "value" just is whatever a person is willing to give up for it. Thus a Harper's value is at least $5,000 to me, while at the same time less than that to you; the Nolan Ryan card is worth less than $5,000 to me, but at least that to you. The values, then, are determined by the valuing agent, not the valued object. Hence the name "subjective value."

The case for this concept of value was made by a series of Austrian economists in the nineteenth century who broke with the Ricardian and Marxian notion that *labor* was what gave things their value.[22] Although labor had seemed promising as an objective criterion of value, examination revealed that it in fact contained a host of problems. To start, labor is difficult to measure, and it varies from person to person: two people who worked for the same amount of time on something might not have expended the same amount of "labor," and it might take different people different amounts of "labor" to create precisely the same thing. Moreover, a labor theory of value has some recalcitrantly odd results: in easily imaginable cases it can turn out that a person expended a great deal of labor on something most people would agree is quite worthless. And what do we do about the location of a thing's value? Do we say that the labor creates value *in* a thing, meaning that the thing is what is now valuable, not the labor? Would this mean that an idle person is without value? Or do we say that labor itself is what is valuable? Then what is the metaphysical operation by which the labor infuses itself into an object? When I buy a Harper, I am buying a painting, not "labor." If it was Harper's labor that had value, however, then her labor must somehow be *in* the painting. But how, and what is the metaphysical entity that is or contains the value as it is being transferred?

---

[22] See Ricardo's 1817 *On the Principles of Political Economy and Taxation,* esp. chap. 1; and Marx's 1867 *Capital,* esp. Part I, in Tucker, *Marx-Engels Reader,* pp. 302–29. Adam Smith also seems to rely on labor as a determinant of value: see his *Wealth of Nations,* esp. bk. I, chaps. 4 and 5.

Beginning with Carl Menger's 1871 *Principles of Economics* and proceeding through the work of Christian von Ehrenfels, Eugen von Böhm-Bawerk, Friedrich von Wieser, and Ludwig von Mises, the "Austrian School" of economists argued that the notion of inherent value imbued in an object by labor was incoherent.[23] In its stead, they set out the detailed and systematic case of their new discovery, the principle of diminishing marginal utility (PDMU), and the subjective theory of value it entailed. The PDMU holds that for any good or service a person wants, the $n + 1$st unit he receives is ceteris paribus less valuable to him than the nth unit.[24] This principle is meant to be a description of human valuing, and it is based on the belief that people tend to put the first unit of any good or service to what they judge to be its most important use, the second unit to its second most important use, and so on, until eventually another unit is worth practically or actually nothing to them. Think of glasses of water for a thirsty person: the first is worth a great deal to him, the second is worth less, and so on, until, say, the fifth glass is worth nothing to him; perhaps the first two glasses he himself drinks, the third he gives to you, the fourth he uses to water his plant, and the fifth he dumps out.

What is important about the PDMU for our purposes is that it posits individual valuation. It shows that human beings value things based on personal preferences, and this valuation is what creates and determines a thing's value. As Ehrenfels argues, "we do not desire things because we grasp in them some mystical, incomprehensible essence 'value'; rather, we ascribe 'value' to things because we desire them."[25] Similarly, there is no "just" price, as for example St. Thomas Aquinas argued in the thirteenth century, and no "intrinsic" price, as for example Richard Cantillon argued in the eighteenth.[26] A single thing can in fact simultaneously have indefinitely many values, each indexed to a particular valuing agent. Because the use to which a thing will be put is determined by an individual's unique circumstances and unique schedule of preferences, it makes no sense to speak of one person's valuation of the thing applying to another

---

[23] For a good discussion of the Austrian School's lineage and its development of the subjective theory of value, see Barry Smith, *Austrian Philosophy*, chap. 9. For discussions of how this school has influenced modern economic thought, see James M. Buchanan, *Cost and Choice*, and Karen I. Vaughn, *Austrian Economics in America*, esp. chaps. 1–3.

[24] See Carl Menger, *Principles of Economics*, pp. 122–8, esp. the chart and Menger's explanation of it on pp. 126–7. For critical discussion of the PDMU, see, for example, Harry G. Frankfurt, "Equality as a Moral Ideal."

[25] In *System der Werttheorie* (1897–8), as cited in Smith's *Austrian Philosophy*, p. 283.

[26] See, respectively, St. Thomas's 1266–73 *Summa theologica*, Question 78 on "Usury," and Richard Cantillon's 1755 *Essay on the Nature of Commerce in General*, pp. 15–17.

person: even if two people in a particular case are willing to sacrifice the same amount for something, their respective valuations will be the result of different calculations based on different variables; hence one's valuation cannot substitute for the other's (and no third party's valuation can substitute for either of the other's). It follows that the value of the thing to one person cannot be compared to its value to the other.

Each act of valuation is relative, then, to a particular agent. That means that not only might two agents value a given thing at different rates, but they might value it relative to other things differently. So I value the Harper more than you do, and we both value a Harper more than, say, an Elvis-on-black-velvet print for sale in front of Wal-Mart, which means that we would both trade an Elvis print for a Harper. But how many Elvis prints would we be willing to give up for a Harper? I would presumably trade more than you would, but how many more? The subjective theory of value says that there is no single "objectively correct" answer to how many should be traded, and that there is no way to calculate an exact value of a Harper based on the number of Elvis prints, because people do not judge value in terms of an objectively quantifiable criterion. They judge, rather, on the basis of their unique set of preferences, as driven by their present desires. Thus the actual value of a Harper to me may not only not be the actual value of a Harper to you, but because our respective judgments of its value are informed by our respective unique sets of preferences, the judgments themselves are not commensurable on any single standard or criterion. Their value may not even be the same to *me* at one time as compared with a later time—there was a time, for example, when I did not appreciate Harpers as much as I do now. Thus the valuations simply cannot be compared. Asking which is "objectively" worth more is, then, incoherent.[27]

How does this relate to giving money overseas? The first step is to show that the Singerian position needs the "strong" version of Singer's

---

[27] I have given only a sketch of the subjective theory of value and the problems attendant on rival theories. For further investigation, see, for seminal classic accounts, Ralph Barton Perry, *General Theory of Value*, and Ludwig von Mises, *Human Action*. For more recent studies of various aspects, see Mark Addleson, " 'Radical Subjectivism' and the Language of Austrian Economics," Israel M. Kirzner, "Another Look at the Subjectivism of Costs," and Gerald P. O'Driscoll Jr. and Mario J. Rizzo, "Subjectivism, Uncertainty, and Rules," all in Israel M. Kirzner's edited *Subjectivism, Intelligibility, and Economic Understanding*; and Eric Mack, "Agent-Relativity of Value, Deontic Restraints, and Self-Ownership," in R. G. Frey and Christopher W. Morris's edited *Value, Welfare, and Morality*. For criticism of this theory of value, see Robert Nozick, *Philosophical Explanations*, pp. 403–570 and the references contained therein.

principle, which involves comparisons of value. Recall that the "strong" version requires that one help if, by helping, one does not sacrifice anything of *comparable* moral significance, while the "moderate" version requires that one help if, by helping, one does not sacrifice *anything morally significant*. The subtle change in wording makes for a substantial change in meaning. But the "moderate" version turns out to be insufficient because its operative notion—"morally significant"—is too vague, allowing for too broad a range of interpretation. People will have sharply different views about what level of sacrifice begins to be "morally significant," and until one can locate a specific, concrete criterion, one would have to live with some people, perhaps most people, not giving any money to overseas relief agencies on the (plausible) grounds that their own local concerns are morally significant. So if one wants to motivate real change in people's behavior, one will have to resort to the "strong" version of the principle after all. (Singer seems to recognize as much, by the way: in later writings his principle is given in only the "strong" version.[28])

One might think that the "strong" version of the principle provides the necessary objective criterion we have been looking for, namely, *comparable moral significance*. The second step in the argument is now to suggest that Pond Cases provide support for Overseas Aid Cases via the "strong" principle only by relying on an interpersonal comparison of value that the above discussion shows to be incoherent. For it relies on the reader's being moved by a rhetorical question such as this one: Is that trinket you are about to spend money on worth more to you than getting a meal is worth to a hungry Bengali? The intended answer is, of course, clear. But no such direct comparison can be made, and the Singerian argument trades on a crucial ambiguity. What the Singerian wants the reader to ask himself is whether, if the reader were in the Bengali's shoes, the reader would want some other wealthy person to buy another trinket or pay the same amount to feed him. Again the answer is obvious. This kind of comparison of cases is coherent, however, because it relies in *both* cases on the *reader's own* personal valuations. But the question the Singerian asks instead is whether the trinket is worth more *to the wealthy person* than the meal is *to the Bengali*. This kind of comparison is what the subjective theory of value disallows as incoherent because it calls for comparison of

---

[28] Cp. *Practical Ethics,* 1st ed., p. 168, and *Practical Ethics,* 2nd ed., p. 229. Cullity agrees that Singer's argument requires the "strong" version; see Cullity, "International Aid and the Scope of Kindness," p. 126.

incommensurable subjective judgments of value. There is simply no way to answer the question of which is "objectively" worth more.

To clarify my argument, let me pause for a moment to address a couple of potential objections.[29] First, it may be thought that my argument necessarily implies an ethical subjectivity: if I cannot compare my valuations to your valuations, is there nothing more to be said about moral judgments than that I value certain things at one level, whereas you value them at another? So, for example, perhaps I value other people's 'personhood,' but you don't. Is there no way to resolve such an impasse? This is a good question, but the answer is unequivocally: No, the incoherence of interpersonal comparisons of value (ICVs) does not necessarily imply a subjective theory of morality. It does not follow from the fact that one cannot compare the value of $15 to A to its value to B that therefore there is no basis for judging, say, that the genocides conducted in Russia under Stalin were (1) morally execrable and (2) morally worse than (probably) any morally bad thing you or I have ever done. The argument that ICVs are incoherent might imply that one cannot compare the value of preventing future such genocides to me with its value to you—that is, what I would be willing to sacrifice to ensure their prevention as opposed to what you would be willing to sacrifice for the same thing, declaring one of us "correct" and the other "incorrect" in his valuation—but it does not imply that one cannot make moral judgments like (1) and (2) above. Moral judgments such as these might be based on any of several criteria—perhaps the judgment of an imagined impartial spectator or an objective utility calculation[30]—and thus are distinct from, and can be entirely independent of, subjective judgments of value.

A second potential objection is that perhaps Singer's argument depends not, in fact, on an ICV, but rather only on the reader comparing his own respective valuations—that is, their value to himself only—of, on the one hand, $15 for a trinket and, on the other, $15 for food when he is hungry. I'm not sure that suggestion rescues Singer's argument. Consider that whichever judgment were reached would by hypothesis apply

---

[29] For an interesting discussion of the topics that follow, see J. C. Lester's *Escape from Leviathan*, chap. 4. See also my review of Lester's book, http://www.independent.org/tii/content/pubs/review/books/tir61_lester.html. (You might also be interested to see Lester's reply to my review, http://www.khcc.org.uk/la/otteson.htm, both accessed December 13, 2005.)

[30] I say "objective" utility calculation to emphasize that, whatever other problems such calculations might face, it need not be based on subjective judgments of value. Such a calculation might instead be based on what actually and in fact leads to greater happiness for all concerned, what actually and in fact allows more people to flourish, and so on.

only to the person making the judgment: it would mean that *I* value money for food over money for trinkets when the two conflict, but it says nothing about anyone else—and in particular nothing about the person who really counts for Singer, namely, the hungry person overseas. But Singer's argument is meant to motivate me to take action with regard to others, not just myself, and for that I will have to compare, or at least draw an analogy between my valuation of my own case and what would be another person's valuation of his case. That brings us right back to the problem of ICVs. So if it is true that the Singerian argument relies only on a single person's making two subjective valuations and comparing them with one another, then the argument would not in the end motivate the conduct that the Singerian wants to motivate, namely, sending money to help overseas poor. Otherwise the argument faces the problems I have suggested with ICVs.

Now it may well be that a wealthy person who spends his money on trinkets is engaging in a vicious—though not unjust (more on that momentarily)—waste of money. My argument here is only that to the extent that the Singerian position relies on this kind of comparison of value, the argument fails. The extreme nature of Pond Cases calls up intuitive sentiments that are strong enough to mask the philosophical problems underlying the use to which they are put, but that does not mean the problems go away. There is no coherent way to compare one person's judgments of value, or his schedule of values, with those of any other person; and there is no single objective criterion of value by which both can be judged that is not beset with fatal problems. Regardless of our intuitions to the contrary, there is no way to decide whether money spent in one way is worth more or less to one person than the same money spent another way is to another person. It may still be proper to blame the wealthy person for spending money on trinkets rather than helping the poor—that is, to repeat, there may well be objective moral grounds on which to base a negative judgment of such a person. But that judgment will have to be on grounds other than the wealthy person's making a morally culpable mistaken judgment of value.

CENTRAL PROBLEM NUMBER THREE: VICE VERSUS JUSTICE

The final problem I wish to raise with the Singerian position is that it conflates two central notions of moral philosophy that should be kept separate: justice and virtue. The Singerian says that a person who does not save the child in the Pond Case is immoral, full stop. Drawing on the distinction drawn in chapter 1, however, I suggest that the person would be *vicious,* but not *unjust;* and it is only injustice that warrants initiating coercive action against a person. The same judgment applies to Overseas Aid Cases: the worst we could conclude about the wealthy person who does not give to overseas relief agencies is that he is vicious. We are not, however, thereby licensed to conclude that he is acting unjustly—and, hence, we are not justified in adopting anything other than rhetorical weapons against him.

This distinction between virtue and justice is based on the account given by Adam Smith in his 1759 *Theory of Moral Sentiments* (hereafter referred to as TMS). Smith argues that the rules of other virtues are like the rules of style, whereas the rules of justice are like the rules of grammar: the former are multiple, vague, and indefinite; the latter are few, precise, and well known. Indeed, we can capture 'justice' adequately with just three simple rules: do not invade another person's life, do not impinge on another person's liberty, and do not transgress on another person's property (TMS, p. 84). These rules are all negative, and it is true, as Smith puts it, that one might fulfill them all completely by sitting still and doing nothing (TMS, p. 82). That does not mean that a person doing nothing would be particularly *virtuous,* however, for full virtue requires indefinitely many positive actions, all situation-specific and guided by judgment and not by precise rules. As I argued in chapter 3, because no society can exist in which its members do not respect the rules of justice, society is justified in enforcing them, coercively if necessary. On the other hand, society is not justified in enforcing other virtues with coercive measures, because doing so would lead to inquisitions, public battles, division, and strife, not to mention ongoing violations of people's personhood.

Since I have already defended this conception of justice and virtue, I won't do so again here. But let me point out two considerations that recommend it in the present context: first, it fits with our everyday moral judgments better than the Singerian picture does; second, it avoids a distasteful consequence of the Singerian position. Take these in turn.

Singer talks of a person's "duty" to give (FAM, p. 27), he speaks of great personal sacrifice not as supererogatory but as obligatory (FAM, p. 28), and he thinks the state ought to take money from private hands and redistribute it if voluntary private donations are not forthcoming (FAM, p. 23). All of this suggests a single-place conception of morality: either one is moral or one is immoral. If one does not help suffering people, one is immoral; if one does, one is (at least on this count) not immoral. As I argued in chapter 1, however, we routinely recognize a two-place conception of morality in our everyday dealings with people. We say that I think your words are vile, but you have a right to say them; we say that what you have done with your life is a waste, but that is your business; we say that you are making a mistake to pay that price for that car, but it is your money. We do not say, however, I think you should not kill an innocent person, but that is your business; we do not say I think you should not rape a person, but that is your business; we do not say I think you should not steal from others, but that is your business. This way of looking at people and their actions assumes the distinction between justice and injustice, on the one hand, and other virtues and vices, on the other: we allow people to be otherwise vicious as long as they are not unjust, but the moment they cross the line of injustice we feel justified in stepping in. We express disapproval of viciousness, but we do not initiate force because the vicious person is doing no "real and positive hurt" to anyone. On the other hand, murder, rape, and theft all do "real and positive hurt" to others, thus are all breaches of justice, and thus justify interference.

Relate this now to the Pond Case. Singer would have us judge the passerby simply to be immoral if he does not help the child. I suggest instead that the proper judgment is that the person is vicious but not unjust. Because he did no "real and positive hurt" to the child, he deserves only disapprobation; since he is not unjust, we would not be justified in initiating force against him (by, say, fining him or throwing him in jail). *Causing* a person's suffering is another matter, of course—that is indeed to act unjustly—but that is not what we are considering here. We imagine a case only of neglect or indifference, which, assuming there was no previous obligation in place—it was not the child's parent, for example, or the child's paid, on-duty lifeguard—could not turn into injustice.[31] However discreditable the idle passerby's actions would be, and however we might justifiably shun and publicly execrate him, his actions remain within the bounds of justice. Therefore, out of respect for his personhood, we are not allowed to force him to do otherwise or coercively punish him.

Besides fitting our everyday moral judgments better, the distinction between virtue and justice is also germane to the Singerian position in another way. Advocates of this position typically think that governments should pick up where private donation ends. This tends to be the practical import of Singer's saying that giving in the Overseas Aid Case is our "duty." Almost all defenders of Singerian positions make similar calls for

---

[31] I defended this notion of causation in chapter 1.

state action; a typical example is Onora O'Neill's *Faces of Hunger,* which asks for state-enforced worldwide wealth redistribution. But this would be to advocate coercive measures to punish people for insufficient virtue—which is disallowed as inconsistent with respecting people's personhood. Because the Singerian tends to think that a person not giving money to overseas aid agencies is immoral, period, he believes he is therefore justified in calling on governments to secure from otherwise unwilling private parties the money that he judges necessary to alleviate suffering. How much money would that be? Singer mentions "40 percent of our Gross National Product" (FAM, p. 32). Now, federal, state, and local governments *already* consume more than one-third of America's GNP. Estimates vary, but one conservative estimate reports that the total effective tax rate—that is, including federal, state, and local taxes—was 32.7 percent in 2001.[32] But putting that complication to one side, the Singerian ends up here in effect arguing for a substitution of his own judgment about whether, to whom, and how much one should give for everyone else's, backing his judgment up with the coercive apparatus of the state. This is the distasteful consequence to which I referred earlier, distasteful because it disrespects others' judgment and thus their personhood.

I suggest that such a governmental policy is inconsistent with a society of 'persons' (1) because it violates the sanctity of private property by not allowing people to do with their own whatever they want, so long as they do no "positive hurt" to others in the process, and also (2) because it violates the sanctity of one's private judgment by not allowing people to contribute their time, money, or other help as they privately judge proper. The decision to give is, after all, based on one's beliefs about deeply important things—such as what constitutes the good life and how one should attain it—and thus falls within the scope of the sanctity of one's private judgment. Advocating government action in this regard ignores the violation of these two central building blocks of a just society. And I suggest this violation is especially incautious given the uncertainties attendant on giving money to overseas aid agencies and the impossibility

---

[32] See http://taxfoundation.org/files/8aeOffb685f381da2b2fc6c035513ac7.pdf. For comparison, in 1925 it was 9.3 percent, in 1950 it was 24.6 percent, and in 1975 it was 28.9 percent. Others calculate that the total government cost is much higher; see, for example, economist Robert Higgs's "Lies, Damn Lies, and Conventional Measures of the Growth of Government," http://www.independent.org/tii/media/pdf/tir_09_1_9_higgs.pdf, and Stephen Moore's "The Most Expensive Government in World History," http://www.ipi.org/ipi%5CIPIPublications.nsf/PublicationLookupQuickStudy/6505E3B3E90495EC86256B4D003EB1A9 (all sites accessed December 13, 2005).

of making the kind of interpersonal comparison of value on which the Singerian bases his judgment.

It should also not go unmentioned in this connection that one considerable virtue of the society entailed by the concept of personhood I have defended is its limitations on the power of the state over the individual. The twentieth century's string of the most bloody political regimes in the known history of the world is a potent reminder of the importance of circumscribing the power of government, particularly as it pertains to private property and private conscience. Just how bloody the twentieth century was is shocking and arresting. R. J. Rummel, the political scientist who has done the most to get the hard numbers, refers to the phenomenon as "democide": in his *Death by Government,* Rummel estimates that during the twentieth century a total of 169,198,000 noncombatants were killed for political reasons by their own governments. Re-read that last sentence. These are not soldiers killed in wars: these are people who were targeted and eliminated—Lenin's word was "liquidated"—solely for reasons of political expediency, by their own governments, those very institutions supposedly charged with ensuring their well-being. As bloody as previous eras or regimes in history have been, no other century in history comes close to this level of carnage. Now there might be cases in which we think that impinging on people's freedoms is proper or required. But prudence indeed dictates that those cases should be few and carefully, publicly scrutinized. And in light of the risks that were horrifically realized during the last century, we would do well to mind the maxim that whatever power we give the state to do *for* us we also give it to do *to* us. One conclusion I think is therefore justified is that not being beneficent enough is a dubious justification for an undertaking as dangerously precedent-setting as asking the government to use force against those who do not agree with or measure up to one person's, or one group's, judgment of "beneficent enough."

Lest I be misunderstood here, I am of course not suggesting that Singer or any others who support Singerian positions are advocating the creation of a brutal totalitarian state. My suggestion is rather that there are often unintended consequences involved in state action. This is not an idea new to me. In his 1888 essay "Democracy and Plutocracy," William Graham Sumner wrote: "Hence we see one fallacy of nearly all the popular propositions of 'reform': they would not be amiss, perhaps, if the change which they propose could be made and everything else remain the same. . . . In the proposition it is assumed that everything else is to remain the same. But it is inevitable that other things will not remain the same; they will all of them adjust themselves to the new elements which are introduced."[33] In his 1884 essay "The Coming Slavery," Herbert Spencer made a similar argument when he wrote:

Legislators who in 1833 voted £30,000 a year to aid in building school-houses, never supposed that the step they then took would lead to forced contributions, local and general, now [in 1884] amounting to £6,000,000; they did not intend to establish a principle that A should be made responsible for educating B's offspring; they did not dream of a compulsion which would deprive poor widows of the help of their elder children; and still less did they dream that their successors, by requiring impoverished parents to apply to Boards of Guardians to pay the fees which School Boards would not remit, would initiate a habit of applying to Boards of Guardians and so cause pauperization.... But the "practical" politician who, in spite of such experiences repeated generation after generation, goes on thinking only of proximate results, naturally never thinks of results still more remote, still more general, and still more important than those just exemplified.... [H]e never asks whether the political momentum set up by his measure, in some cases decreasing but in other cases greatly increasing, will or will not have the same general direction with other like momenta; and whether it may not join them in presently producing an aggregate energy working changes never thought of. Dwelling only on the effects of his particular stream of legislation, and not observing how such other streams already existing, and still other streams which will follow his initiative, pursue the same average course, it never occurs to him that they may presently unite into a voluminous flood utterly changing the face of things.[34]

Adam Smith had expressed the same idea in a famous passage from the 1759 *Theory of Moral Sentiments:*

The man of system, on the contrary, is apt to be very wise in his own conceit; and is often so enamoured with the supposed beauty of his own ideal plan of government, that he cannot suffer the smallest deviation from any part of it. He goes on to establish it completely and in all its parts, without any regard either to the great interests, or to the strong prejudices which may oppose it. He seems to imagine that he can arrange the different members of a great society with as much ease as the hand arranges the different pieces upon the chess-board. He does not consider that the pieces upon the chess-board have no other principle of motion besides that which the hand impresses upon them; but that, in the great chess-board of human society, every single piece has a principle of motion of its own, altogether different from that which the legislature might chuse to impress upon it. (pp. 233–4)

And as I argued (with examples) in chapter 2, government agencies regularly tend to grow and extend their power and authority, and often end

---

[33] In *On Liberty, Society, and Politics,* p. 139.
[34] In *The Man versus the State,* pp. 40–3.

up going well beyond what their original descriptions and justifications would allow or predict. Hence I think we must keep that strong tendency in mind when we ask the state, as Singer and others do, to mind our obligations of beneficence. Who can say for sure where an agency created with such purposes would end up?

I should also point out that the objection I am here raising to Singer's argument targets only one part of Singer's overall argument. He is most interested in reforming *individual* behavior; state action is a secondary, if still real, concern. The objection I here raise stymies only the call for state action. The previous two objections I raised target the larger, central part of the Singerian argument.

LIVING, AND DYING, BY INTUITIONS

The three clusters of problems I have raised with the Singerian position each focuses on a particular part of it: the absence of the knowledge required to make competent judgments about whether and how to help, the incoherent notion of value employed in comparing what something is worth to one person to what it is worth to another, and the failure to distinguish justice from other virtues in evaluating a person's conduct. Let me now close the discussion of this position with a more general challenge to the intuitions on which the position is ultimately based.

Singer argues that employing the "comparable moral worth" criterion of giving means that one must give to the point of "marginal utility"— that is, to the point at which the next unit given will make the giver worse off than the recipient (FAM, p. 32). This would for most Americans mean a drastic change in lifestyle, considering how great the difference is between their own standards of living and that of most third-world nations. But Singer says this sacrifice would not be supererogatory, or above and beyond the normal requirements of everyday morality, but, rather, morally *required* of everyone. This level of sacrifice, according to Singer, is entailed by the principle and the "comparable moral worth" criterion, each of which he supports by an appeal to common intuition.

An implication of the Singerian position is that I am immoral if I buy a gift for my wife on her birthday, or if I pay for my son to have piano lessons, or if I buy a ribbon for my daughter to put in her hair—let alone if I send my children to college, buy them a car, or pay for them to study abroad. For none of these things would seem to pass the "comparable moral worth" test. I have few intuitions, however, as strong as that which tells me that a person who does such things is not immoral because he does so. And I bet you have the same intuition. A person who relies on common intuitions as justifications for moral principles—as do Singer, Peter Unger, James Rachels, and many others who take similar positions based on what they guess or assume will be our intuitive reactions to various hypothetical scenarios—must, then, take this as a serious challenge. Indeed, a moral position that makes a father immoral for buying his daughter a ribbon for her hair so stretches the limits of common moral intuition as to suggest a refutation by reductio ad absurdum. If we then add the fact that the Singerian position renders immediately immoral virtually every American, including even America's *poor*—according to the federal government's standards, the 2003 poverty level in America for one person is anyone whose annual income is at or below $8,980,[35] which is almost *five times* the *average* 2003 purchasing power parity in Bangladesh[36]—then the principle becomes an even stronger candidate for dismissal by reductio.

CONCLUSION: AREN'T WE FORGETTING ONE WEE THING?

Even if Otteson is right about the problems with the Singerian argument, aren't we forgetting one wee thing—namely, *what are our obligations to the poor?* In other words, *so what* if the Singerian argument fails? Wasn't the real point in taking up this issue our concern for the actual well-being of the poor? Don't we still have to take up the topic of which policies, legal circumstances, and so on lead to better conditions for poor people, and which lead in the opposite direction? We must also not forget the role that luck and various social forces outside individuals' control play in influencing people's positions and successes (and failures) in life. Isn't it true, after all, that very few wealthy people in the world got that way without their family connections or without other benefits—such as a good education? In other words, don't we still need to address squarely the situations and fortunes of those who begin life at the bottom, not the top, of life's scale of advantages?

We should not too hastily depreciate the significance of calling the Singerian position into question: it has been, as I said at the beginning of this chapter, enormously influential, at least in academic circles. Still, these

---

[35] See http://www.ocpp.org/poverty/poverty2003.htm (accessed December 13, 2005).

[36] According to the World Bank, Bangladesh's 2004 purchasing power parity in international dollars was $1,980. See http://siteresources.worldbank.org/DATASTATISTICS/Resources/GNIPC.pdf (accessed December 13, 2005).

are all excellent questions. It turns out that wealthy people do not, in fact, usually inherit their wealth—historically, the majority of them, especially in the United States, have actually begun relatively poor and worked their way up.[37] It is apparently also the case that the majority of people who have made the greatest accomplishments in the arts and sciences—such as Shakespeare and Michelangelo, for example—also came from humble backgrounds.[38] But be that as it may, we do indeed need to take up the question of which social institutions are most conducive to people's well-being, including in particular that of the poor. That is the subject of the next chapter.

Bibliography

Addleson, Mark. "'Radical Subjectivism' and the Language of Austrian Economics." In *Subjectivism, Intelligibility, and Economic Understanding.* Israel M. Kirzner, ed. New York: New York University Press, 1986.

Aiken, William, and Hugh LaFollette, eds. *World Hunger and Moral Obligation.* Englewood Cliffs, N.J.: Prentice Hall, 1977.

Aquinas, St. Thomas. *Summa theologica* (1266–73). Http://www.newadvent.org/summa, accessed December 13, 2005.

Arthur, John. "World Hunger and Moral Obligation: The Case against Singer." In *Vice and Virtue in Everyday Life,* 4th ed. C. Sommers and F. Sommers, eds. New York: Harcourt Brace, 1997.

Bethell, Tom. *The Noblest Triumph: Property and Prosperity through the Ages.* New York: St. Martin's Press, 1998.

Buchanan, James M. *Cost and Choice: An Inquiry in Economic Theory.* Chicago: Markham, 1969.

Cantillon, Richard. *Essay on the Nature of Commerce in General.* New Brunswick, N.J.: Transaction, 2001 (1755).

Courtois, Stéphan, et al., eds. *The Black Book of Communism: Crimes, Terror, Repression.* Cambridge, Mass.: Harvard University Press, 1999.

Cullity, Garrett. "International Aid and the Scope of Kindness." *Ethics* 105 (October 1994): 99–127.

Cullity, Garrett. *The Moral Demands of Affluence.* Oxford: Oxford University Press, 2004.

"Ex-President of United Way Guilty of Fraud." *Chicago Tribune,* April 4, 1995.

Feinberg, Joel, and Russ Shafer-Landau, eds. *Reason and Responsibility: Readings in Some Basic Problems of Philosophy,* 10th ed. Belmont, Calif.: Wadsworth, 1999.

Feldman, Fred. "Comments on *Living High and Letting Die.*" *Philosophy and Phenomenological Research* 59, no. 1 (March 1999): 195–201.

---

[37] See, for example, Stanley and Danko's *The Millionaire Next Door.*

[38] See, for example, Murray's *Human Accomplishment.* For a nineteenth-century account detailing the lowly, indeed sometimes abject, beginnings of many of the greatest figures in British and European science, arts, politics, and business, see Samuel Smiles's *Self-Help.*

Frankfurt, Harry G. "Equality as a Moral Ideal." In his *The Importance of What We Care About.* Cambridge: Cambridge University Press, 1988.

Frey, R. G., and Christopher W. Morris, eds. *Value, Welfare, and Morality.* Cambridge: Cambridge University Press, 1993.

"Graft Fears Stalk Indonesia Tsunami Aid Efforts." Reuters, January 11, 2005. Http://www.freerepublic.com/focus/f-news/1320463/posts, accessed December 13, 2005.

Gwartney, James, and Robert Lawson. *Economic Freedom of the World.* Vancouver, B.C.: Fraser Institute, 2004. This report is compiled and issued annually. Http://www.freetheworld.com/release.html, accessed December 13, 2005.

Higgs, Robert. "Lies, Damn Lies, and the Growth of Government." *Independent Review* 9, no. 1 (Summer 2004): 147–53. Http://www.independent.org/tii/media/pdf/tir_09_1_9_higgs.pdf, accessed December 13, 2005.

James, Susan. "The Duty to Relieve Suffering." *Ethics* 93 (1982): 4–21.

Kekes, John. "On the Supposed Obligation to Relieve Famine." *Philosophy* 77 (2002): 503–17.

Kirzner, Israel M. "Another Look at the Subjectivism of Costs." In *Subjectivism, Intelligibility, and Economic Understanding.* Israel M. Kirzner, ed. New York: New York University Press, 1986.

Kirzner, Israel M., ed. *Subjectivism, Intelligibility, and Economic Understanding.* New York: New York University Press, 1986.

"Leftist Uses U.S. Aid for 'Dictatorship.'" *Washington Times*, August 12, 2005. Http://www.washtimes.com/world/20050811-100703-3158r.htm, accessed December 13, 2005.

Lester, J. C. *Escape from Leviathan: Liberty, Welfare, and Anarchy Reconciled.* New York: St. Martin's, 2000.

Lester, J. C. "Give Me That Old Time Justificationism... Not!" Http://www.khcc.org.uk/la/otteson.htm, accessed December 13, 2005.

Lomborg, Bjørn. *The Skeptical Environmentalist: Measuring the Real State of the World.* Cambridge: Cambridge University Press, 2001.

Mack, Eric. "Agent-Relativity of Value, Deontic Restraints, and Self-Ownership." In *Value, Welfare, and Morality.* R. G. Frey and Christopher W. Morris, eds. Cambridge: Cambridge University Press, 1993.

Malthus, Thomas. *An Essay on the Principle of Population.* New York: Norton, 2003 (1803).

Marx, Karl. *Capital.* In *The Marx-Engels Reader,* 2nd ed. Robert C. Tucker, ed. New York: Norton, 1978 (1867).

Menger, Carl. *Principles of Economics.* J. Dingwall and B. F. Hoselitz, trans. New York: New York University Press, 1981.

Mises, Ludwig von. *Human Action: A Treatise on Economics.* New Haven: Yale University Press, 1949.

Moore, Stephen. "The Most Expensive Government in World History." Austin, Tex.: Institute for Policy Innovation, 2002. Http://www.ipi.org/ipi%5CIPIPublications.nsf/PublicationLookupQuickStudy/6505E3B3E9049 5EC86256B4D003EB1A9, accessed December 13, 2005.

Murray, Charles. *Human Accomplishment: The Pursuit of Excellence in the Arts and Sciences, 800 B.C. to 1950.* New York: HarperCollins, 2003.

Nozick, Robert. *Philosophical Explanations*. Cambridge, Mass.: Harvard University Press, 1981.

O'Driscoll, Gerald P., Jr., and Mario J. Rizzo. "Subjectivism, Uncertainty, and Rules." In *Subjectivism, Intelligibility, and Economic Understanding*. Israel M. Kirzner, ed. New York: New York University Press, 1986.

O'Neill, Onora. *Faces of Hunger*. London: Allen and Unwin, 1986.

Osterfield, David. "The Failures and Fallacies of Foreign Aid." *The Freeman: Ideas on Liberty*, February 1990. Http://www.fee.org/publications/the-freeman/article.asp?aid=560, accessed December 13, 2005.

Otteson, James R. "Limits on Our Obligation to Give." *Public Affairs Quarterly* 14, no. 3 (July 2000): 183–203.

Otteson, James R. "Private Judgment, Individual Liberty, and the Role of the State." *Journal of Social Philosophy* 33, no. 3 (Fall 2002): 491–511.

Otteson, James R. Review of J. C. Lester's *Escape from Leviathan*. *The Independent Review* 6, no. 1 (Summer 2001). Http://www.independent.org/tii/content/pubs/review/books/tir61_lester.html, accessed December 13, 2005.

Perry, Ralph Barton. *General Theory of Value: Its Meaning and Basic Principles Construed in Terms of Interest*. New York: Longmans, Green, 1926.

Rachels, James. *The Elements of Moral Philosophy*, 4th ed. New York: McGraw-Hill, 2002.

Ricardo, David. *Principles of Political Economy and Taxation*. New York: Prometheus, 1996 (1817). Http://www.econlib.org/library/Ricardo/ricP.html, accessed December 13, 2005.

Rummel, R. J. *Death by Government*. New Brunswick, N.J.: Transaction, 1994.

"Salary of United Way's Detroit Chief Questioned." *Chicago Tribune*, March 18, 1992.

Sen, Amartya. "Population: Delusion and Reality." *New York Review of Books*, September 22, 1994, pp. 62–71.

Simon, Julian L., ed. *The State of Humanity*. Cambridge, Mass.: Blackwell, 1995.

Singer, Peter. "Famine, Affluence, and Morality." In *World Hunger and Moral Obligation*. William Aiken and Hugh LaFollette, eds. Englewood Cliffs, N.J.: Prentice Hall, 1977.

Singer, Peter. *Practical Ethics*, 1st ed. Cambridge: Cambridge University Press, 1979.

Singer, Peter. *Practical Ethics*, 2nd ed. Cambridge: Cambridge University Press, 1993.

Smiles, Samuel. *Self-Help: With Illustrations of Character, Conduct, and Perseverance*. New York: Oxford University Press, 2002 (1859).

Smith, Adam. *An Inquiry into the Nature and Causes of the Wealth of Nations*. Indianapolis, Ind.: Liberty Classics, 1981 (1776).

Smith, Adam. *The Theory of Moral Sentiments*. Indianapolis, Ind.: Liberty Classics, 1982 (1759).

Smith, Barry. *Austrian Philosophy: The Legacy of Franz Brentano*. LaSalle, Ill.: Open Court, 1994.

Spencer, Herbert. "The Coming Slavery." In *The Man versus the State: With Six Essays on Government, Society, and Freedom*. Indianapolis, Ind.: Liberty Fund, 1981.

Stanley, Thomas J., and William D. Danko. *The Millionaire Next Door: The Surprising Secrets of America's Wealthy*. New York: Pocket Books, 1998.

Sumner, William Graham. "Democracy and Plutocracy." In *On Liberty, Society, and Politics: The Essential Essays of William Graham Sumner*. Robert C. Bannister, ed. Indianapolis, Ind.: Liberty Fund, 1992 (1888).

Tucker, Robert C., ed. *The Marx-Engels Reader*, 2nd ed. New York: Norton, 1978 (1867).

Unger, Peter. *Living High and Letting Die: Our Illusion of Innocence*. New York: Oxford University Press, 1996.

"United Way Admits to 'Excesses,' Says Laws May Have Been Broken." *Chicago Tribune*, April 4, 1992.

Vaughn, Karen I. *Austrian Economics in America: The Migration of a Tradition*. Cambridge: Cambridge University Press, 1994.

Whelan, John M., Jr. "Famine and Charity." *Southern Journal of Philosophy* 29 (1991): 149–66.

World Bank. *World Development Report 1994*. Oxford: Oxford University Press, 1994.

5

The Wealth of Nations

The goal of helping poor people is not to make them more comfortable in their poverty or to help them adopt a Stoic *apátheia*—indifference or impassive resignation—toward it. Nor is the goal to make them dependent on the help of others. Nor, finally, is the goal simply to assuage the consciences of wealthy people by doing something, anything. The goal, rather, is to enable the poor to become independent and themselves wealthy. This is the only goal that is consistent with respecting their personhood and, I would add, with common human decency. So the central remaining question is: How do we do it? How do we help the poor while respecting personhood?

I made what I called a "principled" case for the classical liberal state in chapters 2 and 3, and I argued in chapter 4 that the influential argument of the Singerians does not defeat it. In this chapter let us ask the "consequentialist" question of what exactly are the actual effects on life under such a state. This is an empirical question, after all, so, is there evidence out there that can recommend a course of action? It turns out that economics and history do have something to contribute to the discussion— quite a lot, in fact. For not only has history yielded some fairly definitive recommendations, but economics has in addition gone a considerable way toward explaining why what worked in the past did so.

WHAT ARE THE FACTS OF THE MATTER?

As I argued in chapter 4, the Singerian fails in the attempt to argue that we are just as morally obligated to give money to distant peoples as we are to help a child in front of us drowning in a pond. But what about the more general question of what we should do to help poor people to become independent and wealthy? If we are not morally obligated to give our money to overseas relief agencies, and if the state may not take our money away from us against our will, does that mean that morality requires *nothing* of us? Does it mean that neither we nor our government should do *anything*? Does it mean that poor people's governments should do nothing?

What we should do is encourage all governments to adopt those policies, structures, and institutions that history and empirical investigation have shown to be most conducive to human success and flourishing. They should adopt those institutions that have allowed some nations and areas of the world to become wealthy and prosperous, so that others too can become wealthy and prosperous. The good news, indeed the great news, is that evidence has largely settled the matter. We do not need to speculate about what institutions will have the desired effects. We now *know* what they are. And the still greater news, at least to my mind, is that they are fully consistent with the concept of personhood and its entailed limited government that I defended in the first few chapters. The evidence shows that what is needed is (1) recognition of private property and (2) an exact administration of justice. That's it. There is nothing more that the state need do, and nothing more it should do. If it respects people's private property, enforces that respect among enemies foreign and domestic, and constrains itself to defending it and punishing breaches of it, the state will have fulfilled its complete duty and proper function—and, as history has shown over and over again, the people under that state, including most especially the poor among them, will flourish.

There is so much evidence converging on these same recommendations, from so many disciplines and angles and perspectives, that it can be overwhelming. Since it would be impossible to survey all of it, I propose instead simply to indicate a few central findings of this evidence—enough, I hope, to make the recommendations plausible, but not so much that one cannot wade through it all. The reader who wants to pursue this investigation further is reminded to consult the bibliography at the end of the chapter, where suggestions about where to continue are made.

THE CONTEST

Those countries that respect private property and efficiently administer justice prosper, and those that do not do not. It is as simple as that. Let me begin my case for this by taking the two historical figures who are perhaps most associated with nearly opposite forms of government—Adam Smith and Karl Marx—and constructing a historical challenge. In his seminal 1776 *An Inquiry into the Nature and Causes of the Wealth of Nations,* Adam Smith made several predictions about what would happen in a society that adopted the "obvious and simple system of natural liberty" he recommended, a system that correlates quite closely with what I have defended in respecting private property, administering justice, keeping taxes and tariffs low, allowing free trade, and restricting state interventions in the economic lives of individuals to a minimum. In his 1848 *Manifesto of the Communist Party,* Karl Marx, who read and studied Smith's *Wealth of Nations,* similarly made a series of predictions about what would ensue if a society adopted Smithian recommendations as opposed to the centralized and nationalized economic recommendations Marx made. Remarkably, in several instances, the respective recommendations are nearly exactly opposite. This affords us a singular historical opportunity because we can now, more than two centuries after Smith and one and a half centuries after Marx, look back over the historical record and ask: Who was right—Smith or Marx?

Here are Marx's four central predictions, all made in the *Manifesto:* (1) Smithian-style capitalism will concentrate power and property in the hands of a few and eventually create a society of only two classes, the *propertied* and the *propertyless;* (2) under the "ideologies" of free trade and free competition, capitalism will increasingly enslave the worker, ultimately leaving the worker few or no rights or powers against employers; (3) over time, workers' wages will steadily decline to "subsistence" levels, and their standard of living will hence also decline; and (4) we would all, especially the working poor, be better off if instead of leaving matters to greed-driven and "alienating" "market forces," the "most advanced and resolute" intellectuals "wrest" in a "despotic" fashion "all capital from the bourgeoisie" and "centralize all instruments of production in the hands of the state."

In each case, Smith makes virtually the opposite prediction in his *Wealth of Nations:* (1) the "obvious and simple system of natural liberty" will enable more and more people to ascend out of poverty, creating a large and thriving middle class; (2) free trade, free competition, and the abolition of special privileges (such as state-enforced monopolies) will allow steadily increasing economic prosperity for everyone, including workers; (3) over time, employer competition will lead to steadily *increasing* wages, benefits, and overall standards of living for workers; and (4) because prosperity depends on people exploiting their local knowledge, decentralized markets will precipitate greater prosperity than centrally planned economies will.

Well, who is right? Answer: Smith is. On every count.

Let us take the United States as our test case. The United States has not by any means perfectly instantiated the Smithian (or Ottesonian) recommendations, and over time it has tended away from its original Jeffersonian, Washingtonian, and Madisonian vision of limited government—which was quite similar to, and indeed influenced by, Smith[1]—and has moved rather toward the authoritarian state with a command-and-control economy envisioned by Marx and other advocates of state centralization. But it is nevertheless still the case that America has come closer to embodying the Smithian ideal than have most other countries, and it has done so for a longer time. How, then, have Marx's predictions fared in America?

To begin, the middle class dominates economic life, and its standard of living has steadily improved. Consider, as one initial indicator of the former fact, the size of the respective markets for Ford automobiles, on the one hand, and Jaguars, on the other: the former sold 7.4 million cars in 2000, whereas the latter sold 98,500. Consider similarly the relative market sizes of Wal-Mart Stores versus the high-end stores on Rodeo Drive in Beverly Hills, of luxury yacht manufacturers versus that of fishing boats, and so on. As to the second fact, consider that over the last two centuries, working conditions in America have steadily improved; these conditions are now at previously unimaginable levels—and dramatically better than that of most other countries today. Indeed, one is inclined to say that there is in relative terms no poverty at all in the United States today. For even the officially designated "poor" in America have, for example, access to the finest medical care in the world free of charge, can easily procure three hot meals and a hot shower every day, and can enjoy charity- or state-subsidized housing for an indefinite length of time. Consider moreover the following facts about America's "poor":[2]

- In 1995, more than 40 percent of all American "poor" households owned their own homes. The average home owned by "poor" people has three bedrooms, one and a half baths, a garage, and a porch

---

[1] See, for example, Douglass Adair's "Fame and the Founding Fathers" and Samuel Fleischacker's "Adam Smith's Reception among the American Founders, 1776–1790."

[2] I got the following facts from the Bruce Bartlett's National Center for Policy Analysis's (NCPA) report, "How Poor Are the Poor?" http://www.ncpa.org/ba/ba185.html; Robert Rector's "Census Baloney," http://www.city-journal.org/html/10_1_sndgs03.html and "America Has the World's Richest Poor"; and Robert Rector and Sarah Youssef's "How Poor Are America's Poor?" http://www.heartland.org/Article.cfm?artId=797. Since studies such as these are widely available on the internet now, they are easily corroborated by other sources.

or patio. Over 750,000 "poor" persons own homes worth more than $150,000, and nearly 200,000 own homes worth more than $300,000.

- Only 7.5 percent of "poor" households are overcrowded, and nearly 60 percent have two or more rooms per person. The average "poor" American has one-third more living space than the average Japanese and four times as much living space as the average Russian—and that is the *average* person in Japan or Russia, not the average *poor* person.

- Some 70 percent of "poor" households own a car; 27 percent own two or more cars.

- Two-thirds of "poor" households have air conditioning.

- Some 97 percent of "poor" households have a color television, and 92 percent of those on federal welfare have color TVs. Nearly half own two or more color televisions. Some 60 percent have a VCR; almost 20 percent have two VCRs. Some 64 percent own microwave ovens, half have a stereo system, over a quarter have an automatic dishwasher, and 7.4 percent have personal computers.

- Some 84 percent of the "poor" report that their families have "enough" food to eat; 13 percent state they "sometimes" do not have enough to eat; while only 3 percent report they "often" do not have enough to eat. Note that that is not 3 percent of American families; it is only 3 percent of officially designated "poor" families—which means that, even by the government's inflated figures, less than one-half of 1 percent of Americans claim they "often" do not have enough to eat. (I say that the government's figures are "inflated" because they frequently are based on polls asking overly vague questions, such as, "Do you ever go hungry?" Who cannot answer "yes" to that?)

- The "poor" are in fact quite well fed. For example, American "poor" are more likely to be overweight than are middle-income Americans. Nearly half of America's "poor" adult women are overweight. They may not be eating all the right foods, but their overall caloric intake is high enough to put them well out of the range of the rest of the world's poor. Moreover, consider the following fact about overall nutrition.

- The average consumption of protein, vitamins, and minerals is virtually the same for "poor" and middle-income children, and in most cases is well above recommended norms for all children. Most "poor" children today are in fact "super-nourished," consuming on average *double* the recommended level of protein. "Poor" boys today grow up to be an inch taller and ten pounds heavier than the GIs who fought in the Second World War.

To put the state of America's "poor" in somewhat larger perspective, compare their position with that of citizens of European countries. A few suggestive comparisons:[3]

- In 1991, ownership of automatic dishwashers was lower among all people living in the Netherlands, Italy, and the United Kingdom than among "poor" Americans.
- Ownership of clothes dryers among all people in Sweden was about equal to that among "poor" Americans.
- Among citizens in all of Europe, only in the United Kingdom was ownership of VCRs higher than that among "poor" Americans.
- America's "poor" had greater ownership of microwave ovens than *all* citizens in *every* country of Europe.

Extending our comparison to include people in places such as Africa makes for an even more startling contrast:[4] in 1991–3, Guinea, Guinea-Bissau, Kenya, Madagascar, Niger, Nigeria, Senegal, South Africa, and Zimbabwe all had more than half their populations living on less than $2 per day. This was true of more than 90 percent of the populations in Guinea-Bissau and Madagascar. These millions of people would scarcely be able to imagine the life filled with indoor plumbing and running water, food, medicines, schooling, benefits, scholarships, and other opportunities that routinely characterizes the lives of America's "poor."

Does this mean that there are no truly poor people in the United States? No, but the evidence does indicate several things. First, if you are in America and you are poor, chances are overwhelmingly high that you either just got to this country, you are hiding your assets, or you do not want to avail yourself of the opportunities open to you. In the first case, as economists such as Thomas Sowell and Walter Williams have shown,[5] just wait a few years: in America, today's poor are tomorrow's middle class are the day after next's rich. As Stephen Moore put it recently, "Workers

---

3 NCPA, "How Poor Are the Poor?"
4 See the World Bank's "Poverty Lines in African Countries," http://www4.worldbank.org/ afr/poverty/measuring/cross_country_poverty_lines_en.htm.
5 See Sowell's *Applied Economics*, esp. chap. 5, and *Basic Economics*, esp. Part III; see Williams's *Do the Right Thing*, chap. 2. See also the Federal Reserve Bank of Dallas's 1995 annual report, "By Our Own Bootstraps: Economic Opportunity and the Dynamics of Income Distribution," http://www.dallasfed.org/fed/annual/1999p/ar95.pdf; Arnold Kling's "The Rich and the Poor," http://arnoldkling.com/econ/richpoor.html; Alan Reynolds's "For the Record"; D. Mark Wilson's "Income Mobility and the Fallacy of Class-Warfare Arguments against Tax Relief," http://www.heritage.org/Research/Taxes/BG1418.cfm; and Stanley and Danko's *The Millionaire Next Door*.

[today] earn in less than four days a week what their parents earned in five, and they make in three days on the job what their grandparents earned in five."[6] And respect for your personhood means that we do not have to worry about the second or the third group of people: in both these cases people are making individual choices and therefore themselves must face their consequences.[7]

A few more facts about life in America. Markets and competition have led to unprecedented economic growth, steadily falling prices, and substantially higher standards of living. The average worker today enjoys wealth, accommodations, and opportunities surpassing what was available to even the wealthiest quarter of the population just two generations ago; today's worker routinely has access to wealth that no one could have dreamed of only a century ago. Andrew Carnegie, for example, was one of the world's richest men at the end of the nineteenth century (he sold his empire to J. P. Morgan in 1901 for $480 million—an even more astronomical sum then than today), but all his money could not enable him to prevent his beloved mother from dying of pneumonia[8]—something even the poorest of the poor could today get cured easily and free of charge in any hospital in America. Today workers' wages, benefits, and standards of living are arguably better in America than anywhere else in the world, certainly better than most places in the world, and fantastically better than what people for most of human history enjoyed. Free market–based economies have utterly dwarfed centrally planned economies in productive power. We now know, to take one example, that the impressive numbers published during the Cold War by the Soviet Union of its economic production were often distortions or just outright fabrications.[9]

Free economies have led to prosperity for everyone, including especially the poor, who are far better off in market-based economies than in centrally planned economies. Here is why. The natural course of things in market-based economies is for goods to become more plentiful and for prices therefore to go down. That means that even those in the lowest economic strata are able to afford ever more and more. Some examples illustrating this trend, according to W. Michael Cox and Richard

---

[6] In his "The Wages of Prosperity."

[7] I note, for example, a recent article in the *New York Times* that investigates the choices Europeans have tended to make more than Americans to opt for leisure time rather than work more. See Katrin Bennhold, "Love of Leisure, and Europe's Reasons."

[8] See Peter Krass's *Carnegie,* chap. 17.

[9] See Tom Bethell's *The Noblest Triumph,* chaps. 1 and 10, and Richard Pipes's *Property and Freedom,* chap. 4, and *Communism,* chap. 5.

G. Alm's *Myths of the Rich and Poor:* a three-minute phone call from New York to San Francisco cost 90 *hours* of labor in 1915; in 1999 it cost 1.5 *minutes*. Three hearty meals in 1919 cost 9.5 hours; today only 1.6 hours. Housing cost 7.8 hours of work per square foot in 1920; today, 5.5—and with much higher quality and better amenities (including indoor plumbing, central heating, and so on). In 1900, scissors cost the equivalent in today's money of $67, baby carriages cost $913, bicycles cost $2,222, and telephones cost $1,202. In the early 1900s, only the super-rich had automobiles; today, over 90 percent of American households have cars, 60 percent have two or more, and America may soon be the first nation with more automobiles than people. As Cox and Alm have shown, despite the steadily growing slice of their incomes that federal, state, and local taxes have taken, Americans now have to work much less to provide their basic necessities than they once did.[10] That means that Americans are not only more comfortable now than ever, but they also have more time left to spend as they wish than they have ever had.[11]

This final fact suggests another indicator of the fabulous wealth Americans have been able to accumulate under Smithian polices: the amount of leisure time they enjoy. Juliet B. Schor's *The Overworked American* argues that as "time on the job" has increased over the last twenty years, leisure has dwindled. But Schor's claims have been challenged by a number of more recent studies. For example, in their *Time for Life,* John P. Robinson and Geoffrey Godbey show that in fact Americans are today working less than they did in 1965, having gained nearly a full hour of free time per day. Now it is true that many people use much of their free time to "work"—to do things that, for example, are difficult or that supplement their income—but although Schor includes such activities in her "on the job" estimates, they should not be considered such because this is time people do not *need* to work to provide themselves the necessities of life. Indeed, people do not themselves consider it "work"; it is instead time they choose to "work" for other reasons, often because they simply like doing it. One other indicator of contemporary Americans' leisure: conservative estimates have it that Americans average twenty-eight hours per week watching television alone—which, at over sixty days per year, is

[10] See the summary of their data at http://reason.com/9808/fe.cox.shtml (accessed December 14, 2005). See also Mark Skousen's "Everything Is Cheap—and Getting Cheaper."

[11] For further evidence supporting this claim, see Julian L. Simon's *The State of Humanity,* pp. 20–1 and 224–30; Stephen Moore's "The Wages of Prosperity"; Stephen Moore and Julian L. Simon's, "The Greatest Century That Ever Was," http://www.cato.org/pubs/pas/pa-364es.html (accessed December 14, 2005), and *It's Getting Better All the Time;* and Robert W. Fogel, *The Fourth Great Awakening.*

far more than the average of any other nation.[12] A population that spends about one-quarter of its waking hours sitting still and doing nothing is one wealthy leisured class indeed!

The conclusion is that protections of private property, open markets, and free trade have enabled us to work far less for far more, creating thereby unprecedented levels of prosperity in America, for rich and poor alike.

One might wonder, however, whether the income gap between America's wealthy and poor has increased during this time. It is difficult to say definitely whether or not this is so, owing to the number of variables at work and the many different ways of measuring, but it probably is true.[13] If the gap has increased, however, it has only done so while the status of the poorest in America has gotten substantially better in absolute terms. So: yes, the rich might be richer, and their "lead" on the poor might have increased. But if we are concerned with the welfare of the poor, we should celebrate this fact since in absolute terms the poor are far better off than they were, and the evidence suggests that they are better off than they would have been under most other scenarios.[14] And remember that the "poor" are not the same people over time. Many of the wealthy today are the second- or third-generation descendants of the poor from before. Hence although today's poor do not have as much as today's wealthy, just give them time—and opportunity, of course.

HAS THE STATE CONTRIBUTED?

But what role has the state played in the indisputably impressive creation of wealth in America? Growing prosperity here has, after all, been correlated with growing economic intervention: over the twentieth century as Americans have gotten richer, their government has steadily grown

[12] According to Nielsen Media Research, the television is on in an average American household 7 hours and 40 minutes per day; see http://www.tvturnoff.org/images/ facts&figs/factsheets/FactsFigs.pdf (accessed December 14, 2005).

[13] See, for example, Philippe Van Kerm's "Linking Income Mobility and Inequality: A Re-assessment of American and German Inequality Trends," http://www.wider.unu.edu/ conference/conference-2003-2/conference%202003-2-papers/powerpoint% 20presentations/Philippe%20Van%20Kerm.PDF (accessed December 14, 2005).

[14] See Niels Veldhuis and Jason Clemens's "A Rising Tide Lifts All Boats," http://www. fraserinstitute.ca/admin/books/chapterfiles/A%20Rising%20Tide%20Lifts%20All% 20Boats-Jan04fftide.pdf; James R. Hines Jr. et al.'s "Another Look at Whether a Rising Tide Lifts All Boats," http://www.nber.org/papers/w8412.pdf; Aart Kraay's "When Is Growth Pro-Poor? Cross-Country Evidence," http://econ.worldbank.org/ working papers/33614; and Dollar and Kraay's "Growth Is Good for the Poor," http:// econ.worldbank.org/working papers/1696 (all sites accessed December 14, 2005).

from consuming about 10 percent of their net national product to today approximately 40 percent, and it has slowly but steadily extended its regulation of markets and private property. So perhaps, one might reasonably suggest, America's wealth has been at least partly *because* of state intervention, not *in spite* of it.

This too is a tricky matter to sort out empirically, but evidence suggests that this is in fact not the case. Strong evidence comes from the *Economic Freedom of the World* (EFW) reports compiled annually by economists James Gwartney and Robert Lawson, based on data from the United Nations, the World Bank, and other international sources. Data have been collected for some 120 countries, and what has been charted is their historical correlation between, on the one hand, "economic freedom"— which is defined as the extent to which the country's people enjoy private property rights, freedom of exchange and trade, low taxes, and an effective system of enforcing justice—and, on the other hand, wealth or poverty. So the EFW index's question is what our question has been: What kind of government is most conducive to material prosperity?

The countries most free according to 2004 EFW are, in order: Hong Kong; Singapore; New Zealand, Switzerland, United Kingdom, and United States (tied); Australia and Canada (tied); Ireland; and Luxembourg. The least free are Russia, Burundi, Republic of Congo, Guinea-Bissau, Algeria, Venezuela, Central African Republic, Democratic Republic of Congo, Zimbabwe, and, bringing up the rear, Myanmar. Some other notable countries and their economic freedom rankings: Chile, Germany, Hungary, Sweden, and Taiwan, 22 (tied); Japan, 36; France, 44; Mexico, 58; India, 68; Brazil, 74; Bangladesh, 83; and China, 90.

As this list suggests, the answer to our question seems clear. These historical surveys of countries around the world show that wealth is inversely correlated with size and intervention of government—meaning that the more decentralized or Smithian a country's government is, the wealthier it tends to be; and the more centralized or Marxian a country's government is, the poorer it tends to be. Governments limited in the way I have argued is consistent both with respecting people's 'personhood' and with Smithian recommendations are, moreover, positively correlated with:[15]

- *Per capita income.* The top quintile of "economically free" countries enjoy income that is larger than that of the bottom quintile by nearly a factor of *ten*.

---

[15] See http://www.freetheworld.com/2004/efw2004ch2.pdf (accessed December 14, 2005).

- *Economic growth.* The economies of the bottom quintile are *shrinking* by an average of 1.25 percent annually and those of the top quintile are *growing* by an average of 2.25 percent annually.
- *Development.* The top quintile scores more than twice as high on the United Nation's "Development Index"—which measures life expectancy, adult literacy rates, school enrollment, and per capita incomes—than does the lowest quintile.
- *Life expectancy.* People living in the top-quintile countries enjoy fully *twenty years* longer average life than those living in the bottom quintile.
- *Child nutrition.* Countries in the bottom quintile have more than three times as many children suffering from malnutrition than do countries in the top quintile.
- *Health care.* Approximately 60 percent of those living in countries in the bottom quintile have access to health care, while countries in the top quintile average better than 95 percent access.
- *Food production.* Countries in the top quintile produce three times as many kilograms of cereal grains per hectare than is produced by countries in the bottom quintile.

Economic freedom is thus positively correlated with all these variables, and in addition with infant survival, access to safe water, literacy rates, and percentages of gross domestic product dedicated to research and development. Two more correlations that I want to single out: the more a country's economic system approximates the classical liberal conception I have been defending, (1) the cleaner its environment tends to be and (2) the greater is its long-term political stability.

A word of explanation might be required for these last two benefits. There is an enormous amount of evidence that people take care of what is their own better than they take care of something that belongs to someone else (or that is owned communally or publicly). We might argue about *why* that is the case, but *that* it is the case seems by now beyond dispute.[16] That in a nutshell explains why economies based on private property tend to have far better records in taking care of their environments than do economies based on publicly owned or communally owned property. Under the former, people own their own property, which means they themselves enjoy the benefits if they take good care of it and suffer the consequences if they exploit it, harm it, or let it go to waste. Under the latter, by contrast, since "the public" or "the country" or "the community"

---

[16] For evidence, see Bethell's *The Noblest Triumph*, chaps. 1–4; De Soto's *The Mystery of Capital*, chaps. 1–3; Richard Epstein's *Simple Rules for a Complex World*, chap. 3 and passim; and Pipes's *Property and Freedom*, chap. 2.

owns it, no individuals stand to lose if they plunder the resources or let it go to waste. We explore this familiar "logic of the commons" further in chapter 8. For now, the important point is the fact that the more closely a country approximates the classical liberal model, the better does its treatment of its environment tend to be; and the further away from that model a country is, the worse its treatment of the environment tends to be.[17]

The last listed benefit, stability, also warrants a word of explanation. Economically free countries enjoy decentralized power, whereas the power in economically unfree countries is centralized. That is, in the former, individuals tend to have power over themselves and what they own, and groups, associations, organizations, and so on will also have power over whatever they own. That creates many different loci of power, each under the authority of different, though of course possibly overlapping, individuals or groups of individuals, and the scope of those individuals' or groups' discretion extends only to the limits of whatever it is they own. In unfree countries, by contrast, decisions tend to be made by one person or a small group of people for the whole of the country. This contrast is of considerable moment. For if an individual or a group in the former case makes a bad decision, the bad consequences redound upon only himself or themselves, or is in any case bounded by the scope of their respective authority; the other loci of power and authority remain (relatively) unaffected. In unfree, authoritarian states, however, if the leader or leaders make a bad decision, its consequences can redound upon the entire country. The result is that the social organization in a decentralized system of order—the economically free countries—is far more robust and able to withstand repeated (localized) bad decisions. Social organizations in a centralized system of order, however, are far more fragile and can collapse utterly under inept or corrupt leadership.[18] This is the explanation for the relative levels of stability enjoyed by the two kinds of society: economically free countries are more politically stable because they are decentralized and thus robust, whereas economically unfree countries are more politically unstable because they are centralized and thus fragile.

Now, one might be inclined to be skeptical of the argument if it were based on only one or two of the correlations listed above. Correlations are

---

[17] See Mikhail S. Bernstam's "Comparative Trends in Resource Use and Pollution in Market and Socialist Economies"; Bethell's *The Noblest Triumph,* chap. 18; and Epstein's *Simple Rules,* chap. 15.

[18] See Maria Pia Paganelli's "Adam Smith: Why Decentralized Systems?"

not causations, after all. But when statistically relevant correlations are found with *all* of them—well, this is a statistician's dream come true. And it makes the case very difficult to refute. It must also be pointed out that the correlations go all the way down the line. That is, wherever a country falls on the scale of economic freedom, that is approximately where it will fall on the scale of relative wealth or poverty: a top-ten country in economic freedom turns out to be top-ten in the above variables as well, a middle quintile country in economic freedom is in the middle in these variables, and so on. This implies, then, that in fact material prosperity proceeds, if at all, despite, not because of, government intervention. State intervention beyond the protections indicated by the classical liberal state therefore cannot make a people rich, at least not directly, but it certainly can make a people poor.

ARE WE STILL CONVENIENTLY OVERLOOKING THE WORLD'S POOR?

One might still be suspicious that the benefits of economic freedom accrue mainly to people already at the upper echelons of wealth. The old refrain "the rich get richer and the poor get poorer" is usually repeated here: is there any truth to it? In a word, no. That has not been true in the United States for almost all of the twentieth century, during which time *both* the rich and the poor got richer;[19] and as evidence now readily available shows, it is not true for the rest of the world, either, when Smithian policies are adopted.

Again, what is the evidence? For starters, according to a March 2001 study by the World Bank, which looked at data from fully 137 countries:[20] "private property rights, fiscal discipline, macro stability, and openness to trade increases the income of the poor *to the same extent* that it increases the income of other households in society" (p. 7; see also pp. 8, 10, and 32; emphasis added). The report specifically adds that this is not a "trickle-down" process: the benefits for rich and poor are created "contemporaneously" (p. 8). Another significant discovery of this study is that

[19] See, for example, Douglass C. North's *Institutions, Institutional Change and Economic Performance*, esp. part 3; Richard K. Vedder's *The American Economy in Historical Perspective;* Vedder and Lowell E. Galloway's *Out of Work;* and Jude Wanniski's "Memo on the Margin: A History of the 20th Century," http://www.polyconomics.com/searchbase/12-31-99.html (accessed December 14, 2005).

[20] These citations come from the page given in parentheses in Dollar and Kraay's "Growth Is Good for the Poor," http://econ.worldbank.org/files/1696_wps2587.pdf.

Smithian policies correlate with rising income among the poor more than do other factors one might wish to credit, including "government social spending, formal democratic institutions, primary school enrollment rates, and agricultural productivity" (pp. 8–9). Take another look at that: economic freedom helps the poor *more than government spending* on them does and *more even than having democratic institutions does*—defying precisely the recommendations of many of the campaigners for worldwide poor, including for example Peter Singer.

Of course, the people who recommend government spending and democratic institutions have good intentions, and so if their recommendations did not have consequences in actual human suffering, we might be inclined to forgive them as merely harmless or naïvely idealistic. But it turns out, according to the World Bank, that "reducing government consumption and stabilizing inflation are examples of policies that are 'super-pro-poor'" (p. 8)—meaning that they disproportionately benefit the poorest quintile in a country. Thus, reducing government spending, not increasing it, helps the poor. The report continues: "Social spending as a share of total spending has a *negative* relationship to income share of the poor that is close to statistical significance" (p. 9; emphasis in the original). The EFW index also comes to the same conclusion: it shows that the poorest tenth of the countries in the bottom quintile of economic freedom earn on average only 12 percent of what the poorest tenth in the freest quintile earn on average—$823 annually for the former versus $6,877 annually for the latter.[21] By advocating increased government spending, then, Singerian advocates of the poor actually advocate policies that promote poverty. Some friends.

Consider moreover that since 1965, the United States has spent some $5.4 trillion in its "War on Poverty."[22] That is about $20,000 for every man, woman, and child in the United States, a sum equal to the total 2002 gross domestic products of Germany, the United Kingdom, France, and Italy combined. Yet if the World Bank analysis is correct, it will have had no significant beneficial effect on the poor. Think about that—five and a half *trillion* dollars, and no help at all! Even the federal government has effectively admitted as much, since its official reports on American poverty levels have held them to be relatively constant over the last four

---

[21] See *Economic Freedom of the World: 2004 Annual Report*, p. 23.
[22] See Stephen Moore's "The Most Expensive Government in World History," http://www.ipi.org/ipi%5CIPIPublications.nsf/PublicationLookupQuickStudy/6505E3B3E90495EC86256B4D003EB1A9.

decades. Indeed, according to the World Bank argument, all that government spending would have had a *negative* effect, since that $5.4 trillion would otherwise have been in the private sector, stimulating the economic growth that all the evidence shows *would* have helped the poor.

And there even exists evidence that the poor have in some ways been made *worse* off since the launching of the War on Poverty. Charles Murray's *Losing Ground: American Social Policy, 1950–1980,* chronicles, in fact after dismal fact, just how systematically the welfare state has failed poor people, including blacks in particular, in America. The welfare state has not only led to new, unintended, and unforeseen problems; it did not even help in the specific areas it explicitly undertook to make better: by virtually every measurable criterion, America's poor, especially its black poor, were doing better and were on better trajectories in the 1950s than during the '60s, '70s, and '80s when the state officially undertook to make their lives better.[23] Walter Williams's *The State against Blacks* makes the same case about blacks, expanding the evidence to cover a wider sweep of American history as well as evidence from other countries, notably, South Africa.[24] And Theodore Dalrymple's powerful *Life at the Bottom: The Worldview That Makes the Underclass* makes the same case yet again, this time for the "underclass" in Britain. Dalrymple does not employ the facts and figures that Murray and Williams do; he relies instead on his anecdotal experience as a physician in the slums and prisons of England. But although his experience is anecdotal, it is a far larger sample than what one normally gets from any individual: over his years he has seen tens of thousands of cases, and he has recorded thousands of people's stories. The patterns crystallize with pellucid clarity. There is no real sense anymore, Dalrymple argues, in which one can claim that the British underclass is poor, since they all have, courtesy of the state, minimally adequate housing, food, medicine, and so on. Yet they remain an underclass and continue to lead disastrously self-destructive lives. Why?

As Dalrymple shows for the English underclass,[25] and as Murray and Williams show for the American underclass, one of the central root causes in both cases is the absence of individual initiative, common sense, and

[23] Tanner's recent *The Poverty of Welfare* updates and further substantiates Murray's analysis. See also the Federal Reserve Bank of Dallas's 1995 annual report, "By Our Own Bootstraps," and Alan Reynolds's "For the Record."

[24] For a brief recent discussion, see Myron Magnet's "Freedom vs. Dependency," http://www.opinionjournal.com/editorial/feature.html?id=110005395.

[25] See also James Bartholomew's "The Failure of the British Welfare State," http://www.fee.org/vnews.php?nid=6459, and Amy L. Wax's "What Women Want."

prudence that comes with having developed sound judgment. By not requiring them to work and think for themselves and face and learn from the consequences of their decisions and actions, the state has gradually enervated their judgment and extinguished their independence. By treating them as if they were not persons, it has effectively rendered them things.

WINNING THE ECONOMIC, AND INTELLECTUAL, CONTEST

Places that have approximated the limited governments for which I have argued have prospered, while those that have adopted expansive centralized governments have not. That is the answer to the question posed by that great economist and philosopher (and comedian), P. J. O'Rourke: "I have one fundamental question about economics: Why do some places prosper and thrive while others just suck?"[26] O'Rourke goes on to contrast the United States with Albania, Cuba, and Russia, and Hong Kong with Tanzania—in both cases drawing the obvious lessons. Alternatively, think of the different respective political and economic paths taken by places such as North versus South Korea, by China versus Hong Kong, or by "Little Havana" (Miami, Florida) versus Cuba. Each of those pairs has enjoyed similar climates, natural resources, and cultures, but their economic histories—and their levels of prosperity—could not be more different. Again, think also of the centralized authoritarian regimes of the natural resource–rich former Soviet Union, Cambodia, Mongolia, or India, and then consider the grinding poverty pervasive in each.

The economic contest has therefore been won, but the news of the victory has not reached everyone. So intellectual battles still have to be fought. Consider, for example, U.N. Secretary-General Kofi Annan's September 2, 2002, op-ed in the *Washington Post,* in which he set out what he believes should be the world's agenda for the twenty-first century. He says we face "the twin challenges of poverty and pollution," and that if we are to end the "wanton acts of destruction and the blithe self-delusion that keeps too many from seeing the perilous state of the Earth and its people," we must organize a world-wide effort. "Action," Annan gravely intones, "starts with government." Annan's position is a common one, especially among political leaders (who—pardon the cynicism—are thereby giving themselves steady work), but given what we have seen in

---

[26] In his book *Eat the Rich,* p. 1.

this and the previous chapters it is hard to imagine how a single article could go wrong in more ways.

Here are Annan's claims: (1) "We have filled the atmosphere with emissions that now threaten havoc in our lifetime"; (2) "We have felled forests, depleted fisheries and poisoned soil and water alike"; and (3) while some countries have grown rich, "too many people—in fact, the majority of humankind—have been left behind in squalor and despair."

Take these claims in turn. First, is it true that we have brought our atmosphere to this perilous state? Well, no. Although systematic evidence does not go back for more than about a century, all measurements of average concentrations of dangerous particulate matter shows them decreasing for the last several decades, despite growing populations and economies. This is true for total suspended particles, for lead, for SO_2, for ozone pollutants, for nitrous oxides, and for carbon monoxide. According to a 1992 World Bank study, "Air quality in OECD countries is vastly improved."[27] That same study cites an OECD study showing that since 1970, lead concentrations have dropped by almost 100 percent, suspended particulate matter by 60 percent, and SO_2 by 38 percent.[28]

How about the second claim? Is it true that we have depleted or poisoned our resources as Annan claims? Again, no. It is of course true that some forests have been felled and that some fisheries are being depleted, but on neither count are we anywhere near disaster. Global forestation has dropped about 20 percent within historical times but has remained relatively constant during the latter half of the twentieth century, even increasing marginally from 30.04 percent global forest cover in 1950 to 30.89 percent in 1994.[29] Indeed, forestation in North America has actually *increased* since the day Columbus arrived.[30] And Amazonian rainforest, the loss of which is much lamented, still retains about 87 percent of what it was when man first arrived there; the rate of its loss is declining as well, currently standing at only about one-half of 1 percent per year.[31]

[27] See Bjørn Lomborg's *The Skeptical Environmentalist*, p. 175.
[28] See the World Bank's *World Bank Development Report 1992: Development and the Environment*, p. 40.
[29] See the Food and Agriculture Organizations of the United Nations, *The Global Forest Resources Assessment 2000: Summary Report*, ftp://ftp.fao.org/unfao/bodies/cofo/cofo15/x9835e.pdf (accessed December 14, 2005).
[30] See Stephen Moore and Julian Simon's *It's Getting Better All the Time*, p. 204.
[31] See Lomborg, *The Skeptical Environmentalist*, pp. 114–17.

The world's total fish catch has increased steadily in the last fifty years, but the 90 million tons or so of fish mass now annually taken out of the oceans is estimated to be about 10 million tons *less* than the total sustainable amount. Thus the oceans overall are in relatively good shape;[32] and the private property voucher schemes created in places such as New Zealand, Iceland, and Australia, which have led to over 80 percent of their fish habitats at or above sustainable rates, once again demonstrate the ability of markets to succeed where government edict fails.[33] Moreover, like our atmospheric quality, both soil and water quality are, by virtually any measurement, getting better worldwide.[34] That is not to say that there are not problems, of course, or that things could not be improved—only that strong and credible evidence suggests that Julian Simon was indeed right when he claimed repeatedly that things are getting better and better.[35]

But what about those places where there *are* still problems? What about the places in the world where there are local problems with water, forests, fisheries, and so on? This brings us to the other major error in Annan's article. He notices that most of these problems are in developing, not developed, countries. But Annan fails to realize what is the most important difference between them: property rights, markets, and relatively less government regulation. If the evidence suggests anything, it is that the remedies for poverty Annan proposes—government regulation of industry, markets, and the environment—are precisely the things that have slowed and even stunted progress in developing countries. These cures are worse than the disease.

One could illustrate the point with the histories of any of the countries listed at the beginning of this section, but perhaps the recent case of Ireland will suffice. For centuries Ireland has had a negative immigration rate, meaning that more people left Ireland than came to it. It has been one of the economic backwaters of Europe for many generations. Suddenly, however, things have turned around: the immigration patterns have reversed, investment dollars are rolling in, and the economy has been growing at a robust 9 percent—far outstripping the anemic growth

---

[32] See John P. Wise's "Trends in Food from the Sea."

[33] See, for example, "A Fish Story," *Wall Street Journal Online*, November 6, 2003.

[34] See Julian L. Simon's edited *The State of Humanity*, chaps. 40, 43, and 45, and Lomborg, *The Skeptical Environmentalist*, chap. 19.

[35] For a mountain of further evidence, see Steven Hayward's *2004 Index of Leading Environmental Indicators*.

of other countries in Europe.[36] This has raised the ire of the European Union, which has reprimanded Ireland for the "reckless" policies that are siphoning off business, investment money, and talented people from the rest of Europe.

What has caused this sudden and stark about-face and turned Ireland into the "Celtic Tiger," as it is now called? Has it been the economic intervention, the managed markets, and the globally organized world governments that the Secretary-General of the United Nations recommends? No. Ireland lowered its taxes. Ireland cut its capital-gains tax from 40 percent to 20 percent and its top marginal personal income tax rate from 48 percent to 42 percent, and it reduced its corporate tax rate to 12.5 percent, one of the lowest rates in the developed world.[37] In so doing, it signaled to investors and entrepreneurs around the world that it is a place of opportunity. As the evidence presented in this chapter suggests, wherever there is opportunity, entrepreneurs will come—and wealth will follow them.

Kofi Annan says he is concerned about the poor, and he claims that governments must come to their rescue by taxing wealthy nations and giving some of those proceeds to poorer nations. But that means is inconsistent with the end. What the mounting evidence indicates is that what the poor need is secure property rights and markets—and then they will take care of themselves.

A MATTER OF MORE THAN JUST MONEY

Deciding what system of government to adopt is thus directly related to how much its citizens will prosper: decentralized systems based on markets and private property allow the most prosperity, whereas centralized systems based on regulation, bureaucracy, and "welfare" agencies precipitate economic stagnation and actually retard the poor's ability to escape poverty. That makes the issue not just a matter of economic concern, but one of considerable moral importance as well. But nothing mentioned so far takes into account the substantial human toll that is not based on money.

The relative comparisons invoked thus far do not count, for example, the approximately *one hundred million innocents killed* during the twentieth

---

[36] See Ben Powell's "The Celtic Tiger," http://www.techcentralstation.com/091002M.html (accessed December 14, 2005).
[37] See Brian M. Carney, "The Secrets and Perils of Ireland's Success."

century in the name of Marxian or quasi-Marxian ideals. Some of the execrable highlights:[38]

- *The Soviet Union.* Lenin, 1917–24: 4,017,000 dead; Stalin, 1929–53: 42,672,000 dead. The Soviet slave-labor system created by Lenin and expanded by Stalin killed almost 40 million people in about seventy years—more than twice as many as killed by four hundred years of brutal African slave trade.
- *China.* Mao Tse-tung, 1927–76: 37,828,000 dead. The actual number might be even higher, since, unlike the case with the former Soviet Union, China has not yet opened its archives to Western researchers, and so the hard numbers remain difficult to get. Some scholars suspect the final tally will have Mao surpassing Stalin in total number of people murdered.
- *Cambodia.* Pol Pot, 1968–87: 2,397,000 dead. In absolute terms, Pol Pot's number of killed is only a fraction of Stalin's or Mao's, but controlled for population size, he was the most lethal murderer in the twentieth century: from 1975 to 1979, he killed 8 percent of his population annually. In less than four years of governing, his Khmer Rouge killed 31 percent of all men, women, and children in Cambodia; the odds of any person surviving during those four years were only 2.2 to 1.

The state that is consistent with respecting people's 'personhood,' that is economically free, and that adopts Smithian recommendations has therefore more to recommend it than one might have suspected: it may literally mean the difference between life and death. This kind of society will not be perfect—no society ever will be—but morality and history combine to show that it is superior to any other known alternative. If you want to help the world's poor and oppressed, then, do not lobby for government aid, do not lobby for massive wealth transfer, and do not, God forbid, advocate the expansion of government powers over individuals. Lobby instead for free trade, for markets, for private property, for punishment of injustice, and for the widest possible scope of individual liberty compatible with everyone else enjoying the same liberty. As I argued in chapter 3, this is the vision of government going back at least to the Magna Carta in the thirteenth century, through the Levellers and John Locke in the seventeenth century, and adopted and endorsed by

[38] These numbers are principally from Robert Conquest, *Reflections on a Ravaged Century*, chaps. 1 and 3–7; Stéphane Courtois's edited *The Black Book of Communism*, parts 1, 2, and 4; and R. J. Rummel's *Death by Government*, chap. 1.

Adam Smith and America's founders in the eighteenth century. History has now declared them the winners of this debate, so there is no longer any empirical question at stake.[39]

But this is not a merely academic debate since actual human lives and actual human suffering are at stake. Perhaps you and I are lucky enough to live in one of the wealthiest countries, lucky—and wealthy—enough to enjoy the luxury of not really noticing the other-side-of-the-world effects of our imprudent politics. But others do feel those consequences, and they do not have the luxury of ignoring economic, political, and historical reality with impunity.

INCENTIVES: EXAMPLES

I spoke in chapters 2 and 3 of *incentives* and how it matters considerably how they are aligned. People take notice when they suffer from the consequences of their own bad decisions, and they are thereby induced to seek out and try alternative courses of action. This *natural necessity* disciplines them to overcome their inclinations to otherwise not bother to pay attention and to do nothing. On the other hand, if this connection between decision making and responsibility is severed, if this natural necessity is absent, people lose this discipline and their natural inclinations to laziness can lead them into profligacy.

Departments of motor vehicles are good illustrations. Their incompetence is legendary. Consider how much time you have had to spend waiting in line—hours, no doubt—to do things that should have taken only minutes, and that you probably should have been able to do online. Why are they so bad? They are *so* bad, in fact, that true stories about them sound for all the world like Monty Python-esque satires. Take the recent goings-on in Nevada. Waits in the Nevada DMV offices were getting so long recently—in 1999 the average wait was an incredible

---

[39] I would be remiss if I did not name some recent criticisms of the view I am defending. Some influential ones are Amy Chua's *World on Fire,* John Gray's *False Dawn,* Joseph Stiglitz's *Globalization and Its Discontents,* and Erik Olin Wright's *Class Counts.* Since the majority view among politicians and academics (outside economics) strongly favors government intervention and aid rather than the classical liberal state, other critics of my view are very easy to find. One reason I have focused primarily on evidence and work supporting my view is that, again outside economics, it is typically far less familiar. For other work that in various ways supports the conclusions I reach, see that of (details in the bibliography): Barber, Bauer, Bhagwati, Hicks, Higgs, Jones, Lal, Landes, Norberg, North, North and Thomas, Rosenberg and Birdzell, Seabright, Surowiecki, Weede, and Wolf.

three to five hours—that some Nevadans started threatening DMV workers, telling them that they were going to kill them or that they should
watch out when they leave work. I think we can all understand the frustration involved with queuing for an hour, only to be told that one has
to wait in another line, for another hour of course, then only to be told
that our forms were not properly filled out and we will have to come
back another day—a weekday, meaning yet another day off work. What
was Nevada governor Kenny Guinn's solution to this problem? Was it to
abolish all those tedious, Soviet-style make-work forms that everyone is
required to fill out? Or to fire all the unmotivated incompetents who staff
the offices? Or perhaps to end Nevada's "sick time" policy that leads to
state worker absenteeism rates averaging an unbelievable 49 percent? Oh
no. Instead, according to an editor of the *Las Vegas Review-Journal,* "The
governor . . . asked members of the Legislature's Interim Finance Committee to provide funding for armed guards in the Las Vegas and Reno
DMV offices, to keep these unruly peasants in line."[40] So it is not that
anything has to change with the DMV; no, the governor's comical conclusion is that the citizens must be "persuaded"—by the threat of armed
guards, of course!—simply to grin and bear it.

Now, in fairness to Governor Guinn and Nevada's DMVs, a concerted,
and expensive, effort has now been made to reduce average waiting times,
with the result that in 2001, according to the director of the Nevada DMV,
"eighty percent of residents now wait an hour or less in lines" and they
have "come close" to meeting the one-hour average wait goal set by the
governor.[41] Approaching a one-hour wait time average is a substantial
reduction from the three-to-five-hour average wait time of just two years
earlier, but it is still waiting for an hour! Ask yourself this: when was the
last time you had to stand in line for an hour waiting to get your purchase
refunded or exchanged at a department store? Or to have your Visa card
transaction completed? My guess is the answer is "never." The Nevada
DMV director points out in his agency's defense that they have to process
about one thousand transactions per day. That seems like a lot—until
you find out that Visa, for example, processes almost one hundred *million*
transactions worldwide per day, or about five thousand per second, each

---

[40] Vin Suprynowicz, "And Now . . . Armed Guards at the DMV," *Las Vegas Review-
Journal,* December 8, 2000. Http://www.billstclair.com/blog/vin/001208.html (accessed
December 14, 2005).
[41] See Ed Vogel's "Report to the Legislature: DMV Nears Guinn's Hour-Wait Goal," *Las
Vegas Review-Journal,* January 27, 2001.

taking only seconds and enjoying a nearly perfect accuracy rate of almost 100 percent.

Other government ventures fare similarly badly. Despite increasing ticket revenues, Amtrak, America's government-owned and government-operated passenger railroad system, lost $903 million in 1999 and $2.5 billion over the previous three years.[42] Since its creation in 1970, Amtrak has received almost $25 billion in subsidies from the U.S. federal government, and still it has lost money; and this despite carrying only 0.3 percent of intercity passengers, running more slowly than trains ran on the same routes fifty years ago, and posting consistently abysmal on-time performance ratings. But what is the solution that the people in charge of Amtrak offer? Yet more state money. Amtrak president David Gunn threatened Congress in 2003 that without a *doubling* of its current subsidy, bringing it up to $2 billion per year, and without several billion additional dollars for maintenance and repairs, Amtrak might not survive even one more year.

The U.S. Post Office, to take one final conspicuous example, is the largest civilian government agency in America; it enjoys a state-enforced monopoly on the delivery of first- and third-class mail and on the use of mailboxes; it pays no federal, state, or local taxes; and any private competitor must by law charge more than double what the USPS charges for the same service.[43] Under such extraordinarily favorable competitive circumstances, who, you might think, could possibly fail? Well, the USPS fails, and impressively. The Post Office has over the last four decades taken

---

[42] See "Amtrak Continues to Lose Money," *Memphis Business Journal,* July 25, 2001, http://www.bizjournals.com/memphis/stories/2001/07/23/daily22.html?t=printable. Other sources for the information I present about Amtrak include Pamela Hasterok's "Public Trains in Public Hands"; Iain Murray's "Privatizing Rail, Avoiding the Pitfalls: Lessons from the British Experience," http://www.cei.org/gencon/025,04546.cfm; "National Corridors Initiative: Interviewing David Gunn of Amtrak," July 31, 2002, http://www.nationalcorridors.org/features/gunn073102.shtml; Joseph Vranich and Edward L. Hudgins's "Help Passenger Rail by Privatizing Amtrak"; and Joseph Vranich, Cornelius Chapman, and Edward L. Hudgins's "Time to Liquidate Amtrak," http://www.cato.org/dailys/02-14-02.html (all sites accessed December 14, 2005).

[43] Sources for information about the U.S. Post Office include James Bovard's "Slower Is Better: The New Postal Service," http://www.cato.org/pubs/pas/pa-146es.html; Collinge and Ayers's "First-Class Mail, Third-Class Competition"; "Going L'Postal," *Wall Street Journal Online,* July 23, 2004; Edward L. Hudgins's "A Holiday Gift: Post Office Going Private?"; Robert Knautz's edited "Privatizing the Post Office," http://www.free-market.net/features/spotlight/9901.html; and Brian Summers's "The Postal Monopoly," http://www.libertyhaven.com/theoreticalorphilosophicalissues/economics/monopolyandindustrialorganization/postalmono.html (all sites accessed December 14, 2005).

progressive steps toward considerably easing its workload by abolishing Sunday mail pickups, moving final mail pickup times back from 5 P.M. to 4 or even 3 P.M., reducing service hours, and phasing out individual home delivery and instead relying increasingly on "cluster boxes" where many people's mail is deposited and the individuals must then retrieve it themselves. Despite all this, however, and despite the tremendous gains in technology at its disposal, the Post Office's average delivery times have actually gotten *longer.* Benjamin Franklin announced a goal in 1764 of delivering mail between New York City and Philadelphia in two days; one hundred years ago the Postmaster General said that it should be the goal of the Post Office by the middle of the twentieth century to deliver mail from anywhere to anywhere in the country in two days. Yet in 1991 the USPS claimed it a "success" to be able to deliver mail between New York City and neighboring Westchester County in two days. The private company Federal Express, by contrast, will guarantee *overnight* delivery to any location in the United States, and many locations elsewhere in the world. Since 1969 the average delivery time for a first-class letter has increased 22 percent, and for this increasingly poor service Americans have had to pay increasingly more: first-class stamp rates have increased over 300 percent, from 6 cents to 39 cents. The Post Office's delivery rates have gotten so bad, in fact, that it has stopped publishing its failure rates and claims the information is now "proprietary." Watchdog groups estimate, however, that the Post Office struggles to successfully deliver mail by advertised deadlines 85 percent of the time; Federal Express, by contrast, has a 99.82 percent worldwide delivery success rate, and that is with the majority of its packages being guaranteed for next-day delivery. One study estimates, "The Postal Service is probably losing or throwing out over a billion letters a year"; at about 0.5 percent of its total volume, that is roughly fifty times the loss rate of Federal Express.

One could multiply such examples. The question, again, is why these state-run affairs routinely do so poorly, especially when compared with private competitors. The answer in large part is incentives. State-enforced monopolies give all the wrong incentives by divorcing punishment and reward from actual production. If a private company is consistently incompetent, consistently loses money, consistently loses out to competition, or consistently frustrates and displeases its customers, it will soon have no more customers and it will go out of business. That creates strong incentives to look for ways to please customers, to remain competitive, and to continually reduce costs. But the state-run enterprises face no such market incentives. They get money no matter what, and often their very failures are used as reasons to justify increasing their subsidies rather than cutting them off. Despite their own best intentions, people are inclined by nature to be lazy: if they are not forced by natural necessity to innovate, compete, strive, and contend, they will tend not to. The state-enforced monopoly is just the security they need to rest on their laurels without facing any real repercussions, and the predictable result is exactly what we do in fact see: increasing and widespread stagnation, waste, and incompetence.

I cannot resist adding one more spectacular example that has recently come to the world's attention. The Scottish Parliament, which gained limited independence from England's in 1999, decided that it needed a new, august building that could properly house its new, august self. It began construction in 1997—before the body was even officially elected, in anticipation of the event—on an impressive facility in its capital city Edinburgh, right next to Holyrood Palace, the Scottish home for the monarchs of the United Kingdom. At the time of breaking ground the total projected cost of the edifice was £40,000,000, or about $68,000,000. Now, several years and countless "setbacks," "unforeseen problems," "accounting errors," hearings, and investigations later, the total final cost will be over £450,000,000—a greater than ten-fold increase![44] That is approximately £90 for every man, woman, and child in Scotland, for just this one single government project. Lots of people are upset about this, of course, and the newspapers editorialize against it; many different people have been fingered for the blame and there has been an admirable display of righteous indignation, of shock and horror, and the obligatory promises for reform. But no one has been fired, no one has been jailed, and no one has been shot, guillotined, hanged, or even run out on a rail. So construction and profligacy continue unabated. Who knows how much it will actually cost when the final accounting is completed, if it ever is? But the crucial point to make is: should we really have expected anything different? The parliamentarians are not spending their *own* money, and naturally, therefore, no expense is spared and no luxury omitted: a "brilliant" and "imaginative" design from Enric Miralles, an "avant-garde" Catalonian architect; state-of-the-art technology and exotic materials throughout; unique and nonstandard windows, walls, desks, doors,

---

[44] There is now an official inquiry under way, whose activities can be tracked here and which provides an overview of the spectacle so far: http://www.holyroodinquiry.org/index.htm. One wonders how much the blue-ribbon inquiry itself will end up costing. Here is yet another story about yet another recent "delay": http://news.scotsman.com/topics.cfm?tid=276&id=844122004 (both sites accessed December 14, 2005).

bathroom fixtures, chairs, and so on—all raising the cost, of course. No one is so generous as when he is spending someone else's money. And all this, it must be remembered, is for a parliament that is still partially under the authority of the Parliament in London: four hundred million pounds for a largely advisory board to contemplate and discuss Scotland's future! Had I known, I would have told them that I was available for half that price. All kidding aside, this case perfectly captures the perverse incentives involved in state-run enterprises, and it amply demonstrates why we should restrict them, or perhaps beat them back bodily, to the smallest number and the fewest responsibilities humanly possible.[45]

That is not to imply that in the private sector market forces *guarantee* constant innovation or perfect customer service. Human beings are fallible and imperfect, and any human system of organization will reflect that. The comparison is rather with actual alternatives: under which system— state-run or privately run—should we expect better service overall? History and everyday experience confirm that it is in the private sector, and the respective alignment of incentives explains why. An entire field in economics, called "public choice," has arisen in the last forty years or so, complete now with its own Nobel laureates—a founding father of public choice economics, James Buchanan, won the Nobel prize for economics in 1986 for his pioneering work in the field[46]—to study exactly how such incentives influence behavior in government and private sectors, and a now impressively large body of data has been assembled that validates exactly this conclusion. No system is perfect, but waste and incompetence multiply in the security provided by the "public" or government sector, and they are punished and reduced in the produce-or-perish arena of the "private" sector.

---

[45] Lest it appear I am being overly critical of the Scots, I bring to the reader's attention just one contemporary example from the United States—and as one might expect from America, a waste of public monies on an even more colossal scale: Boston's so-called Big Dig underground highway construction project. Here is *Governing Magazine*'s recent summary: "The Bay State [has] embarrassed itself with its handling of the fiscally mismanaged 'Big Dig,' the Boston highway project that ran up the largest capital cost overrun in U.S. history. The Big Dig was originally supposed to cost slightly more than $2 billion and ended up with a price tag closer to $15 billion. Even when the project was largely finished and seemed to have survived its troubles, it began developing new ones. In the past few months, a series of leaks in its Interstate 93 tunnel have been making news." Http://governing.com/gpp/2005/ma.htm (accessed December 14, 2005).

[46] Perhaps the founding document in the field is Buchanan and Tullock's *The Calculus of Consent*.

BUSINESS POWER VERSUS STATE POWER

It is an element of commonly received wisdom that politics is a sordid affair, and that, despite the occasional notable exception, most politicians are crooked and most bureaucrats are surly, pampered, and lazy petty tyrants. Though widely held, these beliefs do not noticeably deter most people from a seemingly inextinguishable faith that the *next* batch of politicians will straighten it all out, because the new ones, we are always sure, will be imbued with the noble sentiment of "public service" people speak of so reverently. This faith is especially apparent when discussion turns to public schooling, where hope does indeed spring eternal. We reserve discussion of public schooling until chapter 6, but even on the basis of the examples mentioned here—departments of motor vehicles, Amtrak, the Post Office, and the Scottish Parliament building—one can probably safely say that although one suspected that government enterprises were not exactly paragons of virtue and efficiency, the actual extent of their corruption and waste is still shocking to behold. When one generalizes this level of failure to the other arms of the government (have another look at the Appendix to chapter 2), one begins to get an inkling of just how large the *unseen* damage is.

In a famous 1850 essay entitled "What Is Seen and What Is Unseen," French economist Frédéric Bastiat highlighted the "unseen" in economics by pointing out a common fallacy.[47] If a thug throws a rock through a baker's window, some people say it is actually a good thing, since now the glazier who will replace the window gets some work. But the glazier's new work, Bastiat says, is what is *seen;* what is *unseen* is what the baker would have done with the money he now has to give to the glazier. Perhaps he would have bought himself a new suit, and thus given work to the tailor; perhaps he would have saved it in a bank, freeing funds to help an entrepreneur start a new venture; perhaps he would have helped pay for his child's tutor. The point is that all that people usually see is the immediate effect—the glazier gets work—while not pausing to consider, partly because it is "unseen" and thus requires thought to understand, all the things that might instead have taken place and that, because they would have been what the persons in question *wanted* to do instead of what they *had* to do, would have constituted a far greater satisfaction of their interests. Bastiat's lesson is a sound one. Politicians and publicists

---

[47] In *Selected Essays on Political Economy*, pp. 1–50.

routinely, or conveniently, forget it, but since the unseen damage is in lost opportunities for actual people, for you and me, we, at least, would do well to remember it.

Yet some argue that despite government's failures and the further fact that its failures are coercively enforced, one should not forget that business too has failures and that business can often exercise power over people as well. A recurring charge from critics of business is that unregulated markets can lead to monopolies, to people losing their savings in bad investments, and to periods of "boom and bust"; and that businesses and their advertisers can carefully shape or indeed manipulate consumers' preferences so that consumers come to believe that they "absolutely must have" or "just cannot live without" whatever the company wants to sell them.[48]

This argument reminds one of what P. T. Barnum is reputed to have said, that a sucker is born every minute. People can indeed be talked into all sorts of things, and as I have had occasion to mention elsewhere, the world has an apparently endless supply of con men and charlatans who are only too happy to help part a fool and his money. Con men will never go away, however, no matter how many times we outlaw them; so the only real question is how can we minimize their effectiveness. The answer, I propose, is by encouraging people not to be so gullible and to develop a healthy skepticism—in other words, to develop good *judgment*. And how do we help people do this? Precisely by not rescuing them every time they make a bad decision, and by thus introducing natural incentives for them to wise up. You will never make people wise or give them good judgment by protecting them from the consequences of their bad decisions or from trying to prevent them from being able to make bad decisions in the first place. That would be like trying to teach people how to be skilled mountain climbers by never letting them get near mountains for fear they might fall and hurt themselves. People will make mistakes, yes, and some people will pay high prices for their mistakes—there is no getting around that, under my scheme or any other you can think of. The only matter at issue is how to hold those mistakes to a minimum, and I submit to you that our best chance to do that is by encouraging each individual to develop judgment on his own.

---

[48] For a discussion sympathetic to the notion of business power, see John Christman's *The Myth of Property*. For a good general discussion of some of the issues involved here, see Anne Cunningham's "Autonomous Consumption"; see also James Stacey Taylor's "Autonomy, Coercion, and Distress."

But what about monopolies and manipulative advertising campaigns? Let us take a clear-eyed look at the matter. There are monopolies, but probably every successful monopoly known to man has been successful only because it has been chartered, supported, or defended by the coercive sword of the state.[49] Governments grant monopolies all the time and have always done so; in America today we have state-granted monopolies in utilities, schooling, broadcasting, and so on, effected by licensing restrictions, outlawing competition, or prohibitive tariffs and subsidies. Some of these monopolies are indeed successful, but only because coercive measures are adopted to enforce them. Strip them of their special legal protections, and see how long they can continue to monopolize their respective markets. And that is exactly what we see in actual, that is to say, free markets: successful monopolies in competitive markets are as rare as the proverbial bird. At one time in America everyone worried about the "monopoly" of U.S. Steel and how we would soon all be beholden to it; there were congressional hearings, talk of government anti-trust action, and much general fright. Then what happened? Other companies started making steel for less money—and guess what: all of U.S. Steel's vaunted and feared "power" just evaporated. Similarly, we have been nervous about General Motors, about IBM, about AT&T, about Microsoft; we have similarly held congressional hearings and talked of (and sometimes acted on) taking legal measures. And what happened in each case? Again, a little competition goes a long way: the Japanese made small, cheap, and efficient cars; Apple computers came along; Sprint appeared and then Lord knows how many cellular phone companies; the internet happened— and *poof!* all that power just went away. Those companies might well have had, and some still do have, a lot of money, but when it comes down to it, what does all that money really matter if you and I and everyone else can just go right next door and buy from someone else? The fact of the matter is that no business can retain its market share unless it continues to please the customer, and does so better than others. Consumers are exquisitely demanding—exasperatingly so, if you ask any businessman— and their loyalty is to the satisfaction of their own interests above all else, above anything they feel for any company, business, or brand. If they do not like your product, they drop you like a hot potato without batting an

---

[49] For both theoretical and historical analysis of monopolies and monopolistic behavior, see the works of (details in the bibliography): Armentano, Bork, McChesney and Shugart, Posner, and Vedder and Galloway. For a classic account, see Adam Smith's *Wealth of Nations*, pp. 78ff., 630ff., 647ff., 740–1, and 755; and *Lectures on Jurisprudence*, pp. 471–2, 497–8, and 529.

eye. Today's business "monopoly" is tomorrow's historical artifact and case study in a business class. When it comes to markets, the consumer really is king.[50]

And that gives the lie, I believe, to claims about our being manipulated or even brainwashed by advertising. If an advertiser defrauds people, that is one thing, and it is true that the difference between putting a "positive spin" on something and offering a "misleading" description can sometimes be hard to tell. But the thousands and thousands of failed businesses, the fact that indeed one out of every three new business ventures fails within two years, and the fact that advertising companies themselves have among the highest turnover and failure rates in business amply demonstrate that if businesses have the power to manipulate and brainwash, they apparently are not aware of it. They might well trigger a new desire in you, but there is nothing forcing you to act on it. I did not have a desire for a Lamborghini Countach sports car before I first saw a picture of one years ago in *Car and Driver* magazine, but that does not mean that I suddenly had no choice in whether to buy one or not. Okay, I cannot afford a Lamborghini, but the point holds for other things too. You might not have wanted a pair of Nike shoes until you saw Michael Jordan wearing them or a VCR before you saw one; and you probably never could have imagined how important e-mail could be to your life until you began to use it, and now you cannot imagine *not* having it. All of that is true, but none of it means that you had no choice in the matter. Could you do without a VCR? Of course. You probably have a DVD player instead now anyway. Could you do without a cell phone or without e-mail? Again, of course you could: the fact that you choose not to do without them does not mean you *couldn't* (there were a few human beings who existed before cell phones and e-mail, after all); and remember that there are always options about *which* cell phone company to use, which internet service provider to use, and so on. Finally, do not forget the fact that there are lots and lots and lots of things that you would *never* buy no matter how slick the ad campaign was or how many other people you know did. There is some breakfast cereal, for example, that will never be in my house; likewise with some music, some movies, some books, some kinds of alcohol, and, for that matter, some people, and I could not care less what their advertisers or supporters or spokesmen have to say on their behalf. And the same holds true, I am sure, for you.

---

[50] I borrow this phrase from Ludwig von Mises's "The Sovereignty of the Consumers," in his *Human Action*, pp. 270–3. See also George Reisman, *Capitalism*, chap. 6.

I think we should bear those considerations in mind when we hear someone going on about the "power" that businesses have over you.[51] If you do not like the product your department of motor vehicles is giving you, you have little choice since they have legally enacted their own monopoly; similarly with Amtrak, with the Post Office, and with every other agency of the state. If you decide, for example, that you do not like what your tax dollars are going to support in the National Endowment for the Arts, what choice do you have? Try not paying that portion of your taxes: the state will (eventually) look you up and want to have a word with you. If you persist in your obstreperousness, in the end men with guns will come and take you away. *That* is power to make you do what they want. You might hate Bill Gates and wish that Linux or Apple or whatever were used by more people than use Microsoft products, but if you decide to go with Apple, Bill Gates does not, and cannot, send men with guns to take you away.

The natural state of business power is thus temporary, dependent, and only provisionally granted at the pleasure of individual consumers; the natural state of government power, by contrast, is irresistible, absolute, and indifferent to what any individual citizen wishes. To succeed, a business must convince me to choose it, and in so trying it is respecting my personhood; by contrast, however, to succeed, a state simply makes me do what it wants, and in so doing it disrespects my personhood. Now, it is sometimes claimed that the right to vote in a democratic or quasi-democratic society is what constitutes respect for my personhood. Not quite.[52] If the vote does not go my way in politics, people do not shrug their shoulders, say "live and let live," and leave me to my own devices; no, they send their men with guns to make me comply or take me away. On the other hand, if a majority of the people prefer Microsoft while I prefer Linux, well, I can still go get Linux. Even if there were no alternative to Microsoft—something that could hardly happen in a market with open competition, since there are always entrepreneurs out there looking for ways to get a slice of the market's profit by catering to people unsatisfied with what is already available—I am still free to not buy Microsoft.

---

[51] See Thomas Sowell's "Economic 'Power,'" http://www.townhall.com/columnists/thomassowell/ts20031211.shtml (accessed December 14, 2005).

[52] For a good discussion of the lack of "causal" power of voting in contemporary democratic regimes, see Gordon Graham's *The Case against the Democratic State*, chaps. 2–4. You might also have a look at my review of Graham's book: http://www.independent.org/tii/content/pubs/review/books/tir91_graham.html (accessed December 14, 2005).

Many historians have credited the success of Europe and its colonies in the last five hundred years or so to its increasing adoption of what is often called a "contract" society and its gradual abandonment of a "status" society. The contract society is one based on people entering into voluntary transactions and agreements with one another; it is the society based on limited government, markets, and social power. The status society, on the other hand, is the one run by political power. In the former, people succeed by innovation, enterprise, industry, perseverance, and self-discipline, and by finding ways to please and not frustrate or alienate or force or imprison or kill others; in the latter, people succeed by conquest, by force or threat of force, and by ingratiating themselves to those in power. What these historians have argued is that the evidence suggests that societies of the former type are vibrant, growing, and diverse; societies of the latter type are adversarial, bellicose, and stagnating. Economist Nathan Rosenberg made this case in his 1986 *How the West Grew Rich;* economist David Landes made the case again in his 1999 *The Wealth and Poverty of Nations;* historian Jacques Barzun made it again, though in a different way, in his massive *From Dawn to Decadence: 1500 to the Present: 500 Years of Western Cultural Life;*[53] and social scientist Charles Murray has made the case yet again, in a different way, in his 2003 *Human Accomplishment.* Jared Diamond's chapter "From Egalitarianism to Kleptocracy," from his Pulitzer Prize-winning 1999 *Guns, Germs, and Steel: The Fates of Human Societies,* shows how even a person antithetical to market economies nevertheless recognizes how differently societies of contract versus societies of status fare, how much of human progress in the last half-millennia or so can be attributed to the opportunities and incentives provided by the former, and how the existence of the latter slows and retards progress, sometimes with catastrophic results.

Numerous other studies have reached similar conclusions; I list more in the bibliography. I bring this up not only in the hopes that it will encourage you to have a look at some of these studies, but also to highlight the difference between social and business power, on the one hand, and political power, on the other. Reliance on the former, and thus on the society of contract based on it, is the only one consistent with respecting personhood and with wanting everyone to prosper. The latter, and the society of status based on it, is a society fit not for 'persons' but for 'things,' and of course for the conquerors, exploiters, pirates, and brigands who hope to bend them to their own ends.

---

[53] You may be interested to see my review of Barzun's book: http://www.bama.ua.edu/~jotteson/barzun.pdf (accessed December 14, 2005).

Grand Unification Social Theory

I predict that many people on thus coming to the conclusion of Part I of this book will remain skeptical about the limited government it recommends. They may still have lingering doubts about its practicality, or they may continue to think that respecting people's personhood must somehow mean using the state's coercive apparatus to do positive things for them, not just relying on their capacity to do things for themselves or using only the voluntarily offered help of other private individuals and organizations. Or, finally, they may think that while the classical liberal state may perhaps have sufficed in the eighteenth century or for America's founding, nevertheless it is—or somehow must be—outdated or otherwise inapplicable now. I understand these hesitations, even if I no longer share them. I once did share them, though, and it was only after long investigation and consideration that I came to adopt the views I have defended here. Like Robert Nozick, whose 1974 *Anarchy, State, and Utopia* articulated and defended a libertarian state similar in part to the classical liberalism I have defended here, I am quite aware that the position I have adopted puts me in the minority, especially among academics.[54]

But having conducted these investigations, having looked into the actual functioning of so many state programs, agencies, bureaus, and institutes, and having compared their relative levels of success with the levels achieved by private individuals and private organizations, I have found that the discrepancies could not be more pronounced. The local knowledge argument, natural necessity and incentives, and the nature of decentralized versus centralized systems of order—all these *explained* the discrepancies. And when I realized that the classical liberal political vision that is presupposed by the private, decentralized systems of order is also consistent with a true respect for the humanity, the 'personhood,' of others, then the pieces of the puzzle fell into place. It therefore forms, I believe, a quite powerful argument. Nothing beyond the classical liberal state is consistent with respect for persons, and, in a spectacular piece of good fortune, it turns out that human beings are also far more able to succeed and flourish under precisely that kind of state than under any

---

[54] I note, for what it is worth, that Nozick went on in later work to raise doubts about his own position. See, for example, the chapter "The Zigzag of Politics," in his 1989 *The Examined Life* (though he apparently never abandoned the core principles of *Anarchy, State, and Utopia:* see Roderick Long's "Robert Nozick, Philosopher of Liberty"). Economist Daniel Klein has recently offered an intriguing hypothesis to explain why people, especially academics, tend to oppose political positions calling for limited government. See his "The People's Romance."

other. At the end of the day, then, the most compelling guiding principle of morality—respect for personhood—turns out to make precisely the same recommendations that empirically the most beneficial system of government—classical liberalism—does. It is a grand unification theory for human social life, and, in my estimation at least, it is just as deserving of awe and admiration as what Einstein struggled in vain to discover would have been.

Bibliography

Adair, Douglass. "Fame and the Founding Fathers." In *Fame and the Founding Fathers: Essays by Douglass Adair.* Trevor Colbourn, ed. Indianapolis, Ind.: Liberty Fund, 1998.

"A Fish Story." *Wall Street Journal Online,* November 6, 2003.

"Amtrak Continues to Lose Money." *Memphis Business Journal,* July 25, 2001. Http://www.bizjournals.com/memphis/stories/2001/07/23/daily22.html, accessed December 14, 2005.

Annan, Kofi. Op-ed. *Washington Post,* September 2, 2002.

Armentano, Dominick T. *Antitrust and Monopoly: Anatomy of a Policy Failure,* 2nd ed. Oakland, Calif.: Independent Institute, 1996.

Armentano, Dominick T. *Antitrust: The Case for Repeal,* rev. 2nd ed. Auburn, Ala.: Ludwig von Mises Institute, 1999.

Barber, Benjamin R. *Jihad vs. McWorld: How Globalism and Tribalism Are Reshaping the World.* New York: Ballantine, 1996.

Bartholomew, James. "The Failure of the British Welfare State." December 8, 2004. Http://www.fee.org/vnews.php?nid=6459, accessed March 15, 2005.

Bartlett, Bruce. "How Poor Are the Poor?" Washington, D.C.: National Center for Policy Analysis, 2001. Http://www.ncpa.org/ba/ba185.html, accessed December 14, 2005.

Barzun, Jacques. *From Dawn to Decadence: 1500 to the Present: 500 Years of Western Cultural Life.* New York: HarperCollins, 2000.

Bastiat, Frédéric. "What Is Seen and What Is Not Seen." In *Selected Essays on Political Economy.* Irvington-on-Hudson, N.Y.: Foundation for Economic Education, 1968 (1850).

Bauer, Peter. *The Development Frontier: Essays in Applied Economics.* London: Harvester Wheatsheaf, 1991.

Bauer, Peter. *From Subsistence to Exchange and Other Essays.* Princeton, N.J.: Princeton University Press, 2000.

Bennhold, Katrin. "Love of Leisure, and Europe's Reasons." *New York Times,* July 29, 2004.

Bernstam, Mikhail S. "Comparative Trends in Resource Use and Pollution in Market and Socialist Economies." In *The State of Humanity.* Julian L. Simon, ed. Oxford: Blackwell, 1995.

Bethell, Tom. *The Noblest Triumph: Property and Prosperity through the Ages.* New York: St. Martin's Press, 1998.

Bhagwati, Jagdish. *In Defense of Globalization*. Oxford: Oxford University Press, 2004.

Bork, Robert. *The Antitrust Paradox: A Policy at War with Itself*. New York: Free Press, 1993.

Bovard, James. "Slower Is Better: The New Postal Service." *Cato Policy Analysis No. 146*. Washington, D.C.: Cato Institute, 1991. Http://www.cato.org/pubs/pas/pa-146.html, accessed December 14, 2005.

Buchanan, James, and Gordon Tullock. *The Calculus of Consent: Logical Foundations of Constitutional Democracy*. Indianapolis, Ind.: Liberty Fund, 1999 (1962).

Carney, Brian M. "The Secrets and Perils of Ireland's Success." *Wall Street Journal Online*, May 30, 2001.

Christman, John. *The Myth of Property: Toward an Egalitarian Theory of Ownership*. New York: Oxford University Press, 1994.

Chua, Amy. *World on Fire: How Exporting Free Market Democracy Breeds Ethnic Hatred and Global Instability*. New York: Doubleday, 2002.

Collinge, Robert A., and Ronald M. Ayers. "First-Class Mail, Third-Class Competition." *The Freeman: Ideas on Liberty*, April 1995. Http://www.fee.org/publications/the-freeman/article.asp?aid=3571, accessed December 14, 2005.

Conquest, Robert. *Reflections on a Ravaged Century*. New York: Norton, 2001.

Courtois, Stéphane, et al., eds. *The Black Book of Communism: Crimes, Terror, Repression*. Cambridge, Mass.: Harvard University Press, 1999.

Cox, W. *Myths of the Rich and Poor: Why We're Better Off Than We Think*. New York: Basic Books, 1999.

Cox, W. Michael, and Richard G. Alm. "Buying Time." *Reason* (August/September 1998). Http://reason.com/9808/fe.cox.shtml, accessed December 14, 2005.

Cunningham, Anne. "Autonomous Consumption: Buying into the Ideology of Capitalism." *Journal of Business Ethics* 48, no. 3 (December 2003): 229–36.

Dalrymple, Theodore. *Life at the Bottom: The Worldview That Makes the Underclass*. New York: Ivan R. Dee, 2001.

De Soto, Hernando. *The Mystery of Capital: Why Capitalism Triumphs in the West and Fails Everywhere Else*. New York: Basic Books, 2003.

Diamond, Jared. *Guns, Germs, and Steel: The Fates of Human Societies*. New York: Norton, 1999.

Dollar, David, and Aart Kraay. "Growth Is Good for the Poor." *Journal of Economic Growth* 7, no. 3 (September 2002): 195–225.

Epstein, Richard A. *Simple Rules for a Complex World*. Cambridge, Mass.: Harvard University Press, 1995.

Federal Reserve Bank of Dallas. "By Our Own Bootstraps: Economic Opportunity and the Dynamics of Income Distribution." Annual Report, 1995. Http://www.dallasfed.org/fed/annual/1999p/ar95.pdf, accessed December 14, 2005.

Fleischacker, Samuel. "Adam Smith's Reception among the Founders, 1776–1790." *William and Mary Quarterly*, 3rd Series, 59, no. 4 (October 2002): 897–924.

Fogel, Robert W. *The Fourth Great Awakening*. Chicago: University of Chicago Press, 2000.

Food and Agriculture Organizations of the United Nations. *The Global Forest Resources Assessment 2000: Summary Report.* Ftp://ftp.fao.org/unfao/ bodies/cofo/cofo15/x9835e.pdf, accessed December 14, 2005.

"Going L'Postal." *Wall Street Journal Online,* July 23, 2004.

"The Government Performance Project: Grading the States '05: Massachusetts: C+." *Governing Magazine,* February 2005. Http://governing.com/ gpp/2005/ma.htm.

Graham, Gordon. *The Case against the Democratic State.* Charlottesville, Va.: Imprint Academic, 2002.

Gray, John. *False Dawn: The Delusions of Global Capitalism.* New York: New Press, 1998.

Gwartney, James, and Robert Lawson. *Economic Freedom of the World.* Vancouver, B.C.: Fraser Institute, 2003.

Hasterok, Pamela. "Public Trains in Public Hands." *Daytona Beach News-Journal,* August 6, 2003.

Hayward, Steven F. *2004 Index of Leading Environmental Indicators.* San Francisco, Calif., and Washington, D.C.: Pacific Research Institute for Public Policy and American Enterprise Institute for Public Policy Research, 2004.

Hicks, J. R. *The Theory of Economic History.* Oxford: Oxford University Press, 1969.

Hicks, J. R. *Causality in Economics.* Oxford: Blackwell, 1979.

Higgs, Robert. *Crisis and Leviathan: Critical Episodes in the Growth of American Government.* New York: Oxford University Press, 1987.

Hines, James R., Jr., et al. "Another Look at Whether a Rising Tide Lifts All Boats." National Bureau of Economic Research, August 2001. Http://papers. nber.org/papers/w8412, accessed December 14, 2005.

Hudgins, Edward L. "A Holiday Gift: Post Office Going Private?" Washington, D.C.: Cato Institute, December 23, 2000. Http://www.cato.org/dailys/12-23-00.html, accessed December 14, 2005.

Jones, Eric L. *The European Miracle.* Cambridge: Cambridge University Press, 1981.

Jones, Eric L. *Growth Recurring.* Oxford: Oxford University Press, 1988.

Kerm, Philippe Van. "Linking Income Mobility and Inequality: A Re-assessment of American and German Inequality Trends." Http://www.wider.unu.edu/ conference/conference-2003-2/conference%202003-2-papers/powerpoint% 20presentations/Philippe%20Van%20Kerm.PDF, accessed December 14, 2005.

Klein, Daniel B. "The People's Romance: Why People Love Government (as Much as They Do)." *Independent Review ,* 10, no. 1 (Summer 2005): 5–37.

Kling, Arnold. "The Rich and the Poor." Http://arnoldkling.com/econ/ richpoor.html, accessed December 14, 2005.

Knautz, Robert, ed. "Privatizing the Post Office." January/February 1999. Http:// www.hazlitt.org/spotlight/9901.html, accessed December 14, 2005.

Kraay, Aart. "When Is Growth Pro-Poor? Cross-Country Evidence." Washington, D.C.: World Bank, 2004. Http://poverty.worldbank.org/library/view/15173, accessed December 14, 2005.

Krass, Peter. *Carnegie.* Hoboken, N.J.: Wiley, 2002.

Lal, Deepak. *Unintended Consequences: The Impact of Factor Endowments, Culture, and Politics on Long-Run Economic Performance.* Cambridge: MIT Press, 1998.

Landes, David S. *The Wealth and Poverty of Nations: Why Some Are So Rich and Some Are So Poor.* New York: Norton, 1999.

Lomborg, Bjørn. *The Skeptical Environmentalist.* Cambridge: Cambridge University Press, 2002.

Long, Roderick. "Robert Nozick, Philosopher of Liberty." *The Freeman: Ideas on Liberty,* September 2002. Http://www.fee.org/publications/the-freeman/article.asp?aid=4335, accessed December 14, 2005.

Magnet, Myron. "Freedom vs. Dependency." *Wall Street Journal Online,* July 25, 2004. Http://www.opinionjournal.com/editorial/feature.html?id=110005395, accessed December 14, 2005.

Marx, Karl, and Friedrich Engels. *Manifesto of the Communist Party.* In *The Marx-Engels Reader,* 2nd ed. Robert C. Tucker, ed. New York: Norton, 1978 (1848).

McChesney, Fred S., and William F. Shugart II, eds. *The Causes and Consequences of Antitrust: The Public-Choice Perspective.* Chicago: University of Chicago Press, 1995.

Mises, Ludwig von. *Human Action: A Treatise on Economics.* New Haven, Conn.: Yale University Press, 1949.

Moore, Stephen. "The Most Expensive Government in World History." Austin, Tex.: Institute for Policy Innovation, 2002. Http://www.ipi.org/ipi%5CIPIPressReleases.nsf/PublicationLookupPressRelease/3F0943043CA454C085256BB1005A52ED, accessed December 14, 2005.

Moore, Stephen. "The Wages of Prosperity." *Wall Street Journal,* August 29, 2005, p. A9.

Moore, Stephen, and Julian L. Simon. "The Greatest Century That Ever Was: 25 Miraculous Trends of the Past 100 Years." Cato Institute Policy Analysis 364, December 15, 1999. Http://www.cato.org/pubs/pas/pa-364es.html, accessed December 14, 2005.

Moore, Stephen, and Julian L. Simon. *It's Getting Better All the Time: 100 Greatest Trends of the Last 100 Years.* Washington, D.C.: Cato Institute, 2000.

Murray, Charles. *Losing Ground: American Social Policy, 1950–1980,* 2nd ed. New York: Basic Books, 1995.

Murray, Charles. *Human Accomplishment: The Pursuit of Excellence in the Arts and Sciences, 800 B.C. to 1950.* New York: HarperCollins, 2003.

Murray, Iain. "Privatizing Rail, Avoiding the Pitfalls: Lessons from the British Experience." Competitive Enterprise Institute, May 19, 2005. Http://www.cei.org/gencon/025,04546.cfm, accessed December 14, 2005.

National Center for Policy Analysis. "How Poor Are the Poor?" 2001. Http://www.ncpa.org/ba/ba185.html, accessed December 14, 2005.

National Corridors Initiative Incorporated. "National Corridors Initiative: Interviewing David Gunn of Amtrak." July 31, 2002. Http://www.nationalcorridors.org/features/gunn073102.shtml, accessed December 14, 2005.

Norberg, Johann, et al. *In Defense of Global Capitalism.* Washington, D.C.: Cato Institute, 2003.

North, Douglass C. "Institutions and Economic Growth: An Historical Introduction." *World Development* 17, no. 9 (September 1989): 1319–32.

North, Douglass C. *Institutions, Institutional Change and Economic Performance.* Cambridge: Cambridge University Press, 1990.

North, Douglass C., and Robert P. Thomas. *The Rise of the Western World.* Cambridge: Cambridge University Press, 1973.

Nozick, Robert. *Anarchy, State, and Utopia.* New York: Basic Books, 1974.

Nozick, Robert. "The Zigzag of Politics." In *The Examined Life: Philosophical Meditations.* New York: Simon and Schuster, 1989.

O'Rourke, P. J. *Eat the Rich: A Treatise on Economics.* New York: Grove/Atlantic, 1998.

Otteson, James R. Review of Jacques Barzun's *From Dawn to Decadence: 1500 to the Present: 500 Years of Western Cultural Life. Continuity: A Journal of History* 25 (Fall 2001): 131–36. Http://www.bama.ua.edu/~jotteson/barzun.pdf, accessed December 14, 2005.

Otteson, James R. Review of Gordon Graham's *The Case against the Democratic State. Independent Review* 9, no. 1 (Summer 2004). Http://www.independent.org/tii/content/pubs/review/books/tir91_graham.html, accessed December 14, 2005.

Paganelli, Maria Pia. "Adam Smith: Why Decentralized Systems?" *Adam Smith Review* (forthcoming).

"Parliament Building Faces Another Delay." *Scotsman.com News,* July 23, 2004. Http://news.scotsman.com/topics.cfm?tid=276 & id=844122004, accessed December 14, 2005.

Pipes, Richard. *Property and Freedom.* New York: Vintage, 1999.

Pipes, Richard. *Communism: A History.* New York: Modern Library, 2001.

Posner, Richard. *Natural Monopoly and Its Regulation.* Washington, D.C.: Cato Institute, 1999.

Posner, Richard. *Antitrust Law,* 2nd ed. Chicago: University of Chicago Press, 2001.

Powell, Ben. "The Celtic Tiger." Techcentralstation-Europe 9/10/2002. Http://www.techcentralstation.com/091002M.html, accessed December 14, 2005.

Rector, Robert E. "America Has the World's Richest Poor People." Http://www.stevenxue.com/ref37.htm, accessed December 14, 2005.

Rector, Robert E. "Census Baloney." *City Journal* (Winter 2000). Http://www.city-journal.org/html/10_1_sndgs03.html, accessed December 14, 2005.

Rector, Robert E., and Sarah Youssef. "How Poor Are America's Poor?" Chicago, Ill.: Heartland Institute, 1998. Http://www.heartland.org/Article.cfm?artId=797, accessed December 14, 2005.

Reisman, George. *Capitalism: A Complete and Integrated Understanding of the Nature and Value of Human Economic Life.* Danvers, Mass.: Jameson, 1996.

Reynolds, Alan. "For the Record: Despite What You May Read in the Papers, the American Dream Is Alive and Well." *Wall Street Journal Online,* May 18, 2005. Http://www.opinionjournal.com/editorial/feature.html?id=110006704, accessed December 14, 2005.

Robinson, John P., and Geoffrey Godbey. *Time for Life: The Surprising Ways Americans Use Their Time.* University Park: Pennsylvania State University Press, 1997.

Rosenberg, Nathan, and L. E. Birdzell, Jr. *How the West Grew Rich: The Economic Transformation of the Industrial World.* London: I. B. Taurus, 1986.

Rummel, R. J. *Death by Government.* New Brunswick, N.J.: Transaction, 1994.

Schor, Juliet B. *The Overworked American: The Unexpected Decline of Leisure*, rpt. ed. New York: Basic Books, 1993.

Seabright, Paul. *The Company of Strangers: A Natural History of Economic Life*. Princeton, N.J.: Princeton University Press, 2004.

Simon, Julian L., ed. *The State of Humanity*. Cambridge, Mass.: Blackwell, 1995.

Skousen, Mark. "Everything Is Cheap—and Getting Cheaper." *Freeman* 8, no. 12 (December 1998). Http://www.fee.org/publications/the-freeman/articles. asp?aid=3785, accessed December 14, 2005.

Smith, Adam. *An Inquiry into the Nature and Causes of the Wealth of Nations*. Indianapolis, Ind.: Liberty Classics, 1981 (1776).

Smith, Adam. *Lectures on Jurisprudence*. Indianapolis, Ind.: Liberty Classics, 1982 (1762–3).

Sowell, Thomas. *Basic Economics: A Citizen's Guide to the Economy*. New York: Basic Books, 2000.

Sowell, Thomas. *Applied Economics: Thinking beyond Stage One,* 2nd ed. New York: Basic Books, 2003.

Sowell, Thomas. "Economic 'Power.'" Creators Syndicate, Inc., December 11, 2003. Http://www.townhall.com/columnists/thomassowell/ts20031211. shtml, accessed December 14, 2005.

Stanley, Thomas J., and William D. Danko. *The Millionaire Next Door: The Surprising Secrets of America's Wealthy.* New York: Pocket Books, 1998.

Stiglitz, Joseph. *Globalization and Its Discontents*. New York: Norton, 2003.

Summers, Brian. "The Postal Monopoly." *Freeman* 26, no. 3 (March 1976). Http://www.libertyhaven.com/theoreticalorphilosophicalissues/economics/ monopolyandindustrialorganization/postalmono.html, accessed December 14, 2005.

Suprynowicz, Vin. "And Now... Armed Guards at the DMV." *Las Vegas Review-Journal,* December 8, 2000. Http://www.billstclair.com/blog/vin/001208.html, accessed December 14, 2005.

Surowiecki, James. *The Wisdom of Crowds: Why the Many Are Smarter than the Few and How Collective Wisdom Shapes Business, Economies, Societies, and Nations.* New York: Doubleday, 2004.

Tanner, Michael. *The Poverty of Welfare: Helping Others in Civil Society*. Washington, D.C.: Cato Institute, 2003.

Taylor, James Stacey. "Autonomy, Coercion, and Distress." *Social Philosophy and Policy* 20, no. 2 (June 2003): 127–55.

Vedder, Richard K. *The American Economy in Historical Perspective*. Florence, Ky.: Wadsworth, 1976.

Vedder, Richard K., and Lowell E. Galloway. *Out of Work: Unemployment and Government in Twentieth-Century America*. New York: New York University Press, 1997.

Veldhuis, Niels, and Jason Clemens. "A Rising Tide Lifts All Boats." January 2004. Http://www.fraserinstitute.ca/admin/books/chapterfiles/A%20Rising% 20Tide%20Lifts%20All%20Boats-Jan04fftide.pdf, accessed December 14, 2005.

Vogel, Ed. "Report to the Legislature: DMV Nears Guinn's Hour-Wait Goal." *Las Vegas Review-Journal.* January 27, 2001.

Vranich, Joseph, and Edward L. Hudgins. "Help Passenger Rail by Privatizing Amtrak." *Cato Policy Analysis No. 419*. Washington, D.C.: Cato Institute, November 1, 2001. Http://www.cato.org/pubs/pas/pa-419es.html, accessed December 14, 2005.

Vranich, Joseph, Cornelius Chapman, and Edward L. Hudgins. "Time to Liquidate Amtrak." Washington, D.C.: Cato Institute, February 14, 2002. Http://www.cato.org/dailys/02-14-02.html, accessed December 14, 2005.

Wanniski, Jude. "Memo on the Margin: A History of the 20th Century." Polyconomics, Inc., December 31, 1999. Http://www.polyconomics.com/searchbase/12-31-99.html, accessed December 14, 2005.

Wax, Amy L. "What Women Want." *Wall Street Journal,* August 29, 2005, p. A8.

Weede, Erich. "The Diffusion of Prosperity and Peace by Globalization." *The Independent Review* 9, no. 2 (Fall 2004): 165–86.

Williams, Walter E. *The State against Blacks.* New York: McGraw-Hill, 1982.

Williams, Walter E. *Do the Right Thing: The People's Economist Speaks.* Palo Alto, Calif.: Hoover Institution, 1995.

Wilson, D. Mark. "Income Mobility and the Fallacy of Class-Warfare Arguments against Tax Relief." March 8, 2001. Http://www.heritage.org/Research/Taxes/BG1418.cfm, accessed December 14, 2005.

Wise, John P. "Trends in Food from the Sea." In *The State of Humanity.* Julian L. Simon, ed. Oxford: Blackwell, 1995.

Wolf, Martin. *Why Globalization Works.* New Haven, Conn.: Yale University Press, 2004.

World Bank. "Poverty Lines in African Countries." Http://www4.worldbank.org/afr/poverty/measuring/cross_country_poverty_lines_en.htm, accessed December 14, 2005.

World Bank. *World Bank Development Report 1992: Development and the Environment.* Oxford: Oxford University Press, 1992.

Wright, Erik Olin. *Class Counts: Comparative Studies in Class Analysis.* Cambridge: Cambridge University Press, 1996.

PART II

APPLYING THE PRINCIPLES

The chapters of Part I were intended to sketch both a principled and an empirical case for the classical liberal state. The principled case drew on the notions of human 'personhood' and 'judgment,' and on the notion of 'justice' and the General Liberty principle they implied. The empirical case showed that evidence supports the classical liberal state as well: on balance, everyone, including the poor, does better in states approximating the classical liberal ideal than in other kinds of states.

Now, in Part II, I turn to a handful of presently vexing practical moral and political problems, and I investigate how the conceptual tools and empirical evidence developed in Part I can address them.

Part II is not by any means exhaustive: there are a number of other problems I might have discussed. My hope instead is that by addressing these few it will become clear how the general position I defend would address other issues not explicitly discussed.

6

Schooling, Religion, and Other Things You Should Be in Charge Of

One of the most important issues adults face in their lives is education and schooling, since what kind of schooling a child gets is instrumental in creating chances for a better life later on. Yet the traditional tracks and mainstream options routinely short-change students. Partly that is because, as entailed by the 'local knowledge' argument developed in earlier chapters, it is not possible for a distant third party to know which form of schooling is best for you or your children. Only you can know that, based on your knowledge of yourself, of your children, of your conception of the good life, of your schedule of values, and of the resources and opportunities available to you. Since with respect to you I too am one of those distant third parties, in this chapter I do not attempt to lay out a curriculum of education that you or anyone else should follow. Indeed, on my argument, there is no single path everyone should follow. Instead I try to convince you here of two things: first, a child's schooling is more deserving of his parent's personal attention than is sometimes assumed; second, the current American system of educational provision needs radical reform.

WHAT EXACTLY IS THE SUGGESTION?

In Part I, I staked out and defended a conception of moral personhood, and the freedom and responsibility it entails, as well as a conception of government that I argued was necessarily limited by that conception of personhood. You might have found some of the implications I drew from the concept of personhood unsettling, but they were supported by reasons and considerations that I hope made them plausible. I would like to warn you now that in this chapter my argument may well unsettle you again. I argue that all public schooling should be abolished. And yes, I really mean it. By the time you reach the end of this chapter I hope you will think so too.

To avoid any misunderstandings, let me first state my position exactly. By "public schooling" I mean schooling that is subsidized or paid in full by the state through taxation. To avoid terminological confusion—in Britain, for example, a "public school" is what in America would be called a "private school"—I refer to state-subsidized education as "government schooling." By saying it should be abolished I mean that the state should cease having anything to do with it. It should neither subsidize it nor regulate it nor tax for it. I do *not* mean that the state should forbid the creation or existence of schools or that there should be no education. The argument I defend has sometimes been interpreted in this way, but it does not follow from the claim that there should be no government education that there should be no education. I argue the former, not the latter. (How *could* I argue the latter given my chosen profession, for heaven's sake?)

So before even beginning we can head off the objection that my position either is or amounts to a rejection of education altogether. The nineteenth-century French economist Frédéric Bastiat pointed out that this objection is a typical rhetorical strategy employed by people pushing certain state programs (he actually said it was the typical "socialist" strategy, reflecting the political persuasion of the opponents he faced; but people who make such arguments today come under many more flags than just the "socialist" one). Bastiat wrote, "Socialism, like the ancient ideas from which it springs, confuses the distinction between government and society. As a result of this, every time we object to a thing being done by government, the socialists conclude that we object to its being done at all."[1] He continued:

We disapprove of state education. Then the socialists say that we are opposed to any education. We object to a state religion. Then the socialists say that we want no religion at all. We object to a state-enforced equality. Then they say that we are against equality. And so on, and so on. It is as if the socialists were to accuse us of not wanting persons to eat because we do not want the state to raise grain. (p. 29)

Bastiat admitted to some puzzlement, as well as frustration, at how the obvious logical mistake this objection makes—inferring a universal

---

[1] In his 1850 *The Law*, p. 29.

objection to something from an objection to a single particular form of it—could be pointed out again and again, all apparently to no avail. Regardless, let me repeat my own position so that there is no confusion or question: I do not oppose *education;* I oppose *government* education.

GETTING THE CASE OFF THE GROUND

Government education has had a fairly long run in the United States, and it has had an awful lot of money and resources—not to mention a seemingly boundless measure of public faith and forgiveness—and yet it has managed to get itself into an exceedingly bad way. Government education in America is indeed so bad overall, I suggest, that only radical reform has any hope of making things better. The insubstantial tinkering that the education establishment has permitted over the last several decades is so much rearranging of deck chairs on the *Titanic.*

Despite repeated examples of its failures, however, people usually find ways to defend government schooling nonetheless. One sometimes wonders what it would take for people to lose their faith in the necessity, or in the benevolence and beneficence, of government schooling. Would it be overwhelming evidence of its systematic incompetence? Would it be almost daily reports of embezzlement, mismanagement, waste, and even outright robbery? Would it be the regularly recurring battles required to stem the education establishment's relentlessly bad judgment about educational curricula and standards? Would it be their transparently self-serving defenses, their political special pleading, their outright dismissals of criticisms and ad hominem attacks on critics? Would it be that they force unwilling nonusers of their services to pay for them no matter what religious, moral, or other objections those nonusers have to what they do? Would it be that they routinely do not fire but rather defend incompetent teachers, that a majority of their teachers have no academic degree in the discipline they teach, that most of their teachers and their administrators come from "education schools" notorious for being havens both for the worst students and the worst faculty? Would *all* of this suffice?

I argue indeed that all of these problems beset the government education establishment in America, and that therefore continuing to support this failing system is not what we should do. A more radical course is called for. Before I give the particular counts of the indictment, however, let me first present an argument that I hope will give pause even to those inclined to be unmoved by the empirical evidence. That argument is that state intervention in education violates the same moral principle that

state intervention in religious matters does, namely, violation of personhood because it violates private conscience.

FREEDOM OF CONSCIENCE: RELIGION *AND* EDUCATION

Government support for education is analogous to government support
for religion, which means that the moral acceptability, or unacceptability,
of the one is going to be the same as that of the other.[2] The reason for
this is that they both fall under the scope of *freedom of conscience,* which
itself falls under the General Liberty principle entailed by people's 'personhood.' By "freedom of conscience" I mean the freedom to think or
believe whatever one wishes. Since anything a person might think or
believe cannot by itself constitute a violation of justice, and is moreover a
function of and an integral part of one's judgment, I argue that it should
be protected on the same principle requiring protection of people's personhood generally.

One of the freedoms protected by the classical liberalism I have
defended is freedom of conscience. Many other protections are means to
the end of protecting this one. Private property rights, for example, can
be defended by arguing that allowing individuals to maintain personal
jurisdiction over a specified area of things (beginning with themselves)
enables them to act on their beliefs about the good life without interference from others. Actions are, after all, the product of beliefs about the
world, and so the claim that people should enjoy this liberty of action
on private property is an extension of the belief that persons are alike in
having action-guiding private beliefs—which effectively amounts to saying that people are 'persons.' It can then be argued that the beliefs themselves should be protected because a person cannot live a truly human
or truly happy life—that is, cannot truly exercise his personhood—unless
he is allowed to hold *and act on* his own beliefs. Because private property,
by providing a realm or arena in which a person can act and associate
according to his beliefs, is necessary for maintaining and acting on one's
private beliefs, it is thus protected as a necessary means to the end of protecting one's private conscience. And since one's private conscience is a
function of, and necessary prerequisite for developing, one's judgment,
and judgment is itself in turn an integral component of personhood, the
protection of private property and thus private conscience turn out to be
required by respect for people's personhood.

---

[2] The following is based in part on my "Freedom of Religion and Public Schooling."

Several other political principles follow from the requirement to protect private conscience. Arguments for freedom of the press, freedom of speech, and freedom of association can all be plausibly construed as the claim that the private consciences of individuals must be protected, and that these various freedoms are required to do so. Even people who argue for "freedoms" that go beyond the 'negative' freedoms included in the protections of justice I have defended often do so (if inconsistently in my view) on similar grounds.[3] So, for example, state-provided universal health care has been defended on the grounds that good health is a necessary prerequisite to leading a happy, flourishing life. The connection between the two is thought to be that good health grants a person the peace of mind to work out, adopt, and maintain private beliefs about the good life, as well as the soundness of body to act on those beliefs. Again, however, since the actions are dependent on the beliefs, it turns out that to create a sanctuary for private beliefs is the ultimate end of supporting universal health care.

These examples license our drawing the general moral principle that because of the crucial role one's private conscience plays in the exercise of personhood, it must be protected against interference. Although I subscribe to this principle, I will not defend it here more than I already have. But I do want to emphasize that it is already widely accepted. It is explicitly at work, to recur to an earlier example, in the widespread belief in the freedom of the press. Since John Milton's early statement of the argument in his famous speech to the English Parliament that was published in 1644 under the title *Areopagitica,* the claim has been that ideas are crucially important to living a flourishing and good life. The reason is that part of the experimental nature of human life is the trying out and exploring of different possibilities. One way to do this is to write and publish ideas and expose them to public scrutiny.[4] Thus freedom of the press is protected as one means of expression of privately held beliefs.

My suggestion is that because they both fall under the principle of freedom of conscience, both education and religion are analogous in all the morally relevant ways. For parents this means that they should have the freedom and authority to determine which sort of schooling their

---

[3] See notes 32 and 33 of chapter 2 for examples of people making arguments like these.

[4] Another classic early defense of this position is *Cato's Letters* no. 15, written by Thomas Gordon in 1720, entitled "Of Freedom of Speech: That the Same is Inseparable from Public Liberty" (in *Cato's Letters,* vol. 1, pp. 110–17).

children get, just as they have the freedom and authority to determine which religious education their children get. And for adults, the freedom of conscience that is entailed by their personhood means they should have the freedom and authority to make the same decisions for themselves—though, of course, only for themselves. This freedom should therefore disallow state intervention in educational practice, including subsidies drawn from taxes, compulsory attendance laws, and mandatory curriculum standards, just as it disallows religious subsidies drawn from taxes, compulsory church attendance, and state-prescribed religious ceremonies, rites, or doctrines. Hence "public schooling" should be abolished on exactly the same grounds that state-enforced "public religion," wherever it exists, should be abolished.

Let me take a moment to address a concern one might have here. One might be willing to grant that respect for personhood and private conscience entails that the state may not *forbid* educating children, just as it may not forbid imparting to them religious beliefs; but one might nevertheless question how that means that the state may not *subsidize* education, tax for it, and so on. Even if the state makes me pay to support a religion in which I do not believe, I am still free to believe whatever I want—and hence the state would not be violating the sanctity of my private conscience. Or so one might argue. My argument to the contrary is that by making me pay to support a belief system that I do not accept, whether educational or religious, the state fails to respect my *judgment*. For it thereby takes from me the opportunity to decide whether to give, how much to give, and to whom to give. Instead, the state makes those decisions for me, thus substituting its judgment for mine. Now it is true that if the state, say, taxes me 10 percent of my income to support its schooling (or religious) program, I still have the other 90 percent to dispose of as I judge fit: on this basis one might again claim that I am still free to believe, and support monetarily, whatever I want. Again I disagree. Taking that 10 percent from me and putting it in the service of beliefs I do not hold—or disagree with or perhaps even believe to be immoral—is just like the case contemplated in chapter 2 of an employer using my forced labor for only part of the day. Being coerced into working for you for, say, "only" one hour per day is better than if I were forced to work for you for ten hours per day—but it still violates my personhood. The same holds, I suggest, in the case of state-mandated tithes. Part of personhood is exercising judgment, and part of exercising judgment is acting on one's own beliefs. This is what state support of either religion or education denies, and why it is therefore unacceptable.

AN ARGUMENT DIVIDED CANNOT STAND

I believe that settles the matter. And I believe most people's actions tend already to be consistent with my judgment. For example, we try for the most part not to allow the state any influence over religious matters. The fervor—one is tempted to say secularized religious zeal—with which some elements of today's American political scene pursue even the merest hint of, for example, Christianity in government or, especially, in government schools suggests that many will brook absolutely no connection between church and state.[5]

Of course, not everyone in America believes that religion should have nothing to do with government. Indeed, a plausible argument has been made, for example, that liberal American legal institutions exist in part because they are descended from arguments made by Christians in Europe about the sanctity of the individual.[6]

More recently, one of the first things the second Bush administration initiated on taking office was what it called "Faith-Based and Community Initiatives," which, according to its own description, aims "to help faith-based and community organizations build upon and expand their good works"; it claims it will do this by

working legislatively to encourage the good works of faith-based and community organizations and give them the fullest opportunity permitted by law to compete for Federal funding; identifying and eliminating improper Federal barriers to the full participation of faith-based and community-serving programs in the provision of social services; [and] encouraging greater corporate and philanthropic support for faith-based and community organizations, through public education and outreach activities.[7]

Should the government be doing these things? To be honest, it is hard to say for sure, since, as is typical of government verbiage, it is difficult to know from the descriptions what exactly these "initiatives" will be.[8] It

---

[5] For discussions from various perspectives, see David Limbaugh's *Persecution;* the American Civil Liberties Union's defense of "religious liberty," Http://www.aclu.org/ReligiousLiberty/ReligiousLibertyMain.cfm; and the efforts of the Americans United for the Separation of Church and State, http://www.au.org/site/PageServer (both sites accessed December 14, 2005).

[6] See, for example, John Danford's *Roots of Liberty,* M. Stanton Evans's *The Theme Is Freedom,* Alan Macfarlane's *The Origins of English Individualism,* my edited collection *The Levellers,* and Rodney Stark's *For the Glory of God.*

[7] See http://www.whitehouse.gov/government/fbci/ (accessed December 14, 2005).

[8] For an insightful discussion of the philosophical issues involved here, see Tomasi's "Should Political Liberals Be Compassionate Conservatives?"

follows from my argument above that if the government places barriers or hindrances in the way of people pursuing their private religions, then those barriers or hindrances should be removed. Respect for people's personhood entails that we should respect people's decisions to practice, or not practice, religion as they see fit, the practice being, as I argued before, an integral part of exercising one's judgment with respect to these matters. The other side of this same principle, however, is that the government may also not endorse any religion or subsidize it with money; it may not even endorse or subsidize *all* religions or "faith-based initiatives" generally because that would be to violate the personhood of those whose judgment leads them to agnosticism or atheism. The Bush administration's documents endorsing its "faith-based initiatives" argue that local faith-based organizations are the best vehicles for helping those among us who need help, and that may well be true. Since they would operate on their local knowledge, they are far more likely to be effective and efficient than anything run by a distant centralized state. But that is just one more reason why the state should stay out altogether of the business of having anything to do with religion.

My suggestion, then, is that the moral case for freedom of religion stands or falls with that of freedom of education. That means that a society that champions freedom of religion but at the same time countenances systematic state regulation of education has some explaining to do.

OTHER ARGUMENTS AGAINST STATE RELIGION

A number of ways to defend government schooling against my objections will have occurred to you, but before considering them—which we do below—let me first ask which *other* arguments there are to oppose state meddling in religion. I said above that I think the compelling case has already been made, but in case you are not yet convinced, I propose now to look at the central typical arguments against state support of religion. To let the cat out of the bag: afterwards I will suggest that all the arguments one might marshal in favor of government regulation or support of education must, since the cases are analogous, face the same objections raised against government regulation or support of religion. So my strategy is to bring out the objections to government religion, and thereby challenge government schooling as well. I try to capture the most common arguments presented in opposition to state-supported religion, hoping that you will subscribe to or be convinced by at least one of them, and then attempt to show that the same arguments can, without substantive alteration, be raised in opposition to state-supported education.

Objections to state intervention in religious matters fall chiefly under four heads: (1) government support for religion is forbidden by the Constitution or other fundamental legal documents or judicial decrees; (2) government support for religion leads to various bad consequences; (3) religion is too important a matter to be left to politicians or to decisions made by political processes; and (4) government support for religion violates people's rights.

Because I would like to pursue a general moral principle, rather than base my argument on a necessarily limited legal claim, I exclude from consideration arguments based on the American Constitution. Interpreting the Constitution is a tricky, not to mention highly contested, business— even for something as seemingly clear as the First Amendment—so I would prefer to sidestep it altogether. As I hope the following shows, we can build a compelling case without recourse to the Constitution. Let us then consider the other arguments in turn.

1. Government Support for Religion Leads to Bad Consequences

This argument can be constructed in several ways. A religious believer might argue, for example, that true faith cannot be had by coercion: the strength of a person's faith is diminished if he is *forced* to believe, instead of choosing to believe on his own. Now, it may be impossible to force someone actually to hold a belief, as opposed to merely behaving as if he held the belief. This argument claims that a person is less likely to hold religious beliefs if he is forced against his will to act as though he believes them. A person must instead come to hold them on his own and to take responsibility for them himself. Hence, this argument concludes, government support of religion actually works against the religion by disinclining people to believe it or even inclining them to oppose it. This is John Locke's argument in his 1685 *Letter Concerning Toleration,* in which he argues:

In vain therefore do princes compel their subjects to come into their Church communion, under pretense of saving their souls. If they believe, they will come of their own accord; if they believe not, their coming will nothing avail them. How great soever, in fine, may be the pretense of good will and charity, and concern for the salvation of men's souls, men cannot be forced to be saved whether they will or no. And therefore, when all is done, they must be left to their own consciences.[9]

A differing believer's voice is Blaise Pascal's, who argues in his 1660 *Pensées* that "Custom is our Nature. Anyone who grows accustomed to faith believes it, and can no longer help fearing hell, and believes nothing else" (p. 153). Part of Pascal's famous "wager"—by which he argues that belief in God is a rational bet, even irrespective of belief in God's existence— depends on the assumption that people who make the conscious and intentional decision to act as though they believe in God because it is a rational bet to do so will, despite this perhaps less-than-earnest beginning, come in time to actually hold the beliefs. But it should not be supposed that Pascal therefore supports state enforcement of religion: he is quite clear that his aim is to persuade his readers rationally.

This argument can also be construed in light of the effect state inter- vention might have on parents, who are charged with the task of passing on proper beliefs to their children: if the government takes over the responsibility of maintaining correct beliefs, then parents might relax their own commitment to the important job of religious education of their children. This can have the undesirable unintended consequences both of weakening the parents' own faith and of weakening the fabric of the religious community that is based on the joint efforts in faith of whole families.

Now it is true that supporting a religion is not the same thing as coerc- ing belief, so one might argue that a state policy of, perhaps, giving equal amounts of money to all religions, or of giving out generic vouchers for church donations, would not be affected by this consideration. Perhaps these are the sorts of policies envisioned by the Bush administration's "Faith-Based Initiatives." It is what Iceland, for example, currently does: Iceland's official religion is Lutheranism, and all citizens are taxed to support the Lutheran church; since Icelanders are free to support or attend other churches too, however, the Icelandic government never- theless claims that it is not restricting its citizens' freedom of religion.[10] But I doubt many Americans would accept the Icelandic government's argument. How can people still be considered to enjoy religious free- dom when they are forced to support a particular church whether they want to or not? A proponent of the argument we are contemplating now

---

[9] In David Wootton's edited *John Locke: Political Writings*, p. 410. See also Locke's 1693 *Some Thoughts Concerning Education.*

[10] See Gordon Graham's *The Case against the Democratic State*, chap. 5.

should respond that one important element in coming to hold one's own beliefs is the initial decision of *whether* to believe. If Pascal is right that practice leads to belief, then when the government takes money from citizens through general taxation and earmarks some of it for support of or donation to churches or other religiously based organizations, it preempts each taxpayer's initial decision of whether to donate and thus whether to believe. That decision was instead made by the state. And even if Locke is right—that is, if making a person support religious doctrines in which he does not believe will not, in fact, lead to true belief—then a believer may still argue that if the government has decided to support religion, then its imprimatur gives a credence to a set or sets of beliefs that people will thus be more inclined to accept uncritically. But the believer may argue that the proper relation to such important beliefs cannot be maintained if the beliefs were not adopted freely and after due consideration. Hence, the believer might conclude, the government must not prejudice people, as it inevitably would, with its official stamp of approval.

A believer might also be concerned by the very real possibility that the government could support the *wrong* religion or religions. So even the believer who thought it would lead to *good* consequences if his own religion were supported (if, say, you were a Lutheran in Iceland) might well think it would lead to bad—indeed, perhaps disastrously bad—consequences if some other, false religion were supported (if, say, you were a Muslim in Iceland). This is the core of the argument that some Christians make today when they charge public schools with pushing a specific secularized moral vision.[11] Since there can be no guarantee that the government will choose correctly—the decisions will be made politically, after all—the prudent conclusion for the believer is that the state should abstain altogether from supporting religion. Let individuals keep their money and use it to support, or not support, which church or religious organization they judge proper.

On the other side, nonbelievers have at least two clear reasons for believing that government support of religion would lead to bad consequences. First, it might propagate beliefs that the nonbeliever holds to be false, which is not only undesirable in itself but also might stand in the way of cultural and scientific progress. Carl Sagan, for example, argued in his *The Demon-Haunted World: Science as a Candle in the Dark* that today's religions are tomorrow's superstitions; and since we want to encourage

---

[11] For an example, see Limbaugh's *Persecuted*. See also Zimmerman's *Whose America?* chap. 7.

knowledge, which for Sagan means science, and not superstition, which for him means religion, the last thing we should allow our government to do is to support religion. Consider, as Sagan argues, that the money that would go to support the contemporary equivalent of belief in witches might have gone to support research into space exploration and colonization, gene therapy, cancer research, or any number of other enterprises far more conducive to human welfare. The second argument a nonbeliever would make is that state support of religion might propagate not just false beliefs but dangerous or counterproductive ones. In addition to slowing the growth of knowledge, it might, for example, lead people to put less stock in improving life on earth, to be less concerned with "merely temporal" suffering, or inclined to believe that whatever happens is God's will. In any of these cases a believer might hence develop an apathy or resignation that inclines him not to work as hard to change a contemporary, earthly situation that the nonbeliever thinks should be changed.

2. Religion is Too Important to Be Left to Politics and Politicians

This second argument is often supported by both the believer and nonbeliever. Its claim is that one's religious beliefs, whatever they are, are a foundational element of one's worldview—perhaps even the single most important element, the one that fixes and orders all the others. As such they should bear an intensely personal relationship to the person holding them: they should be consciously and deliberately weighed, accepted, and endorsed by the person himself. If the state played an active role in supporting religion, however, it would tend to divorce a person from his beliefs by giving him the dangerously complacent attitude that someone else is taking care of such things for him. As soon as he starts thinking that, the potential believer loses the personal commitment to religion that many maintain is the sine qua non of true belief. Because of the supreme importance of these beliefs, then, we should be even more suspicious and wary of political influence here than we might be in other, less important areas of our lives.

Often coupled with this argument is a general claim about the inefficiency, incompetence, or moral or religious failings of politicians and political bureaucrats.[12] Hence even if government influence did *not* have

---

[12] For examples of the following arguments, see Buchanan and Tullock's *Calculus of Consent,* Mill's *On Liberty,* Nock's *Theory of Education in the United States* and "Anarchist's Progress,"

the effect of dissociating people from beliefs to which they should be personally attached, the last people we should entrust with the care of matters as important as religion are agents of the state. Here one might marshal a public choice–style argument that such people do not have the proper incentives to encourage them to actually work in the best interest of individual people and their religious beliefs; their incentives might rather incline them only to ensure steadily increasing pay and minimal work for themselves, regardless of its effect on people and their beliefs. One might also make a local-knowledge argument that religious beliefs can be properly maintained only by people who have close personal knowledge of the people holding or potentially holding those beliefs. One might thus conclude that parents, priests, pastors, rabbis, or other personal mentors are better equipped to handle this task than any remote stranger, as an agent of the state would necessarily be. A final possibility is an argument based on the fact and value of human diversity. Even if state agents could somehow have all the knowledge about people that is requisite to know how best to maintain proper religious beliefs, it would be impossible to establish a single set of rules, laws, or programs that would be best for everyone: some simplification would necessarily be required, limiting thereby the range of "allowable" religious belief. One might then argue that since human diversity is good, artificially limiting it is bad. And of course one should also point out that if not all religious observation gets supported, it might be one's own that gets left out—not a small consideration.

The upshot is that fallible politicians are not competent authorities on the ultimate good for others, and thus they should not be entrusted with the power to make decisions about such matters for others. Each person must instead be allowed to take his chances on his own, which means that he should have the freedom to make what he can of his own and his children's religion, without the coercive interference of the state.

3. Government Support for Religion Violates People's Rights

Perhaps the most powerful and most widely held argument against government support of religion is that it would violate people's rights. A potential rights violation in this case can be seen in at least two aspects: a violation of the right to free speech and a violation of property rights.

Resch's "Human Variation and Individuality," Rogge and Goodrich's "Education in a Free Society," and West's *Education and the State.*

First, one can argue it would infringe on a person's right to free speech to make him support beliefs he does not hold.[13] Requiring a person to support a religion in which he does not believe is equivalent to requiring him to support any other position, institution, or view in which he does not believe. Since, as I argued earlier, freedom of speech is protected not as an end in itself but rather as a means to protecting one's private conscience, the close connection between religious practice and "speech" licenses bringing the protection of the former under the scope of the latter. Thus, requiring a person to support a religion in which he does not believe violates his right to freedom of conscience. If it is true that one's religious beliefs are of central importance to one's life, then such a violation would be especially egregious.

This argument recalls Thomas Jefferson's famous claim in his 1779 *Act for Establishing Religious Freedom in the State of Virginia* that "to compel a man to furnish contributions of money for the propagation of opinions which he disbelieves, is sinful and tyrannical."[14] If you are tempted to think

[13] As the American Civil Liberties Union argues. See http://www.aclu.org/ReligiousLiberty/ReligiousLibertyMain.cfm. See also its page "Government-Funded Religion," http://www.aclu.org/ReligiousLiberty/ReligiousLibertylist.cfm?c = 37 (both sites accessed December 14, 2005).

[14] In *The Life and Selected Writings of Thomas Jefferson*, p. 312. Jefferson in fact goes on to raise several of the objections articulated here, so his statement is worth quoting at length:

"Well aware ... that to compel a man to furnish contributions of money for the propagation of opinions which he disbelieves, is sinful and tyrannical; that even the forcing him to support this or that teacher of his own religious persuasion, is depriving him of the comfortable liberty of giving his contributions to the particular pastor whose morals he would make his pattern, and whose powers he feels most persuasive to righteousness, and is withdrawing from the ministry those temporal rewards, which proceeding from an approbation of their personal conduct, are an additional incitement to earnest and unremitting labors for the instruction of mankind; that our civil rights have no dependence on our religious opinions, more than our opinions in physics or geometry; that, therefore, the proscribing any citizen as unworthy the public confidence by laying upon him an incapacity of being called to the offices of trust and emolument, unless he profess or renounce this or that religious opinion, is depriving him injuriously of those privileges and advantages to which in common with his fellow citizens he has a natural right; that it tends also to corrupt the principles of that very religion it is meant to encourage, by bribing, with a monopoly of worldly honors and emoluments, those who will externally profess and conform to it; that though indeed these are criminal who do not withstand such temptation, yet neither are those innocent who lay the bait in their way; that to suffer the civil magistrate to intrude his powers into the field of opinion and to restrain the profession or propagation of principles, on the supposition of their ill tendency, is a dangerous fallacy, which at once destroys all religious liberty, because he being of course judge of that tendency, will make his opinions the rule of judgment, and approve or condemn the sentiments of others only as they shall square with or differ from his own; that it is time enough for the rightful purposes of civil government, for its officers

that Jefferson exaggerates the risks involved, consider what your reaction would be to the creation of a new government program called, let us say, the "Patriotic Political Freedom Fund" to which you are required to contribute—don't worry, though: the mandatory contribution is nominal, only 1 percent of your earnings (initially)—and among the recipients of this money will be the American Civil Liberties Union, the Christian Coalition, the North American Man/Boy Love Association, Operation Rescue, and the presidential campaigns of Newt Gingrich, Ted Kennedy, Ralph Nader, and Pat Buchanan. Do you still think Jefferson exaggerates?

Government support of religion is also a violation of property rights insofar as that support is in the form of money taken from taxation revenues. On a Lockean view of property rights, for example, it is illegitimate to tax a person in order to support something he does not expressly or tacitly consent to support. Now, the notion of "tacit" consent is a tricky one, as Locke is aware. Locke writes in his 1690 *Second Treatise of Government* that "every Man, that hath any Possessions, or Enjoyment, of any part of the Dominions of any Government, doth thereby give his *tacit Consent,* and is as far forth obliged to Obedience to the Laws of that Government, during such Enjoyment, as any one under it" (§119; emphasis in original). As I suggested in chapter 2, Locke's position strikes me as overly broad since it sets a pretty demanding standard to meet if one wants not to be "consenting" to whatever the government does. Does it mean I have to actually move out of the country if I don't want to "consent" to what the government does? What if I do not have the resources to do that? And by the way, this is as much my country as it is yours—why do you get to demand that I leave if I disagree with something? In any case, it seems

to interfere when principles break out into overt acts against peace and good order; and finally, that truth is great and will prevail if left to herself, that she is the proper and sufficient antagonist to error, and has nothing to fear from the conflict, unless by human interposition disarmed of her natural weapons, free argument and debate, errors ceasing to be dangerous when it is permitted freely to contradict them.

Be it therefore enacted by the General Assembly, That no man shall be compelled to frequent or support any religious worship, place, or ministry whatsoever, nor shall be enforced, restrained, molested, or burdened in his body or goods, nor shall otherwise suffer on account of his religious opinions or belief; but that all men shall be free to profess, and by argument to maintain, their opinions in matters of religion, and that the same shall in nowise diminish, enlarge, or affect their civil capacities.

And though we well know this Assembly, elected by the people for the ordinary purposes of legislation only, have no powers equal to our own and that therefore to declare this act irrevocable would be of no effect in law, yet we are free to declare, and do declare, that the rights hereby asserted are of the natural rights of mankind, and that if any act shall be hereafter passed to repeal the present or to narrow its operation, such act will be an infringement of natural right."

clear that a person who did not enjoy the benefits of any religious institution, or especially if he expressly renounced any such benefits, would
not, even on Locke's view, have either expressly or tacitly consented to be
taxed to support it. Hence taking a person's money to support a religion
to which he otherwise would not give his money is violating his right to
do with his legitimately acquired property as he chooses. On the Lockean
view, this would be for the government to overstep its legitimate authority.

Moreover, as I have already argued, it would also violate the rules of
'justice' that I defended in Part I because it violates the personhood of
those it requires to pay. The taxpayers would be allowed to exercise their
judgment neither in the decision of whether to support this or any other
religion nor in the decisions of (1) how much to support them, as opposed
to supporting other causes, (2) in which way to support them—whether,
for example, with one's time or one's money, nor, finally, (3) at which
point they no longer deserve or need to be supported, perhaps because
they have served their purpose or because they have become corrupt.

AGAINST GOVERNMENT EDUCATION

I now wish to argue that the same three clusters of arguments that are
brought against state intervention in *religion* also count against government support of *education:* government support of education leads to
various bad consequences, education is too important a matter to be left
to politicians or decisions made by political processes, and government
support for education violates people's rights.

One might also here again make the argument that state support and
regulation of schooling is a violation of the U.S. Constitution, in this case
basing the argument on the Ninth and Tenth Amendments in conjunc-
tion with Article I, Section 8. This argument would claim that Congress's
legitimate powers are enumerated in Article I, Section 8, of the Constitution, and are thus limited to what is listed there. Since there is nothing
there empowering Congress to support or regulate schooling, however,
and given that the Ninth and Tenth Amendments hold, respectively, that
the "enumeration in the Constitution of certain rights shall not be construed to deny or disparage others retained by the people" and that the
"powers not delegated to the United States by the Constitution, nor pro-
hibited by it to the States, are reserved to the States respectively, or to
the people," the natural conclusion seems to be that the federal government exceeds its constitutionally legal limits when it undertakes to
have anything to do with education. The only government interference

in education that would be licensed by the Constitution would be under the auspices of local or state governments.[15]

I believe this is an argument worthy of consideration, but for the reason I gave earlier I put constitutional questions to one side for the sake of this discussion. Let us instead see whether there is in fact the close analogy I allege between the arguments offered against state support and regulation of religion and state support and regulation of education. Again, consider the arguments in turn.

1. Government Support of Education Leads to Bad Consequences

Government support of education leads to bad consequences similar to those raised in discussing government support of religion: people's personal commitment to education is weakened by the government's relieving them of the responsibility of educating themselves or their own children; the government runs a significant risk of supporting a bad system of education; and the government runs an again significant risk of supporting a system of education that propagates dangerous or counterproductive attitudes. Each of these charges has been leveled against government schools by recent critics, including those who otherwise support government schooling.

As an example of the first charge, in his *Separating School and State,* author and editor Sheldon Richman argues that true education requires above all else personal initiative and commitment, and that government schooling tends to deaden personal commitment by depriving people of the responsibility of providing for their own or their own children's education. The result, Richman argues, is that the burden of educating children tends to fall on the shoulders of politicians and bureaucrats who lack the proper incentives or knowledge required to do the job well.[16] Second, in his *The Closing of the American Mind,* philosophy professor and social critic Allan Bloom argues that government schools from the elementary through the college level operate under the rubric of badly flawed theories of knowledge and truth loosely based on the views of Nietzsche and Dewey. Bloom argues that these theories inform educational practices that encourage an unsophisticated epistemological and moral relativism, severely impeding both scientific progress and moral growth. And third,

---

[15] For a recent detailed case for interpreting the Constitution this way, see Randy Barnett's *Restoring the Lost Constitution.*

[16] See also Flew's *Social Life and Moral Judgment,* chap. 6.

in his *Inside American Education,* economist and historian Thomas Sowell argues that public schools across the nation pursue educational policies that foster the dangerous mix of high self-esteem, ignorance, and moral vacuity—which has led, quite predictably, Sowell argues, to the amoral monsters we see increasingly often today, not to mention the fact that in the most important cutting-edge scientific and technological positions Americans are slowly but steadily being supplanted by people from other countries. And one should not make the mistake of thinking that these are uncommon criticisms: in each case numerous other critics make similar claims.

I shall not defend each of these claims; the authors do a fine job of that themselves. But I will point out that a large body of evidence exists indicating that public schools have been steadily declining in quality for at least four decades, despite the facts that (1) expenditures per pupil have steadily *risen* in real terms over the same time period and that (2) class sizes have steadily *decreased* during the same time period.[17] In 1955 the average number of pupils an American public school teacher had was 26.9; in 1995 it was 17.1, fully a one-third reduction. Moreover, between 1959 and 1990, the annual cost of public education rose from $1,710 per child to $5,233 in constant 1991 dollars, a more than three-fold real increase. The increase is even larger if the timeline is expanded: over the period of 1920 to 1996, American public schools saw a *fourteen-fold* increase in constant-dollar per pupil spending (indeed, some studies argue that a proper accounting reveals the increase to be over *twenty-fold*[18]). It would take a massive, dramatic improvement in educational quality over that period to justify an increase of that scale.

And what in fact do we have to show for this? Well, not only have we *not* seen the dramatic improvement in quality that we should expect given the rise in funding and the reduction in class sizes, but by virtually every objective measure public schooling has indeed gotten worse. I would argue that that is no coincidence—that given the nature of state-run organizations, as well as their past performances, we should expect that they would not meet their lofty stated goals and expectations—but be that as it may, the fact that government schools are failing their students in nearly every respect cannot be gainsaid. But that of course has not stopped people from doing just that. David Berliner and Bruce Biddle, for

[17] This information and what follows is widely available. For one excellent detailed resource, see Coulson's *Market Education;* see also Brimelow's *The Worm in the Apple,* Gatto's *The Exhausted School,* Sowell's *Inside American Education,* West's *Education and the State,* and Zimmerman's *Whose America?*

[18] See Coulson, *Market Education,* pp. 205–6.

example, authors of *The Manufactured Crisis,* point out that the proportion of people receiving high school diplomas has increased in the last forty years, a fact they say is "marvelous."[19] But this argument is specious since it fails to note that the requirements for getting those diplomas have ebbed significantly, in many places amounting to little more than attendance.[20] There is nothing marvelous about having more high school graduates if the increases come in the form of not being able to do long division or read and comprehend a book like this one.[21]

Am I exaggerating the decline in quality of government schooling? Just how bad is it? A 1992 study by Harold Stevenson compiled a decade's worth of international studies comparing educational performance and attitudes in the United States, China, Taiwan, and Japan.[22] The study showed that American children had the worst performance: by the fifth grade, for instance, the *best* American schools had math scores lower than the *worst* schools from all three other nations.[23] The study also showed, however, that, due apparently to a systematic campaign of misinformation by their schooling representatives, the American parents were overall the most satisfied with the job their local schools were doing! A 1996 National Assessment of Educational Progress study found that students' *perceptions* of their own writing abilities and their overall levels of self-esteem showed slight but statistically significant increases over the same 1984–95 period during which their actual knowledge and abilities declined markedly.[24]

Studies have even shown that overall levels of public literacy have not benefited from the huge amounts of money the state has spent on

---

[19] See ibid., p. 26. See also Tyack's recent *Seeking Common Ground,* which defends public schools on several of the grounds I here contest.

[20] See, for example, Brimelow's *The Worm in the Apple* and Gatto's *The Exhausted School.* See also the National Association of Scholars' 2002 report "Today's College Students and Yesteryear's High School Grads: A Comparison of General Cultural Knowledge," http://www.nas.org/reports/senior_poll/senior_poll_report.pdf (accessed December 14, 2005), and Sommer's edited collection, *The Academy in Crisis.*

[21] See Mulroy's *The War against Grammar,* chaps. 1–4, for illustrations of how bad things have gotten. Berliner and Biddle claim that virtually all of the problems besetting American public education are mere "myths" constructed and propagated by people with "conservative" political agendas. I find their dismissals of the evidence unpersuasive (and at times offensive: they often characterize their opponents as "con men" and "charlatans," even suggesting their motives are similar to Adolf Hitler's! (p. 8)), but a person wanting a view different from mine might consider consulting their book.

[22] "Learning from Asian Schools" in *Scientific American.*

[23] For further recent corroboration, see the *New York Daily News's* "Duh! 81% of Kids Fail Test"; the *Wall Street Journal's* "America's C–"; and the *Washington Post's* "In a Global Test of Math Skills, U.S. Students behind the Curve."

[24] See "The NAEP 1996 Technical Report," http://nces.ed.gov/nationsreportcard//pubs/main1996/1999452.asp (accessed December 14, 2005).

schooling. Indeed, there is evidence that overall levels of literacy are actually *lower* now than they were before spending on public schooling began
its steep increase, especially among underprivileged populations.[25] American blacks, for instance, had a higher rate of literacy, and the rate was
increasing, in 1960 than they did in 1990.[26]

Perhaps even more worrying are the socially divisive effects of government schooling. One of the arguments routinely marshaled in support
of government schooling is that it provides a community cohesion that
our society would otherwise lack: by requiring children from all walks of
life to come together and study, read, and learn together, we break down
social, class, and racial barriers that would otherwise stratify and rend
society. That is a pleasant myth. The reality is that government schools
have historically been among the most aggressive instruments for per-
petuating political oppression and enforcing conformity to fashionable
moral, political, or religious—and often bigoted—views. Consider how
Andrew Coulson summarized his comprehensive study of the history of
government education:

> Few institutions have caused as much strife and conflict as public schools. They
> have been used to beat down minorities of every color and creed, setting family
> against family and community against community. Protestants in both France
> and the United States used them to attack Catholicism, and Catholics, when they
> achieved the upper hand in French politics, turned them against Protestantism.
> U.S. whites used the public schools to segregate African Americans. Instead of
> welcoming immigrants in a spirit of mutual respect, government schools often
> sought to extinguish their cultures and beliefs. Far from promoting social har-
> mony, government schools in the U.S. undermined it, forcing Catholics to set up
> their own schools in order to avoid the discrimination they suffered at the hands
> of the state system, and breeding resentment among many other immigrant
> groups who felt that their traditions were derided in the public schools. Blood was
> shed and property destroyed in disputes precipitated by the "common schools."[27]

A similar picture has recently been painted by Jonathan Zimmerman,
whose 2002 *Whose America? Culture Wars in the Public Schools* sets out in
painstaking and painful detail the social division, the racial, religious,
and class antagonisms, and the callous disregard of minority interests

---

[25] See West's *Education and the State*, esp. chaps. 9–11.

[26] See, for example, Clint Bolick's "A Lot More to Learn," James J. Heckman and Amy
L. Wax's "Home Alone," Kirsch et al.'s *Adult Literacy in America*, and Thomas Sowell's
"Black Education: Achievements, Myths, and Tragedies," in his *Black Rednecks and White
Liberals*.

[27] Coulson, *Market Education*, pp. 104–5.

that have marked government schooling's unsavory history in America.[28] The ever-continuing cavalcade of stories about outright theft and gross misappropriation of funds on the part of public school administrators is just salt in the wound.[29]

The problems are exacerbated by the fact that the persecuted minorities often cannot escape the schools, owing to mandatory attendance laws in many districts, and in any case they certainly cannot avoid paying for the schools even if their children do not attend. If you can afford to send your children to a private school, good for you: but you still have to pay taxes supporting the government schools. How many more people would be able to send their children to schools of their own choosing, schools that match and support their own cultures, traditions, and values, if they did not *also* have to pay for the government schools? The number cannot be known for certain—they are part of Bastiat's "unseen"—but their existence cannot be denied and must be counted among the undesirable consequences of state-enforced subsidization of schooling.

One could continue to adduce examples of government schooling problems almost indefinitely, but of course it is not true that *every* government school is bad or *every* government school teacher is bad. On the contrary, there are occasional stories of heroic schools and teachers, managing somehow to soldier on in almost uncomprehendingly bad conditions. Dunbar High School in Washington, D.C., for the first half of the twentieth century and St. Augustine in New Orleans are examples of excellent schools, and John Taylor Gatto and Sherry Sheffield Davis are examples of excellent teachers. But the argument here depends on overall trends, which are quite indisputable. These exceptions prove the rule.

One final fact will illuminate the reality of government schooling. Here is a partial list of books that were most frequently banned from American public school libraries from 1990 to 2000, according to the American Library Association:[30]

1. Maya Angelou, *I Know Why the Caged Bird Sings*
2. Nathaniel Hawthorne, *The Scarlet Letter*

---

[28] See also Katz's *History of Compulsory Education Laws,* Richman's *Separating School and State,* chap. 3, Rochester's *Class Warfare,* Rothbard's "Historical Origins," and West's *Education and the State.*

[29] Stories of these misdeeds are legion and recur in every state in the United States. One recent story that came to my attention is the *New York Times*'s "Audit Describes 8 Years of Looting by L.I. School Officials."

[30] See http://www.ala.org/ala/oif/bannedbooksweek/bbwlinks/100mostfrequently.htm (accessed December 14, 2005).

3. Aldous Huxley, *Brave New World*
4. Harper Lee, *To Kill a Mockingbird*
5. Herman Melville, *Moby Dick*
6. Toni Morrison, *Beloved*
7. J. D. Salinger, *Catcher in the Rye*
8. William Shakespeare, *Twelfth Night*
9. John Steinbeck, *Of Mice and Men*
10. Mark Twain, *The Adventures of Tom Sawyer*
11. Alice Walker, *The Color Purple*

The full list is longer; these are just some of the highlights. But they make the point: when the government is in charge of schooling, decisions about educational form and content will reflect the reigning political atmosphere of the moment, with all the stupidity, short-sightedness, and prejudice that implies. It may be that these consequences of governmental oversight of education were unintentional, but, really, they can hardly be surprising.

2. Education Is Too Important to Be Left to Politics and Politicians

The education of children is one of the most important tasks facing parents and communities. Yet the same objections to government support of religion also dog government support of education: it dissociates people from something to which they should have an intensely personal commitment, and it is unreliable because of the inefficiency, incompetence, or moral or religious failings of state agents and bureaucrats.

A common complaint of conscientious parents involved in the operations of their children's government school is that there are disappointingly few parents similarly involved. Low parental involvement is a chronic and perennially lamented problem, but why are so few parents involved? One plausible explanation is that when the state takes on the responsibility of providing for the education of children, parents correspondingly, and quite understandably, stop concerning themselves with it. The present system of government schooling—with its compulsory monetary support by taxation, compulsory attendance, compulsory certification of teachers, and compulsory curricula—attempts to cover almost every aspect over which parents might otherwise have exercised any independent judgment. Parents do not decide on their own how much they are willing to pay or to whom, whether their children should or should not continue to attend school, what qualifications teachers or administrators should have, or what the curriculum is. With so little, then, for which parents are personally responsible, and moreover dissuaded from attempting to become personally involved by the knowledge that they will not likely be able to accomplish anything,[31] it is not surprising that they tend to dissociate themselves from what should be a matter of great personal attention and commitment. Taking responsibility for one's children's education requires a lot of energy, after all. If someone else is looking after it for you whether you asked for help or not, it is only human nature to allow one's vigilance to relax.

Plato was perhaps the first person to make a systematic case for the crucial importance of carefully designing the educational system of children, and he made sure not to leave such matters to just anybody. Indeed, this was a matter that could be properly handled only by the "wisest" human beings: the philosophers.[32] But Plato by no means stands alone: a succession of thinkers over the centuries has maintained the great importance of education and the even greater importance of removing responsibility for it from parents and putting it in the hands of "experts" enjoying a state-enforced monopoly. Various reasons are given for this, but most revolve around the central claim that education is necessary for a person to live a flourishing or truly good life and thus cannot be left to the benighted souls who populate society. But note that exactly the same claim could be made for religion: since having the correct religious beliefs is crucially important to leading a good life—and, one might add, having a good afterlife—it cannot be left in the hands of your average Joes. No, discovering the true will of God or the gods must be the exclusive province of shamans, witch doctors, clerics, and mystics, all of whom have secret ceremonies and mysterious rites and speak or communicate with the other world in strange tongues. Your job is to accept unconditionally what they say—it was divinely inspired, after all—and to obey without question.

If we take away the rhetorical flair, this is not at all unlike the position adopted by those running government education in America. Education of children is too important to be left to their parents; indeed, we must actively, though often clandestinely, seek to minimize or destroy altogether the influence on children that their racist, sexist, classist, homophobic, parochial, eurocentric, capitalist, speciesist, and

---

[31] This is partly because school administrators often deliberately shut parents out. See, for example, Brimelow's *The Worm in the Apple* and Maranto's "No Class: Why Are 'Public' Schools Closed to the Public?"

[32] *Republic,* bks. 4 and 5.

superstitious parents have. Children's education must instead be overseen and directed by experts from "education schools" where things are taught that you just would not understand, and where people write in language you would barely recognize as your own. Moreover, we shall have to require attendance at our schools by law; we shall discourage those trying to opt for schools outside our purview by making them pay twice; we shall resist innovations such as homeschooling or vouchers with demonization, vilification, and vigorous pursuit of legal hindrances to them; we shall undertake to convince every citizen, starting of course with their children in our charge, that public schooling is necessary for the good of the country and for the good of the children and that the country and the children cannot be served in any other way; and we shall campaign against any critic or reformer, resist any studies or data critical of us, and minimize the chances of ever losing our monopoly by treating all substantive dissension from our wisdom as unpatriotic, un-American, anti-poor, and generally immoral.[33]

Does that about cover it? Now do not object that not every single member of the government schooling establishment—not every single teacher, every single administrator, every single school board member—consciously believes all this and deliberately acts in the service of these low ends. Of course not: it bears repeating that some teachers are quite competent and well intentioned, even surprisingly so given the conditions in which they work. But the lowest, not the highest, common denominator usually prevails. Consider this question: what *other* fundamental organizing theory, what other systematic educational worldview, is better able to explain what the government education establishment—as a whole, if not every single member—does?[34]

I agree with Plato and the education establishment about the importance of children's education, and that is precisely why I argue that it should not be left to the dynamics of political processes. And this is the same argument made in the case of religion. If, therefore, the importance of religion warrants that decisions regarding it be removed from the arena of political decision making, the same conclusion should follow, I argue, for education.

[33] See Brimelow's *The Worm in the Apple* and Gatto's *The Exhausted School* for numerous examples.

[34] Some critics draw strongly negative conclusions about the general moral character of these educational institutions, as well as of the administrators who oversee them. See, for example, David Limbaugh's *Persecution*, Val MacQueen's "'Frankly, I Blame the Schools,'" and Thomas Sowell's *Inside American Education*.

3. Government Support for Education Violates People's Rights

Finally, government support for education also commits whatever rights violations that government support for religion does. It infringes upon a person's right to free speech to make him support an educational system with which he disagrees, on exactly the same grounds given in the case of religion. And if a person has beliefs about religion, morality, or politics that differ from what is taught in the government schools, forcing him nevertheless to support that school system involves the same rights violation as does forcing him to support a religion in which he does not believe.

Educational policies and curricula are ultimately dependent on our views about deep matters of conscience—such as conceptions of the good life or religious commitments[35]—and hence they are protected by the same freedom of conscience that would protect our beliefs about matters of religion. You simply cannot have it both ways. You cannot with consistency endorse state supervision of education but object to state supervision of religion. Emerson's quip that "a foolish consistency is the hobgoblin of little minds" is aimed, and rightly so, at those who insist on consistency regarding the trivial matters that occupy little minds; but it is not aimed, as indeed the quotation implies, at weighty matters such as these.

OBJECTIONS

A handful of objections typically arise and should be addressed. The first is that the cases of religion and education are not in fact analogous because whereas everyone supports education, not everyone supports religion; thus one might claim that government support for education enjoys a prima facie justification that government support for religion does not. I suspect, however, that the widespread endorsement of "education" is the joint product of two things: *vagueness* and *habit*. Everyone supports "education" partly because the term is vague enough to mean very different things to different people. But that support evaporates once details of a specific program are fleshed out. Indeed, the endless and ongoing battles over public school curricula would seem to be evidence that in fact there is exceedingly little general agreement about what the form and content of "education" should be.

---

[35] See Resch's "Human Variation and Individuality."

If you ask people a question like "Do you oppose or support education?" the answer will of course be obvious. But try asking these more specific, and thus dispositive, questions instead:

- "Do you oppose or support mandatory prayer in public schools?"
- "Do you oppose or support instruction on the use of condoms, on masturbation, on homosexuality, and on anal sex in the fifth grade?"
- "Do you oppose or support the abolition of class rankings?"
- "Do you oppose or support teaching that Christopher Columbus was a great man who discovered America (or was a racist imperialist exploiting indigenous peoples)?"
- "Do you oppose or support teaching that homosexuality is natural (or that opposing homosexual rights is a vice like racism, or that homosexuality is a sin)?"
- "Do you oppose or support teaching creation science (or intelligent design or evolution)?"

And so on. The point is clear, but I would add that these examples were chosen specifically because American public schools take stances on each of them. The battles fought over these topics are epic and legendary, and they and others like them recur annually in school districts throughout the country. As long as the government is in charge of education, and thus imposes a one-size-fits-all policy, battles like these will continue to be political, rather than educational, issues. And they will never go away.[36]

These considerations also dispatch a related objection to my argument, namely, that whereas the state cannot secure religious conviction, it can provide education. The above considerations demonstrate that the state could provide "education" only as long as the term "education" is not defined with any precision. The moment one begins to specify what actually constitutes education, the irreconcilable differences indicated above come flooding in. There might be general agreement that the first step in any educational program is mastery of the three "Rs"—reading, writing, and arithmetic. But that can be accomplished by the third or fourth grade. It is what happens for the subsequent ten years of mandatory government schooling that is at issue. Hence although it might be true that in (sufficiently vague) principle the government can provide education, any particular actual program of government schooling will conflict with substantial numbers of people's own conceptions of what constitutes education.

---

[36] See Dianne Ravitch's "Ethnomathematics" and Jonathan Zimmerman's *Whose America?*

The other main factor contributing to the semblance of consensus about education is that since the close of the nineteenth century, an almost continuous succession of influential people in America, beginning with Horace Mann, Edward Ross, and John Dewey, has argued that "public schooling" is required to mold children into the kind of citizens a "twentieth-century democracy" needs.[37] The result is that by now most people are so thoroughly steeped in belief in the necessity of such schooling that the notion of its abolition never surfaces. As is the case with other beliefs that are held on the basis of deeply ingrained habit and inculcation, their advocates tend to meet searching questioning not by considering, contemplating, and weighing it but by ignoring it or dismissing it, often with a dose of invective and contumely thrown in for good measure.

Thus the vagueness in what the term "education" is perceived to indicate and the long-standing, habitual acceptance of the necessity and benevolence of public schooling combine to give the impression of universal support for education. But that impression is only apparent.

Another objection to my argument is that, regardless of whatever merits it might have, no self-respecting society should contemplate abolishing public schooling because of the disastrous effects this would have on the poor. Public schooling gives the poor a chance; without it, only the children of the rich would get an education, and we would thereby condemn the poor to remain a permanent underclass. Hence we must make an exception to the normal rules of justice in this case.

I argued in chapter 3 that one should not make an exception to the rules of justice for politicians or agents of the state, an argument I would apply here as well. But a number of other responses to this objection also present themselves, including disputing that such bad consequences would in fact ensue from the abolition of public schooling. Before considering them, however, let me make two points about this objection. First, I believe it underestimates the resourcefulness of poor people. This argument assumes, rather condescendingly I think, that if they do not get an expensive state-designed education, they will be "uneducated"; and if someone does not provide an education for them, they will not be able to get it for themselves. But poor people, like everyone else, have

---

[37] For rehearsals of this history, see the work already cited of Coulson, Richman, Rochester, Rothbard, West, and Zimmerman. For Dewey's own statements of his views, see his essays "What Is Freedom?," "Ethical Principles Underlying Education," "Progressive Education and the Science of Education," "American Education and Culture," and "The School and Society," all contained in the edited collection *John Dewey on Education.*

strong natural incentives to procure the means requisite to their ends,[38] and I would suggest that they are at least as capable of doing this as your average local school board member or "education school" graduate. Remember too that going, for example, to a fancy university is not the best educational route for everyone—far from it. Some would be much better served by trade schools, vocational schools, or apprenticeships. As with paths to happiness, no single path of education is appropriate for everyone. The right path for any given individual, poor or not, can be determined only by exercising his own (or his parents' own) judgment based on local knowledge of his situation. State agents, who will not have this knowledge, are thus better advised, once again, to mind their own business.

A second response to this objection draws strictly on the analogical argument I have made above. The objection posits this disanalogy between the cases of religion and schooling: whatever may be the case with religion, schooling is simply too important to be left to the vagaries of the market, where class antagonisms, "old boy" networks, exploitation of the disadvantaged, crass self-interest, or other vices are the order of the day. The state is thus justified, on grounds of what might be called "social justice," if not plain old regular justice, in intervening in educational matters and correcting the inconsistencies, instabilities, or inequities to which markets and private enterprise lead.[39]

But there is no real disanalogy here after all, because supporters of religion can make precisely the same claims on behalf of religion: they too can argue that holding correct religious beliefs is simply too important to be left to the hurly-burly of the market and must therefore be guaranteed by the state. For what argument would block the religion-statist's claim that would not simultaneously block the education-statist's claim? Not the argument that everyone supports education but not religion, for the reasons already discussed. Moreover, the education-statist's confidence that he is *correct* in his estimation of the importance of education, whereas the religion-statist is *incorrect* in his estimation of the importance of religion, is also insufficient: besides suffering from a lack of supporting evidence, such a claim would be just as hotly contested by the religion-statist as the reversed claim would be by the education-statist.

---

[38] For evidence of this, see West's "Economic Analysis, Positive and Normative" and *Education and the State*, chap. 17.

[39] See "Edison's Discovery," *Wall Street Journal Online*, August 25, 2004.

THE EMPIRICAL QUESTION

Let us not shrink, however, from the empirical issue broached in the objection. Would the abolition of government education in fact help or hinder the poor in their attempts to escape poverty? Another way of putting the objection is to claim that the private sector would simply not be up to the task of educating the entire populace. Sometimes this is alleged to be because its resources are too meager, other times because it is so shot through with moral or religious or other prejudice that the disfavored classes, whatever they are, would simply be left out in the cold. We must confess to a certain amount of speculation here—though no more than is ever involved in economic forecasting (and, by the way, that holds true for the person pressing this speculative objection too). Instead, we must rely on whatever suggestive historical evidence there is. Is there evidence that can give us confidence in predicting what would happen if the state stopped subsidizing and regulating education, and took all the hundreds of billions of dollars it currently takes out of the private sector to spend on this enterprise annually and instead returned it to the people from whom it takes it? Thankfully, yes—and a mountain of it. There is actual evidence, actual experience, actual data out there that address this worry—and it all supports the expectation that *the private sector would serve the needs of everyone, including especially the poor, better than the government education establishment does now.* Indeed, the evidence on this point is so strong that this is perhaps the single best argument for abolishing government education.

I do not list all the evidence here: that would be impossible, since there is so much (I do, however, list several sources of more information in the bibliography at the end of the chapter). Most of the evidence crystallizes in support of four main contentions: (1) public schooling has historically gotten progressively worse despite real increases in funding; (2) public schooling does a worse job than does private schooling, even though the latter typically has only about half the funding; (3) it is precisely among the poorest students where public schooling is at its worst; and (4) private enterprise and market-based economies have historically benefited all income classes, including in particular the poor, and thus would be expected to perform equally well in this case as well. I have already given some evidence of the first claim, so I do not repeat it here; and the fourth claim I defended at length in chapter 5. That leaves us with the second and third claims.

A CONTROLLED EXPERIMENT

Ideally, what one would want is a controlled experiment to test these hypotheses. Suppose, for example, we could take a public school district made up principally of poor students whose facilities and academic performances were typically subpar, and over a substantial length of time, say a decade or so, give them all the funding the administrators deemed necessary and all the local control and oversight they wished to make the school into whatever they wanted. If we could give them everything the local educators desired in terms of teachers, facilities, books, whatever, and let them put all that money and all their creativity to work, then the results would be telling indeed. Then we could see just how much of poor public schools' performance is due to factors outside their control—such as chronically underfunded budgets—and how much of it is actually due to the incompetence that critics allege. Would that not be an illuminating experiment?

Well, we need not dream. The claim that public schools' woes are due to lack of money or hamstringing policies was dramatically disproved by the twelve-year experiment conducted in the Kansas City, Missouri, school district by federal judge Russell Clark.[40] In 1985 Judge Clark found that the Kansas City school district was abysmally bad, and because it was populated by mostly black students, he ruled that it violated the "equal protection" clause of the Fourteenth Amendment of the United States Constitution. He therefore ordered that the state of Missouri immediately begin massive subsidization of the Kansas City schools. He asked the local school district officials what they wanted, telling them to "dream" and not let money be an object, and then he ordered that the state provide funding for *everything* they wanted.

The results were magnificent. Over the next twelve years, the state gave the Kansas City district some $2 billion over and above their locally realized funds. What did these princely sums buy? First and foremost it allowed the school district to spend upwards of $11,700 per pupil, which is more money per pupil in adjusted dollars than what any of the other largest 280 school districts in America spent. It got the Kansas City district a dramatic 40 percent increase in teachers' salaries, fifteen

---

[40] The following facts are again widely available. One excellent study is Ciotti's "Money and School Performance: Lessons from the Kansas City Desegregation Experiment." See also Coulson, *Market Education,* chap. 6; Hollingsworth's "Judge Ends Kansas City Desegregation Case"; the *Wall Street Journal*'s "Jayhawk Judgment"; and Wildavsky's "Kansas City Schools Learn the Hard Way"

new schools, fifty-six "magnet" schools, and facilities that included, as one reporter summarized it, "an Olympic-sized swimming pool with an underwater viewing room, television and animation studios, a robotics lab, a 25-acre wildlife sanctuary, a zoo, a model United Nations with simultaneous translation capability, and field trips to Mexico and Senegal. The student-teacher ratio was 12 or 13 to 1, the lowest of any major school district."[41] The new $32 million Central High School boasted the very latest technology and computer equipment; even its athletic teams enjoyed all the latest equipment. Its fencing team, for example, was now coached by the former head of the Soviet Union's Olympic fencing team.

You might be wondering what the educational results were amid all this magnificence. The truth is almost too much to bear: there was *no* improvement in the students' reading or math scores, the gap between white students' achievement in other districts and black students' achievement in this district did not close and in some cases actually *increased,* and the drop-out rate actually *rose* to 60 percent. Defenders of the government education establishment had at the beginning of Judge Clark's project hailed it as a controlled experiment that would finally prove once and for all that, contrary to their critics' claim that money is not the problem, money was in fact the central problem and that once that problem was solved everything else would fall into place. When, however, in 1997 even Judge Clark realized that the experiment had been a complete failure, he took himself off the case—but not before having saddled Missouri with the huge monetary cost and the not insubstantial social cost associated with the disruptions and divisions his mandates introduced into the affected communities.

What general conclusion does this case license? Several, I believe, but the one that is relevant here is that money is not the problem with public schools. If money could save them, it certainly would have done so in this riotous orgy of spending.[42]

---

[41] Ciotti, "Money and School Performance," p. 1.

[42] There is a great deal of evidence supporting the general claim that more money alone is not the answer, and some evidence even suggesting a negative relationship between increased state funding and student performance. For some examples, see Childs and Shakeshaft's "A Meta-Analysis of Research on the Relationship of Educational Expenditures and Student Achievement"; Coulson, *Market Education,* chap. 6; and Hanuschek's "The Economics of Schooling" and "Impact of Differential Expenditures on School Performance." See also Gary Orfield's 1994 Harvard University Study, which concludes by saying, "Just putting money into schools is not likely to produce benefits"; and Mary Jordan's "Study Finds Separate Still Unequal—Extra Money Not Seen to Aid Segregated Schools."

ARE PRIVATE SCHOOLS REALLY ANY BETTER?

One often hears the claim that private schools do a better job than public schools, and one often hears in response that private schools have
advantages that public schools do not—for example, that private schools
can expel troublemakers, that they do not have to deal with "special
needs" children, and that they have more money. False on all counts. Private schools do indeed outperform government schools on virtually every
measure, but they do so despite enormous handicaps that the government
schools do not face. Why? There is a greater level of the crucial parental
involvement in private schools, even among poor parents, than there is
in government schools; private schools create a greater feeling of shared
enterprise and community than government schools, again even among
the poor parents and children; and teachers in private schools tend to
have better morale than those in government schools, despite being
paid on average only *65 percent* what their government school peers get
paid.[43]

Consider for a moment the single largest private schooling enterprise
in the United States, that conducted under the aegis of the Roman
Catholic church. Catholic private schools average only one-tenth the
bureaucrats and administrators that their government school counterparts have when controlled for the number of students in their care, and
yet Catholic school students significantly outperform their government
school counterparts on standardized tests. Again, why? Studies indicate it
is because students in Catholic schools spend more of their in-school time
on academic subjects than do government school students; they average,
in fact, approximately 25 percent more time on subjects such as foreign
languages, mathematics, and science. When controlled for family background, ethnicity, and overall economic status, the Catholic school kids
simply trounce the government school kids, *especially* for underprivileged
minorities.[44]

It is furthermore an exaggeration to claim that Catholic schools are
far more restrictive in admissions or expel far more students than government schools. Nationwide, Catholic schools accept on average 88 percent
of those who apply, only one-third of them maintain waiting lists, and

---

[43] See Coulson, *Market Education*, chap. 8, and West's *Education and the State*, chap. 17.
[44] See Sowell, *Inside American Education*, chap. 1. For a competing view that I find quite
unpersuasive, see Sarah and Christopher Lubienski's "A New Look at Public and Private
Schools."

they suspend or dismiss only a small handful of students per year. This is a difference, but it does not account for the full discrepancies—especially when it is revealed that many public schools artificially inflate their students' scores by omitting from the data pools precisely the scores their "special needs" and "troubled" students make. Many Catholic schools on the contrary take it as part of their moral mission to minister to the poor and troubled of their communities, and studies indicate, consistent with this stated mission, that they routinely give scholarships and subsidies to poor students and take extraordinary measures to help troubled ones. Other studies indicate that poor and troubled or "at-risk" students are more likely to drop out, start taking or dealing drugs, join gangs, have teenage and unwed pregnancies, and engage in criminal activity if they go to government schools than if they go to Catholic schools—even the Catholic schools that are in exactly the same neighborhoods, sometimes just down the block.[45]

To dispel another pernicious myth: it turns out that government schools are on average significantly more racially segregated than Catholic or other private schools.[46]

The final fact, and perhaps the coup de grace: private schools cost on average only *half as much* as government schools: $3,116 per student for the former as compared with $6,653 per student for the latter in 1994 dollars.[47] Even taking into account the subsidies that some private schools get from their associated congregations and the donations they get from their alumni, private schools still cost only 60 to 65 percent of what the government schools cost. Thus the facts just will not go away: private schooling outperforms government schooling, it does so at a lower cost, and it does so, incredibly, despite the existence of a nationwide government-enforced monopoly against which it must compete.

[45] See the *American Enterprise's* group of articles under the title "Race, Broken Schools, and Affirmative Action"; Bolick's "A Lot More to Learn"; Chira's "Where Children Learn How to Learn: Inner City Pupils in Catholic Schools"; Davidson's "Private Schools for Black Pupils Are Flourishing"; Hill et al.'s *High Schools with Character;* Putka, "Education Reformers Have New Respect for Catholic Schools"; Sowell's "Black Education" and *Inside American Education,* chap. 1; Steers's "The Catholic Schools' Black Students"; and "Urban Minorities Benefit Most from Catholic Schools," in the *University of Chicago Chronicle.*

[46] See Coleman's *Equality and Achievement in Education* and Greene's "Integration Where It Counts."

[47] Coulson, *Market Education,* p. 277.

PUBLIC GOODS AND BADS

A final defense of government schooling holds it to be what economists call a "public good," or something that provides benefits to others without requiring or being able to require those other beneficiaries to pay for it. Typical examples of "public goods" are clean air and national defense. In both cases, once the good in question has been produced—once there is clean air or a national defense—it is difficult to prevent everyone from benefiting from it, even those who did not contribute to or pay for it, and one person's enjoyment of it does not measurably diminish the ability of others to enjoy it as well. Given this definition you can probably imagine lots of other potential "public goods." Perhaps this book is one: even if you paid for your copy, I cannot prevent you from photocopying it or lending it to your friend. The argument as it applies here is that public schooling counts as a 'public good' and therefore the government is justified in making everyone pay, just as it makes everyone pay for environmental regulations and cleanups and for national defense. Now, people argue about what actually count as public goods, but let us skip over that debate here and focus instead on the case of government schooling.

So: how does government schooling count as a public good? It would seem, first of all, that whatever its benefits are, they are concentrated in the students themselves. They themselves are the ones, after all, who stand to make more money in the future and lead more fulfilling lives if they become educated. Moreover, if you want to exclude someone from enjoying the benefits of government schooling who does not pay for it, the easy solution is either not to let him in or to make him pay for it. Thus government schooling seems to be rather one of those kinds of goods that can easily and appropriately be paid for by its users, and hence not a "public good" at all. Government schooling defenders dispute this claim, however. They argue that everyone benefits from public schooling, whether they themselves go there or have children who go there or not. Why? Because, they argue, government schooling provides things we all benefit from: an educated electorate, citizens prepared to deliberate democratically, a shared cultural heritage.[48] The argument is that whether you realize it or not you benefit if your neighbors are and have these things, and that means that even if you enjoy no *direct* benefit from government schools you do nevertheless *indirectly* benefit. The defenders conclude that therefore the government may "ask"—that is, force—you

---

[48] For presentations of each of these claims, see Tyack's *Seeking Common Ground*.

to pay for government schools regardless of whether you or your children go there.[49]

Yet this argument fails in numerous ways. Begin with the fallaciously inferred conclusion. The argument assumes that it follows from the fact that if you benefit from X, then others may (1) forcibly manage X in your life and (2) force you to pay for X (and their management of it). But those conclusions do not follow. Grant that exercising is good for me. Does it follow that you may appoint yourself my Exercise Administrator, develop an exercise regimen for me, and then force me to pay both for you and your regimen, whether I abide by it or not? Does it follow that the state may do these things? Or grant that marriage would be good for me (as empirical evidence does indeed suggest, especially for men[50]), and then ask the same questions. One could make the argument that each of us benefits from any number of things others provide: perhaps everyone is better off because of the existence of philosophy professors, or people carrying concealed weapons, or Southern Baptist ministers, or Good Samaritans, or children playing in the park next to your office, and so on. Again, does that mean you should be made to pay these people?

One is reminded here again of Plato's justification for the scheme of compulsory education laid out in his *Republic,* the goal of which was to control all the nonphilosophers and give them correct—though not necessarily *true*—beliefs. Plato dubbed these politically expedient teachings "noble falsehoods." He thought that the philosophers would have to tell them to everyone else in his ideal city in order to make sure that all the dimmer souls appreciated and docilely accepted the place in the community assigned to them by their "noble" leaders.[51] So you and I would be told myths, stories, and legends designed to habituate us to believe in, among other things, the necessity and goodness of our leaders' control of our lives. One detects a whiff of the noble falsehood odor, I think, in the "public goods" argument for government schooling. Like some in the education establishment, Plato might himself have had only the best of intentions—perhaps he really did believe in something called the Good that only select humans, the "philosophers," could apprehend, thereby justifying their rule over the rest of us and the necessity of our

---

[49] For a classic defense of this position, see Friedman's *Capitalism and Freedom,* chap. 6. For a rebuttal, see West's *Education and the State,* chaps. 3–7.

[50] See, for one recent example, the BBC's "Being Single 'Worse than Smoking,'" http://news.bbc.co.uk/1/hi/health/2195609.stm (accessed December 14, 2005).

[51] *Republic,* bk. 3.

unquestioning obedience. But the practical upshot of arguments like these is to put manifestly mortal and imperfect human beings into positions of considerable power over others, while providing them a meretricious rationalization of their lordly rule.

Is that not what this "public goods" argument does? Am *I* not, after all, the one who should judge whether I benefit from the existence of government schooling? What if I do not believe I do? What indeed if I believe that government schools train pupils in a dangerous and poisonous mix of ignorance, amorality, and high self-esteem? What if I therefore judge that government schooling is in fact a public *bad*, one that I pay for in more ways than one? Should the enormous costs associated with prisons and policing be added into the equation, for example? There are people who believe precisely these things, and as we have seen they have reason to do so.[52] By what justification, then, do we ignore their beliefs and force them to pay nonetheless? Because *we* believe in government schooling? Then let *us* pay for it, and allow those who wish to opt out do so—and let us do the honest thing and let them take their money (and their children) with them. One cannot respect the personhood of another by any other course of action.

But what of the worst-case scenario, the poorest of the poor, who would simply have no option for themselves or their children? Let us first of all not forget that these are precisely the people who are already failed the worst by the current system.[53] We must not compare the scenario I propose against an imaginary and ideally perfect system; we must rather compare *actually available alternatives*. Since the world is imperfect, some children will be disserved under any scenario. The question, then, is not which scenario is most perfect in its hypothetical description, but, rather, which of the actually practicable scenarios will do the best to minimize the failures and maximize the successes. And here, I suggest, the evidence is clear.

One final point. Is it impolite to point out that you fail in your moral duty to the poor if you charge the state with taking care of it for you—and that, on the contrary, you can fulfill your duty only by making a *personal* effort to help those who need it? If there are children who need help with their schooling, then help them! Find them, figure out what help they need, and do your best to give it to them. Do not take the inadequate, if

---

[52] See, for example, Rogge and Goodrich's "Education in a Free Society."

[53] See above, nn. 36–46 for evidence. For a recent, albeit indirect, illustration of this point, see Levitt and Dubner's *Freakonomics*, chap. 3.

easy, route of endorsing a political apparatus that forces others to attend to your moral responsibilities for you.

PRIVATE VICES, PUBLIC VENEERS OF VIRTUE

We should not forget that, just as for centuries kings, priests, and Parliaments have known that controlling both the state and the religion was the key to controlling people, compulsory government schooling was explicitly introduced for exactly the same reason: control. Exhibit A is Plato's recommendation that society's leaders use "noble falsehoods" to keep us ignorant and unwashed masses in line. Similarly, modern public schooling has its roots in sixteenth-century attempts by Protestant church leaders who wanted to forcibly train people in correct religious beliefs. As historians such as Andrew Coulson, Sheldon Richman, Edwin G. West, and Jonathan Zimmerman have shown, controlling people for correct religious, moral, or political beliefs and behavior has continued to be the driving, frequently explicit motivation behind public school advocacy. Now, some might agree that it is a good idea to mold children in accordance with correct religious, moral, or political beliefs, and hence they might be sympathetic to this motivation behind government schooling. But that no more establishes the acceptability of the practice than would the widespread acceptance of the king's official religion among those who already happen to subscribe to it. And of course it does not address the numerous other objections raised in this chapter to state intervention in education.

I close this chapter by sharing a personal observation based on my own experience with people defending government education against the objections I raise in this chapter. They often fall into three groups. First, there are those who are simply unaware of the actual facts of how public schools perform, which policies they pursue, how much money they waste, and so on. Their position instead merely reflects the decades of public cheerleading about the goodness and necessity of government schools. The next group contains those people whose support for public schools is the product of a political or moral ideology, and as such is impervious to facts or argument. In this they are like religious believers who could not even in principle be dissuaded. The third and final group is those who are themselves part of the government education establishment or who benefit from it in some way. This group includes the teachers, administrators, counselors, advisers, secretaries, administrative assistants, executive assistants, and school board members; the contractors, vendors, groundskeepers, and maintenance personnel; the politicians who take donations from teachers' unions or have spouses or other family members who are otherwise employed somehow in government education; the leaders of the teachers' unions who take their salaries from those unions; the police and other security guards, the metal-detector manufacturers, the doctors and nurses who administer all those psychoactive drugs and the pharmaceutical companies who supply them; the politically sensitive textbook manufacturers and their hundred-million-dollar state-wide government school contracts; the public school graduates who cannot bring themselves to think ill of their own school or of the training they themselves received; and so on. There are no doubt other groups I have forgotten. When you add them up, that is quite a lot of people—and it goes some way, does it not, toward explaining why it is so difficult for so many people even to consider major change in the government schooling establishment.

The opinion of anyone who belongs to any of these categories, however, should be viewed with a measure of skepticism. I invite you to review your own experience in this regard or to take notice when the subject comes up in the future of who is making what argument. Perhaps you too will begin to wonder exactly what the public's considerable faith and credit in the government schooling system actually rest on.

Bibliography

American Library Association. "The 100 Most Frequently Banned Books, 1990–2000." Http://www.ala.org/ala/oif/bannedbooksweek/bbwlinks/100mostfrequently.htm, accessed December 14, 2005.

"America's C–." *Wall Street Journal Online*, December 15, 2004.

"Audit Describes 8 Years of Looting by L.I. School Officials."*New York Times*, March 3, 2005.

Barnett, Randy. *Restoring the Lost Constitution: The Presumption of Liberty.* Princeton, N.J.: Princeton University Press, 2003.

Bastiat, Frédéric. *The Law.* Irvington-on-Hudson, N.Y.: Foundation for Economic Education, 1998 (1850).

BBC News. "Being Single 'Worse Than Smoking.'" August 15, 2002. Http://news.bbc.co.uk/1/hi/health/2195609.stm, accessed December 14, 2005.

Berliner, David C., and Bruce J. Biddle. *The Manufactured Crisis: Myths, Fraud, and the Attacks on America's Public Schools.* New York: Perseus, 1996.

Bloom, Allan. *The Closing of the American Mind: How Higher Education Has Failed Democracy and Impoverished the Souls of Today's Students.* New York: Simon and Schuster, 1987.

Bolick, Clint. "A Lot More to Learn: Make 'No Excuses' for Schools That Fail Black Americans." *Wall Street Journal Online*, October 9, 2003. Http://www.opinionjournal.com/1a/?id=11000437, accessed December 14, 2005.

Brimelow, Peter. *The Worm in the Apple: How the Teacher Unions Are Destroying American Education.* New York: HarperCollins, 2003.

Buchanan, James, and Gordon Tullock. *The Calculus of Consent: Logical Foundations of Constitutional Democracy.* Ann Arbor: University of Michigan Press, 1962.

Childs, Stephen, and Charol Shakeshaft. "A Meta-Analysis of Research on the Relationship between Educational Expenditures and Student Achievement." *Journal of Education Finance* 12, no. 4 (Fall 1986): 249–63.

Chira, Susan. "Where Children Learn How to Learn: Inner City Pupils in Catholic Schools." *New York Times,* November 20, 1991, p. A14.

Ciotti, Paul. "Money and School Performance: Lessons from the Kansas City Desegregation Experiment." *Cato Policy Analysis No. 298.* Washington, D.C.: Cato Institute, 1998.

Coleman, James. *Equality and Achievement in Education.* Boulder, Colo.: Westview Press, 1990.

Coulson, Andrew J. *Market Education: The Unknown History.* New Brunswick, N.J.: Transaction, 1999.

Danford, John W. *Roots of Freedom: A Primer on Modern Liberty.* Wilmington, Del.: ISI Books, 2000.

Davidson, Joe. "Private Schools for Black Pupils Are Flourishing." *Wall Street Journal,* April 15, 1987, p. 37.

Dewey, John. *John Dewey on Education: Selected Writings.* Reginald D. Archambault, ed. Chicago: University of Chicago Press, 1964.

"Duh! 81% of Kids Fail Test." *New York Daily News,* May 10, 2005.

"Edison's Discovery." *Wall Street Journal Online,* August 25, 2004. Http://cob.jmu.edu/doylejm/ec201docs/WSJ`com%20-%20Edison's%20Discovery.htm, accessed December 14, 2005.

Evans, M. Stanton. *The Theme Is Freedom: Religion, Politics, and the American Tradition.* Washington, D.C.: Regnery, 1996.

Flew, Antony. *Social Life and Moral Judgment.* New Brunswick, N.J.: Transaction, 2003.

Friedman, Milton. *Capitalism and Freedom.* Chicago: University of Chicago Press, 1962.

Gatto, John Taylor. *Underground History of American Education: A Schoolteacher's Intimate Investigation into the Problem of Modern Schooling.* New York: Oxford Village Press, 2000.

Gatto, John Taylor. *Dumbing Us Down: The Hidden Curriculum of Compulsory Schooling,* 10th ed. New York: New Society, 2002.

Gatto, John Taylor. *The Exhausted School: Bending the Bars of Traditional Education,* 2nd ed. Berkeley, Calif.: Berkeley Hills Books, 2002.

Graham, Gordon. *The Case against the Democratic State.* Exeter: Imprint Academic, 2002.

Greene, Jay P. "Integration Where It Counts: A Study of Racial Integration in Public and Private School Lunchrooms." *Texas Education Review,* Spring 2000. Http://www.educationreview.homestead.com/Integration.html, accessed December 14, 2005.

Hanushek, Eric A. "The Economics of Schooling: Production and Efficiency in the Public Schools." *Journal of Economic Literature* 24, no. 3 (1986): 1141–77.

Hanushek, Eric A. "Impact of Differential Expenditures on School Performance." *Educational Researcher* 18, no. 4 (1989): 45–51.

Heckman, James J., and Amy L Wax. "Home Alone." *Wall Street Journal Online*, January 23, 2004.

Hill, Paul T., Gail E. Foster, and Tamar Gendler . *High Schools with Character.* Santa Monica, Calif.: RAND Corporation, 1990.

Hollingsworth, Heather. "Judge Ends Kansas City Desegregation Case." *Kansas City Star,* August 14, 2003.

"In a Global Test of Math Skills, U.S. Students behind the Curve." *Washington Post,* December 7, 2004, p. A01.

"Intel Struggling to Fill New Jobs."*Seattle Times,* March 4, 1996.

"Jayhawk Judgment." *Wall Street Journal Online,* June 22, 2005, p. A10.

Jefferson, Thomas. *An Act for Establishing Religious Freedom in the State of Virginia.* In *The Life and Selected Writings of Thomas Jefferson.* Adrienne Koch and William Peden, eds. New York: Modern Library, 1944 (1779).

Jordan, Mary. "Study Finds Separate Still Unequal—Extra Money Not Seen to Aid Segregated Schools." *Seattle Times,* April 7, 1994.

Katz, Michael S. *A History of Compulsory Education Laws.* Bloomington, Ind.: Phi Delta Kappa Education Foundation, 1976.

Kirsch, I. S., et al. *Adult Literacy in America.* U.S. Department of Education. Washington, D.C.: National Center for Education Statistics, 1993.

Levitt, Steven D., and Stephen J. Dubner. *Freakonomics: A Rogue Economist Explores the Hidden Side of Everything.* New York: William Morrow, 2005.

Limbaugh, David. *Persecution: How Liberals Are Waging War against Christianity.* Washington, D.C.: Regnery, 2003.

Locke, John. *Some Thoughts Concerning Education.* In *John Locke: On Politics and Education.* Roslyn, N.Y.: Walter J. Black, 1947 (1693).

Locke, John. *Second Treatise of Government.* Peter Laslett, ed. Cambridge: Cambridge University Press, 1988 (1690).

Locke, John. *Letter Concerning Toleration.* In *John Locke: Political Writings.* David Wootton, ed. Indianapolis, Ind.: Hackett, 2003 (1685).

Lubienski, Sarah Theule, and Christopher Lubienski. "A New Look at Public and Private Schools: Student Background and Mathematics Achievement." *Phi Delta Kappan* (May 2005): 696–99.

Macfarlane, Alan. *The Origins of English Individualism.* Oxford: Basil Blackwell, 1978.

MacQueen, Val. " 'Frankly, I Blame the Schools.' " *Tech Central Station,* June 9, 2005. Http://www.techcentralstation.com/060905C.html, accessed December 14, 2005.

Maranto, Robert. "No Class: Why Are 'Public' Schools Closed to the Public?" *Wall Street Journal Online,* September 16, 2004. Http://www.opinionjournal.com/extra/?id = 110005625, accessed December 14, 2005.

Mill, John Stuart. *On Liberty.* Stefan Collini, ed. Cambridge: Cambridge University Press, 1989 (1859).

Milton, John. *Areopagitica: A Speech of Mr. John Milton for the Liberty of Unlicensed Printing, to the Parliament of England.* New York: Grolier Club, 1890 (1644).

Mulroy, David. *The War against Grammar.* Portsmouth, N.H.: Boynton/Cook, 2003.

National Assessment of Educational Progress. "The NAEP 1996 Technical Report." Http://nces.ed.gov/nationsreportcard//pubs/main1996/1999452.asp, accessed December 14, 2005.

National Association of Scholars. "Today's College Students and Yesteryear's High School Grads: A Comparison of General Cultural Knowledge." December 18, 2002. Http://www.nas.org/reports/senior_poll/senior_poll_report.pdf, accessed December 14, 2005.

Nock, Albert Jay. *The Theory of Education in the United States*. New York: Ayer, 1969 (1932).

Nock, Albert Jay. "Anarchist's Progress." In *The State of the Union*. Charles H. Hamilton, ed. Indianapolis, Ind.: Liberty Press, 1991 (1927).

Orfield, Gary. "Deepening Segregation in America's Public Schools." Harvard University, 1994. Http://www.news.harvard.edu/gazette/1997/04.10/NationalStudyFi.html, accessed December 14, 2005.

Otteson, James R. "Freedom of Religion and Public Schooling." *The Independent Review* 4, no. 4 (Spring 2000): 601–13.

Otteson, James R., ed. *The Levellers: Overton, Walwyn and Lilburne,* 5 vols. Bristol: Thoemmes, 2003.

Pascal, Blaise. *Pensées*. A. J. Krailsheimer, trans. New York: Penguin, 1966.

Plato. *Republic*. G. M. A. Grube, trans. Indianapolis, Ind.: Hackett, 1992 (ca. 380 B.C.).

Putka, Gary. "Education Reformers Have New Respect for Catholic Schools." *Wall Street Journal,* March 28, 1991, p. 1.

"Race, Broken Schools, and Affirmative Action." *The American Enterprise,* April/May 2003.

Ravitch, Dianne. "Ethnomathematics." *Wall Street Journal Online,* June 20, 2005.

Resch, H. George. "Human Variation and Individuality." In *The Twelve-Year Sentence: Radical Views on Compulsory Education*. William F. Rickenbacker, ed. LaSalle, Ill.: Open Court, 1974.

Richman, Sheldon. *Separating School and State*. Fairfax, Va.: Future of Freedom Foundation, 1995.

Rochester, J. Martin. *Class Warfare: Besieged Schools, Bewildered Parents, Betrayed Kids and the Attack on Excellence*. San Francisco, Calif.: Encounter, 2002.

Rogge, Benjamin A., and Pierre F. Goodrich. "Position Paper: Education in a Free Society." In *Education in a Free Society*. Anne Husted Burleigh, ed. Indianapolis, Ind.: Liberty Press, 1973.

Rothbard, Murray N. "Historical Origins." In *The Twelve-Year Sentence: Radical Views on Compulsory Education*. David Boaz and William F. Rickenbacker, eds. San Francisco, Calif.: Fox and Wilkes, 1999 (1974).

Sagan, Carl. *The Demon-Haunted World: Science as a Candle in the Dark*. New York: Ballantine Books, 1997.

Sommer, John W., ed. *The Academy in Crisis: The Political Economy of Higher Education*. New Brunswick, N.J.: Transaction, 1995.

Sowell, Thomas. *Inside American Education: The Decline, the Deception, the Dogma*. New York: Free Press, 1993.

Sowell, Thomas. "Black Education: Achievement, Myths and Tragedies." In *Black Rednecks and White Liberals*. San Francisco: Encounter, 2005.

Stark, Rodney. *For the Glory of God: How Monotheism Led to Reformations, Science, Witch-Hunts, and the End of Slavery.* Princeton, N.J.: Princeton University Press, 2003.

Steers, Stuart. "The Catholic Schools' Black Students." *This World*, December 23, 1990, p. 8.

Stevenson, Harold W. "Learning from Asian Schools." *Scientific American* 267, no. 6 (December 1992): 70–6.

Tomasi, John. "Should Political Liberals Be Compassionate Conservatives? Philosophical Foundations of the Faith-Based Initiative." In *Morality and Politics.* Jeffrey Paul, ed. Cambridge: Cambridge University Press, 2004.

Trenchard, John, and Thomas Gordon. *Cato's Letters: Or Essays on Liberty, Civil and Religious, and Other Important Subjects,* 2 vols. Ronald Hamowy, ed. Indianapolis, Ind.: Liberty Fund, 1995 (1720–3).

Tyack, David. *Seeking Common Ground: Public Schools in a Diverse Society.* Cambridge, Mass.: Harvard University Press, 2003.

"Urban Minorities Benefit Most from Catholic Schools." *University of Chicago Chronicle* 16, no. 12 (March 6, 1997). Http://chronicle.uchicago.edu/970306/catholic.shtml, accessed December 14, 2005.

West, Edwin G. "Economic Analysis, Positive and Normative." In *The Twelve-Year Sentence: Radical Views of Compulsory Schooling.* William F. Rickenbacker, ed. San Francisco, Calif.: Fox and Wilkes, 1999 (1974).

West, Edwin G. *Education and the State: A Study in Political Economy,* 3rd ed. Indianapolis, Ind.: Liberty Press, 1994.

Wildavsky, Ben. "Kansas City Schools Learn the Hard Way." *U.S. News & World Report,* May 8, 2000.

Zimmerman, Jonathan. *Whose America? Culture Wars in the Public Schools.* Cambridge, Mass.: Harvard University Press, 2002.

7

Moral Hobgoblins

Inclusion and Exclusion

A number of issues that currently occupy a large place in discussions about ethics, particularly discussions about "practical" or "applied" ethics, are rendered significantly less prickly and intractable if we apply the concepts and tools developed in Part I of this book. Thus if we keep in mind the central principles of what it means to be a *person*, what *judgment* is, and what are matters of *justice* and what are matters of other *virtues*, I think we shall find we can navigate many new and unfamiliar waters with confidence. Let us then take up a few of these vexed issues and see, based on the tools we have, what we can make of them. In this chapter the focus is a few of the ways human beings include or exclude others.

WATCH YOUR LANGUAGE

Let us begin with an issue that, if judged by the number of people who address it in one way or another, is of great general concern: gender-specific, or gender-exclusive, language. Worry about things like whether writers use a "generic 'he' " relies on the fallacy that words determine reality, rather than the other way around. If I refer to you as the *chairman* of my department, I am not asserting that you are a chair, or a man, or some combination: I am asserting that you are the head or leader or director of my department. Your sex is not implicated in the term, any more than whether you are a piece of furniture is. Similarly with *mailman, foreman, policeman, fireman,* and so on.[1] If this were not so, then *chairperson*

---

[1] One venerable source supporting my position is Strunk and White's *The Elements of Style,* pp. 60–1. For an alternative view, see Warren's "Guidelines for Non-Sexist Use of Language," http://www.apa.udel.edu/apa/publications/texts/nonsexist.html.

would be no improvement, since the word "person" contains the word "son," which is male after all.

Yet those who a few decades ago began to call attention to these words as words and to decry some of their uses offered theories about their origins that conflict with my claim. Their theories typically hold that such terms are reflective of the historically patriarchal organization of most human societies—that is, of (unjustifiable) male dominance. It is because they believe such language to be symbolic or reflective, or perhaps partly constitutive, of this larger unjust social order that they believe it is important enough to address squarely and publicly, and to work to change it.[2]

My own layman's suspicion is that the terms at issue arose rather as a joint product of (1) the fact that most of the posts in question have historically been held by men and (2) the fact that "man" is shorter, and thus easier to affix and say, than, for example, "person." It must be admitted, however, that most speculations about word origins are little more than guesswork, since the historical beginnings of words—noble and useful efforts like that of the *Oxford English Dictionary* notwithstanding—remain mostly shrouded in mystery. That is why there are so many competing accounts of word origins. Go to any good bookstore and you will find lots of books offering rival accounts of the origins of words and phrases. Thus most of this species of learning falls into what the eighteenth-century Scottish philosopher Dugald Stewart called "conjectural history": not what *was* the case, since we do not know for sure, but, rather, what *might have been* the case, based on patchy circumstantial evidence and what seem to us plausible conjectures. Claims, for example, that Homer was really two, or ten, or indefinitely many persons, and that Shakespeare was really the nobleman Edward de Vere, are of this type.[3] They are utterly otiose, of course, since the reasons we read Homer and Shakespeare ultimately have nothing to do with such questions, even if they are of some curiosity.

In any case, the explanation that the language reformers offer simply can't be correct, since it rests on a now-exploded theory of language.

---

[2] See, for example, Vetterling-Braggin's *Sexist Language*. For discussion, see Pinker's chapter "The Language Mavens" in his *The Language Instinct* and the articles contained in the "Free Speech" section of Hugh LaFollette's edited collection, *Ethics in Practice*. For exploration of some of the political issues involved, see Bernstein's *You Can't Say That!*, Sunstein's *Democracy and the Problem of Free Speech* and *Why Societies Need Dissent*, and Levy's "Literacy, Language Rights, and the Modern State."

[3] For a discussion of the theories about Homer, see Bernard Knox's "Introduction" to Robert Fagles's translation of the *Iliad;* for an argument that Shakespeare was not Shakespeare, see Joseph Sobran's *Alias Shakespeare*.

Indeed, it gets the truth of the matter exactly backward. People do not first decide what kind of language they want to have, then create one, and then apply it to their experiences and use it to understand or manipulate the world. On the contrary: they first have the experiences, and they then develop language to try to communicate their experiences. A word such as *mailman*, for example, would not have first been deliberately invented—as part of, say, a larger effort to keep women in their place—and then intentionally used to induce men to become carriers of mail and women not to. It would rather have developed with the quite localized intention of naming, understanding, and communicating a familiar experience. That is how words get made, change, develop, accumulate new meanings, then fade away and die—as reflections of people's experiences and as functions of their desires and their attempts to satisfy those desires.[4] Words do not, in other words, have Platonic essences that are eternally fixed and thus objective in some transcendent fashion, able to be deduced by a priori analysis or apprehended in a flash of insight. Like the rules of etiquette, they are earthly, mortal affairs, driven by actual human experience in the actual world.

The important point is that words do not *create* reality: they *reflect* it, or they reflect at least our attempts at understanding it. A word such as *woozy*, for example, is an instance of our commonplace experience of being unable to quite characterize something we nonetheless know. You probably know immediately what *woozy* means, but I bet you would have a hard time explaining it. There are lots of similar terms in English (*love* is a notorious one), as there are in every language. A diverting and instructive exercise is locating them and trying to give them proper Socratic definitions; if you are ambitious, you might also try defining them in or translating them into other languages. But since you will never arrive at a definition that would satisfy Socrates, this is ultimately a futile activity—except, of course, insofar as you find the attempt amusing. Words such as *woozy* and *love* are evidence of the primacy of experience to words: we *first* have an experience, and we *then* try to understand it and describe it. Of course we do not try to name or describe every experience we have, but the more frequently we have an experience or the more common it is, the more likely we are to try to identify and name it.[5] Words are thus not out there somewhere waiting to be discovered and loosed,

---

4 See Keller's *On Language Change*, Jespersen's *Growth and Structure of the English Language*, and Pinker's *The Language Instinct*.

5 Adam Smith saw this already in the eighteenth century: see his short essay, "Considerations Concerning the First Formation of Languages." For discussion of Smith's project, see my "Adam Smith's First Market: The Development of Language."

fully developed with prefashioned meaning and armed with swords to slay miscreants who misuse them.[6] They are instead the results of our fallible attempts to understand our world as we experience it and our desire to communicate our experiences as we perceive them.

Thus the reformers base their injunctions on the false theory that language works the other way around. Since language is a reflection of people's attempted understanding of their experiences in the world, it is getting the cart before the horse to try policing it with moral reproach. One should instead try to get people to *experience* or *understand* things differently. But those are far tougher nuts to crack. The strength and durability of people's habits are formidable, especially when based on common experience. I set myself no light task if, for example, I want you to think just as easily of a man as of a woman when I say "consider a nursery school teacher." But it is sometimes possible: witness the virtual disappearance in America of the honorific *Miss*. But the difficulty of changing people's usage of a handful of terms is itself an indication of the reformers' false theory: since the words were a reflection of people's experience, the mandate to change long-standing habitual usage could make headway only when it became accompanied by a threat to something people hold dear. It was thus not until the reformers succeeded in making people feel socially backward or chauvinistic that their efforts began to take hold. But you see that people's experience had to be changed before their language would follow suit. Trying to go in the opposite direction is like thinking you can talk birds out of flying on the theory that birds developed wings because they wanted to fly.

Should one, then, disobey the directive to use terms like *chairperson, police officer, service personnel* (instead of *soldiers*), *foreperson* or *forewoman*, *spokesperson* or *spokeswoman*, and so on? Let me be definite: yes and no. Start with "no": use these terms if you like. If they serve an end of yours—perhaps fitting in with the times or current fashion, indicating your enlightenment, signaling your solidarity with oppressed peoples, or smashing patriarchy or "the man"—then by all means, go ahead. I certainly would not presume to tell you that it is morally wrong to use them, since I do not think it *is* morally wrong to use them. I will admit to some puzzlement that more women do not object to the apparent implication

---

[6] Thinking otherwise can lead to the dilemma Rousseau posed in his 1754 *Discourse on the Origins of Inequality*, a dilemma Rousseau thought inescapable, namely, that generalization is possible only if we already possess general words, but it is possible to possess general words only if one already possesses the power to generalize.

that they are oppressed by, and thus must be protected from, words like *chairman*, but that is beside the point here. If stopping the use of such words is important to you, then I encourage you to stop using them, and even to try by your example to get other people to stop using them as well. That indeed is how the marketplace of human life works. And if recent history is any indication, many people respond well to shaming about their language and are willing to comply with such exhortations.[7]

On the other hand, I confess I do find most of the suggested neologisms manifestly unsightly. I am one of those curmudgeonly English speakers who thinks that the language is, or can be, beautiful. In the hands of a master—a David Hume, for example, a Keats, or an Albert Jay Nock—its power and beauty surpass just about every other language going. For that reason I view using a word like *forewoman* as an absolute abomination. Quite regardless of its alleged gender specification, the word is just damned ugly—as almost all words invented for political purposes must be. Perhaps in time we shall grow accustomed to hearing words like that and their ugliness will fade, in the way that much contemporary "performance art" just does not shock us any more. Perhaps. I fear for civilization when *forewoman* does not offend English speakers' tastes, but that might just be my own aesthetic stubbornness. For what it is worth I note that I am also quite repulsed at much modern architecture, which often strikes me as an attempt to realize some bizarre, other-worldly ideal, come hell or high water, and at the same time to inconvenience and menace actual people as much as possible.[8]

Putting aesthetic matters to one side, however, introducing these neologisms into your writing can also have the disastrous consequence of diverting your reader's attention *away* from your subject and *to* you the writer, or to this "feminist" issue itself—which, unless you are writing an autobiography, an article on the use of "the generic 'he,' " or feminist critiques of language, is irrelevant to your purpose. When one comes across "he or she" or "s/he," one is immediately transported to any number

---

[7] Steven Pinker argues, however, that people often just transfer the negative connotation to the newly preferred terms. An example he cites is "the replacement of formerly unexceptionable terms by new ones: *Negro* by *black* by *African American*, *Spanish-American* by *Hispanic* by *Latino*," and so on; he continues: "Linguists are familiar with this phenomenon, which may be called the euphemism treadmill. People invent new words for emotionally charged referents, but soon the euphemism becomes tainted by association, and a new word must be found, which soon acquires its own connotations, and so on" (*The Blank Slate*, p. 212; emphasis in original).

[8] Consider, for example, the work of Le Corbusier, or, to recur to an example from an earlier chapter, the new Scottish Parliament building in Edinburgh.

of thoughts, perhaps good, perhaps bad, but probably none connected with your thesis. And then your hold on the reader is lost. Whatever else you have to say, your novel usage itself, as well as speculations about your motives for having done so, are now present in the reader's thoughts. Losing your reader's attention defeats the whole purpose, even if you manage to avoid causing the reader to develop a general suspicion of your judgment.

What I suggest is that the issue of which word or phrase or term to use for something is more a matter of conformity to common usage and good taste than of moral injunction. There are plenty of areas that require moral condemnation and contempt, and Lord knows human beings need constant reminding about things like minding their own business, keeping their hands to themselves, and keeping their promises. But though moral condemnation can be a powerful tool if used skillfully, it is, like spanking a child, a volatile and potentially unwieldy instrument: it works only when used sparingly and judiciously, in just the right situation, and in reference to just the right objects. It is easily overplayed, whereupon all its real effectiveness vanishes, however much apparent compliance it commands in the moment. Hence it should be husbanded jealously and brought out only when good sense indicates it has a chance of success. And that will almost never be the case in word usage.

Despite, then, the earnestness and no doubt quite commendable, if misguided, intentions of the reformers, they are in the end atwitter about a thing of little importance. We all want people to have a world full of opportunities, we all condemn and execrate the summary closing of doors to certain kinds of people, we all regret whenever a person is denied a chance he deserves because of some truly irrelevant fact about him— in all this we are all wholeheartedly in union with the reformers. But language is at best a symptom of the problems they want to address, at worst entirely irrelevant; and in any case it is probably impossible to render it completely consistent with our political ideals. It may be a bitter pill to swallow, but I think we must accept and keep ever before our minds Kant's maxim that perfection cannot be fashioned out of so crooked a timber as humanity.[9] So let it go. Save your moral indignation for those few cases where it can matter. When you resolve to do so, you will find yourself relieved of a burden, and the world will not be the worse for it. Indeed, since *you* will be the better for it, the world might marginally profit as well.

[9] In his 1784 essay "Idea for a Universal History with a Cosmopolitan Purpose."

WHAT WAS THE POINT?

If I'm right that the use, or nonuse, of "gender-specific" language is not worth the attention currently paid to it, why did *I* spend so long talking about it? That's a fair question. The first answer is because there are others who take it quite seriously, and it has for many become a "moralized" issue, rather than, as I suggest it should be, an issue of taste or prudence. Smoking was at one time considered by almost everybody to be a matter of individual preference, or perhaps of prudence given health concerns, but not any longer. Increasingly many people now view the choice to smoke or not as a *moral* choice, and they stand ready to condemn morally those who make the wrong choice—even, depending on where you live, to put you in jail for it.[10] Similarly with "gender-specific" language. People are not, as far as I know, prepared yet to put people in jail for using it, but it has nevertheless become something that will incur moral condemnation; and there are academic journals, newspapers, magazines, and publishing houses that will not accept manuscripts that use such language, regardless of any other merits the manuscript might possess.

But the other main reason this issue was worth discussing is that it points toward a larger argument of this book, namely, that social orders are, or tend to be, reflective of people's actual experiences and their attempts to realize their ends based on their unique local knowledge of their situations. That was one argument I marshaled in Part I in defense of limited government: since no third-party interposer will be in possession of this 'local knowledge,' third-party interposition in otherwise "natural" social orders is generally a bad idea. Language is an example of a relatively orderly but unplanned social order: it arises to serve people's local ends, and it will change over time as their ends change and as they find newer, better ways to effect those ends with language. Because language, like other unplanned or unintentional—or "spontaneous"[11]—social orders

---

[10] As I write, measures prohibiting smoking in public and even some private venues are either being enacted or contemplated in, among other places, England, Ireland, California, and Maryland.

[11] Friedrich Hayek has made the term "spontaneous order" the standard appellation for such social orders; see, for example, his *Constitution of Liberty*, chap. 10. There is now a large and growing literature from a number of disciplines exploring the implications of "spontaneous order" explanations of social orders. For a few recent discussions from various disciplinary perspectives, see Infantino's *Ignorance and Liberty*, Lal's *Unintended Consequences*, Otteson's *Adam Smith's Marketplace of Life*, Skyrms's *The Stag Hunt and the Evolution of Social Structure*, Sober and Wilson's *Unto Others*, and Young's *Individual Strategy and Social Structure*.

bears this relation to people's attempts to satisfy their ends, it too is an area of social life that third parties should for the most part leave alone. Or perhaps somewhat better put, it is something third parties should not get their moral backs up about.

SEXUAL HARASSMENT

Sexual harassment is a far more vexing matter than deciding which pronouns to use, and it should be treated accordingly. The first step is to distinguish between sexual *harassment* and sexual *assault*. The latter clearly falls within the scope of breaches of justice, properly so-called, and thus justifiably invokes prevention and punishment, coercive if necessary. But sexual harassment is a different animal, and it therefore requires a different treatment. Perhaps we should begin with this question: What exactly *is* sexual harassment? It may turn out to be difficult, even impossible, to define it once and for all, but people who write codes of conduct to prohibit it or file lawsuits to punish alleged instances of it typically include as examples things like sexually explicit jokes, sexually demeaning remarks, and comments that take notice of a person's sex and that at least some people find offensive. My university defines "harassment" not atypically as "unwelcome conduct, whether verbal, physical, or visual, that is based upon a person's protected status, such as sex, color, race, ancestry, religion, national origin, age, physical or mental disability, citizenship status, or other protected status"; it further stipulates that it "will not tolerate harassing conduct that affects tangible job or education benefits, that interferes unreasonably with an individual's work or academic performance, or that creates an intimidating, hostile, demeaning, or offensive working or learning environment."[12]

Whew! That covers a lot of territory. Indeed, taking this definition at its letter would seem to prohibit a substantial portion of normal human social interaction. For example, I have colleagues who put articles, comic strips, spoofs, bumper stickers, and so on outside the doors of their offices that lambast, sometimes in a rather pointed fashion, people whose political or religious positions differ from their own. Does that create an "intimidating, hostile, demeaning, or offensive working or learning environment" for those students and professors who are the intended targets?

---

[12] This is from the "General Employment Practices" in my university's *Staff Handbook*, http://hr.ua.edu/empl_rel/staff_handbook/#harass. See also its "Sexual Harassment Policy," http://eop.ua.edu/sex.html.

Remember that the word *or* in the definition means that it counts as "harassment" if any *one* of the listed adjectives applies, not necessarily all of them. Thus it seems it would not take much for this definition to get away from us altogether. And I shall not pause here to regale the reader with any of the seemingly endless cases in which universities across America that have similar policies about harassment have enforced them with an almost comic zealotry against certain kinds of "harassment," but have remained utterly inactive in the face of obvious instances of different kinds of "harassment." There have been, and continue to be, so many such instances that whole cottage industries have arisen to document and publicize them[13]—yet despite the embarrassing exposure of duplicity, university administrators continue their double-standard enforcement. Whatever else this shows, the definition of "harassment" at work seems not fully adequate.

It might also be added that in restricting certain kinds of "verbal conduct," even for the purpose of creating or maintaining "civility" or "civil discourse," these policies are in fact restricting the liberty of speech; and that is something, it would seem, that we should be wary of. The eighteenth-century Scottish philosopher Adam Ferguson put the argument this way:

But if a vigorous policy, applied to enslave, not to restrain from crimes, has an actual tendency to corrupt the manners, and to extinguish the spirit of nations; if its severities be applied to terminate the agitations of a free people, not to remedy their corruptions; if forms be often applauded as salutary, because they tend merely to silence the voice of mankind, or to be condemned as pernicious, because they allow this voice to be heard; we may expect that many of the boasted improvements of civil society, will be mere devices to lay the political spirit at rest, and will chain up the active virtues more than the restless disorders of men. (*Essay on the History of Civil Society*, p. 210)

Perhaps we can fill out our picture of what counts as sexual harassment by asking what is *not* included in it. Here again examples are illustrative. Fondling, groping, grasping, or otherwise physically handling a person do not count. These kinds of activity are, if wanted, not harassment of any kind; and if unwanted, then they count as assault, not harassment. It is important to see that assault is not just a bad case of harassment. Assault involves a breach of conduct that puts it into a different category

---

[13] Perhaps the best recent work on this topic is Kors and Silverglate's *The Shadow University*. Of the numerous other treatments, one might also consult Adams's *Welcome to the Ivory Tower of Babel* and Shapiro's *Brainwashed*.

from harassment, even if one can imagine some cases that are on the margin between the two. As a rule of thumb, if you have laid your hands on another and attempted thereby to get that person to do something he did not want to do, you are probably guilty of assault; if you did not put your hands on anyone, then your actions can probably count only as harassment.

But what about hugging someone, or putting one's arm around another, or perhaps saying "You look nice today" while smiling in a way that admits of more than one interpretation? What about telling a sexually oriented joke that some people find offensive but others do not? What about talking business in the locker room, to which members of the opposite sex, whichever it is, do not have access? What about using sexual language that pretty much everyone would find offensive, but in a private e-mail that a co-worker, who was not its intended recipient, espied over the writer's shoulder and took offense at? Let me be definite again: it depends. Whether cases like these count as harassment, even on the somewhat expansive definitions some want to give it, simply cannot be determined a priori or without familiarity with the local facts of the particular case in question. There is no finite set of rules that will infallibly capture when a statement or action should count as harassment and when not. We will need to know more than what was said or done: we also need to know who was involved, what their relationships to one another were, and what the circumstances were. And these facts are not trivial. That they decisively determine the character of the incident is clear upon reflection. An example makes the point. Consider how differently the use of the word *nigger* should be taken in the contexts of (1) reading *Huckleberry Finn*, (2) listening to contemporary hip-hop music, or (3) listening to a speaker at a white supremicists' rally.

The first problem, then, with sexual harassment codes and laws is that they are blunt instruments that cannot be sensitive to the subtleties of context that determine the character of social interaction. The expansive and vague definition of "harassment" used by my university reflects this problem. For example, what on earth would count, or *not* count, as "visual conduct"? What is needed instead is *judgment*, the skill that is honed by repeated application, testing, and correction against reality, and based on local knowledge of the situation. Because sexual harassment, unlike sexual assault, does not involve doing another positive harm or bodily injury, it counts as *vicious* but not *unjust*. And as I have argued, what counts as vice, as well as what counts as virtue, is a pragmatic and particular affair that can be adjudicated only on a case-by-case basis by people of good judgment. Since justice, by contrast, pertains only to a few, definite things, its few rules can be specified with relative precision and applied relatively straightforwardly—though even here good judgment is still required. Other virtues and vices, by contrast, cover a far larger range of possible human action, and hence rules here will be far more limited in their usefulness and local judgment will play a far larger role.

The upshot, then, I suggest, is that we should get rid of official, written harassment codes. Instead, we should for the most part leave these matters to the discretion of the individuals involved. They are the ones with the relevant local knowledge necessary to know whether a remark or gesture was, given the context, appropriate or not, objectionable or not, deserving of condemnation or not. Here again third parties usually do not have the requisite contextual knowledge and thus are generally not in a good position to make accurate judgments. The prudent thing to do, therefore, seems to be to let individuals sort out such matters themselves. That is also, I should add as a bonus, the *proper* thing to do, inasmuch as it shows a respect for the personhood of everyone concerned and seems entailed by the General Liberty principle—which, as argued in chapter 5, would include freedom of speech.

NO REMEDIES?

If official rules or laws are inappropriate to settling allegations of sexual harassment, and instead we should leave the matter to the judgment of the individuals involved, have we left victims of sexual harassment to hang out to dry by allowing them little hope of relief? Have we in effect consigned them to simply suffer? No. It is luckily the case, first of all, that this area where law and punishment by the state or other official agencies are inappropriate is also an area in which, to repeat, people are not done real or 'positive' harm. This is no coincidence. However offended a person might be at another's remark, such offense is of a different species from being physically assaulted or robbed; similarly, however vicious it might be to refuse to hire an applicant on account of the applicant's sex, an applicant is not, except in extraordinary cases, legally or morally entitled to the job. So a co-worker's caddish remarks can reveal his low character, just as an employer's sexually based decisions can reveal his own low, not to mention imprudent, character; and the auditor or applicant can be disappointed, disaffected, or otherwise justifiably displeased. But in neither case can there be claimed an injury to life, to liberty, to possession, or to what is due from the promises or contracts of others.

The other consideration that is apposite here is that the target of sexual harassment has a powerful, and often decisive, defense: his voice. There is nothing preventing a person who is offended at someone's remarks or jokes, or who does not want to be touched in this or any other way, or who is being treated in an unwanted way because of his sex, from speaking up and saying so. And there is nothing preventing a third party who is privy to the exchange from speaking up in the person's defense. Again I suggest that this is an area in which what I have called *social power* can be quite effective. I would wager that that co-worker would smarten up fast if matter-of-factly told something like "I don't think that's funny." And if the market forces of losing out on competent workers do not ruin him, the sexually discriminating employer will almost always respond to the public voicing of one's recognition and disapproval of what he is doing.

But perhaps one fears that this underestimates the difficult and uncomfortable position in which sexual harassment can put a person. Let us consider two cases. In the first case suppose that a woman's co-worker greets her every day with a lewd remark or sexual innuendo. She dislikes and is made uncomfortable by these remarks. What should she do? Given the argument so far, it seems her first step should be to tell him that she dislikes his remarks and ask him to please stop it—and she should make sure she does this in a way that no one, not even the cad in question, can misinterpret what she says as "really saying 'I like it.' " Suppose he persists nonetheless—what then? Before answering this question, it should be pointed out that the number and proportion of people who would make daily lewd comments must be low, but the number and proportion who would *continue* to make them after having been informed in no uncertain terms that they were unwanted, disliked, and perceived to be improper must be very small. I make this point not to suggest that when it does happen it is unimportant or trivial, but simply to register the concern that we must be careful not to focus only on a small number of hard cases and draw inferences from them to cover all the other cases from which they are exceptions. As we have seen before, that can be a serious mistake because it can lead to judgments or policies that are inappropriate or even do violence to all the other cases.

With that caution in mind, let us continue with our line of questioning: what should the woman do if she finds herself in one of the rare cases when her co-worker persists in his rudeness or lewdness? It seems that if the situation warrants it, the next step is to go to her boss (or, if it is her boss who is the cad in question, go to *his* boss) and make her complaint, demanding that he put a stop to the behavior. There should be no reason why she should not do this, and it would seem a rather patronizing underestimation to suggest that women are not capable of taking this step. In all but the most extraordinary cases nothing more should be required. The caddish co-worker might now be angry toward the woman, or think she has overreacted, but if his boss tells him to stop, he will. How can I be so sure about this? Well, I can't be completely sure, but what I do contend is that the "desire for mutual sympathy of sentiments," as Adam Smith calls it[14]—or what we might describe as the nearly universal desire to have others agree with our sentiments—is a central, powerful motivation factor in human life.[15] This is not just peer pressure: it is also that our happiness partly depends on comfortable, reaffirming relationships with others, and that feeling socially isolated is unpleasant and almost everyone wishes to avoid it. I return to this below, but for now let me suggest that this desire for mutual sympathy of sentiments is stronger than often realized, and that the threat of its absence—as when it becomes clear that no one but you thinks your joke is funny—is a surprisingly powerful incentive to change one's tune.

But let us not rest here: let us push to the hardest case, however unlikely, that the co-worker is such a thorough blackguard that his lewd behavior still continues. Perhaps the boss (and his boss?) are complicit as well. What then? A different but similarly serious case is one in which a worker's boss makes it clear that he wants sexual favors in return for continued employment or advancement. Suppose, furthermore, to make the case more pointed, if still more unlikely, that the boss has arranged things so that if the worker talks to anyone else—like the boss's own boss, for example—he will somehow get off scot-free and she will suffer bad consequences. What then?

At this final iteration in both these cases the woman employee in question has still another option, which would at this stage seem the wisest thing to do in any case: quit. These are places that have proved manifestly unwelcome to and unsuitable for her, and even if someone this late in the game should come in and try to end the behavior, the atmosphere is probably so poisoned as to make it unsalvageable for her. Quitting is a big step to take, and we should not trivialize the disruption it can cause in a

---

[14] In his 1759 *Theory of Moral Sentiments*, pp.13–16 and passim.
[15] This fact has been reconfirmed in a number of recent studies. See, for example, Brown's *Human Universals*, Pinker's *The Blank Slate*, Ridley's *The Origins of Virtue*, and Wright's *The Moral Animal*.

person's life. But it can also be a blessing—and in extreme cases like what we are contemplating, it might well be that the employee in question would find far better opportunities elsewhere. It must be added, however, that life is full of disruptions. The best-laid schemes, one might say, o' mice an' men gang aft agley. There are and always will be people who do not behave the way one would like, who do not speak the way one would like, whose low thoughts, actions, or sentiments offend one's sensibilities. Part of becoming emotionally and morally mature is learning to cope with such people, learning to deal with such disruptions, and not letting them unduly affect the rest of one's life. If you find yourself faced with an exceptionally obstinate cur who lacks the normal sensitivities to social pressures and incentives, then it seems the prudent thing to do is quit the situation, move on, ply your skills and services elsewhere, and entertain no regrets. Life is too short, and there are too many important things that require one's attention, to squander one's energies worrying about such mean and base people.

Of course, it is also true, on the other side, that the rest of us can reasonably expect you to use your judgment and common sense. If you are a woman and you decide to take a job as the only female in the stevedoring company's dockyard office, do not be surprised if you are subject to or overhear salty, colorful, or sexually oriented language. If you feign shock and offense in this kind of situation, people will be suspicious of you on the reasonable grounds that you should have known what you were getting into. Yet even in a situation like this, standing up for yourself with confidence and insistence just once might do the trick: you may well gain a respect from them, and perhaps even ingratiate yourself in such a way that will awaken their latent chivalry. Who knows? Before long you may have them doffing their hats when they come into your presence, addressing you as "ma'am," and themselves chastising any of their uninitiated brethren who display coarse manners around you. It is no secret to most women that this so-called weaker sex can, when it chooses, wield an almost occult power over men. Many men may not be conscious of its influence, but it is the rare man indeed who is immune to it.

A final point. It is neither sexist nor insensitive, nor is it unjustly "blaming the victim," to point out that a woman should not pretend that she can act or dress any way she pleases in any circumstances without any regard for what might happen. This is simple common sense. Do not act or dress in suggestive ways if you do not intend to make suggestions. If you are assaulted or raped, of course the assailant or rapist must be held responsible for his actions. But both prudence and good judgment recommend that you take precautions and not put yourself in situations where things like this are likely. Steven Pinker argues:

> The suggestion that women in dangerous situations be mindful of reactions they may be eliciting or signals they may inadvertently be sending is just common sense, and it's hard to believe any grownup would think otherwise—unless she has been indoctrinated by the standard rape-prevention programs that tell women that "sexual assault is not an act of sexual gratification" and that "appearance and attractiveness are not relevant."[16]

Camille Paglia makes a similar argument, though more bluntly:

> For a decade, feminists have drilled their disciples to say, "Rape is a crime of violence but not sex." This sugar-coated Shirley Temple nonsense has exposed young women to disaster. Misled by feminism, they do not expect rape from the nice boys from good homes who sit next to them in class. . . .
>
> These girls say, "Well, I should be able to get drunk at a fraternity party and go upstairs to a guy's room without anything happening." And I say, "Oh, really? And when you drive your car to New York City, do you leave your keys on the hood?" My point is that if your car is stolen after you do something like that, yes, the police should pursue the thief and he should be punished. But at the same time, the police—and I—have the right to say to you, "You stupid idiot, what the hell were you thinking?"
>
> I mean, wake up to reality.[17]

One more citation on this point, this one from Wendy McElroy:

> The fact that women are vulnerable to attack means we cannot have it all. We cannot walk at night across an unlit campus or down a back alley, without incurring real danger. These are things that every woman *should* be able to do, but "shoulds" belong in a utopian world. They belong in a world where you drop your wallet in a crowd and have it returned, complete with credit cards and cash. A world in which unlocked Porsches are parked in the inner city. And children can be left unattended in the park. This is not the reality that confronts and confines us.[18]

We must keep in mind that we are dealing here with human beings, not hyper-rational robots who will respond immediately—and "rationally"— to one's words or wishes exactly as one would like them to. If you behave or talk or dress in a way that leads others to develop natural or obvious expectations, they do not bear sole responsibility for those expectations: you share some of it too. Like other animals, human beings have natures

---

[16] In his *The Blank Slate*, p. 369.
[17] In her *Sex, Art, and American Culture*, pp. 51 and 57.
[18] In her *Sexual Correctness*, p. 33.

that come complete with instincts, drives, and desires. It's true that human beings also have the ability, as I have been at pains to argue, to redirect, channel, diminish, sometimes even thwart altogether some of these natural inclinations, and that good judgment, and good character, requires they often do so; but, as I have also been at pains to argue, that takes a lot of work, and one would be displaying awfully bad judgment simply to assume that all human beings are perfect masters of their desires. Human rationality is sometimes a rather slender reed with which to hope to stem a tide of powerful desire. Indeed, David Hume went so far as to claim, "Reason is, and ought only to be the slave of the passions."[19] It reminds one of the politicians and military commanders who were shocked—shocked!—when they found out that stationing female personnel on previously all-male submarines and aircraft carriers resulted in a high incidence of pregnancy.[20] How is that possible, the politicians and commanders asked with feigned incomprehension, when they were all under strict orders to refrain from any fraternization? And then they bring serious charges and punishments against the personnel in question! Is it impertinent to ask them, well, what did you expect?

I conclude, then, that the donnybrooks over sexual harassment, and especially over the speech and behavior codes that have been written in light of it, are mostly needless and misplaced. Remember too that such policies can be abused just as easily as they can be used: a person can deliberately defy the spirit, but not the letter, of such policies if he has a mind to, and then use the policy itself to defend his actions. ("See, here is the list of 'harassment' activities, and what I did is not included among them. It doesn't say anything about playing that kind of music out a dorm window over the quad. . . . ") Given the counts against them, then, what I recommend is an end to these kinds of policies, an abolition of any laws about them, and a vacating of any lawsuits brought in regard to them. Remove them, in other words, from the realm of legal and state action, a realm that is ill-equipped to deal with them in any case. The claim is not, then, that such activities are not wrong, only that the state is the wrong vehicle for addressing them.

Instead of seeking legal and state measures, button yourself up and set your social power to work. If you suffer, or observe, what you think

---

[19] In his *Treatise of Human Nature*, bk. 2, pt. 3, sec. 3, p. 415.

[20] See, for example, "Marine Had Baby on Ship in War Zone," *Washington Times*, June 11, 2003, http://www.washtimes.com/national/20030611-120105-9326r.htm (accessed December 15, 2005).

is objectionable conduct, tell the offender that you will not stand for it. Encourage a person suffering it who does not have your fortitude to stand up and be counted. Adam Ferguson expressed the point nicely:

If forms of proceeding, written statutes, or other constituents of law, cease to be enforced by the very spirit from which they arose; they serve only to cover, not to restrain, the iniquities of power: they are possibly respected even by the corrupt magistrate, when they favour his purpose; but they are contemned or evaded, when they stand in his way: And the influence of laws, where they have any real effect in the preservation of liberty, is not any magic power descending from shelves that are loaded with books, but is, in reality, the influence of men resolved to be free; of men who, having adjusted in writing the terms on which they are to live with the state, and with their fellow-subjects, are determined, by their vigilance and spirit. (*Essay on the History of Civil Society*, p. 249)

Such individual action, provoked as it is by local knowledge of individual cases, will be far more sensitive to nuance and detail than third-party legal attempts to regulate social conduct from afar. If you object that social power will not always be successful, and that hence some bigots, scoundrels, and curs will get away with it, well, you are surely right about that. But then again *nothing* will ever be completely successful, and that includes state or legal action. Given, however, (1) the flexible, peculiarly adapted, and on-the-spot dynamics of social power, (2) the nearly universal desire for mutual sympathy of sentiments, and (3) the way individual actions can give rise to habits and then principles of behavior, we can predict that individual responses will ultimately have more influence than the people calling for official legal remedies suppose.

DISCRIMINATION AND AFFIRMATIVE ACTION

To the related question of whether it should be legal to discriminate on the basis of sex, or any of the other bases listed in my university's definition of harassment, the answer is clearly: yes. No one has a right to a particular job, a fact that can be seen immediately once it is realized that a right to a job entails a right to someone else's property—and that is a violation of justice, of each person's legitimate claim to be left unmolested in his person and possession. Similarly, no one has a right to anybody else's friendship, acquaintanceship, or even politeness. If someone is assaulting you, that is one thing; if someone just does not want to eat lunch with you, or go to the mall with you, or invite you to his birthday party, or play on your softball team, or go to your church—well, in all these cases he may be acting rudely or insensitively or inconsiderately, but he has committed no injustice and hence is within his rights under the General Liberty principle. Just as *you* are when *you* routinely do not eat lunch with some people, go to some people's churches, and so on. And remember that like everyone else you too do all of these things, even if you are not always aware of it or do not do it maliciously.

You will have noticed that I did not argue that people should be hired, students should be admitted, and so on, solely on the basis of *merit*. Merit is important, of course. Indeed, it should be emphasized that not only is there such a thing as merit, but it is also far more important to recognize and reward it than an increasing number of people today profess to believe. The trend to depreciate merit is an alarming one because progress in civilization largely depends on merit. I have said that in order for judgment to get better it is necessary that its achievements receive reward and its failures receive their appropriate consequences. An analogous point obtains with respect to merit: if we do not reward it, or if—as is today often the case in public schools, for example—we reward everyone whether they demonstrate merit or not, we will get increasingly less of it. It is hard, after all, to be good at something. It takes practice, discipline, and perseverance in the face of failure; and to be really good, to be at the top of the game, what is almost always required is *years* of practice, discipline, and perseverance in the face of failure. Given natural human laziness, however, most of us are simply not going to be inclined to put out this enormous effort unless there is the possibility of reward commensurate with what we manage to accomplish (and even then most of us still won't do it). Since the progress of civilization rests on the shoulders of people who accomplish things, by depreciating merit we effectively diminish the vigor and vitality of this progress. And the long-term consequence of that is, in the words of Rabelais, a terrible thing to think upon.[21]

Hence encouragement of, recognition of, and reward for merit are all of vital importance. But at the same time merit is not the only thing. For example, when a university academic department hires, decisions must first be made about what specialties to look for. Those decisions are typically not made by arguing that one specialty is more meritorious than another; they are made rather on a range of factors, including what specialties are already represented well in the department, what specialties would best serve the students' and department's needs, and

---

[21] For discussion of this point, see Barzun's *From Dawn to Decadence*, Landes's *The Wealth and Poverty of Nations*, and Murray's *Human Accomplishment*.

so on. When it comes down to selecting among the candidates that meet the initial screening criteria, then a department may be hard-nosed in looking principally for merit. Even here, however, when there are twenty or thirty excellent candidates roughly equal in merit—and that is not uncommon—they may consider things like collegiality or friendliness, which again are not strictly merit. That means therefore that although the decision process is based *largely* on merit, it is not based *solely* on merit. But that is all right; there is nothing wrong with making decisions in this way. If a philosophy department is searching for a person whose specialty is, say, philosophy of religion, that may mean that exceptionally qualified—even, possibly, better-qualified—applicants whose specialty is, say, ancient Greek philosophy will be overlooked. It would be true in such a case that the ancient Greek specialist was discriminated against, but it was without malice, and in any case the department would have done no 'positive harm'—remember that merely refraining from giving someone a good is not the same as taking his good away from him. So although the ancient Greek specialist might be justifiably disappointed, he can have no legitimate grounds for complaint.

Now one complication this example raises is what to do about *public* schools or other entities that receive some portion of their funding from the state: may they discriminate on the basis of any of the "protected statuses" listed in my university's harassment policy? Here we leave the realm of what people should be allowed to do morally, and enter the realm of what they are in fact allowed to do legally. By introducing the state into the mix, we necessarily inject its political processes—with all the cumbersome baggage that accompanies them—into the decisions. I shall have nothing to say here about whether this or that kind of discrimination is legal or not according to the United States Constitution, to the Fourteenth Amendment, or to the 1964 Civil Rights Act, and so on. In my view most discussions of these topics miss the point. Although it may well be that hiring professors at a state-funded university requires discriminating or not on the basis of any number of criteria as specified by law or judicial fiat, the first question, it seems to me, is whether the state should have anything to do with such matters at all. Should the state be regulating private associations? Should it be involved in taking some people's money away from them in order to pay for the education of others? The answer to both these questions is no. I defended this answer at length in the previous chapter, so I shall not rehearse the arguments here. Suffice it to say that by answering these questions in the negative we have effectively eliminated the complicating factor that state funding introduced into the discussion. If there is no state funding, or if there should not be any, then we can focus our argument on the real point at stake, which is private discrimination.

Thus we can sidestep the twin hornets' nests of giving an account of the nature and proper role of merit and of determining relevant legality simply by recalling that, as I argued in chapters 1 and 2, respecting people's 'personhood' entails letting them associate peaceably with whomever they choose. A and B have no legitimate grounds on which to tell C with whom he must associate, and certainly no grounds on which to force C to do what A and B think he should. Carry the opposite view to its logical conclusion: if A and B may have some say in deciding whom C should hire or admit into his (private) school, then why should they not have some say in deciding whom C is friends with, whom he eats lunch with, indeed whom he marries and whom his children are friends with. These might strike you as ridiculous suggestions—I certainly hope they do—but they are not outside the realm of possibility, and they are valid conclusions from the premises marshaled to defend legal prohibitions of discrimination.

PRIVATE DISCRIMINATION

As of 2005 there is a standing policy in America's National Football League that any team hiring a new head coach must consider a certain number of applicants who are not white. And "considering" them entails more than just thinking about it—the teams must fly them out and give them full interviews. Recently, this rule was tested and cited as justification for fining one team $200,000 when it failed to "consider" any "minority" candidate. (I put the word *minority* in quotation marks because although that is the term used, what is meant is people of certain races, or, more particularly, *not* of certain races, namely, white; minority religions, for example, or minority political persuasions do not count as "minority" in this case.) The offending team's defense was that it had indeed contacted several "minority" candidates and invited them to fly out for interviews, but all of them declined. No matter: the NFL commissioner, Paul Tagliabue, did not accept this defense and meted out punishment accordingly, taking the opportunity also to threaten that future such infractions would incur larger fines, up to or exceeding even half a million dollars.[22]

---

[22] See the Associated Press report, "Millen Fined for Not Interviewing Minority Candidate," http://espn.go.com/nfl/news/2003/0725/1585560.html (accessed December 15, 2005).

Commissioner Tagliabue's decision should not have been unexpected. A decade earlier Tagliabue interrupted the normal rotation of locations for the Super Bowl championship game when it was Phoenix, Arizona's turn. He decreed that the 1993 Super Bowl would not be allowed to be played in Phoenix—thereby costing the Phoenix economy a great deal of lost revenue—because the state of Arizona did not have an official holiday celebrating Martin Luther King Jr. More recently, Tagliabue has threatened not to hold similar events in states that fly flags containing Confederate themes.[23]

I cannot resist pausing for a moment to mention an amusing recent event in the NFL connected with race. A well-known white commentator on a sports television program claimed on air that he believed people were refraining from criticizing Donovan McNabb, the quarterback of the Philadelphia Eagles, because he was black, and, the commentator in question alleged, people were anxious to see a black quarterback succeed in the NFL. A firestorm of criticism of this commentator erupted, leading in short order to his resignation from the sports show. I have no idea whether what the commentator said is true or not, but I would point out that the huge number of demands for his dismissal, including in many of the prominent American newspapers and magazines, based their demands on the Orwellian grounds that race no longer does, or should, matter in the NFL. Such are the lengths to which our moral pretenses can lead us.

But to return from our divagation. My argument entails that as a private organization the National Football League can have any commissioner, any hiring policy, and any game-location policy it wants. If it wants commissioners like these who enforce rules like these with potential punishments like these, it is entirely within its rights to have them. I bring the case up only to illustrate the logic, and the implications, of such policies if they are enacted by the state. The difference between a private organization like the NFL and the state is that you can opt out of the former but not the latter. If you do not like the NFL's rules, you are free to leave, to sell your team, to start a rival football league, and so on. If you do not like the state's rules, however, none of these options is available to you: you must follow its rules regardless of your beliefs or preferences. Indeed, the state demands obedience even when its edicts are inconsistent with the desires of every single person involved in a potential exchange: even when the employer, employee, and customer all agree to a certain private

---

[23] See Winkeljohn's "Perdue Comes to Green Bay, Flag Issue Follows," http://www.ajc.com/falcons/content/sports/falcons/0103/05perdue.html.

business arrangement, if the arrangement violates the state's rules, they are not allowed to go forward and they face coercive punishment if they do. That is where the state oversteps its legitimate bounds and treats its citizens no longer as 'persons' capable and thus authorized to make their own decisions but as 'things' incapable of doing so and thus justifiably coerced into serving other people's ends.

Just as private "affirmative action" must therefore be allowed on the basis of respecting people's personhood, then, so too must private discrimination be allowed on precisely the same grounds.[24] It should be pointed out, however, that there may indeed be times when discrimination on the basis of sex or other characteristics is quite reasonable and not based on malice, and hence in no way objectionable. If one is reviewing applicants for combat soldiering or fire fighting, for example, using the applicant's sex as an initial screening is not, despite the occasional exception, unreasonable. The same could be said if one is reviewing applicants for gym teacher or in-residence faculty at an all-girls boarding school. Similarly, there seems no good reason why a director of *Othello* should not be allowed to consider only black lead actors, why an investment company looking for fund managers should not be allowed to discount inveterate gamblers, why a Catholic university should not be allowed to refuse to consider atheist professors, why the director of a ballet company should not be allowed to consider as female leads women of only certain types, why a hospital should not be allowed not to hire as lab technicians people whose religious beliefs forbid them to wash their hands regularly, and so on. Examples of reasonable "discrimination" could be multiplied indefinitely, but what I hope to suggest is that in none of these cases does the person omitted from consideration suffer thereby any 'positive harm,' and hence in none of them does this person have a basis for seeking redress or punishment. To repeat: refraining from giving you something that is mine is not to do 'positive harm' to you; only forcibly taking away from you something that is yours—like your life, liberty, or property—is.

Yet it is also true that some portion of the discrimination that would take place if the state allowed it would in fact be counterproductive and not reflective of rational or prudent assessments of people's local situations. People are not perfectly rational, and they are frequently

---

[24] See Mosley and Capaldi's *Affirmative Action* and Sowell's *Civil Rights: Rhetoric or Reality?* and *Affirmative Action around the World*. See also the section entitled "Affirmative Action" in LaFollette's *Ethics in Practice*.

driven by habitual or unthinking prejudice, bigotry, or bias. So any claim that if we just left everyone to their own devices everything would turn out roses would be naïve at best. But I think there are several considerations pertinent here. First, what is required to distinguish cases that justify taking action from those that do not is a supple instrument that perceives and takes into account all the relevant details of the case. What can qualify for that is good judgment, not the one-size-fits-all state. The reason for this is that the people directing the state do not have, and cannot have, precisely the familiarity with the relevant individuals and their circumstances that would enable an informed decision. As I have argued before, *local knowledge* is hopelessly and discretely scattered in the brains of individuals: no one person has it all, and no one person—and no group of persons—*can* have it all. This is not to disparage politicians or bureaucrats in particular; rather, it is merely an acknowledgment of a natural human limitation. People are of course not infallible in assessing their local situations either, but the nature of human knowledge, and its dependence on actual individual experience, means that a person making decisions about his own situation will stand a much better chance of making a good decision than will any even well-intentioned third party who does not know him from Adam and knows nothing of his particular situation. So we can predict that state action would be as ill-adapted for dealing with such cases as it has in fact proven to be. A look into the actions of the Equal Employment Opportunity Commission, for example, will quickly disabuse even the most hopeful and forgiving statist of the notion that state action does not produce ten absurd travesties for every reasonable judgment.[25]

And by the way, please don't just take my word for this. I invite, nay beg, you to investigate for yourself such agencies and their actions. It is a saddening and disheartening enterprise to see for oneself just how inefficient, inept, and disappointingly short they routinely fall of popular expectation and intention. I know because I speak from my own disillusioned experience. If you have not conducted any such inquiries, then you owe it to yourself to do so before you recommend or endorse state solutions or, heaven forbid, the creation of new state agencies. I predict you too will be disillusioned, but getting a clear idea of the way

---

[25] Critical discussions of EEOC policies and decisions are widely available. Good places to start would be Richard Epstein's *Bargaining with the State* and *Forbidden Grounds*. See also Stanley Kurtz's "Fair Fight: Taking on Preferences," http://www.nationalreview.com/kurtz/kurtz080902.asp.

things really are is worth the price both to yourself and, I add with some measure of self-interested concern, to the rest of us as well.

MARKETS MORAL AND ECONOMIC

This leads to the second point I would make in this connection, which is: do not underestimate the power of the moral and economic marketplace. One of the strongest desires human beings have is, as mentioned earlier, the desire for mutual sympathy of sentiments.[26] That does not mean we want to feel sorry for one another; it means rather that we desire to see our own sentiments, feelings, and thoughts present in, echoed by, and approved by others. We like, in other words, to fit in with our peers, and we hate few things more than feeling isolated or alone in our beliefs. This desire for mutual sympathy is a powerful engine for social cohesion: it acts like a centripetal force driving us toward each other and moderating our sentiments so that they stand a better chance of corresponding, or enjoying a "sympathy" with, those of others. If we know, for example, that our peers would not fully enter into the anger we actually feel on being turned down for a date, then this knowledge acts as an incentive to temper the anger. The same holds true for other sentiments we might feel. Our desire to achieve this sympathy acts as an antidote to excessive self-centeredness and self-indulgence, while at the same time as a fillip to enter into and bring home to ourselves the situations of others. And since everyone feels the pull of the same desire, the result is an ongoing mutual adjusting of sentiments that converges over time on commonly shared habits and standards of judgment and conduct.

The relevance to our discussion here of the desire for mutual sympathy of sentiments is that it is a redoubtable, if often underappreciated, influence for behavioral change. The knowledge that others disapprove of or condemn one's sentiments or actions is a strong, and sometimes decisive, incentive to change. Thus often the best way to change another's sentiments or actions is simply to make clear that you do not sympathize with them, or indeed that you despise them, as the case may be. It is precisely the aggregate of these individual judgments that gives rise over time to a larger system of moral order, and hence every judgment you make—whether approving or disapproving—has some influence, even if you do not or cannot see what it is. My belief is that this kind of social

---

[26] The following draws on my *Adam Smith's Marketplace of Life* and "Adam Smith's Marketplace of Morals."

shunning or shaming is far more effective in many areas of human social life than any legislative enactment can ever be. The exceptions would be those actions involving infractions of justice, as we have defined it. In virtually every other area of social life, however, the "moral marketplace," as one might call it, is surprisingly effective. We can after all far more easily shrug off the abstracted preachings of a faraway legislator than we can the uncomfortable reality of our disapproving neighbor. Consider this test, based on a quite pedestrian but instructive example.[27] Which of the following do you think would be more effective at getting *you* not to tell or laugh at certain kinds of jokes? Would it be having your corporate office or university president send around a memo that states, in typically prolix legalistic prose, that it has now adopted a policy prohibiting those kind of jokes—when you and your friends share a good laugh at the policy itself? Or would it be your friends simply not laughing when you tell one and allowing your laughter to float out utterly alone followed by an awkward silence? Similar influences are at work in other areas of human social interaction, with similar effects.

Thus the moral marketplace operates on incentives, in the form of promised rewards or threatened punishments, which impel us, sometimes willy-nilly, into recognizing, responding to, and taking account of the sentiments and beliefs of others. Just as an open marketplace of ideas tends over time to weed out the bad ones and converge on the good ones, the marketplace of morals, by punishing the bad behavior and rewarding the good with the absence or presence of sympathy with others, also discourages the bad and encourages the good. It is not an infallible mechanism of social progress, to be sure, but then no mechanism is. The question therefore is once again not whether this mechanism fails when compared with an imagined perfect ideal, but rather how it fares in comparison to other actually available mechanisms. In comparison to state intervention in such matters, there are good reasons to believe that the social power at work in the moral marketplace is, or can be, far more effective.

A similar point holds in economic marketplaces, which brings us back to our topic of private discrimination and affirmative action. The incentives of profit and loss encourage people to bring their capital to bear in places and in ways that will satisfy others and thereby satisfy themselves, and to withdraw it from places and ways that do neither. An instance of this mechanism is hiring, firing, and promoting employees. It has been

[27] The example is adapted from Smith's *Theory of Moral Sentiments*, pp. 16–19 and passim.

well said that the only color businessmen see is green, and that fact has the dual effect of tending to direct business into channels that we approve of and desire, and of shielding people from unwanted, irrational, or counterproductive prejudices. There are no guarantees, of course, but the employer who hires on the basis of race, sex, national origin, and so on, irrespective of their connection to actual merit or production, is an employer who probably will not long be in business. And that not because of lawsuits or other legal action, or even because of boycotts or protests, but because those of his competitors who are not prejudiced in the ways he is will snap up those disaffected but promising employees and eventually out-compete him. Business, like nature, is a fiercely competitive environment: small advantages can accumulate and cripple or even ruin an incompetent, while simultaneously rewarding successful competitors. Thus businesses and employers have every incentive, even despite themselves, to search out and try to land the most productive employees without respect to irrelevant features that much anti-discrimination law aims to rule out.

Another football example is apposite. The legendary University of Alabama football coach Paul W. "Bear" Bryant famously announced, after a particularly difficult loss in which a black running back dismantled his all-white defense, that his team simply would not win anymore if it continued its historic practice of not allowing black players on the team.[28] Because winning was more important to him than nursing his prejudices, or those of his school or his state, he resolved to defy tradition, as well as the sensibilities of many Alabamians and University of Alabama alumni, and he recruited, trained, and played black players. The first black person to play football for the University of Alabama was John Mitchell, whose first appearance was in a 1971 game against the University of Southern California, the very team that had previously humiliated Alabama and spurred Bear Bryant's epochal change of mind. Some have suggested, not without reason, that only someone as respected as Bear Bryant was could have gotten away with this crossing of the color barrier when he did, and indeed that he might have done as much for race relations in Alabama as any other single person—and that is saying quite something for the state that was home to Martin Luther King Jr. and Rosa Parks. Be that as it may, however, it did not take long for Alabama football fans to forget all about whatever prejudices they or their forebears

---

[28] For the details of this story, see Allen Barra's *The Last Coach*.

once had. Alabama football has been integrated ever since. In fact, as one of my colleagues has pointed out to me, today the football program may well be the most strictly merit-based, competitive enterprise at the University of Alabama: there are no quotas, set-backs, or privileges there; only the best play, period, and they do not care *what* your color or creed is.

The moral of an example like this is frequently overlooked, forgotten, or underestimated. There may well be some businesses or businessmen for whom prejudices of one kind or another are more important than succeeding in business and making money, but they cannot be many and they must be the minority. They "must be" the minority because the rigors of competitive marketplaces will inexorably hunt them, nose them out, and tear them to shreds, like wolves culling herds of deer. If they could survive an open market at all, it could be only if they are small and localized, and thus hidden from sustained competition. But as anyone with any familiarity with business knows, there are vanishingly few enterprises that would not face competition in an open market. That small number that are weathering market selection while employing non-profit-oriented prejudices are not going to be real players, and their probable moribundity virtually guarantees that they are not long for this world.

Historically the only way for businesses operating on racial or other prejudices to survive has been with the assistance of the government. An example is the Davis-Bacon Act. This act, which was passed by Congress in 1931 and remains in force in the United States today, provides that construction contractors doing work for the federal government must pay their workers "prevailing wages," "prevailing wages" being determined by what local unions pay their workers.[29] This might seem an innocuous, even laudable, piece of legislation, until its intent and motivation— and actual consequences—are disclosed. The problem was that some contractors who had the temerity to hire non-white construction workers were outbidding the all-white union contractors, whose wages had become inflated from legally protected lack of competition.[30] The renegade construction companies paid their black workers below the wages of the union workers, and hence they could get jobs done at lower costs.

---

[29] See Epstein, *Forbidden Grounds*, chap. 2. See also the U.S. Department of Labor's Web page dedicated to the Davis-Bacon Act at http://www.dol.gov/esa/programs/dbra.

[30] For evidence that nineteenth-century businesses generally did not practice racial segregation when they were not forced to do so by law, see Jennifer Roback's "The Political Economy of Segregation" and "Southern Labor Law in the Jim Crow Era."

Rather than responding to the competition from the black workers by cutting their own expenses, however, the unions naturally went to their friends in the United States Congress and demanded that they outlaw the competition—which Congress promptly did in the Davis-Bacon Act. The act's requirement to pay workers "prevailing wages" quashed the competition by effectively outlawing the contractors employing black workers.[31] And the act is the law of the land still today—still today working to prevent lower-skilled, largely minority, workers from competing in the market. The point is that there were in the marketplace entrepreneurs who did not share the prejudices of the all-white unions—or if they did, their desire to turn a profit outweighed them—and so they were willing to break through the color barrier and hire black workers who were, it need hardly be pointed out, more than happy to get the work.[32] As was the case with other legislation at the time, the intent was to keep American blacks low and marginalized, and to protect whites from having to deal with, let alone compete against, them. But the example also shows how innovators will always be looking for opportunities to exploit, and, if allowed to, they will slowly but systematically replace their hidebound competitors who prefer to take comfort in their prejudices instead of reforming their practices.

Now one might object that a person who does not land a job because of his race or sex is indeed harmed, even if not physically. Profound disappointment or perhaps embarrassment are, it may be argued, just as damaging in their own way as physical assault. But the phrase "in their own way" gives the game away. The existence of difficult marginal cases does not change the fact that there are clear and uncontroversial cases of each respective type and that their differences require different responses. There is a clear difference between, on the one hand, the 'positive harm' that a rape, mugging, or robbery causes and, on the other, the unpleasantness caused by an off-color joke or the disappointment in not having landed a job. Respecting the personhood of both the doer and the receiver of discrimination (or harassment, or biased language) requires letting them sort out these matters on their own. Stepping in from afar with force or threats of punishment, by contrast, is to displace the individuals' own judgments—and thus treat them rather as 'things' than as 'persons'—and indeed to threaten them with injustice.

---

[31] See David Bernstein's *Only One Place of Redress*, chap. 4.

[32] For an excellent first-hand account of similar practices somewhat earlier in America's history, see Booker T. Washington's 1901 autobiography, *Up from Slavery*.

SOCIAL PRESSURE VERSUS LEGAL ENACTMENT

I have stated that an implication of my argument is that private companies or other entities may develop and implement affirmative action policies if they like. For the same reasons private companies or other private entities may also develop and implement policies about sexual harassment. For that matter, they are within their rights under the General Liberty principle to develop speech codes, rules requiring or forbidding religious observations, dress codes, or any other behavioral practices they like. The reason is clear. As private associations, they are made up of persons who, as persons, are entitled to respect for their beliefs and decisions and, according to the General Liberty principle, rightly accorded the freedom to do as they please as long as they do not impinge on unwilling others.

When taken to its logical conclusion, this policy of respecting persons can be startling in the breadth it encompasses: it means that people can form a Southern Poverty Law Center, a National Association for the Advancement of Colored People, or a Ku Klux Klan; an American Civil Liberties Union, a People for the American Way, a Jews for the Preservation of Firearms Ownership, and a Christian Coalition; a National Organization for Women, a Family Planning Association, an Individualist Feminists, and a Focus on the Family; and so on. All of these are allowed, as long as they confine their activities to gathering, speaking, writing, publishing, advocating. It need not be repeated that if they begin to violate the rules of 'justice' they may be stopped or punished, coercively if necessary. This freedom may be bracing, and for that reason provoke condemnation. But it is required by respect for justice and personhood. And, in any case, consider what an inspiring diversity it embraces!

Not every organization survives in the marketplace of social life, however. The media coverage that groups like the Ku Klux Klan get, for example, is exaggerated given their actual membership—which is pitifully low—and, more importantly, given their universal condemnation. Do *you* know anyone who sides with the Ku Klux Klan on anything? When they get their members together and stage their marches through Jewish communities or on the steps of city hall, the spectacle of all fourteen or so of them nervously withering under the insults of hundreds, even thousands of protestors verges on the comical. The reporters alone outnumber them. The proper response to such tiny and truly insignificant groups is simply to ignore them. Who cares what they believe or say? At the end of the day I suspect that if we paid no attention to them at all no one would ever hear what became of them. So goes life in the marketplace of society.

This suggests an important point about the nature of social pressure versus legal pressure. As a matter of historical fact, formal legal enactments such as the 1964 Civil Rights Act and various aspects of sexual harassment law were the *results* of previous changes in popular sentiment, not the *causes* of them.[33] Politicians are nothing if not followers of the winds of change, and they are certainly not going to be at the vanguard of societal progress. They are rather like those dogs who get out in front of slow-moving trains and bark, "clearing a path" for the trains: despite what it might look like, the trains are not going where they are going *because* the dogs are barking and clearing the path; it is rather the reverse. To keep with the metaphor, social and popular sentiments are society's moving trains. By the time civil rights legislation came along, by the time politicians got around to having rules about affirmative action and sexual harassment and hostile workplaces, they were indeed bowing to public pressure, not creating it. Businesses, schools, and other organizations had already begun to implement policies regarding these things— all on their own, under the market pressures that go hand-in-hand with popular sentiment—long before the state came along and started claiming credit. Does that mean that all the work was already done and there was nothing left to address? No, of course not. But it does mean that the problems were on the way out already, and that the state's involvement substituted its blunt, inflexible measures where varied individual measures were already producing results. Remember that perfection is not ever a possibility, so the question of which method of addressing social problems—state power or social power—is preferable is one of *relative* effectiveness. I bring to your attention the historical precedence of social pressures in cases like the Civil Rights Act to suggest to you that the contention that state power is necessary to make people behave themselves is historically unjustified.

OTHER MORAL HOBGOBLINS?

I call these issues "moral hobgoblins" because they initially appear to be threatening, perennial, and perhaps unresolvable conflicts of human

---

[33] See Epstein's *Forbidden Grounds*, Sowell's *Affirmative Action around the World* and *Ethnic America*, and Williams's *The State against Blacks*.

social life. But they seem more intractable than they actually turn out to be. In the end human beings are substantially more resilient than those who would protect us from gender-specific language, sexual harassment, or discrimination allow. If you find yourself to be especially sensitive to such matters, that is probably your problem, not the world's. Do not feel yourself unique or privileged if you are offended or excluded: *everybody* gets offended and excluded, and it happens all the time, all around the world.[34] What characterizes good judgment, as well as good character, is precisely the ability to realize that there is often nothing in such cases worth getting offended at. Taking offense, after all, requires time and energy; and if you have ever held a grudge, you know firsthand how psychologically draining it can be. The prudent thing is to reserve one's offense for things that really and indisputably deserve it, those things that you find it well-nigh impossible *not* to take offense at; and not to dissipate it on everything at which one *might* take offense. Preserving your offense in this way will allow you to deploy it with strength and vigor—not to mention credibility—when you really need to, and that is how you will make best use of your moral capital. One other not inconsiderable reason not to spread your offense broadly is that doing so can make you an angry and rather disagreeable person. Since no one, including you, I bet, likes to be around people like that, acting that way is a good recipe for alienating your family, friends, and associates. And this point cannot be emphasized too strongly: you will not be happy if you are alone. Social isolation can be the worst kind of prison, made even more painful by the knowledge that it is readily avoidable.

There are many other activities that can be included as moral hobgoblins. I address another cluster of them in the next chapter, but for the most part I leave them to you to identify. The key in each case is to approach them, and their zealous advocates, with a measure of skepticism. Ask yourself whether the issue in question is one of justice and injustice, or other virtues and vices, and approach it accordingly. Ask yourself whether it is worth the cost to everyone involved, including yourself, of taking offense, and again act accordingly. Or, if you are too close to the issue or are personally implicated in some way, ask yourself what an impartial spectator of the situation would think. In other words, take a moment to use and rely on your considered judgment. And if after the fact you realize you made a mistake, use the instance as instruction and as a means to refine your judgment for future cases.

---

[34] See Sowell's *Affirmative Action around the World, Conquest and Cultures,* and *Race and Culture.*

People become agitated about all sorts of things, but in my experience at least, in the majority of cases their agitation is out of proportion with what sound judgment would indicate. Of course, that goes both ways: people sometimes remain inactive and unmoved when they *should* take action, just as they sometimes take action when indifference, coolness, or even a simple shrug of the shoulders is what is required. This lack of proportion is the result of having poor judgment—which, by the way, is not necessarily correlated with intelligence. An intelligent person might have poor judgment just as easily as good judgment.

As I have had occasion to say before, however, nature is a harsh mistress and will have her way eventually: sooner or later she will exact payment for poor judgment. I announced at the beginning of this book that it was about how to live your life, and that it was motivated by the importance of the goal of a good life, namely, happiness. Poor judgment issues in bad consequences—somewhere, somehow—and hence unhappiness (somewhere, somehow). This is therefore another reason to develop our judgment as best we can, and thus to adopt and implement the respect for personhood and justice articulated in Part I. One's approach to "moral hobgoblins" is not only constitutive of the direction one's life is taking, but it is also, I suggest, a diagnostic test for the quality of one's judgment. It seems, therefore, that one should examine it carefully.

Bibliography

Adams, Mike S. *Welcome to the Ivory Tower of Babel: Confessions of a Conservative College Professor.* Augusta, Ga.: Harbor House, 2004.

Barra, Allen. *The Last Coach: A Life of Paul "Bear" Bryant.* New York: Norton, 2005.

Barzun, Jacques. *From Dawn to Decadence: 1500 to the Present: 500 Years of Western Cultural Life.* New York: HarperCollins, 2000.

Bernstein, David. *Only One Place of Redress: African-Americans, Labor Regulations, and the Courts from Reconstruction to the New Deal.* Durham, N.C.: Duke University Press, 2001.

Bernstein, David. *You Can't Say That! The Growing Threat to Civil Liberties from Antidiscrimination Laws.* Washington, D.C.: Cato Institute, 2003.

Bowen, William G., and Derek Bok. *The Shape of the River: Long-Term Consequences of Considering Race in College and University Admissions.* Princeton, N.J.: Princeton University Press, 2000.

Brown, Donald E. *Human Universals.* New York: McGraw-Hill, 1991.

Epstein, Richard. *Bargaining with the State.* Princeton, N.J.: Princeton University Press, 1995.

Epstein, Richard. *Forbidden Grounds: The Case against Employment Discrimination Laws.* Cambridge, Mass.: Harvard University Press, 1992.

Ferguson, Adam. *An Essay on the History of Civil Society.* Fania Oz-Salzberger, ed. Cambridge: Cambridge University Press, 1995 (1767).

Hayek, Friedrich A. *The Constitution of Liberty.* Chicago: University of Chicago Press, 1960.

Hume, David. *A Treatise of Human Nature,* 2nd rev. ed. L. A. Selby-Bigge and P. H. Nidditch, eds. Oxford: Oxford University Press, 1978 (1739–40).

Infantino, Lorenzo. *Ignorance and Liberty.* London: Routledge, 2003.

Jespersen, Otto. *Growth and Structure of the English Language.* Chicago: University of Chicago Press, 1982 (1938).

Kant, Immanuel. "Idea for a Universal History with a Cosmopolitan Purpose." In *Kant: Political Writings.* Hans Reiss, ed. Cambridge: Cambridge University Press, 1991 (1784).

Keller, Rudi. *On Language Change: The Invisible Hand in Language.* New York: Routledge, 1995.

Knox, Bernard. "Introduction" to Homer's *Iliad.* Robert Fagles, trans. New York: Penguin, 1990.

Kors, Alan Charles, and Harvey A. Silverglate. *The Shadow University: The Betrayal of Liberty on America's Campuses.* New York: Perennial, 1999.

Kurtz, Stanley. "Fair Fight: Taking on Preferences." *National Review Online,* August 9, 2002. Http://www.nationalreview.com/kurtz/kurtz080902.asp, accessed December 15, 2005.

LaFollette, Hugh, ed. *Ethics in Practice: An Anthology.* Cambridge, Mass.: Blackwell, 1997.

Lal, Deepak. *Unintended Consequences: The Impact of Factor Endowments, Culture, and Politics on Long-Run Economic Performance.* Cambridge: MIT Press, 2001.

Landes, David S. *The Wealth and Poverty of Nations: Why Some Are So Rich and Some So Poor.* New York: Norton, 1999.

Levy, Jacob T. "Literacy, Language Rights, and the Modern State." In *Language Rights and Political Theory.* Will Kymlicka and Alan Patten, eds. Oxford: Oxford University Press, 2003.

"Marine Had Baby on Ship in War Zone." *Washington Times,* June 11, 2003. Http://www.washtimes.com/national/20030611-120105-9326r.htm, accessed December 15, 2005.

McElroy, Wendy. *Sexual Correctness: The Gender-Feminist Attack on Women.* Jefferson, N.C.: McFarland, 2001.

"Millen Fined for Not Interviewing Minority Candidate." Associated Press, July 25, 2003. Http://espn.go.com/nfl/news/2003/0725/1585560.html, accessed December 15, 2005.

Mosley, Albert G., and Nicholas Capaldi. *Affirmative Action: Social Justice or Unfair Preference?* New York: Rowman and Littlefield, 1996.

Murray, Charles. *Human Accomplishment: The Pursuit of Excellence in the Arts and Sciences, 800 B.C. to 1950.* New York: HarperCollins, 2003.

Otteson, James R. "Adam Smith's First Market: The Development of Language." *History of Philosophy Quarterly* 19, no. 1 (January 2002): 65–86.

Otteson, James R. *Adam Smith's Marketplace of Life.* Cambridge: Cambridge University Press, 2002.

Otteson, James R. "Adam Smith's Marketplace of Morals." *Archiv für Geschichte der Philosophie* 84 (2002): 190–211.

Paglia, Camille. *Sex, Art, and American Culture: Essays.* New York: Vintage, 1992.

Pinker, Steven. *The Blank Slate: The Modern Denial of Human Nature.* New York: Penguin Putnam, 2002.

Pinker, Steven. *The Language Instinct: How the Mind Creates Language.* New York: Perennial, 2000.

Ridley, Matt. *The Origins of Virtue.* New York: Penguin, 1996.

Roback, Jennifer. "The Political Economy of Segregation: The Case of Segregated Streetcars." *Journal of Economic History* 46, no. 4 (December 1986): 893–917.

Roback, Jennifer. "Southern Labor Law in the Jim Crow Era: Exploitative or Competitive?" *University of Chicago Law Review* 51 (Fall, 1984): 1161–92.

Rousseau, Jean-Jacques. *Discourse on the Origin of Inequality.* In *Jean-Jacques Rousseau: The Basic Political Writings.* Donald A. Cress, ed. Indianapolis, Ind.: Hackett, 1987 (1754).

Shapiro, Ben. *Brainwashed: How Universities Indoctrinate America's Youth.* Nashville, Tenn.: WND Books, 2004.

Skyrms, Brian. *The Stag Hunt and the Evolution of Social Structure.* Cambridge: Cambridge University Press, 2004.

Smith, Adam. "Considerations Concerning the First Formation of Languages." In *Lectures on Rhetoric and Belles Lettres.* J. C. Bryce, ed. Indianapolis, Ind.: Liberty Classics, 1985 (1761).

Smith, Adam. *The Theory of Moral Sentiments.* Indianapolis, Ind.: Liberty Classics, 1982 (1759).

Sober, Elliott, and David Sloan Wilson. *Unto Others: The Evolution and Psychology of Unselfish Behavior.* Cambridge, Mass.: Harvard University Press, 1998.

Sobran, Joseph. *Alias Shakespeare: Solving the Greatest Literary Mystery of All Time.* New York: Free Press, 1997.

Sowell, Thomas. *Affirmative Action around the World: An Empirical Study.* New Haven, Conn.: Yale University Press, 2004.

Sowell, Thomas. *Civil Rights: Rhetoric or Reality?* New York: William Morrow, 1985.

Sowell, Thomas. *Conquest and Cultures: An International History.* New York: Basic Books, 1999.

Sowell, Thomas. *Ethnic America: A History.* New York: Basic Books, 1983.

Sowell, Thomas. *Race and Culture: A World View.* New York: Basic Books, 1995.

Strunk, William, Jr., and E. B. White. *The Elements of Style,* 3rd ed. New York: Macmillan, 1979.

Sunstein, Cass. *Democracy and the Problem of Free Speech.* New York: Free Press, 1995.

Sunstein, Cass. *Why Societies Need Dissent.* Cambridge, Mass.: Harvard University Press, 2003.

University of Alabama. "General Employment Practices." In *Staff Handbook.* Http://hr.ua.edu/empl_rel/staff_handbook/#harass, accessed December 15, 2005.

University of Alabama. "Sexual Harassment Policy." Http://eop.ua.edu/sex.html, accessed December 15, 2005.

Vetterling-Braggin, Mary. *Sexist Language: A Modern Philosophical Analysis.* Totowa, N.J.: Rowman and Littlefield, 1981.

Warren, Virginia L. "Guidelines for Non-Sexist Use of Language." *Proceedings and Addresses of the American Philosophical Association* 59, no. 3 (February 1986): 471–82. Http://www.apa.udel.edu/apa/publications/texts/nonsexist.html, accessed December 15, 2005.

Washington, Booker T. *Up from Slavery*. New York: Dover, 1995 (1901).

Williams, Walter E. *The State against Blacks*. New York: McGraw-Hill, 1982.

Winkeljohn, Matt. "Perdue Comes to Green Bay, Flag Issue Follows." *Atlanta Journal-Constitution*, January 5, 2003. Http://www.ajc.com/falcons/content/sports/falcons/0103/05perdue.html, accessed December 15, 2005.

Wright, Robert. *The Moral Animal: Why We Are the Way We Are*. London: Abacus, 1994.

Young, H. Peyton. *Individual Strategy and Social Structure: An Evolutionary Theory of Institutions*. Princeton, N.J.: Princeton University Press, 1998.

8

More Moral Hobgoblins

Extending Rights

Two things you may have noticed about the discussions so far in this book are that nothing in the arguments has turned or depended on any sort of religious beliefs and that there has been vanishingly little about any notion of natural rights. The reason for the first is not that I discount or disparage religious belief; on the contrary. You may recall from the Preface, however, that one of the four central theses often taught in contemporary "ethics" classes is that there exists no consensus about what a moral life is or what constitutes virtue, and you may also recall that I claimed that this was false. As I have suggested earlier, I believe that there is indeed substantial and widespread agreement about the main contours of a moral life. To be specific, almost everyone believes that 'justice' should be respected. That is, almost everyone subscribes to the view that we should respect one another's person, liberty, and property, at least in our personal associations and dealings with others. Moreover, there is also general agreement about the central elements of 'virtue,' including honesty, courage, and temperance. My contention is that this agreement cuts across political and religious differences. That is why I did not draw on the authority of any particular religious tradition: I did not want to give the misleading impression that only a subscriber to this or that religious view could be persuaded by my arguments or recognize the eligibility of justice, honesty, courage, and temperance. My aim in part has been, rather, to galvanize adherents to various disparate religious, not to mention political, traditions in support of a moral vision I believe—and hope—is attractive to them all regardless of their other differences.

The reason for the second, the lack of natural-rights talk, is more closely connected to the topics of concern in this chapter. I have frequently mentioned rights, as, for example, when I said things such as this or that person is "within his rights" to do such and so. But that was not a reliance on a theory of natural rights; rather, it referred to rights *under the General Liberty principle*. Although it makes clear and uncontroversial sense to speak of "legal" or "positive" rights, meaning those rights one has as specified, granted, or guaranteed by human legal decree, whether there exist such things as "natural" rights, and, if so, what their exact content is, is far more nebulous and quite actively contested. The liberalism I defended in Part I is consistent with the natural-rights tradition articulated by John Locke and adopted in the Declaration of Independence, but it is not dependent on that tradition. It may also be consistent with St. Thomas Aquinas's influential conception of natural law and the rights it entails, but that will depend on how Thomas's position is interpreted. And it will be consistent with some of the uses to which natural rights theory is put today, but it is clearly inconsistent with a lot of its contemporary use. The problem thus is that the notion of "natural rights" admits of more than one interpretation, is put to quite different and at times inconsistent uses, and is denied existence by a significant number of thinkers past and present. Hence I think it is better to leave it out of the argument altogether if possible. As I hope my argument has shown, it is indeed possible. If there are natural rights and if their prescriptions agree with the vision of morality outlined here, then I welcome the additional support. But since I feel on stronger ground with the notions of personhood, judgment, justice, and so on that I have defended here than with any particular conception of natural rights, I will err on the side of caution and sidestep it altogether.

As I argued in chapter 1, the conception of morality on which I have based the argument of this book—that people are 'persons,' that a specific notion of 'justice' follows from personhood, that a specific system of government follows from this notion of 'justice,' and so on—is an empirically based conception following in the tradition of Aristotle rather than an a priori or purely rational conception in the tradition of Plato. In other words, the proof is in the pudding: the basic concepts of morality for which I have argued and the political order they imply are those that have actually proved to be most conducive to human flourishing and happiness. My suspicion is that that is precisely why people are interested to find either religiously based or a priori arguments for them as well: many of us tend to think that if a moral or political system works, it must enjoy higher or purer sanction than merely "it works." And indeed my own intuitions, for whatever they are worth, run strongly in the direction of personhood, independent judgment, and so on. Hence I am attracted to the picture I have argued for here quite apart from its actual effectiveness. As I suggested at the end of Part I, the coincidence of the moral concepts defended and their empirical success is a stroke of considerable luck. One might be inclined to believe the coincidence rather *too* lucky to be merely accidental, but I leave that to the reader to pursue.

In the rest of this chapter, then, I do not rely on a notion of a priori, transcendent "natural rights." When I speak of "rights," what I will have in mind are either (1) *legal rights,* that is, entitlements as specified by human laws, contracts, or judgments; (2) *social rights,* that is, entitlements as specified by a given society's custom or practice, by its social convention, or by the society's commonly accepted morality; or, finally, (3) *moral rights,* that is, what follows from the moral concepts—principally 'personhood,' its correlated 'justice,' and the General Liberty principle they imply— that I have developed and argued for in this book. The relation among the three kinds of "rights" I take to be this: our 'moral rights' are those that follow from the empirically based conception of morality that I have argued is the one that applies to creatures like us and that works—that is, that is most conducive to the flourishing, success, and happiness of creatures constructed as we are and that inhabit the world we do; our 'social rights' and our 'legal rights' are those "rights" that are actually and in fact respected by our social or legal community, and they stand under correction from the 'moral rights' but not vice versa. In other words, we can use our 'moral rights' to criticize a society or legal system that does not allow what it should, but no 'legal' or 'social' right proves anything about what our 'moral rights' are. The questions, then, will be whether a person ought to be respected in this or that activity—whether, that is, the state should enact the legal rights or whether a society should endorse the moral rights in question—and not whether there exists an antecedently given natural right. To be clear: there may also exist the "natural right" in question. I do not deny that possibility; I am only putting it off the table for the present discussion.

I realize I may be skating on somewhat thin ice with my distinction between what I'm calling 'moral rights' and what is frequently understood as "natural rights." I think the difference is important, however, and, despite its fineness, is intelligible.[1] The traditional conception of

---

[1] I draw here on Max Hocutt's chapter "Rights: Literal and Proleptic" in his *Grounded Ethics.* See also Antony Flew's *Social Life and Moral Judgment,* chap. 5.

natural rights holds them to issue from a (usually divine) lawgiver—God or Nature. They are thus standardly conceived to be written in the very fabric of things: changeless, eternal, and ascertainable by a priori reasoning.[2] That reliance on fixed eternality is what I eschew in my discussion—again, not because I deny it, but, rather, because for the sake of the argument here I remain agnostic toward it. What I call 'moral rights' derive instead from the empirically grounded conception of personhood I developed in chapter 1 and comprise the respect—that is, 'justice'—that this 'personhood' requires.[3]

A FINAL PREFATORY REMARK

In this chapter I take up two issues that are of great contemporary concern: so-called alternative sexual lifestyles and the treatment of non-human animals. They have little or no connection to one another, except for the fact that discussions of these issues are usually couched in terms of "rights" talk, with people arguing that certain rights should, or should not, be extended to them. My own hesitance to rely on theories of natural rights, however, means that the discussion of them here may be somewhat out of step with the normal course of contemporary discussions. Nevertheless, I think the conceptual tools we have developed in this book will prove up to the task.

HOMOSEXUALITY

Respect for people's personhood includes respect for the life choices they make as long as those choices do not impinge on the similar freedom to choose of others. That means that 'persons' who want to engage in sexual activity may do so with consenting other 'persons,' regardless of what third parties think, believe, or judge. Homosexuality, sodomy, prostitution, and other practices often outlawed and often somewhat derisively called "alternative lifestyles," again as long as they take place among voluntarily consenting persons, therefore fall within the scope of the General Liberty principle; because they do no injustice to anyone, others may not forcibly prevent them from taking place. If, as some claim, they are sinful or immoral or vicious or imprudent or risky or improper, then one is allowed to use only social power to combat them. One may remonstrate

---

[2] Consider the accounts given in St. Thomas Aquinas's *Treatise on Law,* Locke's *Second Treatise of Government,* or, more recently, in John Finnis's *Natural Law and Natural Rights.*

[3] For a discussion of "natural law" and "natural rights" that I find instructive, see Barnett's *The Structure of Liberty,* chap. 1.

with the persons in question, one may publish one's arguments against the activities, one may even publicly condemn the people who engage in them. But one may not initiate force against them.

Hence the General Liberty principle grants 'persons' the 'moral right' to engage in these activities. But respect for personhood is a two-way street. Suppose a person who condemns any of these activities wants no part of them, wants no part of those who participate in them, and wants not to see, hear, or read about them: is that person acting within the rules of justice as well? The answer is yes. So A and his like-minded associates may not forcibly prevent B and C from engaging in any of these activities: A is barred from doing so out of respect for the personhood of B and C; were A to try to impose on B and C nonetheless, he would thus violate B and C's 'moral rights.' Yet it also follows that A's own 'moral rights' entitle him to decline to hire, admit, or associate with B and C if he so chooses; and of course vice versa.

A may also prevent B and C from performing the activities he dislikes on A's property or at A's expense; and he may do this coercively if necessary. So suppose, for example, that B and C's activities lead to medical or health problems. A is within his 'moral rights' to refuse to help pay for the medical bills, just as he is within his rights to refuse to pay the medical bills for helmetless motorcycle riders, skydivers, narcotic drug users, or others whose activities run high medical risks. All of these people have personhood and so must be respected—that is, *allowed,* though not necessarily approved, supported, or affirmed—if they decide to engage in these behaviors, but the personhood of others who demur must also be respected if they decide to refrain from helping, paying, or remaining silent about their misgivings.

This brief outline addresses much of the contested issues currently surrounding alternative sexual lifestyles, and it gives a general indication of how other related issues might properly be addressed. But it does not clear up everything. It does not address, for example, at what age a person should be considered enough of a 'person' to be able to consent to these (or other) activities. And what about adoption by homosexual individuals or couples—should that be allowed? Should homosexuality be treated merely as a "choice" that one makes, and that thus one might be talked out of, or is it something biologically or genetically determined? Finally, should people be allowed to engage in these activities, or at least promote them, in public forums where even those who disagree or disapprove might see or hear them? These issues are far trickier, but perhaps we can make some headway nonetheless.

The Hydraulic Pressures of Freud

Let us start with the easier questions. Is homosexuality a mere choice or are we in some way biologically or genetically inclined, even determined, to have whatever sexual desires we do? My guess is that homosexuality, like heterosexuality, is heavily biologically influenced; but this is an empirical question and its final answer should thus await empirical determination.

Yet this is also a loaded question because there may be lurking behind it an assumed Freudian conception of desires in the form of quasi-pneumatic "pressures" or "motions" that may be channeled or directed but cannot go away. On this view, a strong emotion is like a high pressure level in a steam boiler: if it is not released the whole thing could blow. When we counsel people not to "bottle up their emotions" or to "let it out," we seem to be operating with this picture in mind, as if body parts would soon be flying in all directions from the explosion if the angry person does not get a chance to "vent" his anger.

This is a popular, and perhaps in some ways useful, metaphor, but it is a false one. People may well be naturally inclined to get angry or happy or sad, but that does not mean they cannot behave in any other way or cannot control those emotions. We can in fact exercise a great deal of self-command if we choose to do so, and our emotions will usually follow suit. Think of a particularly irascible person you know. People often talk of such people as if they have no control over their anger: "that is just the way he is," people say, implying that nothing can be done about it. But ask yourself whether the person you know flies into fits of anger at nothing at all—that is, just randomly, without any cause—or whether in fact there are usually clearly identifiable things at which he got angry. Does he just attack others like a wild animal? Assuming the answer is "no," ask yourself this: has it ever happened that the person *delayed* his anger? Has it ever happened that an event took place that would normally get him angry, but because of the circumstances—perhaps he was in a public place—he waited to express his anger until later, perhaps until you were alone together in the car or until you got home? Then his anger is not so uncontrollable after all, is it? And if the angry person can stay his anger in at least some circumstances, he will be able to stay it in others; and by careful and regular exercise of his will he would be able not only to develop a mastery of his anger but also indeed to diminish the anger itself.[4] Our manner of expressing emotions is susceptible to habits, like

---

[4] See Pinker, *The Blank Slate*, chap. 17.

other aspects of our behavior; if we develop bad habits it is difficult to break free of them, but it is not impossible. Concerted effort to temper one's anger, for example, will lead to the habit of doing so, which in turn will lead to its being easier to do—and that is tantamount to having actually diminished one's anger. Similarly in the other direction: if you are in the habit of reacting too impassively, or having, as Adam Smith put it, "too little spirit,"[5] you can remedy this by repeatedly consciously willing yourself to act the way you want to act and thereby developing the proper habits of behavior.

For an excellent and sobering discussion of people's ability to control their actions and desires when they choose to do so, see Theodore Dalrymple's *Life at the Bottom.* Dalrymple is a British physician who has worked in mostly British inner-city hospitals and prisons for decades; he has seen first-hand the disastrous effects that the idea that people have no control over themselves can have on people's lives. In particular, "underclass" men who believe they can't control themselves do not try to restrain their inclinations to beat their wives or girlfriends, and the wives or girlfriends who believe their men can't control themselves don't hold them responsible for their behavior. Here is one story Dalrymple relates:

Criminals call for therapy for all anti-social behavior—curiously, though, only after it has led to imprisonment, not before. For example, last week a young man finally imprisoned for repeated assaults on his girlfriend and his mother, among others, told me that prison was not doing him any good, that what he needed was anger management therapy. I remarked that his behavior in prison had been exemplary: he was always polite and did what he was told.

"I don't want to be taken down the block [the punishment floor], do I?" he replied, rather giving the game away. He had been violent to his girlfriend and his mother because hitherto there were advantages, but no disadvantages, to his violence. Now that the equation was different, he had no problem "managing" his anger.[6]

Thus contrary to the popular picture, emotions are not necessarily fixed or predetermined. Their objects and their relative strengths are amenable to our conscious direction, even if not completely so. If you ask any of the millions of people who have broken their addictions to various substances or behaviors, you will discover support for both these claims: the people themselves are ultimately in control of their desires and their behaviors, even if some now much weaker desire for the object

[5] *Theory of Moral Sentiments*, p. 77.
[6] *Life at the Bottom*, pp. 217–18; material in square brackets is Dalrymple's.

of their addiction lingers on. Whatever our desires are, then, they behave like other parts of both our psychological and physical natures: regular indulgence strengthens and encourages them, and regular frustration weakens them and makes them atrophy.

Does that mean that we can make ourselves have homosexual desires or heterosexual desires merely by choosing to? Perhaps this is possible in some extreme circumstances—some people in the stressful context of prison, for example, claim to do so—though something as extreme as diametrically changing one's sexual proclivities would seem to be a pretty tall order. The point of this discussion is rather that what one can certainly control is one's *behavior,* regardless of one's desires. We all have many desires that we do not and would not act on. We can also implement that same self-command over the kinds of desires under discussion here. So even if one cannot control one's desires and thus should not be held responsible merely for having them, one can control how one acts in response to those desires, and for that one should be held responsible. And that means that one's sexual *activities* are subjects for persuasion and remonstration, even if one's *desires* are not (though one's actions also influence one's desires, in the sense that regular indulgence of a desire tends to strengthen it whereas regular denial of a desire tends to weaken it). It is not inappropriate for a parent to have rules for his children about their behavior regardless of their desires, for example, and similarly it is not inappropriate for one person to try to convince another person to behave differently with regard to such matters.

That point applies to all sexual desires, heterosexual and homosexual; indeed it applies to all desires, period. So why bring it up now? For two principal reasons. One, to emphasize that all our sexual behavior, if not our sexual desires, is at least potentially under our individual control. We are thus accountable and morally responsible for our behavior, even with regard to our strongest desires—including sexual desires. Two, it under-scores the need for 'judgment.' Merely having desires, and even enjoying the freedom under the General Liberty principle to act on them, does not mean we *ought* to act on them, or that it would be good to do so, or that it would not be vicious to do so. Now that says nothing about whether specifically homosexual activity, to return to our topic, is moral or immoral: it says only that a person who believes it is one or the other acts reasonably and acceptably when he tries to convince others of that, just as the person who believes otherwise acts reasonably and acceptably when he tries to convince others of his view. It is not the case that he is making a mistake about sexual desires by misunderstanding them as mere "choices." Rather, he is understanding our sexual behavior as a result of choices; thus moral praise or blame are applicable to it. Whether homosexuality (like heterosexuality) is "in our genes" or not is, to repeat, an empirical matter;[7] it is an "is" from which no "ought" necessarily follows. Even if a person believes, as some do, that homosexuality is the result of a psychological disorder, such a person is free to promulgate that view and do his utmost to persuade others. As long as the people in question are adult persons, however, he has no 'moral right' to force them to stop, and thus should have no legal or social right either; but neither do others have a 'moral right' not to let him express his views and associate with others (or not) based on them.

Marriage and Other Contracts

We can also address the related questions, then, of whether we should allow homosexual marriages, whether we should allow homosexual couples to take out house loans together, to make each other beneficiaries of insurance policies, and so on. The answer is: who do you mean by "we"? If by asking whether "we" should allow these things you mean whether the *state* should legally forbid them, the answer is clearly no: regardless of anyone's view of them, these activities do no one any injustice and hence are automatically ruled out of being within the state's proper purview. The state should have nothing to do with it whatsoever. The question becomes, then, whether private individuals or companies should be allowed to insure them as joint beneficiaries, lend them money jointly for a house, and so on. And the answer to this is: if the private individuals or companies *want* to. Since private individuals are persons too, whether to do these things is within their discretion. My suspicion is that market incentives would encourage most insurance companies, banks, and so on to do business with homosexual couples—they want to make money, after all—but in the end whether they do so or not is up to them. More likely, in an open market, some companies and individuals would do business with them and some wouldn't, and the profits and losses would sort themselves out naturally. But just as heterosexuals are within their 'moral rights' to marry if they choose, so too should there be no legal barrier to homosexual couples entering into any kind of agreement, contract,

---

[7] For discussion of this and related issues, see articles in John Corvino's edited *Same Sex*, Thomas Schmidt's *Straight and Narrow?*, and the articles in Andrew Sullivan's *Same-Sex Marriage: Pro and Con*.

or other arrangement with willing others that they like. And, to repeat, at the same time there should be no legal requirement forcing others to deal with them if they prefer not to. The key here as elsewhere is respecting the personhood of each person involved. If we use that as the "north" on our moral compass, we should be able to find our way clear of most of these thickets.

So my argument is that homosexuals should be allowed to marry or enter into whatever private, voluntary arrangements they like. Now one might object on the grounds that such an allowance could open the door to unintended bad consequences, chief among them the devaluing of marriage between a man and a woman. Marriage is an extremely important social institution. Although I myself was not raised in a traditional two-parent family, nevertheless evidence shows that men, women, and children all benefit enormously in the contexts of monogamous marriage relationships: they tend to live longer, to be physically and psychologically healthier, and, perhaps most important of all, to be happier; they also tend to suffer in various ways if they do not live in the context of a stable household run by a mother and father.[8] Indeed, the great importance of marriage to people's well-being and even to stable societies generally led the otherwise liberal eighteenth-century philosopher David Hume to make the extraordinary recommendation that divorce should be made illegal.[9] And the strong evidence of their great importance means we should all take the matter of family bonds, child rearing, and spousal relationships quite seriously.[10]

But it seems that these are all concerns once again that should be addressed to our social power, not to state power. They are not matters that the blunt, coercive instrument of the state should settle. Remember that the state makes its determinations as a result of political processes, which are independent of, and often quite at odds with, what good judgment and concerted social power would recommend. Like religion and education, marriage is, in other words, too important to be left to the

---

[8] For an extensive survey of the evidence, from various sides in the debate, see Sullivan's *Same-Sex Marriage: Pro and Con*, chap. 7. See also Steven Baskerville's important "Is There Really a Fatherhood Crisis?" which summarizes a good deal of the evidence as well. Steven Pinker argues that some evidence suggests that children's home family structure is not as important as I suggest it is, with the exception of the importance of having a father; see his *The Blank Slate*, chap. 19, esp. pp. 385–6.

[9] In his essay "Of Polygamy and Divorces."

[10] For more evidence, see David Blankenhorn's *Fatherless America*, Cynthia Daniels's edited collection *Lost Fathers*, Frank Furstenberg and Andrew Cherlin's *Divided Families*, and Whelan's *Broken Homes and Battered Children*.

political machinations of the state. Instead, set yourself, your family, and your community to the task of developing and propagating the right moral attitudes. Given the importance of marriage, one might begin by not letting *oneself* disrespect marriage: one ought not to mock it, enter into it lightly, or hold divorce to be an easy and readily available escape—especially when children are involved. Moreover, one ought not to let others get away with flippant disparagement of marriage, one should counsel them not to enter it lightly or consider divorce a ready escape, and impress upon them the exponentially increased gravity these matters assume when children are involved. To recur to an ongoing leitmotif of this book, morality is an individual, personal responsibility: if there is a matter requiring moral action, propriety requires that one undertake to do it *oneself.* Calling on others—such as the state—to look to it for us does not discharge our own moral duty, and the habit of expecting others—such as the state—to do so may actually weaken our own moral fiber and character for lack of vigorous exercise.[11]

Adoption

Whether homosexual persons or couples should be allowed to adopt children is a more difficult question because it affects others, in particular, the children in question. Contrary to what is sometimes claimed, precisely because it affects others, no one, homosexual or otherwise, has any automatic 'moral right' to adopt a child. For that matter, no one has a 'moral right' to *have* a child either. Under the General Liberty principle, people have the right to engage in "baby-making" activities and to try to adopt, but they would have no claim on anyone else if they were unsuccessful at either one. Speaking now only of adoption, we are not talking about adopting a house plant, after all: it is a child, a future 'person'; thus the stakes are much higher and the deliberations cannot end with having considered only the prospective adopters' interests. The issue in this case should pivot, rather, on what is in the best interests of everyone concerned, including the child, not just the prospective adopters, and that means that considerable deliberation and good judgment will be required. Some of the questions it would thus seem necessary to investigate in any individual case are: What kind of home would the prospective adopters provide? What other alternatives are available to the child in question? Those questions would apply to any adoption; with respect to

[11] See Flew's *Social Life and Moral Judgment,* chap. 3. See also chapters 2 and 3.

homosexual adoption in particular: What short- and long-term effects does being raised by a homosexual person or couple have on children? Are the likely effects any different from other kinds of adoption, or other kinds of child rearing, for that matter? Since the question of homosexual adoption is a relatively new one, little research has as yet been conducted.[12] One presumes that more is forthcoming, and as it does this will put the persons involved in any individual case in a better position to make sound judgments. In the interim, the reasonable position seems to recommend that the persons involved judge on a case-by-case basis using whatever knowledge of the particular local situation that they are able to gather.

Thus the use of good judgment based on local knowledge is crucial once again. We should not, then, simply say that homosexual adoption is good or bad *simpliciter,* and we shouldn't demand a final overarching judgment one way or the other. In other words, we shouldn't call on the state to pass a law or on the courts to make a generally binding judgment. Instead, we should recognize not only the seriousness of the elements involved—the interests and personhood of the prospective adopters, the interests and personhood of the biological parents, and the interests and (future) personhood of the child—but also the uniqueness of each individual case and allow those involved to rely on their 'local knowledge' to weigh them and their respective situations carefully.

Despite our justified reluctance to make any final determinations in the matter, however, perhaps the existing evidence should incline us to adopt as a tentative default a position against homosexual adoption. Making it the "default position" means that though the circumstances of a particular case can overrule it, in the absence of countervailing evidence the judgment will be expected to oppose homosexual adoption. Here is the reason for my suggesting this position. Although there is, as I said, little evidence directly about the effects on children of having been raised by homosexual persons or couples, there is, on the other side, substantial evidence indicating that children tend to fare far better when they are raised by a mother and a father than they are likely to when they are raised by a single mother or father, by stepparents, or by more distant relatives. Growing up in a family with a mother and a father decreases the child's chances of behavioral problems, drug abuse, crime, living in poverty, and going to prison.[13] For these reasons, this arrangement seems to enjoy a strong

---

[12] But see Sullivan's *Same Sex Marriage: Pro and Con,* chap. 7.
[13] See notes 8 and 10 above for citations to evidence for these claims.

presumptive preference.[14] Now, future studies might end up showing that homosexual couples can provide environments similarly conducive, perhaps even superior, to the child's well-being, but until such evidence appears the prudent judgment would seem to find in favor of the home with a mother and father. The reason for this is again simple: because the stakes are so high—the overall well-being of the child, a developing 'person'—we should be extremely wary of deviating from circumstances that experience has shown to be good, and better than other alternatives. We should do so, I suggest, only in cases in which either no other alternative is available or in which there is compelling reason against the default position.

Now the question of who should do all this weighing and considering, and whose responsibility it ultimately is to decide whether a particular homosexual couple, or anyone else, should be allowed to adopt a particular child, should, according to the argument of this book, be determined according to the *familiarity principle* described in Part I. In this case that means that the child's biological parents should decide; if they are unable to do so, the nearest of kin or demonstrably closest caregivers; failing that, more distant family or caregivers, and so on. If no such people are able to make the decision, then perhaps a closely connected local charity might be the next best option. Only in the last resort should it be doctors at the hospital where the baby was delivered (or abandoned) or agents of the state: they are the last resort not on the presumption that they are incompetent or uncaring, but rather because they can be presumed to have the least familiarity with the particulars involved— the least 'local knowledge'—and will also have the least incentive to

---

[14] There may also be indirect evidence counting against male homosexuals adopting, if not against female homosexuals adopting. David Buss, for example, writes, "The most frequent manifestation of male homosexuality is casual sex between strangers. Whereas male homosexuals often cruise the bars, parks, and public rest rooms for brief encounters, lesbians rarely do.... One study found that 94 percent of male homosexuals had more than fifteen sex partners, whereas only 15 percent of lesbians had that many. The more extensive Kinsey study conducted in San Francisco in the 1980s found that almost one-half of the male homosexuals had over five hundred sex partners, mostly strangers met in baths or bars" (*The Evolution of Desire*, p. 84; see also Pinker's *How the Mind Works*, pp. 473–4). This evidence suggests that male homosexual partners do not typically have long-term or stable relationships; given that children seem to fare better in long-term, stable relationships than in other kinds, this might constitute indirect reason to oppose male homosexuals adopting. On the other hand, since female homosexual partners do tend to have long-term, stable relationships, this same objection would not, other things being equal, have force against their adopting.

expend the considerable effort required to make sure that things turn out right.[15]

The Age of Consent

People develop at different rates, some mature before others, and no single rule about age of consent will be appropriate in all cases. Thus if we set the bar at, say, eighteen, before which we do not allow a person to enter into a binding relationship with another person, there will be those who will be disserved by the restriction. On the other hand, it is also true that if we set the bar at, say, fourteen—there are groups who wish to move the age of consent back to twelve, even some to abolish age-of-consent laws altogether[16]—there will again be those who, because of the rule, entered into such arrangements at ages too young and then suffered gravely because of it. The stakes here too are high: the earlier one begins sexual activity the more likely one is to be depressed and unhappy, to have abortions, to have multiple sexual partners, to live in poverty, to have out-of-wedlock children, to attempt suicide, and to have unstable relationships later in life; beginning sexual activity at twelve, thirteen, or fourteen makes the chances of these and other misfortunes increase even more dramatically.[17] These are not matters to be taken lightly.

Hence we must here, as elsewhere, avoid making a few exceptional cases the basis of principles to apply generally. While recognizing that there will be a minority of people who mature unusually early, the default rule should be set not for them but for most people. What we would seem to require is a settled rule that applies generally except in the presence of countervailing evidence in a particular case. And the age on which the rule should settle should be determined by the empirical reality of when

---

[15] For evidence supporting the 'familiarity principle' and the claim that people less related will have less incentive to expend this energy, see Buss, *The Evolution of Desire*, chaps. 2, 5, and 6; Dawkins, *The Selfish Gene*, chaps. 7–9; Pinker, *The Blank Slate*, chap. 14; Ridley, *The Origins of Virtue*, chaps. 6–8; and Wilson, *Consilience*, chaps. 7–9.

[16] A quick internet search turned up several such initiatives and groups worldwide.

[17] Evidence for these claims can be found in the 1995 *National Survey of Family Growth* conducted by the Centers for Disease Control and the U.S. Department of Health and Human Services, http://www.cdc.gov/nchs (accessed December 15, 2005). See also Rector et al., "The Harmful Effects of Early Sexual Activity and Multiple Sexual Partners among Women," "Sexually Active Teenagers Are More Likely to Be Depressed and to Attempt Suicide," and "Teens Who Make Virginity Pledges Have Substantially Improved Life Outcomes."

most people are actually and in fact able to make reasonable judgments about the matter. When is that, exactly? My guess is in the sixteen to eighteen range, maybe earlier for some things and later for others, but I would hesitate to carve my guess in legal stone. This situation seems perfectly suited, then, to the operations once again of human judgment and the community's social power. It may turn out that a default setting for the age of sexual consent will in the end best suit society only if it is indeed erected into (local) law, just as it may similarly turn out that the law should erect a default setting for the age of consent for other contractual arrangements. My hunch, however, is that precisely because there will be exceptional cases that can be properly assessed only on the basis of local knowledge of the cases in question, this is rather a matter best left for individual parents, family, friends, churches, and local communities to settle on and enforce using their social power of persuasion, example, and rebuke. If your daughter is too young, do not let her do so; if your friend's daughter is too young but your friend is wavering, let him know what you think; and do not be shy about voicing your views publicly.

It is a mistake, I suggest, to think that a single exceptionless rule for all mankind is required. It is also a mistake to think that one can't take a stand on an issue unless one can claim either direct divine intervention or an omnisciently exhaustive assessment of all of mankind. Do not worry about what people on the other side of the planet are doing, or even in the next subdivision. Worry about your own children, and leave— and encourage—other parents to worry about theirs. People will make poor judgments, of course, but instances of poor judgment can be just as instructive as instances of good judgment. If we take them as opportunities from which to learn, we can greatly increase our own chances of choosing rightly when the time comes. And improving the lot of mankind by just one instance—namely, yourself or your family—is probably more than can be hoped for from an eternity of insincere bleating from state officials.

Conclusion: "Rights" and Rectitude

Politics is not (thankfully) all there is to human social life. It is in fact a fairly small part of it, hemmed in by the myriad social activities we all engage in that fall under the compass of etiquette and social power. Or at least politics *should* only be a small part: if it gets any larger, it is at the expense of human social power, crowding it out and thus weakening it. Because these are two separate realms, however, we can endorse different rules in each, and if we are to have a vibrant and vigorous community we must keep politics to its barest minimum and give social power—administered, as it is, by lissome individual judgment—the widest scope and most extensive responsibility we can. Hence we can say without inconsistency that in the *political* realm, homosexuality, prostitution, and other "alternative lifestyles" are strictly permitted, just as being a rock star, a Marxist college professor, a Hollywood actor, or any of *those* alternative lifestyles are also permitted. Yet being politically acceptable does not mean being acceptable according to the rules of religion, of etiquette, of propriety, of morality. It is perfectly possible, then, to be a political liberal but a moral conservative: "Yes, you are allowed to be a (fill in the blank), and I will not forcibly prevent you from doing so; but I do not endorse what you do, and I will argue against you at every opportunity." The saying "Though I disapprove of what you say, I will defend to the death your right to say it," apocryphally credited to Voltaire, captures the point here precisely.

It does not follow from the fact that you must respect a person's freedom to choose activities you believe are wrong or reprehensible that you must remain utterly silent and have no grounds on which to voice your disagreement. On the contrary: not only does your own personhood grant you the freedom to speak your mind, but respect for the personhood of the person in question requires you tell him as well. Honest criticism is the highest form of flattery. Moreover, as Shaftesbury wrote about "wit," by which he meant the intellect or the powers of the mind, "I am sure the only way to save men's sense or preserve wit at all in the world is to give liberty to wit. Now wit can never have its liberty where the freedom of raillery is taken away, for against serious extravagances and splenetic humours there is no other remedy than this."[18] He continued:

[W]it will mend upon our hands and humour will refine itself, if we take care not to tamper with it and bring it under constraint by severe usage and rigorous prescriptions. All politeness is owing to liberty. We polish one another and rub off our corners and rough sides by a sort of amicable collision. To restrain this is inevitably to bring a rust upon men's understandings. It is a destroying of civility, good breeding and even charity itself, under pretence of maintaining it.[19]

---

[18] Anthony Ashley Cooper, Third Earl of Shaftesbury (1671–1713), *A Letter Concerning Enthusiasm to My Lord *****, contained in his 1711 *Characteristics of Men, Manners, Opinions, Times*, p. 12.

[19] *Sensus communis, an Essay on the Freedom of Wit and Humour in a Letter to a Friend*, in *Characteristics*, p. 31.

According to Shaftesbury's argument, honest criticism—which is some-times most effectively expressed in the form of intelligent "raillery"—is the surest, perhaps even only, means to moral fortitude and virtue. And it means you respect another well enough to treat him as capable of comprehending and weighing arguments. Since nothing but a 'person' is capable of that, you pay a person a significant compliment indeed if you take the time and trouble to make your case. Consider, alternatively, what it says if you do not bother to address the person at all.

Hence you can respect a political freedom, or "legal right," to do some-thing while at the same time denying the action's moral rectitude. Now you might be concerned that this gives too much free rein to undesirable activities, and that they will thus proliferate; or that this kind of politi-cal latitudinarianism "sends the wrong message" to people, perhaps by giving them to believe that any choice is acceptable or that all choices are equally acceptable; or that a properly civilized or enlightened society must express its moral vision not just privately but also publicly in its laws and institutions; or, finally, you might worry that it will simply be much harder to encourage and enforce the rules of morality or etiquette if we cannot count on the strong arm of the law to back us up. I am not ultimately persuaded by these arguments. It may well be true that it is harder to enforce certain rules of morality and etiquette if one is allowed recourse only to social power and not political power. In the end, how-ever, moral integrity requires reliance on good judgment. The only way to get good judgment is to use it, and the only way to be a person of moral integrity is to develop and exercise the self-discipline required to bring one's actions into line with one's judgment. Thus although it might be possible to get people to act in accordance with moral rectitude by coerc-ing them, and although force used in this way might be more reliably consistent in commanding good behavior (though I am not actually sure about this), nevertheless obedience achieved in this way should not be mistaken for anything approximating actual moral integrity. A carefully trained dog who obeys its master does not thereby deserve praise for hav-ing acted morally: and a scrupulously regulated human being obeying *his* master likewise gives no cause for moral celebration—neither on his own part nor on the part of his master.

THE TREATMENT OF ANIMALS

If one starts a discussion about how we should treat animals with the ques-tion of whether animals have (natural) rights, one has probably doomed the discussion to interminable and fruitless disagreement. As I suggested

at the beginning of this chapter, it is not even clear that *humans* have natural rights, and one cannot simply create them out of thin air by declaring
that they do. So framing a discussion of how people should treat animals
in terms of whether animals have natural rights or not leads inevitably
to some solemnly averring that animals do have them and others equally
solemnly averring that they do not—and ne'er the twain shall meet.[20] If
progress is to be hoped for, however, what is crucial is to begin with common ground. All reasonable parties to the discussion agree that needless
suffering is bad, and they all agree that inflicting needless suffering is also
bad. Let me repeat: nobody—well, with the possible exception of boys
exploring the creeks, fields, and woods behind their houses—nobody, I
say, believes that animals should be tortured or otherwise caused to feel
pain for no good reason. So the debate actually pivots on what counts as a
"good reason" or "sufficient reason" to cause pain. The mere "pleasure of
seeing it" would not seem to count—not because nothing is gained from
this pleasure (the pleasure itself presumably is), but because it won't outweigh the pain caused. But what about, say, scientific or medical research?

I make three claims. First, as I have argued before, 'persons' may use
'things' to their own ends without violating the 'moral rights' of 'things'
since 'things' have no 'moral rights.' That means that we may indeed
use nonhuman animals for our ends, though this will be limited by some
important qualifications. Second, the level of care and concern we should
show for animals varies directly with the ability to sense and suffer of
the animals in question. Third, the more sensitive and sophisticated an
animal is, the higher the standard of importance the reason for causing
it any pain must meet.

Speech Metaphorical and Literal

Let me make a necessary prefatory note before continuing. One frequently hears nowadays that *nature* must be protected, and a great deal
of contemporary "environmentalism" operates on the explicit or implicit

---

[20] Compare, for example, the claims made by People for the Ethical Treatment of
Animals, http://www.peta.org/about/faq.asp (accessed December 15, 2005),
with Carl Cohen's "Why Animals Have No Rights," available at http://www.
responsiblewildlifemanagement.org/carl_cohen.htm (accessed March 15, 2005).
For several good discussions of both sides of this issue, see Sunstein and Nussbaum's
edited collection, *Animal Rights: Current Debates and New Directions*. For fascinating
eighteenth-century discussions of the moral status of animals, whether they have souls,
what their relation to human beings is, and so on, see Aaron Garrett's edited collection
Animal Rights and Souls in the Eighteenth Century.

assumption that nature either has interests or has intrinsic value.[21] Both of these are the result of flabby thinking. One can speak *metaphorically* of nature as an agent, as when one says, for example, "Nature will always maintain her rights, and prevail in the end over any abstract reasoning whatsoever."[22] But that is metaphorical, not literal speech: nature is not an agent—it is not even a single thing—so it cannot have interests or be an agent. If you clear out a forest to create arable land or dump your trash in the nearby river or hunt and kill endangered animals, you may be guilty of any number of vices or crimes, but you have not wronged "nature" per se. You might have trespassed on another's property, you might have violated some contractual agreement, you might have acted cruelly or imprudently or selfishly; again, however, none of this is to have harmed nature or nature's interests. There is no literal sense in which nature is a single whole or has any, let alone united, purposes. Similarly with believing that nature has intrinsic value. Only 'persons,' as self-generating agents and end-pursuers, have intrinsic value; thus they, but only they, have interests that must be respected.[23] Everything else in nature is a 'thing,' which means that they derive whatever value they have from the uses to which persons might put them.

We can of course talk about beautiful vistas and pristine, unspoiled forests, we can hold natural things to be better than artificial things in some ways (though not all: I suspect few human beings would want, for example, to give all bacteria or viruses the opportunity to live "naturally" within their own bodies). Moreover, we can, as Pulitzer Prize-winner and self-described "naturalist" E. O. Wilson argues, lament the loss of species caused by mankind's activities on account of the potential for medicines or other scientific promise they might possess.[24] Wilson also argues that human beings have what he calls *biophilia*, or an inherent love of nature bred into them by evolution.[25] People disagree about the relative values of these, as well as other, uses of nature, but the thing to note here is that they all are relevant to and dependent on valuing agents, that is, 'persons.'

---

[21] See, for example, Callicott's "Intrinsic Value in Nature" and Vilkka's *The Intrinsic Value of Nature*.

[22] This is David Hume in his *Enquiry Concerning the Principles of Understanding*, sec. V, pt. I, p. 41.

[23] I defended this view in chapter 1. See also Lomasky's *Persons, Rights, and the Moral Community*.

[24] See Wilson's chapter "Is Humanity Suicidal?" in his *In Search of Nature*.

[25] See Wilson's chapter "Biophilia and the Environmental Ethic" in his *In Search of Nature*, his *Biophilia*, his *Consilience*, chap. 12, and Kellert and Wilson's edited *The Biophilia Hypothesis*.

Even pure aesthetic enjoyment is a value only to someone, a person. There is no more an "intrinsic" value to nature than there is an "intrinsic" or "just" price for commodities: in both cases the value is determined by the respective valuing agents. That is why one person might value a tree or an owl or a rainforest more than another. Each respective valuation is the result of the respective agent's schedule of subjective values. We might for prudential reasons tell children that "Mother Earth does not like it when you litter," but we adults should not let ourselves be bewitched by such metaphors.[26]

Persons and Animals

This means, then, that we should resist talking about the intrinsically right or wrong way to treat animals, still less of animals having "natural rights." Like all other 'things,' they are valuable only as persons value them, and persons may use them to their (the persons') ends. I hasten to add two qualifications, however. The first is that this claim presumes a clear line of demarcation between *person* and *nonperson*. In the case of human beings and chickens, for example, there wouldn't seem to be much difficulty. I think the available evidence points against chimps, dolphins, or pigs— three species some argue for—counting as 'persons,' but I believe this is an issue that should be settled empirically, not a priori, and so to be on the safe side we might adopt the cautiously open-ended position of saying that 'persons' include any and all animals possessing, or by reasonable estimation potentially possessing (children, for example), the qualities of 'personhood.'

The second qualification is that claiming that 'persons' may use 'things' to serve their (the former's) ends emphatically does *not* mean that we may be cruel to animals. Animal cruelty, like human cruelty, is still vicious, if not unjust. We should strive to treat animals humanely, just as we should other human beings. In the case of nonhuman animals, the proper level of solicitude and care should be dictated by their relative sophistication and level of sentience. So we should take far more care to treat a chimpanzee well than we should an earthworm, more for a dog than a mouse, more for a cat than a catfish, and so on. If an animal can

---

[26] I say this with all due respect to Plato, who, in Book III of the *Republic*, argues that the leaders of his ideal society—that is, the "philosophers"—should tell others an elaborate myth about how the earth gave birth to them in order to instill proper patriotism or proper obedience to the state or some other politically proper beliefs or attitudes.

in fact feel pain, it seems clear that we should, as Peter Singer argues, recognize that fact about it and treat it accordingly.[27] On the other hand, we should not make the mistake of thinking that "all interests are interests, no matter who has them," as some would recommend,[28] because it is simply untrue: a *person*'s interests are more important than those of a nonperson for all the reasons given in chapter 1.[29]

I fear that people who, like the group People for the Ethical Treatment of Animals, make claims along the lines of "the billions of chickens who are murdered in processing plants each year constitutes greater suffering than what occurred in all of Hitler's concentration camps"[30] are actually sabotaging the cause. Most people who hear such claims, even those who like animals (which is just about everybody—E. O. Wilson is probably right about that), will be immediately put off by the outrageousness of the claim. The people killed in Hitler's concentration camps were 'persons,' which means that not only are we unable *not* to sympathize with their suffering more deeply than we would with that of any nonpersons, but it is also untrue, I suggest, that their suffering does not outweigh that of the chickens. This is not a mere matter of counting up heads—X billion chickens versus "only" X million humans. Pain is not an independently existing substance that can have a quantity over and above the individuals that perceive it; thus there is no sense in speaking of "total suffering" if by that is meant the pain suffered by more than one individual added to the pain added to others. There are no discrete units of pain that can be summed across individuals, in the way my baseballs and your baseballs can all be put in one bucket of our "total baseballs." Your pain is necessarily yours, mine necessarily mine. What matters, therefore, is the pain actually felt by the individuals themselves. The people in the concentration camps were capable of perceiving pain far more deeply than could chickens because the former are 'persons' and the latter are not. So their suffering was far worse than anything chickens could possibly suffer. Consider moreover that chickens have no ends and are not in any

---

[27] In his *Animal Liberation*, chap. 1, and in his *Practical Ethics*, chaps. 2 and 3. See also Scully's *Dominion*.

[28] As Singer argues in his *Practical Ethics*, chaps. 1 and 2.

[29] It's not even true that we should take all *humans'* interests equally into account: consider, for example, the different weightings we properly give the terrorist's interests and the innocent victim's interests. On this point, see Kekes's "On the Supposed Obligation to Relieve Famine."

[30] See Carnell's "PETA Launches 'The Holocaust on Your Plate' Campaign," http://www. animalrights.net/archives/year/2003/000052.html (accessed December 15, 2005).

real sense agents; and no one who has ever spent any time with them could conclude anything other than that they are pretty far down the evolutionary scale. It's difficult indeed not to consider it an insult and affront to the personhood of concentration camp victims to suggest any kind of parity, which means one will probably succeed only in causing people to dismiss one completely if one does make such a suggestion. In this way, then, the person concerned about animal suffering is disserved by those who make such claims.

What one should argue is not that chickens deserve human-like treatment, since they are not humans, but rather that they can feel pain in this or that limited way and that thus if there is no need for them to be caused to feel that pain, then they should not. That is an argument with which almost everyone will sympathize—and it may provide the common ground necessary to enable the expanding of our circles of concern, as Singer puts it.[31]

In the larger scheme of things, however, I suggest that the best advice for those of us concerned to reduce suffering in the world is to stop, or at least put off for a while, worrying about things so far down the scale: worry about suffering *humans* first—of which there are plenty, enough to occupy our efforts for some time. Only thereafter, as a distant second, worry about chimps or dolphins or orangutans, or whatever the correct order turns out to be, and so on down the line. To briefly state a point that is elaborated in chapter 9, human love and concern are scarce and limited resources; they must therefore be carefully reserved and deployed only in their most important uses. Consuming your limited supply by worrying for lower animals will only diminish your capacity to address problems higher up. My own sense of propriety makes me hesitate in making the additional point that having the principal object of one's concern be the suffering of chickens is a luxury consequent upon a remarkably affluent and privileged life: if that is all you have to worry about, your life must be, by any worldly standard, pretty darn good. Imagine Mayan Indians in Guatemala, who live hand-to-mouth daily from what they can scrounge from the land, boycotting chicken farms for not taking proper care of the chickens when their own children are undernourished from lack of protein!

Some argue that human beings are not all that different after all from other animals, that life on earth is on a continuum of development and sophistication, and that there are only arbitrary lines of division between

---

[31] In his *The Expanding Circle*. See also Pinker's *The Blank Slate*, chap. 18.

one species and another.[32] Indeed, it has become among some a commonplace to dismiss positions such as that defended here as "anthropocentric" or "speciesist"—that is, as manifesting arbitrary and thus unjustified prejudice in favor of one's own kind. Putting the criticism this way is meant, of course, to invoke images of racism, where people make similarly (it is alleged) arbitrary prejudicial judgments in favor of their own kind and against other kinds. But the claims in this case hold no water. Yes, there are rudimentary biological similarities common to all animals, but it does not follow from that that human beings are not distinct. The claim is often made, for example, that humans share 99 percent (or so) of their DNA with chimpanzees, a fact intended to suggest the close similarity between the two. But that 1 percent makes a pretty big difference! Consider that the average brain size of *Homo sapiens* is 1400 cubic centimeters, which is about 3.5 *times* that of a chimpanzee. For comparison, *Australopithecus afarensis*—one of *Homo sapiens*'s earliest ancestors, living approximately 3–4 million years ago—had an average brain size of about 400 cubic centimeters, a tad larger than the 390 cubic centimeters of today's chimp. One can make a similar point with another example: although many animals have noses, there is nothing in the world that resembles the sophistication of the elephant's trunk, and it would be plain sophistry to claim that it is somehow "pachydermcentrism" to hold that the elephant is special in this regard. Similarly with human personhood. To the "speciesism" charge: well, yes, we do favor our own kind—but, as the evidence adduced earlier in this chapter seems to suggest, we are apparently biologically programmed to do so, so no amount of condemnation or execration will change it. I will add that there are also good reasons to think that we *should* be "speciesist," because this contributes to our ability to be happy; but I will save that argument for chapter 9. Finally, the allusion to racism is an example of what John Kekes in a similar context calls "rampant moralism."[33] The vice of racism is constituted by holding members of other races not to be full 'persons' when they in plain fact are. To liken that case to one in which one holds nonpersons not to be 'persons,' when they in plain fact are not, is to miss the boat entirely.

The Objection of a Thousand Pigs

The skeptic of my position asks: "Are you saying that if I wanted to get a thousand pigs and hook them up to electrodes to torture them merely

---

[32] See Regan's *The Case for Animal Rights* and Singer's *Animal Liberation*.
[33] In his "On the Supposed Obligation to Relieve Famine."

for my twisted amusement, I would have a *right* to?—that no one would have a right to stop me?"[34] That is the wrong question to ask! It's the wrong question because it assumes that the only recourse one could have to condemn a reprehensible act—as torturing the pigs for fun obviously would be—is to claim a "rights" violation. But as I have argued, having a 'moral right' to do something does *not* entail that it is moral to do it. That applies to the Thousand Pigs objection: even if, strictly speaking, one had the 'moral right,' as we have defined the term, to torture the pigs, that does not mean that it is all right to do it. Indeed it is *not* all right to do it: but the reason it is wrong is not because it violates anyone's rights but because it is cruel and inhumane. Period. Full stop.

The Thousand Pigs objection is trying to suggest that a weakness of the view I have defended is that it seems to provide for no absolute trump—for example, no *natural right* (even if there are contingent legal or social rights)—that one can invoke to say that such-and-such treatment of animals is absolutely forbidden, and then on that basis justify forcible action if necessary to make the person cease and desist. We would have justification to take coercive action if the pigs were stolen, if they were bought under false pretenses (perhaps you told the farmer from whom you bought them that you would let them wander freely on your land), if torturing them violates any other contract that might have been entered into, or, finally, if empirical evidence turns out to show that pigs (or any other nonhuman animals) should count as 'persons' after all: in any cases such as these we would in fact have breaches of 'justice,' thereby justifying forcible prevention. But the position I've defended is not as weak as this objection would have it. Even in the absence of coercion-justifying conditions, my argument is that we would still have the full moral authority to condemn behavior that is morally blameworthy. We might not be able to tell someone he doesn't have a "right" to do it, meaning that we could not use that particular species of moral condemnation; but so what? Things can be immoral, reprehensible, blameworthy, or just plain wrong for any number of reasons. And if they are, then we have every right—pardon the expression—to say so.

Thus when faced with a person who wants to torture pigs, we can publicly execrate him, boycott him, and refuse to associate with him. That is, we can bring the considerable force of our social power to bear on him in just those ways that our judgment, based on our local knowledge of the situation, suggests will be most punishing to him. Now, that's not foolproof: there will always be those few among us who are immune to

[34] I thank Torin Alter for formulating this objection for me.

such social pressures. But then again, *nothing* is foolproof against such people. What we can reasonably hope for is to reduce as much as possible such inhumane treatment, cognizant of the fact that nothing will ever guarantee complete eradication. Deploying our social power is remarkably effective, and doing so at the same time respects the personhood of all 'persons' involved.

Private Property and Plundering the Commons

The position I have defended is therefore not as weak as the Thousand Pigs objection presumes. Here is another consideration. I mention above that what would constitute "coercion-justifying" criteria in the Thousand Pigs case would be the pigs having been stolen or bought on false pretenses. In order for a 'person' to have a 'moral right' to use 'things' as he pleases, on my view he would first have to own them—that is, he would have to buy them with his own money, and suffer any losses or enjoy any gains on them himself. That is not a throwaway remark. There is good reason to expect that people treat things they own far better than they do things they do not own. This is exhibited in the by-now famous problem called "the tragedy of the commons," after Garrett Hardin's 1968 article by the same name. The argument is quite simple. If scarce resources are held publicly or "in common"—that is, without clear property divisions among private title holders—then people have strong incentive to misuse, to exploit, and to overuse the resource in question, and they have little or no incentive to conserve it or to worry about other people's use of it. If I am a logger retrieving timber from a public forest, I am monetarily rewarded by taking as much timber as I possibly can. If I decide to hold back and save some for next year or for future generations, that only means more timber for you or other competing loggers to take at my expense. I cannot count on your voluntarily restraining yourself, so as a result I rush in and just take everything I can; you would do precisely the same. This is the "tragedy of the commons": since it is in everyone's interest to get everything possible out of the resource, the resource gets plundered without concern for others or for future generations. And this is not a merely hypothetical scenario. It has been replayed countless times across the world wherever a desired and sought-after resource is not privately owned: overfishing in the seas, killing endangered animals for their tusks or fur, strip-mining, clear-cutting, and so on.[35]

---

[35] For good discussions, see Bethell's *The Noblest Triumph,* esp. chap. 4, and Richard Epstein's *Simple Rules,* chap. 15.

Consider the incentives in the other case, however. If you own something yourself, then you are far more likely to care for it prudently and husband it wisely, since if you plunder it, you will have nothing left—meaning that you yourself will have paid the price of lost value. Again this scenario is constantly realized. Logging companies that take timber only from their own land employ careful reseeding programs; catfish producers who take only from their own lakes carefully restock their supply; and African villagers who have been given private property rights over wild animals have discovered they can make money— usually from Western tourists—by tending them and nurturing them rather than by killing them, so they have done so, and with great success.[36]

Bring the logic of the commons versus private property closer to home: Ask yourself whether you are more likely to pick up trash in a public park or in your own front yard. How likely are you to repair and repaint a water-damaged wall in your apartment, as opposed to in your own house? Which do you take better care of—a rental car or your own car? Which part of the fraternity house do you think will be cleaner—the common living area or the individual, padlocked bedrooms? To make the same point from a different direction, one might point out that it is in precisely those countries where the state controls most of the resources—places such as former members of the Soviet Union, for example—where pollution is worst, where natural resources have been most profligately misused, and where chronic shortages of things such as arable land, livestock, and potable water—not to mention an abundance of trash, human and animal waste, and thus disease—are most acute. And it is in those places where private property has been relatively more extensively realized— such as the United States, for example—where overall levels of pollution are lower, where resources are better managed, and where trash, disease, and so on are under better control.[37]

What exactly does this "logic" of the commons versus private property suggest about the treatment of animals? Given human nature—given, that is, that human beings naturally tend to care far more about something that is their own than about something that belongs to others or is held

---

[36] See, for example, Alessi's "Private Conservation and Black Rhinos in Zimbabwe," Hecox's "Wildlife Management: A Comparative Analysis of Protection versus Utilization, Kenya and Zimbabwe," and Rihory's "HSUS vs. CAMPFIRE."

[37] As Julian Simon, for example, has shown in his edited *The State of Humanity,* the differences in this respect are quite stark. Bjørn Lomborg's *The Skeptical Environmentalist* makes the same case again, though without intending to do so. For further recent evidence, see Hayward's *2004 Index of Leading Environmental Indicators.*

"in common"[38]—one important step we should take if we want to increase the chances of animals being properly cared for is to allow, even demand, that people *own* them.

A specific example illustrates the argument. Through much of the latter half of the twentieth century, a thriving world-wide market in ivory was leading to the killing of elephants and to their numbers dwindling precipitously. Everyone deplored this; the question was what to do about it. East Africa made the decision to outlaw ivory trade, to nationalize the elephants, and to prohibit killing them. What were the results? In the ten years after the ban, the number of elephants in East Africa actually declined by half, from 866,000 to 404,000. In Zimbabwe, by contrast, the decision was made to give individual villages private title to elephant herds that roamed over their lands. Suddenly, the elephants there had a value to them when they were alive, not just when they were dead, and the number of elephants there more than doubled from 32,000 in 1960 to 77,000 in 1992. Rhinoceroses, particularly black rhinos, have seen a similar history. South Africa, for example, now has scores of private rhino farms, where the rhinos are grown for their horns (which are now removed carefully, without leading to the animal's death), for tourist visitation and viewing, and even for controlled hunting safaris. Because of these private efforts, their numbers too are now reversing the decades-long trend and are beginning to climb.

Given what I have suggested about the disparate incentives involved in private versus public ownership, and the tendency to take better care of what one individually owns than of what one jointly owns with many unknown others,[39] the explanation is clear. As long as elephants, rhinos, lions, tigers, and other scarce resources belong to nobody in particular, poachers and exploiters will try to get as many as they can regardless of the long-term consequences; they know that if they do not get them, some other poacher will. Once they are a privately owned asset, however, they cannot be treated with the same reckless abandon. If I have to spend my own hard-earned money to acquire rhinos, or if I can now earn money from their being alive rather than dead, suddenly my tune changes dramatically: I now have the strong incentive to do my best to

---

[38] See Richard Pipes's *Property and Freedom* for further evidence of this.

[39] It is more accurate in most cases of "public" ownership to say that the *state* owns it, not "the people." If you are unsure about this, consider how difficult it is for you to use "public" property for your own purposes—consider the required permissions, permits, authorizations, etc. Try going into a national park, for example, and camping or hiking wherever you please.

make sure they stay alive and are used properly. As Arthur Young said in the eighteenth century, "Give a man secure possession of a bleak rock and he will turn it into a garden; give him nine years' lease of a garden and he will turn it into a desert."

There are many other examples one could site of tragedies in the commons and of successes with private property. Tom Bethell's *The Noblest Triumph* is a good place to start, and further reading is in the bibliography at the end of the chapter. But making animals privately owned will not solve all problems, of course. Animals may still be misused, neglected, exploited, or inhumanely treated—just as humans, too, are. Think, for example, of dogs owned and used for fighting. Sadly, there will always be those among us who exploit others for their own enjoyment. As Theodore Dalrymple writes, while discussing the character Macbeth in Shakespeare's play by that name,

Original sin—that is to say, the sin of having been born with human nature that contains within it the temptation to evil—will always make a mockery of attempts at perfection based upon manipulation of the environment. The prevention of evil will always require more than desirable social arrangements: it will forever require personal self-control and the conscious limitation of appetites.[40]

Thus no system of "social arrangements" can guarantee elimination of evils such as animal mistreatment. Aristotle was right, however, when he argued in criticism of Plato that what private ownership does is *increase the incentives* for taking better care of things.[41] Incentives are not guarantees, and not everyone responds to them the way we might like or predict. But incentives do increase chances, especially "on the margins," as the economists say. Public, common, or no ownership, on the other hand, provides a different set of incentives altogether, and it has historically allowed just what would be predicted, namely, far more extensive exploitation of resources and decimation of species.

Remember moreover that the more we legally restrict supply of something that is desired, the higher its price goes—which creates all that much more incentive for black markets and illegal suppliers. So one should think very carefully before calling for legal bans on owning or exchanging natural resources. The 1973 Endangered Species Act in America, for example, has in many instances created the perverse incentive that is popularly, though clandestinely, known as "shoot, shovel, and

---

[40] In *Our Culture, What's Left of It*, pp. 35–6.
[41] In his *Politics*, bk. 2, chaps. 1–5.

shut up."[42] That is, because the presence of, say, an "endangered" bird on one's property can lead the federal government to take control over all of the property and forbid the owner from profiting from or even using it, owners now suddenly have the incentive to make sure that no one discovers the bird on their property. There have been numerous cases of owners who actually *wanted* to provide havens for animals or to protect them in various ways, only to have the Fish and Wildlife Service discover their efforts, decide, as it inevitably does, that they were somehow lacking, and then take all of the property in question out of the hands of the owners. This not only leads to owners being understandably resentful of the federal government's intrusion, but it also leads, tragically, to the practice already mentioned: if they see an "endangered" animal, they shoot it, bury it where no one can see it, and dare not breathe a word. This is the opposite of what the act was hoping to accomplish, but it is an understandable consequence nonetheless.

Private ownership would remove these perverse unintended incentives, and a growing number of studies have suggested that granting private property rights goes a long way toward solving a host of environmental problems, from overfishing to pollution to water scarcity to protecting endangered wildlife and wetlands.[43] I leave it to you to investigate why this would be so, exactly how such solutions might work, and what their relative strengths and weaknesses would be.

Consistent with what I have argued elsewhere in this book, however, I would argue that if you or I think that certain habitats or areas should be off-limits to people to farm or build on or otherwise exploit, then we should do the honest thing and put our money where our mouths are: we should *buy* the habitat in question and maintain it the way we judge proper. Claiming that we do not have enough money to do so is no excuse. Here's why: there is no end to the things I would do if I did not have to spend my own money to do it—but by using other people's money for my ends I disrespect their personhood. There is a great deal of popular support for environmental causes in the West today. The best

---

[42] See Epstein, *Simple Rules*, chap. 15, and Simmons, "Fixing the Endangered Species Act." For a powerful, if polemical, presentation of the argument, see Suprynowicz's *The Ballad of Carl Drega*, chaps. 3 and 4.

[43] See Adler's "Bad for Your Land, Bad for the Critters," Anderson and Leal's *Free Market Environmentalism*, Kay and Simmons's *Wilderness Ecology*, Schmidtz and Willott's *Environmental Ethics*, Simmons's *Endangered Species*, Simon's *Ultimate Resource 2*, and the *Wall Street Journal* editorial, "A Fish Story."

way to capitalize on it, and all the while respect everyone's personhood, is to take private donations, buy the land or animals we want to protect with the pooled money, and thereby place that land or those animals beyond the reach of encroachment.

If the Sierra Club, Greenpeace, and other similar organizations took the money they spent on lobbying political bodies and funding protests and boycotts, and instead spent it on actually buying up acres of wetlands, natural habitats, and so on, my guess is that everyone concerned would be shocked with just how much they could come to own in no time at all. The Sierra Club has 700,000 members, Greenpeace claims 2.8 million members, and there are of course hundreds of other environmental organizations around the world.[44] That is a lot of potential. Ted Turner himself owns approximately *two million* acres of land in North America[45]—and that is just one person, albeit a very wealthy one. The Nature Conservancy, an organization that does what I recommend here, namely buying acres of land with its own privately donated money, currently owns 116 million acres worldwide and boasts one million supporters.[46] Another such organization is the Montana Land Reliance.[47] It focuses on buying up land in and around Montana and keeping it clean and protected for the native wildlife. They do it not by blowing up buildings or lobbying Congress, but by taking private donations and buying easements and land with their proceeds. They currently own and have thus protected approximately 500,000 acres. Still another organization is Vital Ground, which buys the natural habitat of North American grizzly bears to protect the bears and allow them to continue living on their previously dwindling territory.[48] Vital Ground was founded in 1990 and currently owns and protects more than 120,000 acres of land in Wyoming, Montana, Idaho, and Alaska. They want to buy a lot more, of course, but they have done much already; and the point is that they could do a lot more if concerned individuals concentrated their efforts in places such as this. The Property and Environment Research Center in Bozeman, Montana, is a think tank dedicated to finding ways to protect the environment while

---

[44] See http://www.greenpeace.org/international_en/aboutus (accessed December 15, 2005).

[45] See http://en.wikipedia.org/wiki/Ted_Turner (accessed December 15, 2005).

[46] See http://nature.org/aboutus/ (accessed December 15, 2005).

[47] See http://www.mtlandreliance.org/who.htm (accessed December 15, 2005).

[48] See http://www.vitalground.org/vital_ground/mission.html (accessed December 15, 2005).

respecting private property and personhood: contact them to find out more, or about more such organizations.[49] And just imagine what could be accomplished if more people with similar concerns put their heads, and their wallets, together.

Testing, Research, and Other Uses

It follows from my argument that human beings may use animals (and land) for testing and research. I believe that is a good consequence of the argument, since so many of the medical treatments and everyday products we depend on today would have been impossible without prior testing on animals, and one can only guess just how much human suffering and death has been avoided thereby. But my argument does not imply that people should do just anything they want with any animal they want. Indeed, several qualifications apply.

First, owning an animal does not give one a moral blank check to do whatever one wants with the animal. Even if a person owns an animal and therefore would commit no 'injustice' by treating it badly, that does not mean he should do so, that he is not vicious if he does so, or that the rest of us have to stand by silently while he does so. Here as elsewhere we can remonstrate with him, make public our judgment of his actions, refuse to buy his products, encourage others to similarly refrain, and so on. Here is yet another opportunity for us to exercise our social power muscles.

Second, basic decency requires that people treat animals with as much solicitude as their sophistication and ability to suffer indicates,[50] and the relative level of sophistication of an animal dictates the relative level of importance that a reason must meet if we are to use the animal for testing and research. What that means in practice is, for example, that although one need not reserve testing on mice or rabbits for only extremely important research, one should use chimpanzees only for research that cannot be conducted on other, lower animals. The reason in both cases relates to the respective animals' actual, empirically determined, capacities for pain and suffering. Humane treatment is indicated in all cases, but we should reserve most of our worry over quality-of-life issues for the higher animals since it is they who can most enjoy it or suffer from the lack of it. We should therefore not take the position that all animal testing is

---

[49] See http://www.perc.org/about.php?id=700 (accessed December 15, 2005).
[50] I think Scully's argument in his *Dominion* is compelling on this point.

bad, end of discussion. Such a rule is simple at the price of being simplistic, papering over both the relevant differences among animals and the important purposes that scientific research serves.

Understanding our relationship to and use of animals in this way—as a matter of wise use circumscribed by honest estimations of the animals' conditions and ability to enjoy or suffer from those conditions—as opposed to seeing the relationship as one of adversarial natural rights claims has several further benefits. It allows, first, some progress in the discussion. Instead of merely trading respective absolute injunctions based on assertions of fixed natural rights, we can instead engage argument about exactly how much this or that animal is able to suffer, exactly how much this or that procedure causes suffering, exactly how important this or that use is, and so on. Here too there will be disagreements, of course, but this at least holds out the possibility of progress—we might well come to appreciate the relevant trade-offs and thus reach compromises—whereas little hope for compromise is possible when one person claims a natural right that another claims does not exist. Moreover, once the issue is taken out of the political realm, we no longer have to fear—and hence fight ruthlessly over—a single, one-size-fits-all, coercively enforced political decision. Once a law is passed, it is enormously difficult to change, amend, or challenge it. And woe to you if your opponent gets his position written into law and you do not. If we take this issue out of politics, however, and instead put it in the hands of private property owners, then even if there are some who treat animals in ways you or I disapprove, not everyone will do so; and we can build on those who do things the right way by giving them our encouragement, our business, our money, our good press, and so on.

One final thought. Making this an issue of private property keeps everybody honest. Because the government will not subsidize them and pick up the tab for more animals and equipment, scientists and researchers cannot afford to be profligate in their use of animals or to not worry about their treatment. They will have to take care of those they have because, since they must pay for them on their own nickel, they will not have an unlimited supply. Thus the benevolence they probably already feel toward their animals will be supplemented and strengthened considerably by their own self-interest. And environmental activists, for their part, will not demand the moon—to which they might feel entitled if "the government" bears the costs—but instead will make schedules of priorities and pursue goals in light of the scarcity of resources, unavoidable trade-offs, and second-best solutions that characterize real-world possibilities. Instead of trying to hammer each other into submission with the coercive fist of the state, then, we are required to consider the actual consequences and costs of our views and of our actions, and thus use and appeal to one another's judgment.

Keeping Everybody Honest

The people in organizations called Earth First!, Earth Liberation Front (ELF), and others like them are little better than thugs and terrorists, whatever they try to convince themselves of. I say this not only because their typical modus operandi is destruction of private property in the dead of night but also because if they were serious about preserving forests or other land, they would buy it, and if they were serious about helping animals, they would begin by adopting and neutering the thousands and thousands of animals euthanized in animal shelters around the country every year. Instead, they burn down logging company workers' houses, live in other people's trees for months on end, and firebomb science laboratories.[51] Thus they wish to impose their own valuations of nature and natural resources, and to some extent their economic worldviews, on others by mere use of force or intimidation by threatening force. That makes them enemies of civilized society, and if anything it should galvanize others to oppose, not support, them. In addition to their assaults on 'justice,' then, they systematically disrespect the personhood of everyone who disagrees with them. Ironic for organizations that claim, as ELF does, to be "in defense of all life."

It must be said, however, that in this they are not just crazies who can be summarily dismissed: they have merely taken the mindset of state action to its logical extreme. The existence and ready availability of a state apparatus to enforce certain worldviews about nature, animals, and so on is premised on the idea that people holding the correct view are entitled to force everyone else to agree with their position. But of course the "correct" view in this case is determined by political dynamics, not by actual argument, evidence, or, for that matter, good judgment. And political dynamics are, at bottom, merely the more powerful group forcing its view on the weaker groups. Hence the eco-terrorists can be forgiven

---

[51] See, for example, Schabner's "Already Active ELF Extending Range," http://abcnews.go.com/US/story?id=90151&page=1 (accessed December 15, 2005). ELF's own site is available at http://www.earthliberationfront.com/main.shtml (accessed December 15, 2005). Earth First!'s site is available at http://www.earthfirst.org (accessed December 15, 2005).

if they decide to cut out the middleman—that is, the state—and assume this role themselves. However repugnant we rightfully judge the methods of these groups to be, it is hard to see how we can consistently condemn them and yet at the same time endorse asking the state to enforce our own views.

Instead, let us avoid such unbecoming conduct altogether and resolve not to subsidize loggers or scientists or environmentalists or anyone else through government taxation. Make the loggers buy the land they want to deforest; make the scientists, pharmaceutical companies, and so on buy the animals and equipment they want to use in their experiments; make environmental groups buy the land they want to preserve unspoiled by mankind. Grant titles back to the ranching and farming families who had been using and caring for land for generations before the government took it from them. Allow sport hunting to take place, but only on privately owned preserves. To make all this possible, take those hundreds of millions of acres of land the federal government has unilaterally decreed ownership of and currently uses as so many political footballs, and instead sell it to private use. That will have the simultaneous benefit of immediately removing the "tragedy of the commons" logic that leads to exploitation and overuse, and making both the conservationists and the users face the actual, real-world consequences of what they propose to do with the resources in question. Resources are scarce and cost money. Wishing that were not so, or transferring the costs of one's own use onto others, does not make those costs go away.

In an imperfect world where—excuse the redundancy, but it bears repeating—perfection is impossible, we must instead search out the best among less-than-ideal policies. Private property ownership, by maintaining the connection between freedom and responsibility, has proven again and again to be the best among those imperfect solutions. It has proved its ability to do this even in the issues of environment and animals we are considering here. We will never all agree on how animals and natural resources should be used, but if we make people pay for their respective uses themselves, there is no question that we would see an increase of careful consideration about how best to use, nurture, and preserve these resources for the future—human ingenuity in the face of adversity and necessity is, after all, as Julian Simon called it, our one true "ultimate resource"—and at the same time we would see a great decrease in wanton neglect, callous disregard, and pointless cruelty or endangerment. That is all that one can hope for, I believe, in an imperfect world filled with imperfect human beings. On the other hand, to accomplish even that much would be to realize just about everything that people on all sides of these issues could reasonably want.

Bibliography

Adler, Jonathan H. "Bad for Your Land, Bad for the Critters." *Wall Street Journal Online*, December 31, 2003.

Alessi, Michael de. "Private Conservation and Black Rhinos in Zimbabwe: The Savé Valley and Bubiana Conservancies." Competitive Enterprise Institute, 2000. Http://www.cei.org/gencon/025,01687.cfm, accessed December 15, 2005.

Anderson, Terry L., and Donald R. Leal. *Free Market Environmentalism*. Boulder, Colo.: Westview, 1991.

Aquinas, St. Thomas. *Treatise on Law: Summa Theologica Questions 90–97*. R. J. Henle, trans. Notre Dame, Ind.: University of Notre Dame Press, 1993 (1266–73).

Aristotle. *Politics*. C. D. C. Reeve, trans. Indianapolis, Ind.: Hackett, 1998 (ca. 350 B.C.).

Barnett, Randy E. *The Structure of Liberty: Justice and the Rule of Law*. Oxford: Oxford University Press, 1998.

Baskerville, Stephen. "Is There Really a Fatherhood Crisis?" *The Independent Review* 8, no. 4 (Spring 2004): 485–508.

Bethell, Tom. *The Noblest Triumph: Property and Prosperity through the Ages*. New York: St. Martin's, 1998.

Blankenhorn, David. *Fatherless America: Confronting Our Most Urgent Social Problem*. New York: Basic Books, 1995.

Buss, David M. *The Evolution of Desire: Strategies of Human Mating*, rev. ed. New York: Basic Books, 2003.

Callicott, J. Baird. "Intrinsic Value in Nature: A Metaethical Analysis." *Electronic Journal of Analytic Philosophy* 3 (Spring 1995). Http://ejap.louisiana.edu/EJAP/1995.spring/callicott.1995.spring.html, accessed December 15, 2005.

Carnell, Brian. "PETA Launches 'The Holocaust on Your Plate' Campaign," March 10, 2003. Http://www.animalrights.net/archives/year/2003/000052.html, accessed December 15, 2005.

Centers for Disease Control and the U.S. Department of Health and Human Services. *National Survey of Family Growth*. 1995. Http://www.cdc.gov/nchs/. accessed December 15, 2005.

Cohen, Carl. "Why Animals Have No Rights." Http://www.responsiblewildlifemanagement.org/carl_cohen.htm, accessed March 15, 2005.

Corvino, John, ed. *Same Sex: Debating the Ethics, Science, and Culture of Homosexuality*. Lanham, Md.: Rowman & Littlefield, 1997.

Dalrymple, Theodore. *Life at the Bottom: The Worldview That Makes the Underclass*. Chicago: Ivan R. Dee, 2001.

Dalrymple, Theodore. *Our Culture, What's Left of It: The Mandarins and the Masses*. Chicago: Ivan R. Dee, 2005.

Daniels, Cynthia, ed. *Lost Fathers: The Politics of Fatherlessness in America.* New York: St. Martin's, 1998.

Dawkins, Richard. *The Selfish Gene,* 2nd ed. Oxford: Oxford University Press, 1989.

Epstein, Richard. *Simple Rules for a Complex World.* Cambridge, Mass.: Harvard University Press, 1997.

Finnis, John. *Natural Law and Natural Rights.* Oxford: Oxford University Press, 1980.

Flew, Antony. *Social Life and Moral Judgment.* New Brunswick, N.J.: Transaction, 2003.

Furstenberg, Frank, and Andrew Cherlin. *Divided Families: What Happens to Children When Parents Part.* Cambridge, Mass.: Harvard University Press, 1991.

Garrett, Aaron V., ed. *Animal Rights and Souls in the Eighteenth Century,* 6 vols. Bristol: Thoemmes, 2000.

Hardin, Garrett. "The Tragedy of the Commons." *Science* 162 (December 13, 1968): 1243–8.

Hayward, Steven F. *2004 Index of Leading Environmental Indicators.* San Francisco, Calif., and Washington, D.C.: Pacific Research Institute for Public Policy and American Enterprise Institute for Public Policy Research, 2004.

Hecox, Eric B. "Wildlife Management: A Comparative Analysis of Protection versus Utilization, Kenya and Zimbabwe." Http://www.coloradocollege.edu/ Dept/EC/faculty/Hecox/erichecox/kenzim.html, accessed December 15, 2005.

Hocutt, Max. *Grounded Ethics: The Empirical Bases of Normative Judgments.* New Brunswick, N.J.: Transaction, 2000.

Hume, David. "Of Polygamy and Divorces." In *Essays Moral, Political, and Literary.* Eugene F. Miller, ed. Indianapolis, Ind.: Liberty Classics, 1987.

Hume, David. *An Enquiry Concerning Human Understanding,* 3rd ed. with text revised and notes. P. H. Nidditch, ed. Oxford: Clarendon, 1992 (1748).

Kay, Charles, and Randy T. Simmons, eds. *Wilderness Ecology: Aboriginal Influences and the Original State of Nature.* Provo: University of Utah Press, 2002.

Kekes, John. "On the Supposed Obligation to Relieve Famine." *Philosophy* 77 (2002): 503–17.

Kellert, Stephen R., and Edward O. Wilson., eds. *The Biophilia Hypothesis.* New York: Shearwater Books, 1993.

Locke, John. *Second Treatise of Government.* Peter Laslett, ed. Cambridge: Cambridge University Press, 1988 (1690).

Lomasky, Loren. *Persons, Rights, and the Moral Community.* Oxford: Oxford University Press, 1990.

Lomborg, Bjørn. *The Skeptical Environmentalist: Measuring the Real State of the World.* Cambridge: Cambridge University Press, 2001.

Pinker, Steven. *How the Mind Works.* New York: Norton, 1997.

Pinker, Steven. *The Blank Slate: The Modern Denial of Human Nature.* New York: Penguin, 2002.

Pipes, Richard. *Property and Freedom.* New York: Vintage, 1999.

Plato. *Republic,* 2nd ed. G. M. A. Grube, trans., rev. by C. D. C. Reeve. Indianapolis, Ind.: Hackett, 1992 (ca. 380 B.C.).

Rector, Robert E., Kirk A. Johnson, Lauren R. Noyes, and Shannan Martin. "The Harmful Effects of Early Sexual Activity and Multiple Sexual Partners among Women: A Book of Charts." Washington, D.C.: Heritage Foundation, 2003. Http://www.heritage.org/Research/Family/abstinence_charts.cfm, accessed December 15, 2005.

Rector, Robert, et al. "Sexually Active Teenagers Are More Likely to Be Depressed and to Attempt Suicide." Washington, D.C.: Heritage Foundation, 2003. Http://www.heritage.org/Research/Family/cda0304.cfm, accessed December 15, 2005.

Rector, Robert, et al. "Teens Who Make Virginity Pledges Have Substantially Improved Life Outcomes." Washington, D.C.: Heritage Foundation, 2004. Http://www.heritage.org/Research/Family/cda04-07.cfm, accessed December 15, 2005.

Regan, Tom. *The Case for Animal Rights*. Berkeley: University of California Press, 1985.

"Review and Outlook: A Fish Story." *Wall Street Journal Online*, November 6, 2003. Http://online.wsj.com/article/0,,SB106808072524412900,00.html, accessed December 15, 2005.

Ridley, Matt. *The Origins of Virtue*. New York: Penguin, 1996.

Rihory, Liz. "HSUS vs. CAMPFIRE." 2001. Http://www.naiaonline.org/body/articles/archives/campfire.htm, accessed December 15, 2005.

Schabner, Dean. "Already Active ELF Extending Range." ABC News, January 30, 2001. Http://abcnews.go.com/US/story?id=90151&page=1, accessed December 15, 2005.

Schmidt, Thomas E. *Straight or Narrow? Compassion and Clarity in the Homosexuality Debate*. Downers Grove, Ill.: Intervarsity Press, 1995.

Schmidtz, David, and Elizabeth Willott, eds. *Environmental Ethics: What Really Matters, What Really Works*. Oxford: Oxford University Press, 2002.

Scully, Matthew. *Dominion: The Power of Man, the Suffering of Animals, and the Call to Mercy*. New York: St. Martin's, 2003.

Shaftesbury, Third Earl of (Anthony Ashley Cooper). *Characteristics of Men, Manners, Opinions, Times*. Lawrence E. Klein, ed. Cambridge: Cambridge University Press, 1999 (1711).

Simmons, Randy T. "Fixing the Endangered Species Act." *The Independent Review* 3, no. 4 (Spring 1999): 511–36.

Simmons, Randy T. *Endangered Species*. New York: Greenhaven, 2002.

Simon, Julian, ed. *The State of Humanity*. New York: Blackwell, 1995.

Simon, Julian. *Ultimate Resource* 2. Princeton, N.J.: Princeton University Press, 1998.

Singer, Peter. *The Expanding Circle: Ethics and Sociobiology*. Oxford: Oxford University Press, 1983.

Singer, Peter. *Practical Ethics*, 2nd ed. Cambridge: Cambridge University Press, 1993.

Singer, Peter. *Animal Liberation*, 2nd ed. New York: Ecco, 2001.

Smith, Adam. *The Theory of Moral Sentiments*. Indianapolis, Ind.: Liberty Classics, 1982 (1759).

Sullivan, Andrew, ed. *Same-Sex Marriage: Pro and Con: A Reader*. New York: Vintage, 1997.

Sunstein, Cass R., and Martha Craven Nussbaum, eds. *Animal Rights: Current Debates and New Directions*. Oxford: Oxford University Press, 2004.

Suprynowicz, Vin. *The Ballad of Carl Drega*. Reno, Nev.: Mountain Media, 2002.

Vilkka, Leena. *The Intrinsic Value of Nature*. Amsterdam: Rodopi, 1997.

Whelan, Robert. *Broken Homes and Battered Children: A Study of the Relationship between Child Abuse and Family Type*. London: Family Education Trust, 1993.

Wilson, Edward O. *Biophilia: The Human Bond with Other Species*. Cambridge, Mass.: Harvard University Press, 1984.

Wilson, Edward O. *In Search of Nature*. Washington, D.C.: Island Press, 1996.

Wilson, Edward O. *Consilience: The Unity of Knowledge*. New York: Knopf, 1998.

PART III

THE END

9

What Is Good for the Goose

Throughout this book I have used the dread word *happiness,* and I think an impartial spectator would judge that fact to impose upon me an obligation to say something substantive about what exactly the word means. I have several times talked *about* happiness. I have argued, for example, that people must find their own paths to it and that no two people's paths will be exactly alike, claims that together constitute a large part of the reason why a wide scope of individual freedom is necessary. Indeed, most of the argument of this book has explicitly or implicitly assumed that happiness is everyone's ultimate goal, that, as Aristotle put it, happiness is the one good that is desired for its own sake and not for the sake of anything else.[1] These should not be left to stand as mere assertions, however. That means that the time has come for me to put my money where my mouth is and say something about what I believe human happiness actually is and how it might be achieved. My argument that there is no single good for all people carries with it the implication that one cannot give a single account of "the good," and that might provide an excuse for me to avoid having to address this topic. But that would be a rather weak evasion, I think: if I did not want to address this topic at all, I shouldn't have mentioned it throughout the book!

THE GOOD AND THE HAPPY

I would like to begin by taking up the question of whether a person who is "good" or does "good" things is necessarily happy. But before I can

---

[1] In his *Nicomachean Ethics*, bk. 1, chap. 7.

address that I must first avert a common and easy mistake. Despite the impression one might get from the way we sometimes talk about such matters, speaking about "the good" makes as little sense as speaking about "the happy"—as if there were, in either case, some Platonic entity out there in which all good things or all happy people, actions, or events participated. I do not believe in any such entity, principally because there is no good reason to do so. One does not have to believe in them to be able to use and understand terms such as *good* or *happy;* the Platonic argument that such terms could derive meaning only by reference to some transcendent, fixed, and absolute standard turns out simply to be mistaken. An initial piece of evidence for that is the fact that you and I use and understand those terms all the time without having any idea at all about any transcendent, fixed, or absolute standard they might relate to.

Ludwig Wittgenstein elaborated the argument in the first half of the twentieth century by repeatedly asking philosophers not to ask what "must" be the case about such-and-so, but, rather, simply to look and see what in fact *is* the case.[2] Plato had thought that the resemblance among various uses of words such as *good* implied their reliance on one fixed, ideal standard and that our ability to use such terms in a variety of cases meant that all such uses "must" rely on such a standard: this was the genesis of Plato's famous theory of "forms."[3] Wittgenstein's suggestion, however, was that words gained their meanings simply from the ways they are used. Since the word *good*, for example, is often used in similar ways, its meaning in particular usages often overlaps with its meaning in other particular usages. Wittgenstein suggested the felicitous term "family resemblance": a word's meaning in various usages might bear certain familiar similarities, as the members of a family do to one another, but there may be no single feature that all usages have, just as there may be no single physical feature that all members of a family share. Thus we can use and understand different uses of the same word by habitual associations based on this rough familiarity, but they do not necessarily require or depend on any strict logical or rational relationships. So, for example, the phrases "good watch," "good meal," "good wife," and "good man" might use the word *good* in related ways, but they need not; and we can use and understand these terms regardless.

---

[2] He makes this argument in several places. One should perhaps start with his *Blue and Brown Books* and his *Philosophical Investigations*. See also Taylor's *Good and Evil*.

[3] For Plato's presentation of his argument, see, for example, the *Republic*, bks. 5 and 6, the *Euthyphro*, or the *Meno*.

Wittgenstein's suggestion is simpler and more plausible than Plato's, and a number of people have made the same argument, and in more sophisticated fashion, since then. It is by now a commonplace. If you are a stickler about such things, however, I suppose I should say that although there could possibly be Platonic "forms" that exist in the "intelligible realm," there is nonetheless no reason to assume that there are and no reason to believe there must be. Following Ockham's Razor, which holds that we should not needlessly complicate our explanations, I think we can safely shave away Plato's mysterious metaphysics.

Hence to begin a discussion about happiness and goodness by asking about "the good" and "the happy" is to begin on quite the wrong foot. Instead of asking whether happiness is connected with goodness, we should ask whether a person who does what is good (for him) will be happy. This question is still a general one, but it narrows its focus to individuals rather than to hypothetical collectives or ideal entities. My definite answer to this more tractable question, then, is: it depends. It depends, that is, on what we mean by the terms *good* and *happy*.

I have used the term *good* in this book to refer to what satisfies individuals' interests. So accepting a job offer is a "good" decision if it promotes the person in question's interests, "bad" if it does not; the exchange was a "good" one if it satisfied the interests of the people in question, not if not. In this way happiness will bear the simple relation to goodness that we can presume that if a person manages to successfully promote his interests—that is, achieve "goods"—then he will probably be happy. In his *Nicomachean Ethics* Aristotle seemed to think that a good person would therefore be a happy one, a "good person" for him being one who, among other things, exercised his rational abilities and his uniquely human *phronesis* or judgment.[4] This is a quite pedestrian conception and use of "good," we must admit, and one might think indeed that it is overly pedestrian: can't one after all speak of a "good" painting or a "good" book, without meaning thereby only that it serves this or that person's interests? And by the way, who says that promoting people's interests is necessarily a good thing to do? Some people have pretty nasty interests, after all.

This is why I said this was a "dread" topic. We now enter into a hornet's nest of difficult issues, most of them outside the scope of this book to resolve, not to mention probably beyond my competence to address. But

---

4 See the *Nicomachean Ethics,* bk. 1 and bk. 10, chaps. 6–9. For an excellent discussion of this notion of judgment, see Fleischacker's *A Third Concept of Liberty,* esp. chaps. 1–4.

let me hazard a preliminary stab nonetheless. Yes, we can talk about a good painting or book, but it is somewhat misleadingly put that way because, again, it seems to imply that there is a transcendently fixed standard being adverted to. I suggest on the contrary that what constitutes the standard of goodness in these cases is pragmatic and empirically grounded. It is the answer to the further question, "'Good' at what?"—which will then entail providing a description of the kind of thing we are talking about. If we are talking about a book, for example, the criteria for "good" in this case will depend on what a (or this kind of) book is, what it is for, what it should do, and so on. My suggestion is that these are all empirical matters—to be discovered by actually looking to see what (these kinds of) books are, what they are for, what they should do, and so on, rather than by sitting in one's office and excogitating imaginary idealized standards. I suggest the standards are thus "pragmatic" in the sense that they are linked to and driven by the details of the case in question, and they are "empirical" in the sense that they are discovered by actual experience with cases like the one in question and not invented or apprehended by a disembodied rational intellect.[5]

That does not mean that these pragmatic, empirical standards are arbitrary, however—far from it. They are objective in that they are dependent on the actual facts of the matter, facts such as what actually constitutes human nature, what actually constitutes human experience, what actual ends people pursue and what means to those ends are actually better or more efficient than others, what are the actual historical facts and events that have given rise to usages, beliefs, and practices, and so on. I apologize for repetition of the word *actual,* but the point is frequently mistaken and therefore needs to be emphasized. These facts are often dependent on the actions and beliefs of individuals, but they are not for all that arbitrary or determined by any single individual's idiosyncratic beliefs. So, for example, when I walk into a store in Hong Kong—a long way away from where I live, where I do not speak the language and they do not speak mine, where I do not know the shopkeeper and he does not know me—I can nevertheless hand him a little piece of plastic and he in turn lets me walk out with some of his things. How is that possible? Well, it is possible because of the objective existence of a large web of beliefs and practices concerning what certain pieces of plastic represent and how they are used, how banks operate, what currencies are and what

---

5 See Richards's "A Fitness Model of Evaluation." Much of my discussion here also draws on Taylor's excellent *Good and Evil.*

they do and how they are exchanged, and on and on. All of these beliefs and practices are the result of human action and are thus in some sense "socially constructed," but they are not up to and cannot be changed by any individual.[6] And they are certainly not arbitrary. If you do not believe me, try taking your green piece of paper with the symbol *20* written on it and telling the merchant in question that it is actually worth one thousand Hong Kong dollars—and see how far you get. Or take driving on the right (or left) side of the road: it does not matter which is chosen, but once a choice is made you had better not decide all on your own one day to flout the rule.

Moreover, if it is true that human practices are largely the results of people's trial-and-error investigations into how to achieve their ends in cooperation with others, then those practices will in fact have something else to recommend them besides being merely what everyone currently believes: utility. As people find ways that allow them to successfully negotiate interactions with others, their successes, as well as their failures, are precedents that they will follow in future similar cases. Their success will also be imitated by others who observe them and also want to succeed in similar circumstances. It is in this way that social practices are born, become habits, and sometimes coalesce into principles and rules.[7] If people do come to follow them or view them even as (moral? God's? the gods'?) rules, then it will be because they served people's interests or allowed people to promote their interests—which means they fostered people's welfare and thus served utility. This process of historical winnowing of practices is what ultimately underlies the system of moral concepts that is the foundation of this book, including those political principles that others are inclined to describe as "natural rights" issuing from "natural law."

So a community's long-standing rules of morality or etiquette will reflect the experiments into what is conducive to utility that its members have conducted over many generations. This is the sense in which these rules are not arbitrary: they will bear an actual connection to actual lived experience (that word *actual* again), they will embody the accumulated wisdom of previous generations, and they therefore should not be

---

[6] See Searle's *The Construction of Social Reality*.

[7] See Hayek's *The Constitution of Liberty*, chaps. 3 and 4, and *The Fatal Conceit*, chaps. 1–3; Hocutt's *Grounded Ethics*, pt. 1; Otteson's *Adam Smith's Marketplace of Life*, chaps. 5 and 7; Taylor's *Good and Evil*, chaps. 2 and 3; and Wilson's *Consilience*, chaps. 8, 9, and 11. For classic accounts, see Smith's *Theory of Moral Sentiments*, pts. 1–3, and Hume's *Treatise of Human Nature*, bk. 3, pt. 2, secs. 1–3.

taken lightly or ignored for transient reasons.[8] Of course, since human experience changes over time, and this process of discovery is a product of experimentation and will tend to yield better results over time, the authority of a community's long-standing rules of morality and etiquette is *presumptive* but not *absolute*. These standards thus enjoy a "middle way objectivity": they are not arbitrary or dependent on any single person's private beliefs, but they are also not eternally fixed by any transcendent standard.[9] They are the joint or macro product of individual or micro action.[10] Prudence therefore suggests that while one might test their limits, one should think long and hard before, and have good cause for, disregarding them. John Locke captured this sentiment in his 1690 *Second Treatise of Government*. In response to the charge that his endorsement of the possibility of justified revolution could lead to instability and even anarchy, Locke writes:

[S]uch *Revolutions happen* not upon every little mismanagement in publick affairs. *Great mistakes* in the ruling part, many wrong and inconvenient Laws, and all the *slips* of humane frailty will be *born by the People,* without mutiny or murmur. But if a long train of Abuses, Prevarications, and Artifices, all tending the same way, make the design visible to the People, and they cannot but feel, what they lie under, and see, whither they are going; 'tis not to be wonder'd, that they should then rouze themselves, and endeavour to put the rule into such hands, which may secure to them the ends for which Government was first erected. (chap. 19, §225; emphasis in original)

Thomas Jefferson echoes Locke's sentiments in the 1776 Declaration of Independence: "Prudence, indeed, will dictate that Governments long established should not be changed for light and transient Causes."

Locke's and Jefferson's points—as well as Burke's, Flew's, Hayek's, Hocutt's, Hume's, Otteson's, Smith's, Taylor's, Wilson's, and so on—are that long-standing social institutions have a presumptive authority grounded on their connection to and dependence on lived experience. Adam Smith makes the case by means of three interlocking arguments. First is the *local knowledge argument,* which we have encountered before: given that everyone has unique knowledge of his own "local" situation, including his goals, desires, and the opportunities available to him, each individual is therefore the person best positioned to make decisions for himself about which courses of action he should take to achieve his goals.

---

[8] Edmund Burke makes a similar argument in his 1790 *Reflections on the Revolution in France.*

[9] See Flew's *Social Life and Moral Judgment,* chap. 3, and Otteson's "Adam Smith und die Objektivität moralischer Urteile: Ein Mittelweg."

[10] I adapt this terminology from Schelling's *Micromotives and Macrobehavior.*

Here is the argument in Smith's words: "What is the species of domestick industry which his capital can employ, and of which the produce is likely to be of the greatest value, every individual, it is evident, can, in his local situation, judge much better than any statesman or lawgiver can do for him" (*Wealth of Nations*, p. 456).[11] Second is the *economizer argument,* which holds that as each of us seeks to better his own condition (however each of us understands that), each of us will therefore be led to seek out the most efficient uses of our resources and labor so as to maximize their productive output and return on our investment. Here again are Smith's words:

The uniform, constant, and uninterrupted effort of every man to better his condition, the principle from which publick and national, as well as private opulence is originally derived, is frequently powerful enough to maintain the natural progress of things toward improvement, in spite both of the extravagance of government, and of the greatest errors of administration. (*Wealth of Nations*, p. 343)[12]

Third and finally is the *invisible hand argument,* which holds that as each of us strives to better his own condition, each of us thereby simultaneously, though without intending to do so, betters the condition of everyone else. This happens for at least two reasons: one, when we specialize or concentrate our efforts on some small range of tasks or talents, we usually produce more of it than we can ourselves consume or use, which means we have a surplus that we can trade or sell away—which in turn means that the overall stock of goods and services increases for everyone; two, we seek out behaviors, policies, protocols, forms of contract and trade,

[11] Smith continues: "The statesman, who should attempt to direct private people in what manner they ought to employ their capitals, would not only load himself with a most unnecessary attention, but assume an authority which could safely be trusted, not only to no single person, but to no council or senate whatever, and which would nowhere be so dangerous as in the hands of a man who had folly and presumption enough to fancy himself fit to exercise it" (*Wealth of Nations*, p. 456).

[12] Smith also writes: "But though the profusion of government must, undoubtedly, have retarded the natural progress of England towards wealth and improvement, it has not been able to stop it. The annual produce of its land and labour is, undoubtedly, much greater at present than it was either at the restoration or at the revolution. The capital, therefore, annually employed in cultivating this land, and in maintaining this labour, must likewise be much greater. In the midst of all the exactions of government, this capital has been silently and gradually accumulated by *the private frugality and good conduct of individuals, by their universal, continual, and uninterrupted effort to better their own condition.* It is this effort, protected by law and allowed by liberty to exert itself in the manner that is most advantageous, which has maintained the progress of England towards opulence and improvement in almost all former times, and which, it is to be hoped, will do so in all future times" (*Wealth of Nations*, p. 345; emphasis added).

and so on that serve our local interests, but others will learn from us and imitate our successes and avoid our failures, thereby saving themselves time and energy, thereby enabling them to go yet further than we did in securing their—and thus, indirectly, everyone else's—ends. Here is Smith's phrasing of this argument:

As every individual, therefore, endeavours as much as he can . . . to direct [his] industry that its produce may be of the greatest value; every individual necessarily labours to render the annual revenue of the society as great as he can. He generally, indeed, neither intends to promote the public interest, nor knows how much he is promoting it. . . . [H]e intends only his own security; and by directing that industry in such a manner as its produce may be of the greatest value, he intends only his own gain, and he is in this, as in many other cases, led by an invisible hand to promote an end which was no part of his intention. (*Wealth of Nations*, p. 456) [13]

Note that the argument is not that the unintended social orders that are produced by this invisible-hand mechanism *guarantee* beneficial results. People can make unwise, imprudent, or downright immoral choices, and they can lead to habits, protocols, and standards that are not in fact conducive to everyone's best interests. We are fallible creatures, after all. But *given* that we're fallible, the argument focuses not on what is ideally best but rather on what is the best among what is actually possible. And the argument is that the best way to find that out is by allowing the invisible-hand mechanism to work itself out, and by granting the results of this trial-and-error process of winnowing and culling presumptive, if again not absolute, authority. This invisible-hand mechanism is what Smith describes as "the obvious and simple system of natural liberty." A final passage from Smith. Here is how he concludes the argument:

All systems either of preference or of restraint, therefore, being thus completely taken away, the obvious and simple system of natural liberty establishes itself of its own accord. Every man, as long as he does not violate the laws of justice, is left perfectly free to pursue his own interest his own way, and to bring both his industry and capital into competition with those of any other man, or order of men. The sovereign is completely discharged from a duty, in the attempting to perform which he must always be exposed to innumerable delusions, and for the proper performance of which no human wisdom or knowledge could ever

---

[13] Smith continues: "Nor is it always the worse for the society that it was no part of it [i.e., his intention]. By pursuing his own interest he frequently promotes that of the society much more effectually than when he really intends to promote it. I have never known much good done by those who affected to trade for the publick good" (ibid.).

be sufficient; the duty of superintending the industry of private people, and of directing it towards the employments most suitable to the interest of the society. (*Wealth of Nations*, p. 687)

BACK TO HAPPINESS

But how does the discussion of middle-way objectivity, unintended order, and invisible hands relate to the questions about goodness and happiness? Standards of goodness that might apply to books or paintings or music or anything else are pragmatic, empirical standards, but they are not arbitrary or subjective. They occupy the middle-way objectivity, which means that we can indeed speak of "objective" standards of goodness, as long as we (1) understand that these standards are still pragmatic and empirical, (2) regard them as having historically presumptive authority that is nevertheless always subject to testing and revision, and (3) are dependent on and indexed to the particular thing or kind of thing in question. Because the way such standards are generated means they will typically have an ultimate connection to utility, it may be that the sense of "good" at work in discussions of books, paintings, and so on might end up issuing from a shared source or justification. If they do, although that fact might be consistent with Plato's view, it would not be evidence for it; and in any case whether they do or not is yet another matter that can be determined only by empirical, not a priori, investigation.

Similarly—and here we finally get back to our original subject—what is good for a person is a matter of empirical, not a priori, investigation, and yet it is not arbitrary, even if it cannot be merely apprehended intellectually or known in advance. That is one reason I argued in Part I for the General Liberty principle, that you must be given a broad and wide scope to act freely, using your judgment on your local knowledge, to discover and act on what will, and what will not, promote your interests and thus be "good" for you. The rules and advice and received wisdom of your community should be your starting point, and your community, starting with your parents, has the obligation to pass on and train you in its collected wisdom so that you do not have to start from scratch. You have the same obligation toward others in your community, starting with your children. Contrary to what some well-intentioned but misguided parents think, allowing children to do whatever they want and to come up with whatever rules they happen to hit on is doing them no favor; it is like putting a child out in the woods and hoping it figures out how to survive on its own. The whole point of having parents is so that children do not have to run these same experiments all over again, just as the whole point of taking a physics class is so that future physicists do not have to start by wondering, as Thales did in the sixth century B.C., whether everything is really made up of water. We would never get anywhere that way. If you had good parents, they schooled you in what they and their community had already figured out. As you got older, however, and began to develop your own judgment—and thus became your own 'person'—you probably did what you should have, which is take those rules as guidelines or rules of thumb and tried them out.

What will be good for you will most likely bear a resemblance to what has been good for others, but you will have to discover exactly how close the resemblance is and exactly how you should depart from the course others have charted. Although what turns out to be good for all individuals will, because of common features in human nature, bear a family resemblance, nevertheless the exact signature of each individual person's good will be unique. And that means that the exact signature of each individual person's happiness will also be unique.

SO WHAT *IS* HAPPINESS?

As is implied by the discussion above, one's happiness is intimately connected with one's relative success at promoting one's unique schedule of interests—that is, with achieving one's good. In fact, let me make the stronger statement that a person's happiness is ultimately *constituted by* his having successfully promoted his interests or good. So you are happy if you are living a successful life, and unhappy if you are not.

Now that may be true, and I think it is, but it is only a starting point. It still does not fill out a substantive picture of what the happy human life is. Is there nothing more concrete that we can say? Unfortunately, not really. I can no more tell you exactly what happiness will be for you than I can tell you whom you should marry or what book will be your favorite.

But that does not mean that we can't say anything at all. Given some general facts about human nature and the human condition, it is possible to discover some guidelines about what would be *obstacles* to happiness, and we might be able to make some general hints or take some educated guesses about in what human happiness may consist. These will be about on a par with your doctor saying to you something like: I can't tell you exactly what food you should eat, but I can say that you should absolutely not eat glass or drink Drano; and I can also say that most likely you will be healthiest if you eat a variety of foods, not too much of any one thing, and make sure you get enough protein. That still leaves quite a lot for you to discover on your own, obviously, but it is giving you some guidelines. Without knowing much about you, then, or about what exactly makes you tick, I can make similarly general recommendations that will provide some measure of guidance despite their generality. I thus make a series of assertions now without a whole lot of supporting evidence. But they are offered as prospective descriptions of human reality, so you can test them against your experience.

One thing people need to be happy is deep, loving relationships.[14] These can take different forms, of course, and there is no way that I or anyone else could tell you exactly what kind of deep relationship or with whom is best for you. But what we can say with confidence is that a life without such relationships is a far poorer one, and consequently a far less happy one, than a life with such relationships. Another thing we can say with confidence is that an individual's capacity to form such relationships is limited. Love is a scarce resource, and a deep relationship takes time, energy, and devotion, all of which each of us has in only limited quantities.[15] What that means is that true friends or soul mates are rare and should be treasured, and if you have such a friendship, you should nurture and hold on to it. It also means that you will not be able to have, say, fifty of them. That would be simply impossible—as impossible as being an aficionado of fifty different genres of music at once. Unless you need no sleep or have unlimited energy or both, you will have to make choices, conserve and economize your resources, and concentrate your efforts. You should count yourself lucky and blessed to have two or three soul mates in your lifetime.

The other consequence of this, I believe, is that those ethical theories that preach cosmopolitanism, or the view that you should love or treat every other human being as if he were your own neighbor or brother, are prescriptions, ultimately, for unhappiness. The reason is that they dissipate your scarce resources, leaving you with large numbers of superficial but no deep relations. And human beings simply cannot be happy that way. Moral cosmopolitanism is an attractive ideal, issuing as it does from

---

[14] Here again Adam Smith got it right: "What so great happiness as to be beloved, and to know that we deserve to be beloved? What so great misery as to be hated, and to know that we deserve to be hated?" (*Theory of Moral Sentiments*, p. 113). For a more recent account, see Buss's *The Evolution of Desire*, chaps. 2, 3, and 10.

[15] See Smith again: *Theory of Moral Sentiments*, pp. 229–30 and 236, and *Wealth of Nations*, pp. 26–7. For recent evidence, see Dunbar's *Grooming, Gossip, and the Evolution of Language*, chap. 4, and Barton and Dunbar's "Evolution and the Social Brain."

the reasonable conviction that you should not mistreat or disparage others simply because you do not know them or because they are not part of your inner circle of close friends.[16] Putting this in the terms developed earlier in this book, you owe everyone, even complete strangers, treatment in accordance with 'justice'; in some cases—if, for example, the person is right in front of you or has otherwise insinuated himself into your attention as a concrete individual—decency may require you to display virtues such as generosity, hospitality, or charity. The argument I wish to press here is rather that one should not in the first instance worry oneself unduly about the suffering or hardship that exists "somewhere in the world" or "in the third world" or "among the least of us." The reason for this is not callousness, provincialism, or selfishness. It is instead a recognition of two hard facts of the human condition. First, our capacities to love and show genuine concern are limited. If they are widely scattered, their fruitfulness is diminished, and the more widely they are scattered the less fruitful they will be. Second, love is a resource that must be carefully nurtured to be vital and robust, and part of this nurturing must be with the assistance of the object of our love. That means that deep human attachment is necessarily a mutually reenforcing enterprise and that widely scattered or one-sided love withers and becomes desiccated and lifeless; if this condition persists, one's very ability to have deep, loving relationships might atrophy and eventually die altogether. Although there will be the occasional exception to this—the rare hermit or recluse who can be genuinely happy even in long-term solitude—and although you might be one of these exceptions, nevertheless these cases are so rare that it would be foolish not to seek out people with whom it is possible for you to have such relationships, to focus your energies on fostering them, and to attend to them with delicacy and care. Only thereafter should you focus any remaining energies on people or problems farther away from you.

A moral cosmopolitanism can, then, have the truly unfortunate—and dangerous—unintended consequence of rendering people less able to form the kinds of bonds with others that can make them deeply happy. This danger must be reckoned when considering whether to encourage people to love the whole world as they love their own, rather than merely to love their own but to treat everyone else with justice.

[16] See Singer's *Expanding Circle* for an example of the view I am here criticizing. See also Nussbaum's *Cultivating Humanity* and "Patriotism and Cosmopolitanism." For a classic source, see Cicero's *De officiis*.

I should also point out that the moral cosmopolitanism I am criticizing departs from Jesus's so-called Golden Rule. According to St. Matthew, Jesus said (in the King James translation), "Therefore all things whatsoever ye would that men should do to you, do ye even so to them" (Matthew 7:12). Although some interpret this very expansively, along the lines of "do *everything* for others that you would like done to you," because each of us is different from others, there is little chance that *everything* that is good for us would also be good for others. Thus I think the more plausible reading of Jesus's maxim is that we should show others what we ourselves require and expect from others—and what we can be sure that everyone does in fact require and expect—and that is the 'justice' described in chapters 1 and 2. One argument that modern proponents of moral cosmopolitanism sometimes marshal in their behalf is that their position is based on, or is a refinement of, the Christian Golden Rule. If I am right, however, it is actually a distortion of it. The only true Golden Rule is one that can be applied equally to all people. And that would be the General Liberty principle based on a universal justice.

The danger of moral cosmopolitanism is even more pronounced when we construct moral categories such as "speciesism" and admonish people to treat not only all other humans as we would treat our own loved ones, but even members of other species as well. Six billion people is already an impossibly large number, without adding to that figure, as some would, the billion or so chickens slaughtered every year, the tens of thousands of animals in zoos around the world, and so on.[17] There have been studies suggesting that genuine human concern for others can reach to only approximately 150 entities, and that deep love and close friendship can extend to only approximately eleven.[18] Yes, it is apparently that precise— and that limited. Thus it has been suggested that it is no accident that historically an army platoon has usually had ten to twelve members, that a jury usually has twelve members, that the number of Jesus's disciples was what it was, and so on. Human beings have evolved under specific pressures for survival, and one hypothesis has it that those hominids over the last several hundred thousand years who concentrated all their concern and love on their own small group and family were more likely to survive

---

[17] As suggested by, among others, Tom Regan in his *The Case for Animal Rights*, Peter Singer in his *Animal Liberation*, and Steven Wise in his *Drawing the Line* and *Rattling the Cage*. People for the Ethical Treatment of Animals makes a similar argument; see http://www.peta.org/about/faq.asp (accessed December 15, 2005).

[18] See Barton and Dunbar's "Evolution of the Social Brain," Dunbar's *Grooming, Gossip, and the Evolution of Language*, chap. 4, and Gladwell's *The Tipping Point*, chap. 5.

than those who did not; it turned out, apparently, that communities of about 150 or so and closer, usually family-based units of ten to twelve were optimal. Thus we, today's inheritors of those survivors' genes, may be programmed with specifically limited capacities to show concern and to love; and though some variation exists, as always, nevertheless the bulk of us cluster around the numbers given.

The claim, then, would be that if you use up your store of concern on rock stars or actors, on "all mankind" or unspecified "people in the third world," or on all sentient beings or all God's creatures or all of nature, not only will you put yourself in a state of perpetual nervous anxiety—since you will not be able to actually express or execute your concern for those objects, they being too distant or too numerous—but you also may well not have anything left for your actual neighbor, colleague, or sister-in-law. Similarly, if you discharge your stock of love on "the children" or on "the animals," not only will you again provoke in yourself a constant, unsettling agitation—even more distressing in this case since love is just not the kind of thing that can be shared widely—but you will also deprive both yourself and those who would love you of the bonds that are constitutive of human psychological health and, thus, happiness. How can you love your wife if you are busy loving all mankind? Will you still have time left for your daughter or your son?

None of this, to repeat, implies that one should be indifferent or callous toward others or that it is all right to treat animals cruelly or inhumanely. The argument rather is that psychological distance matters in human happiness and therefore should be figured in when assessing one's moral duties and obligations.[19]

I should take a moment to point out that I don't believe I am committing here the "naturalistic fallacy" of illegitimately deriving an *ought* from an *is*. It is a logical fallacy to derive moral injunctions directly from factual descriptions of human nature. For example, just because we have by nature certain instincts (a factual, or "is" statement), does not by itself mean we should, or should not, act on them (a moral injunction, or "ought" statement). But consider the matter from the other direction, as it were. A moral *ought* implies a *can*, meaning that the things one *ought* to do cannot exceed the things one is *able* to do. But that means—and this is what I want to emphasize—that a *cannot* defeats an *ought*: one does not have a moral duty to do what one is unable to do. So moral exhortations

[19] For interesting discussions of this issue, see Barzilai's "Sympathy in Space(s)," Boltanski's *Distant Suffering,* and Kamm's "The New Problem of Distance in Morality."

to, for example, regard all sentient creatures as equally deserving of your care or concern are, because impossible to realize, therefore defeated at the outset. It would be like someone saying that you are morally required to push that innocent pedestrian out of the way of an oncoming truck, though to do so you would have to run a sub-ten-second hundred-yard dash: since you probably can't do that, it can't reasonably be contended that it is your moral duty to do so. But these impossible moral exhortations are also dangerous because in attempting, necessarily in vain, to realize them, one runs the risk of squandering a crucial element to human happiness, namely, love.

Although we can say, then, that love and friendship are necessary elements of human happiness, no single answer can be given to what exactly constitutes either of them in your case. Even asking about them this way suggests the Platonic fallacy I disputed earlier. Love and friendship take many different forms, and although there will probably be overlap, or family resemblances, among the instantiations, there is no ideal form they must all take or approximate or participate in. All that can be said are the general remarks that a happy life will necessarily include them and that each person will have to investigate and discover the unique contours that peculiarly suit himself.

I will share one speculation I have, however, as long as you bear in mind that it is just a speculation: a true or deep or close friendship will, among other things, necessarily contain a *mutual* seeking of happiness. That is, you and I are not true friends if I do not genuinely desire your happiness and you mine; and this may imply in turn that I will not ultimately be happy unless you, my true friend, are happy as well. I have no evidence that this is true, but somehow I believe it is. I offer it only as something to consider.[20]

Can anything else be said? Perhaps a few more general remarks. I think Marcus Aurelius in his second-century A.D. *Meditations* and Montaigne in his 1575 *Essays* were right when they suggested that happiness is unattainable if it is your *direct* goal: if you are consciously aiming at it, you will miss it. Instead, what you have to do is go about your life in good, reputable, and decent ways, you must occupy yourself with industry and diligence, and then happiness is something that you will simply find yourself enjoying. Much of this book has been concerned with what those good, reputable, and decent ways are. They are all predicated on your having developed independent judgment, which means, therefore, that

---

[20] But see also Cicero's discussion of friendship.

part of what is required for happiness is independence. If you lived your life dependent on others when you did not need to be, if you were always asking, fawning, begging, or even demanding help from others (perhaps with the pseudo-indignation that people sometimes display who are trying to convince themselves they have a "natural right" to something), then your chances of happiness are commensurately diminished. The complement also holds that if you routinely treated others as servile dependents, as inferiors incapable of living as fully fledged independent persons, or, worse, as 'things' that could be manipulated or coerced into serving your or others' ends, this, I predict, will also gnaw at you and eviscerate your happiness, like termites hollowing out an old wooden church.

HAPPINESS WHEN YOU ARE OTHERWISE OCCUPIED

I would add here a word in support of those hoary Victorian virtues of industry and perseverance. There is a lot more to say for them than is usually thought today. As a child I used to hear that "idle hands are the devil's workshop," and I have come to believe that there is considerable truth in that: not just in the fact that people who have little to do will tend to find ways to get into trouble, but also in the fact that a person who is busy doing constructive, creative, productive things often never finds himself feeling the angst or ennui or "lethargy of soul" common to the idle rich, to pampered teenagers, or to some French philosophers.

Samuel Smiles's excellent and tragically neglected 1859 *Self-Help*—which went through numerous editions, was a best-seller in Britain and in America, and by the way is, to this day, the single all-time best-selling book in Japan—is nothing like the syrupy, let's-talk-about-our-feelings-and-wallow-in-self-pity "self-help" books we see today. On the contrary, it chronicles the lives of the great leaders and innovators in numerous walks of life—banking, engineering, biology, geology, mathematics, literature, chemistry, physics, manufacturing, and on and on—and demonstrates with pellucid clarity the central features of their characters that, no matter how different they all were otherwise, were common to them all. What are those features? First and foremost, industry and perseverance. Yes, they had native abilities, but they also worked, all the time, furiously, all day long; they had indefatigable energy and they never let themselves just sit around doing nothing. And, just as important, they did not give in or give up when they failed—and failed they all did, repeatedly. None of the great leaders of human accomplishment became that way by getting it right the first time. They were snubbed, unappreciated, discriminated against, discredited, underestimated, disadvantaged, and abused, and yet despite that, in the face of that, and perhaps even partly because of that, they hardened their will, disciplined themselves, and persevered.[21] Some of the people Smiles describes faced and overcame almost unimaginable hardship on the way to their ultimate success. The great nineteenth-century ornithologist John James Audubon, to take one example, had all his drawings, representing years and years of work, totally destroyed by rats. Here, according to Smiles, is the event in Audubon's own words:

> My absence was of several months; and when I returned, after having enjoyed the pleasures of home for a few days, I inquired after my box, and what I was pleased to call my treasure. The box was produced and opened; but reader, feel for me—a pair of Norway rats had taken possession of the whole, and reared a young family among the gnawed bits of paper, which, but a month previous, represented nearly a thousand inhabitants of air! The burning heat which instantly rushed through my brain was too great to be endured without affecting my whole nervous system. I slept for several nights, and the days passed like days of oblivion—until the animal powers being recalled into action through the strength of my constitution, I took up my gun, my notebook, and my pencils, and went forth to the woods as gaily as if nothing had happened. I felt pleased that I might now make better drawings than before; and, ere a period not exceeding three years had elapsed, my portfolio was again filled. (*Self-Help*, p. 95)

Note again that Audubon proceeded to draw them all again, grateful for the chance to do them all better—and it only took him three years! One cannot help but be awed and humbled, if not outright humiliated, reading the stories of these heroic accomplishers and then reflecting on oneself. Read Smiles's book, and then read it with your children. I promise you will be amply rewarded.

Right now, though, you might be thinking that those Victorian, "bourgeois" virtues are outdated indeed. But I beg you to reconsider. First of all, a considerable amount of recent research has shown that learning and taking to heart these "bourgeois" virtues is poor people's key out of poverty, while not learning is the key to remaining permanently in poverty. Even if people in the top economic classes can afford to flout the virtues of steadiness, perseverance, and industry, poor people emphatically cannot afford to do so—and their growing family and social disintegration, which is due not to lack of money but the other way around, is a high

---

[21] For more recent documentation of the same phenomena, see Murray's *Human Accomplishment*.

price to pay for the freedom to entertain a fashionable upper-class moral libertinism.[22]

Second of all, however, think for a moment how much *you* could accomplish in your life if you took, say, half an hour every day to devote to something. What could you do in, let us say, one year? You could learn ancient Greek, you could commit to memory scores of Shakespearean sonnets, you could learn the Argentinean tango, you could master Scottish history, you could learn how to paint, you could become an expert on the Civil War or Winston Churchill or Thomas Jefferson or Alexander the Great or Leonidas or Mary Queen of Scots or Darwin or Leonardo da Vinci or Pope Innocent III or Catherine the Great, you could find out what quantum mechanics or general relativity or string theory is, what sociobiology or kin selection or punctuated equilibrium is, you could finally figure out what statistical significance is, what irrational numbers do, or how to do multiple regression analysis, you could learn how to cross-stitch or knit or weave or play guitar. And on and on. Consider, moreover, how much you could accomplish if you took your three-and-a-half hours a week, gathered them together, and devoted them to doing something with someone else: you could go to every one of your son's football games, every one of your daughter's dance practices and recitals, you and your spouse could start an at-home business, you could save money by buying the "fixer-upper" house and actually fixing it up, and again on and on. You will have your own list, but I hope the point is clear.

Now do not respond by saying that you simply cannot find half an hour a day to devote to a new project. Ask yourself this: How much time do you spend every day sitting around doing pretty much nothing? How much time do you spend watching TV? How much time do you spend doing nothing of importance on the computer—playing games, idly surfing the net, sending (let us be honest) needless e-mails or silly text messages or pointless chatroom comments? If you claim that you simply cannot carve out of your day one half-hour to devote to some new, creative project that you would in a year or five or ten look back on and thank heaven you did, well, you may be kidding yourself but you're not kidding anyone else. A measure of laziness may be natural to human beings, but so are diseases; it is just as evil and necessary to combat as the plague is. So stop making excuses. Pick something, get to work, and see it through.

What is the point of all this, and what is its connection to happiness? As I suggested earlier, idle time varies directly with whining: the more

---

[22] See Theodore Dalrymple's *Life at the Bottom,* and Amy L. Wax's "Against Neutrality," "The Political Psychology of Welfare Reform," and "What Women Want."

time you spend doing nothing, the more likely you are to complain about everything. And although having more whiners in the world is not exactly an attractive prospect for the rest of us, the point here is that it will make *you* unhappy. If you are busy devoting yourself to something worthwhile, you just will not have time, or inclination, to lie about pondering the world's injustices or growing aggrieved at all the slights you have suffered. Personal industry, diligence, perseverance, and persistence do not just make the world better, then, they also make you better. Those are precisely the virtues of character that will enable you to become independent and to accomplish things that when you are not looking make you happy. Neither I nor anyone else can tell you *what* you should be doing, which projects you should undertake, how you should devote your energy, or what you should focus your attention on. But I can tell you that you need to find *something*. A life of idle inactivity might have provided an anemic pleasure in the moment, but it will provide you only sorry solace and an embarrassed disappointment in your old age. Aristotle was right that man is not only a social and contemplative animal but also a productive one. Happiness attends only upon both.

MAKING THE WORLD A BETTER PLACE

This book is, as stated in the Preface, a *primer*, which means it covers only the basic elements. It has not aimed to answer all the questions, exhaustively examine any topic, or be the final word on anything. I believe it contains sound advice (I wrote it, after all!), but the most that a primer like this can succeed at is in pointing you in the right direction. All the really heavy lifting is left for you: you will have to figure out how to apply it to your own unique circumstances and you will have to investigate troublesome issues or inadequately discussed topics on your own. Despite, then, all the demands that are and will continue to be made on you, despite all the exhortations and remonstrations to be or do this or that, in the end leading a good and happy life begins with one crucial, indispensably necessary element. Before you set out to make the whole world a better place, first present the world with one improved unit: you. You may be surprised how much power one sound example of moral witness can have, how profoundly and extensively one instance of quiet but firm moral resolve can affect others, how greatly others can benefit both directly and indirectly from one inspiring case of steady diligence and perseverance. You will not know exactly how far your example has reached and you will never know exactly whom it has reached, but you can be sure that it has reached somewhere and someone. And toward the end, when your path is taking you to the river, and you look back on your life, there is little in this world that can provide greater and more deserved satisfaction. You may even discover that you were happy.

Bibliography

Aristotle. *Nicomachean Ethics*, 2nd ed. Terence Irwin, trans. Indianapolis, Ind.: Hackett, 2000 (ca. 350 B.C.).

Aurelius, Marcus. *Meditations.* Gregory Hayes, trans. New York: Modern Library, 2003 (A.D. 167).

Barton, Robert A., and Robin I. M. Dunbar. "Evolution and the Social Brain." In *Machiavellian Intelligence II: Extensions and Evaluations.* Andrew Whiten and Richard W. Byrne, eds. Cambridge: Cambridge University Press, 1997.

Barzilai, Fonna Forman. "Sympathy in Space(s): Adam Smith on Proximity." *Political Theory* 33 (April 2005): 189–217.

Boltanski, Luc. *Distant Suffering: Morality, Media, and Politics.* Cambridge: Cambridge University Press, 1999.

Burke, Edmund. *Reflections on the Revolution in France.* J. G. A. Pocock, ed. Indianapolis, Ind.: Hackett, 1987 (1790).

Buss, David M. *The Evolution of Desire: Strategies of Human Mating,* rev. ed. New York: Basic Books, 2003.

Cicero, Marcus Tullius. *On Old Age, on Friendship, and on Divination.* W. A. Falconer, trans. Cambridge, Mass.: Harvard University Press, 1970 (44 B.C.).

Cicero, Marcus Tullius. *De officiis (On Duties).* M. T. Griffin and E. M. Atkins, eds. Cambridge: Cambridge University Press, 1991 (44 B.C.).

Dalrymple, Theodore. *Life at the Bottom: The Worldview That Makes the Underclass.* New York: Ivan R. Dee, 2001.

Dunbar, Robin. *Grooming, Gossip, and the Evolution of Language.* Cambridge, Mass.: Harvard University Press, 1998.

Fleischacker, Samuel. *A Third Concept of Liberty: Judgment and Freedom in Kant and Adam Smith.* Princeton, N.J.: Princeton University Press, 1999.

Flew, Antony. *Social Life and Moral Judgment.* New Brunswick, N.J.: Transaction, 2003.

Gladwell, Malcolm. *The Tipping Point: How Little Things Can Make a Big Difference.* New York: Little, Brown, 2002.

Hayek, Friedrich A. *The Constitution of Liberty.* Chicago: University of Chicago Press, 1960.

Hayek, Friedrich A. *The Fatal Conceit: The Errors of Socialism.* Chicago: University of Chicago Press, 1988.

Hocutt, Max. *Grounded Ethics: The Empirical Bases of Normative Judgments.* New Brunswick, N.J.: Transaction, 2000.

Hume, David. *A Treatise of Human Nature,* 2nd rev. ed. L. A. Selby-Bigge and P. H. Nidditch, eds. Oxford: Oxford University Press, 1978 (1739–40).

Kamm, F. M. "The New Problem of Distance in Morality." In *The Ethics of Assistance: Morality and the Distant Needy.* Deen K. Chatterjee, ed. Cambridge: Cambridge University Press, 2004.

Locke, John. *Second Treatise of Government.* Peter Laslett, ed. Cambridge: Cambridge University Press, 1988 (1690).

Montaigne, Michel de. *The Complete Essays.* M. A. Screech, trans. New York: Penguin, 1993 (1575).

Murray, Charles. *Human Accomplishment: The Pursuit of Excellence in the Arts and Sciences, 800 B.C. to 1950.* New York: HarperCollins, 2003.

Nussbaum, Martha. "Patriotism and Cosmopolitanism." In *For Love of Country.* Joshua Cohen, ed. Boston: Beacon, 1996.

Nussbaum, Martha. *Cultivating Humanity: A Classical Defense of Reform in Liberal Education.* Cambridge, Mass.: Harvard University Press, 1998.

Otteson, James R. *Adam Smith's Marketplace of Life.* Cambridge: Cambridge University Press, 2002.

Otteson, James R. "Adam Smith und die Objektivität moralischer Urteile: Ein Mittelweg." In *Adam Smith als Moralphilosoph.* Christel Fricke and Hans-Peter Schütt, eds. Berlin: de Gruyter, 2005.

Plato. *Euthyphro.* In *Plato: Five Dialogues.* G. M. A. Grube, trans. Indianapolis, Ind.: Hackett, 1981 (ca. 360 B.C.).

Plato. *Meno.* In *Plato: Five Dialogues.* G. M. A. Grube, trans. Indianapolis, Ind.: Hackett, 1981 (ca. 390 B.C.).

Plato. *Republic,* 2nd ed. G. M. A. Grube, trans., rev. by C. D. C. Reeve. Indianapolis, Ind.: Hackett, 1992 (ca. 380 B.C.).

Regan, Tom. *The Case for Animal Rights.* Berkeley: University of California Press, 1985.

Richards, Richard. "A Fitness Model of Evaluation." *Journal of Aesthetics and Art Criticism* 62, no. 3 (Summer 2004): 263–75.

Schelling, Thomas. *Micromotives and Macrobehavior.* New York: Norton, 1978.

Searle, John R. *The Construction of Social Reality.* New York: Free Press, 1997.

Singer, Peter. *The Expanding Circle: Ethics and Sociobiology.* Oxford: Oxford University Press, 1983.

Singer, Peter. *Animal Liberation.* New York: Ecco, 2001.

Smiles, Samuel. *Self-Help: With Illustrations on Character, Conduct, and Perseverance.* Oxford: Oxford University Press, 2002 (1859).

Smith, Adam. *An Inquiry into the Nature and Causes of the Wealth of Nations.* Indianapolis, Ind.: Liberty Classics, 1976 (1776).

Smith, Adam. *The Theory of Moral Sentiments.* Indianapolis, Ind.: Liberty Classics, 1982 (1759).

Taylor, Richard. *Good and Evil,* rev. ed. Amherst, N.Y.: Prometheus, 1999.

Wax, Amy L. "Against Neutrality." *Boston Review* 29, no. 2 (April/May 2004). Http://www.bostonreview.net/BR29.2/wax.html, accessed December 15, 2005.

Wax, Amy L. "The Political Psychology of Redistribution: Implications for Welfare Reform." In *Welfare Reform and Political Theory.* Lawrence M. Mead and Christopher Beem, eds. New York: Sage Foundation, 2005.

Wax, Amy L. "What Women Want." *Wall Street Journal,* August 29, 2005, p. A8.

Wilson, Edward O. *Consilience: The Unity of Knowledge.* New York: Random House, 1999.

Wise, Steven M. *Rattling the Cage: Toward Legal Rights for Animals.* New York: Perseus, 2001.

Wise, Steven M. *Drawing the Line: Science and the Case for Animal Rights.* New York: Perseus, 2003.

Wittgenstein, Ludwig. *The Blue and Brown Books: Preliminary Studies for the "Philosophical Investigations."* New York: Harper Torchbooks, 1960.

Wittgenstein, Ludwig. *Philosophical Investigations,* 3rd ed. G. E. M. Anscombe, trans. London: Routledge, 2002 (1953).

Index

schooling: disagreements over curricula in, 226–8; parental involvement in, 222–3; public, 202; as public good, 234–7; public vs. private, 232–3; Roman Catholic, 232–3; *see also* education
Schor, Juliet B., 69, 166
Schwartz, Barry, 13
Scottish Parliament building, 183–4, 185, 247
Scully, Matthew, 298, 308
Seabright, Paul, 179
Searle, John R., 323
Seldon, Arthur, 115
self-esteem, 67, 218, 219, 236
self-interest, 16–22, 228; children and, 18
selfishness, *see* self-interest
Sen, Amartya, 139–40
sexual harassment, 250–9; codes, 250–3; vs. sexual assault, 250–2; social power and, 258–9
Shafer-Landau, Russ, 130
Shaftesbury, Third Earl of (Anthony Ashley Cooper), xix, 293, 294
Shakeshaft, Charol, 231
Shakespeare, William, 155, 222, 244, 305, 336
Shapiro, Ben, 251
"shoot, shovel, and shut up,"305–6
Shugart, William F. II, 187
Sierra Club, 307
Silverglate, Harvey A., 251, 275
Simmons, Randy T., 306
Simon, Julian, 105, 135, 140, 166, 175, 176, 303, 306, 311
Singer, Peter, ix, xiv, xvi, xviii, 27–30, 129–55, 159, 172, 298–9, 300, 330, 331
Skoble, Aeon, ix
Skousen, Mark, 166
Skyrms, Brian, 249
Smiles, Samuel, 155, 334–5
Smith, Adam, ix, 17, 20, 22, 24, 27–28, 30, 51–2, 74, 103, 104, 109, 142, 148, 152, 160–7, 179, 187, 245, 255, 267, 284, 323, 324–7, 329; vs. Karl Marx, 160–7
Smith, Barry, 143, 157
Sober, Elliott, 19, 249
Sobran, Joseph, 244
social means vs. political means, *see* social power vs. political power
social power vs. political power, 110–16; personhood and, 113–15

social pressure vs. political pressure, 271–2
socialism, 45–56; personhood and, 49–56, 63–4
Socrates, 18, 24, 245
Sommer, John W., 219
Southern Poverty Law Center, 271
Sowell, Thomas, ix, 48, 111, 115, 164, 189, 218, 220, 224, 232, 233, 264, 272, 273
speciesism, 300–1, 331–2
speech, metaphorical vs. literal, 295–7
Spencer, Herbert, 12, 58, 111, 152
Spooner, Lysander, 30
Stalin, Joseph, 56, 133, 146, 178
standards, pragmatic vs. transcendent, 322–4, 327
Stanley, Thomas J., 155, 164
Stark, Rodney, 207
status society vs. contract society, 190
Steers, Stuart, 233
stem-cell research, 66
Sterba, James P., 67
Stevenson, Harold, 219
Stewart, Dugald, 244
Stiglitz, Joseph, 179
Stirner, Max, 17
Stone, Lawrence, 18
Stossel, John, 115
Strunk, William, Jr., 243
Sullivan, Andrew, 286, 287, 288
Summers, Brian, 181
Sumner, William Graham, 58, 107–8, 111, 151–2
Sunstein, Cass, ix, 23, 68, 71, 116–19, 244, 295
supererogatory, 27, 148, 153
Suprynowicz, Vin, 180, 306
Surowiecki, James, 179
Tabarrok, Alexander, 33
Tagliabue, Paul, 262–3
Talley, Brett J., ix
Tanner, Michael, 115, 173
Tax Foundation, the, 59
taxation: forced labor and, 59–60, 62, 109, 206; personhood and, 62–5, 108–9; slavery and, 59–60, 108–9; theft and, 62
Taylor, James Stacey, ix, 29, 38, 186
Taylor, Richard, 320, 322, 323, 324
Taylor, Robert S., 7
Terry, Katherine I., ix

Thales, 328
thing, *see* person vs. thing
third-party interference, 39–40, 72, 249, 259
Thomas, Robert P., 179
Thomas, St., *see* Aquinas
Thousand Pigs, Objection of, 300–2
Tocqueville, Alexis de, 63, 112
Tomasi, John, 207
Tong, Rosemary, ix
tragedy of the commons, 170, 302–8, 311
Tullock, Gordon, 115, 184, 212
Turner, Ted, 307
Tyack, David, 219, 234

Unger, Peter, 130, 131, 139–40, 154
United Nations General Assembly, 67, 168, 177, 231
United Way, 133–4, 135
Universal Declaration of Human Rights, 67–8
University of Alabama, x, 268–9
U.S. Constitution, 106, 209, 216–17, 230, 261
U.S. Department of Agriculture, 33
U.S. Department of Health and Human Services, 291, 312
U.S. Forest Service, 75
U.S. Post Office, 181–2, 185, 189
U.S. Securities and Exchange Commission, 106–7
U.S. Steel, 187

Valdez, Exxon tanker, 55
value, interpersonal comparisons of, 141–7, 151; subjective, 141–4, 297
Vaughn, Karen I., 143
Vedder, Richard K., 171, 187
Veldhuis, Niels, 167
Vere, Edward de, 244
Vetterling-Braggin, Mary, 244
Vilkka, Leena, 296
virtue(s): positive, 22–4, 27, 28, 30, 31, 41; Victorian, 334–7
Vital Ground, 307
Vogel, Ed, 180
Voltaire, 65, 73, 104, 293
Vranich, Joseph, 181

Wallace, Richard, ix
Wall Street Journal, 306
Wal-Mart, 79, 144, 162
Wanniski, Jude, 171
War on Poverty, America's, 172–3
Warren, Melinda, 76
Warren, Virginia L., 243
Washington, Booker T., 270
Wax, Amy L., 173, 220, 240, 336
Weede, Erich, 179
welfare state, 57–8, 71; personhood and, 59–65, 74, 75–9
West, E. G., 213, 218, 220, 221, 227, 228, 232, 235, 237
Whelan, John M., Jr., 130, 139
Whelan, Robert, 287
White, E. B., 243
Wieser, Friedrich von, 143
Wikipedia (Web site), 17
Wildavsky, Ben, 230
Williams, Walter E., ix, 164, 173, 272
Willott, Elizabeth, 306
Wilson, D. Mark, 164
Wilson, David Sloan, 19, 249
Wilson, Edward O., 17, 19, 291, 296, 298, 323, 324
Wilson, James Q., 19
Winkeljohn, Matt, 263
Wise, John P., 176
Wise, Steven, 331
Wittgenstein, Ludwig, 320–1
Wolf, Martin, 179
Wolff, Jonathan, 59
Wolff, Robert Paul, 59, 102
Wootton, David, 210
words, origins of, 243–6
World Bank, 138, 139, 154, 164, 168, 171, 172–3, 175
Wright, Erik Olin, 179
Wright, Robert, 19, 52, 255
Wright, Robert E., 34

Yandle, Bruce, ix
Young, Arthur, 305
Young, H. Peyton, 249
Youssef, Sarah, 162

Zimmerman, Jonathan, 211, 218, 220, 226, 227, 237